AF413073

# DANGER'S DISCIPLE

# DANGER'S DISCIPLE

## SAM HALL

*with*

Larry Hussman

SEABOARD PRESS

JAMES A. ROCK & COMPANY, PUBLISHERS

*Danger's Disciple* by Sam Hall with Larry Hussman

SEABOARD PRESS

is an imprint of JAMES A. ROCK & CO., PUBLISHERS

*Danger's Disciple* copyright ©2008 by Sam Hall

Special contents of this edition copyright ©2008 by Seaboard Press

Cover photo by Evan Howe, Sam Hall's trainer, guide and photographer.



*Address comments and inquiries to:*
SEABOARD PRESS
9710 Traville Gateway Drive, #305
Rockville, MD 20850

**E-mail:**
jrock@rockpublishing.com    lrock@rockpublishing.com
Internet URL: www.rockpublishing.com

Trade Paperback ISBN: 978-1-59663-645-3

Library of Congress Control Number: 2008920278

Printed in the United States of America

First Edition: 2008

*Dedicated to*

*my Mother*

*and*

*late Father*

*Mom, I love you*

*Dad, I miss you*

ACKNOWLEDGMENTS

Many thanks to my co-writer, Dr. Larry Hussman and my pastor, Ron Julian. Very special thanks to my editor, Lilda RockWiley; without her this book would never have been published.

Loving thanks to my wife, Melinda, for never saying "No" and for always urging me to pursue greater deeds for other people.

To my brothers, Mike and Tony, thanks for giving me high morals which set the example for me to live by.

Finally, I would like to express my gratitude to the Humane Society of the United States whose good deeds and devotion to the rescue of animals in the wake of disaster could easily fill another book.

# Past As Prologue

Danger nourishes me. Shows me I'm alive. Always has. When I was three, my father would take me to the pool at the Y. Apparently I kept begging to go to the deep end, even though I couldn't swim a stroke. At twelve I gave my mom heart thumps doing handstands and cartwheels on the roof of my dad's four-story business building in downtown Dayton. At fifteen I readied myself for a coming career as a paratrooper by fabricating a sheet chute to jump off cliffs into the Little Miami River. On my twenty-first birthday my dad shook my hand and said, "Congratulations son, I never thought you'd make it!"

My need to flaunt every red flag landed me in several serious scrapes as a kid, not that I count myself a faultless adult role model either. But I've been taking chances and loving the rush ever since. And there's always been an upside to my urge. For instance, most sensible humans wouldn't think of balancing on a bobbing plank hundreds of feet above what from there looks like a little puddle of water, and then diving for it. That rush bought me my next measure of exhilaration: mounting a fixed platform to accept a 1960 Olympic silver medal. Listening to the *Star Spangled Banner* that day in Rome gave me more goose bumps than you'd find in a whole migration of honkers. Being draped in the flag sparked in me an abiding affection for America. Little did I know then, that I could combine my rage for risk with my patriotism and travel the world in the process. The peril and pride that accompanied doing deeds for other people, well, that was the ultimate fulfillment.

Before I found my way I made a lot of false starts. There was my brief fly-boy gig that ended when I blew out my leg prepping for an Air Force track meet; my mostly boring term as an elected member of the Ohio House of Representatives; my three failed marriages; the jet-setting and woman-winning; a bout with lung cancer and assorted other distractions, including a major drug addiction. Fortunately, my life finally took a radical turn in the right direction. I got off the drugs and found religious faith. That was back in the early eighties. Armed with new conviction, I signed up as a personnel specialist for a Sinai support element of the UN Multinational Forces and Observers that was part of the Camp David Accords. Since my stint with the Air Force hadn't scratched my military itch, I got myself trained as a commando by the Israelis and started helping them take out terrorists. Later, in Africa, I set up a small strike unit called The Free Lancers. We did some serious damage to terrorists there and pulled off a harrowing rescue of a bunch of captured kids. Then I found myself on the front lines helping carry out President Reagan's Iran-Contra strategy, and went on secret missions in El Salvador and Honduras, leading a band of Miskito Indian fighters in Nicaragua.

My last visit to Central America wasn't nearly as rewarding as the earlier ones. I went down to an airbase outside Managua on an N.S.A. spying errand and ended up trying to convince the local authorities that a map hidden in my shoe was really just an arch support. They didn't believe me and I spent time chilling my exposed arch in a Sandinista prison.

You can look it all up in my 1987 autobiography, *Counter-Terrorist*. At the time the book came out it got me my Andy Warhol nanosecond on Good Morning America, the Larry King Show, and other media outlets. But a lot of the daggers-drawn issues of those days have been filed in the history books by now, and though I take some satisfaction in having been a counter-terrorist before counter-terrorism was cool, it's some of the things I've done since my Nicaragua imprisonment that are the source of my deepest satisfaction. That's what I want to tell you about now: what happened to me after the Sandinistas let me loose. About my time as a covert "cutout" for the FBI helping bust drug dealing "big shots." About establishing a 150 million dollar construction business. About getting hooked on helping Hurricane victims in Florida and North Carolina. About serving as a tunnel rat and digger at Ground Zero hours after 9/11. About teaching counterterrorism techniques to first responders, lending a hand in the cleanup after the Columbia space shuttle disaster, helping fight forest fires in the West including California during the 2003, 2006, and 2007 destruction out there. About visiting and supporting a leper colony. About serving with the Salvation Army building hospitals and schools in war torn Iraq and about leading a disaster relief unit after the devastating earthquake in Bam, Iran. About helping out in Sri Lanka after the terrible tsunami. About climbing in the Himalayas toward Mt. Everest. About trying to save the last of the harp seals at the North Pole. About doing dangerous animal rescue work in Africa and in hurricane decimated New Orleans. If that's not enough for you, I'll cover some odds and ends too.

Along the way of all these adventures I discovered that volunteering for duty in danger zones to help others gives me a jolt of God's grace I couldn't have explained twenty years ago. It makes me feel His pleasure, makes me want to do more. But let's get started on the story!

# Autumn 2003

KABOOM ! A big pine 20 feet to my left explodes and shoots flames 200 feet up over the forest canopy near Lake Arrowhead. The smoke is so thick I'm gasping for a little good air and at the same time biting the inside of my fire hood to clamp it closer to my nose. Right about now I ask myself what in this world I'm doing on a California ridge that's part of what must be the biggest inferno north of that other world where sinners supposedly simmer without letup. After all, I could be back in Florida building condos instead of watching them burn out here. Or tapping into a personal fortune that would free me to sail my sixty-six-year-old butt around the seven seas seven times over. But then I remember the reason. It's the personal paradise I bask in when I'm doing something really risky for the greater good. And what a twisting road I traveled to reach that place.

# ONE

Try keeping your balance in the back of a moving van with your wrists cuffed behind your back. I bet it's near impossible. Luckily I didn't have that problem. Sure my wrists were bound, but they had me packed into a makeshift metal pen so tight my shoulders curled forward. The van could have rolled and I wouldn't have budged. I didn't care. Not that forty-nine days in a Managua prison had left me numb. Hell, you could've busted my arm and I wouldn't have noticed, but not because I felt deadened.

The van stopped. Outside, I could hear a muffled roar and shouting, English. Then the door shot open. The roar grew louder, and my captors hauled me out into the bright light. Pure pandemonium.

We'd parked some 400 meters from an idling 737 commercial jet, my ticket to freedom. But a swarm of press blocked the way. Photographers and TV crews pressed against a line of security, threatening to bust loose.

One voice reached me above the shouts. It was Gary Froelich, my family attorney from the States. He'd followed from the prison in a separate car and was now pushing his way through the chaos via escort. The guards removed my handcuffs and nodded.

"Let's get the hell out of here," I said to Gary.

He warned me for about the hundredth time to keep my mouth shut, and we set off at a fast clip toward the security line. At first they all looked like a pack of moving lips, climbing over one another, clamoring to make themselves heard above the jets. But once we were surrounded, the questions fired loudly left and right.

"Sam, were you treated fairly?"

"Are you guilty of spying?"

Gary held my arm and kept saying, "Keep moving. Don't stop."

The camera crews stuck with us, walking backwards as they filmed, until someone tripped and a group of them fell, forming a roadblock of bodies. The reporters closed in.

"What's your take on Ortega?"

"Were you on an assassination assignment?"

"Don't answer," yelled Gary.

The TV people sorted themselves out and we moved again. Hundreds of hands reached toward me. Mikes knocked my chin. Someone called out, "What do you have to say to the people of Nicaragua?"

That's when I stopped. Gary snapped back to me like a rubber band. He was all red in the face and sweating profusely.

"Don't," he implored, but I shot him a look, and he backed off.

I opened my mouth, "I want …"

Every reporter went silent, and the sudden hush startled me. What surprised me more was how calm I felt. Don't get me wrong, I was excited too. I was going home. But I felt at peace. All I could hear was the steady click of cameras—they sounded like insects—and the engines of that big beautiful jet that was going to fly me out of this mess. I took a deep breath and said:

"To the people of Nicaragua, I apologize if I brought you any embarrassment. I didn't come down here to hurt anyone. I only came to get information."

That was the truth and I wanted people there to know it, because there'd been reports to the contrary. Satisfied, I yielded to Gary's tugging arm, and he led me the rest of the way through the mob out onto the tarmac. We ascended the ramp and stepped into the plane. First stop, Costa Rica. Final stop, Miami.

They'd cordoned off the plane's whole first class section for Gary and me, a couple of federal agents and some lucky reporters who'd psyched out my release in advance and guessed the right flight. I had access to the main cabin if I wanted to hit the head or grab some coffee, so long as the two agents flanked me and guarded the john door.

Exhausted, Gary collapsed in his seat and didn't budge. He kept telling me to relax, but I couldn't sit still. I'd been cooped up long enough, not to mention that every time I'd tight-lipped the Sandinista interrogators they'd thrown me in a four-by-two-by-three foot box, 26 feet underground. They called it a prison annex. I called it the freezer. When I wasn't chilling, they'd put me back in my regular eight-foot cell with two plywood bunks, and a ratty mat I named Maggie. I'd piss and shit into a drain hole in the middle of the floor, and on the rare occasion, shower using water that squirted out of a pipe, high on the wall. That same water was supposed to wash away the excrement. Mostly it just made the cement slippery.

I'd passed dark moments there, staring into that fucking hole. I'd gone down to Nicaragua to help the Miskito Indians and the Contras, knowing full well the consequences if I got caught. I was prepared for my government to disavow me. I wasn't fighting for reward or pay. I was serving my country. What I wasn't prepared for was the shame I felt. Between not answering the guards and having my leg whacked repeatedly, I had plenty of time to lie on that stinking plank of a bed and think about all the people I'd let down.

Maybe the guards read my mind, because right away they took my clothes and shoes, even my glasses. All I had were thick canvas shorts and a shirt that I couldn't tear, and a beat-up pair of slippers. The way I figured it, my only shot at killing myself was to dive off the top bunk into that drain hole and snap my neck. It would take a perfect dive, a sure award of ten, Olympic caliber.

Thanks to the guards, I never tried. One guard, really, a big guy named Juan. The interrogations were non-stop at that point. Juan was beating on my leg, when it occurred to me: why bother with the swan dive? All I had to do was attempt an escape and they'd shoot me. I was so relieved to have come up with a new way to commit suicide that when they threw me in the freezer, I started right in on my plan. Later, they pulled me out for more questions, then stuck me back in. Out, in, out, in: that was their mistake.

The more times they shoved me in that ice-box, the more I kept picturing Juan's smiling face as he beat on my leg. All I could think about was how I wanted to take the heel of my right hand, smash down on that prick's nose, and then drive the broken bone up into his brain with my thumb. I stopped thinking about killing myself and started figuring out how to escape for real, taking out as many guards as I could in the process. Before my capture I'd been a workout freak. I could bench-press three sixty and do a thousand sit-ups in 40 minutes. I'd let the routine slide for too long. Time to get back in shape. I'd put my hands on one of the lower bunks and stretch my feet across to the other and do pushups. I'd grab the rail of the upper bunk from underneath and put my feet across to the other upper bunk and do chin-ups. It wasn't long before my strength returned. My attitude changed too. Juan would say, "You're gonna be living here for the next thirty years," and I'd think, *Like hell I am.*

I prayed for strength. I prayed for rescue. I sucked in only positive thoughts and vowed to do good. I know anger's a sin, but anger saved me. It transformed my shame. I went from feeling like a failure to thinking I could start life over if only I could get free, if only I could kill that guard. And then my anger did something else for me. It made me feel guilty for having it in the first place.

I remembered something my pastor once said, "A conduit to God won't be met if you don't first pray for forgiveness for any ill thoughts, jealousies, grudges, or hates against anyone else."

Well, I could take the beatings. I could take the shit smell and all the other fine amenities at the Managua "Hilton," but praying for those pricks … That was the toughest. Yet, I did. And now here I was flying first class back to the good ol' U.S. of A.

No way was I going to sit still. Since my capture, the Iran-Contra scandal had stirred a political storm back home about like the tempest over Teapot Dome in the twenties. My incarceration by the Sandinistas had made news of my light-lifting for President Reagan front-page fodder for every paper around the world. Up 'till now I'd only gleaned pieces of the full story from the few people who'd visited me in the prison.

Mike Wallace had flown down to interview me for "60 Minutes." He'd come packed with an agenda and little seeming interest in my actual story. I didn't know if the piece had aired yet, but I had a good idea it wasn't going to be pretty. I'd like to see him spend two weeks in the freezer and then try giving an interview.

My main interrogator would goad me with newspaper articles. Then there was the visit from Senator Dodd of Connecticut and the group of congressmen: David Coats of Indiana, Alex McMillan from North Carolina, Guy Molinari from New York, and Frank Wolfe from Virginia. Frank was a friend of my congressman brother, Tony. And then of course there was Gary. A deal had been struck between the U.S. and Nicaragua: one of theirs for me. It was what they call in baseball, a "straight player swap," except that I hadn't learned the name of the guy we'd given away.

Now I was talking to the security agents, the flight attendants, even the reporters, starved for information. I wanted to know everything that was happening in the world, everything I'd missed—sports scores, you name it. They were all so friendly. They treated me like a celebrity. I could get used to this, I thought.

About an hour into the Miami leg of the flight, I wandered back to the coach section to kibitz with some more reporters. I was standing in the aisle, sipping my first real decent cup of coffee in months, when from the corner of my eye I saw a slim blonde woman get out of her seat and walk toward me. I couldn't tell how old she was—maybe in her forties—and I didn't look directly at her until she was close. Then I turned and flashed a smile.

"If I'd known Sam Hall was going to be on this plane," she said, her words choked with anger, "I would have brought a gun and shot him."

Before she could add an exclamation point, the agents stepped between us. One put his hand on her shoulder, spun her around with force and marched her down the aisle. His associate nodded for me to return to First Class. Looking back, I could see the woman glaring from her seat now, and the agent beside her with a matching expression, only it was directed at her.

I sat down beside Gary, and he asked what had happened.

"Better get used to it," he said. "Didn't I warn you? I told you not to walk around."

So much for the celebrity treatment.

"To the liberal half of the country, you're the living embodiment of Republican policy run amok," he said.

He adjusted his pillow and shut his eyes. I tried to rest a bit as well, but I could still see that woman's face twisted up with hate. If she was an indication of what I had to look forward to, I was beginning to think I might have a longer life expectancy back in the freezer.

When we landed in Miami, the angry woman debarked first. From the window I could see the agent escorting her down the ramp. He'd stayed at her side the whole rest of the flight—probably wanted to rush her through customs and clear her out of the airport before she could make any more stink.

We were next. They'd wheeled an additional ramp up to the plane just for me, and now there were more agents. The Sandinistas had taken most of my belongings, leaving me little more than a few shirts and my Dopp kit, which fit into a small duffle. I slung the bag over my shoulder and followed Gary and the guards down the aisle to the door. Three guards formed a barrier in front of us in case someone tried to take a shot at me. Another brought up the rear. As we descended the steps to a waiting convergence of black vans and more government agents, I spotted a single white van. Beside its open door were my two brothers.

I stopped to take in the sight of them and drew a deep breath and exhaled. Countless times in the prison I'd envisioned this moment; seen it so clearly in my mind it was like I'd willed it into being. But it was really happening now. My brothers were hurrying toward me. It was the best damn deja-vu I'd ever felt and I lifted my hand from the rail and waved.

Seconds later we hugged. My brothers kept shaking their heads, looking me up and down, like they couldn't believe it was me. No one knew what to say. I'll admit, we shed a few tears, but I couldn't stop smiling.

Tony was the first to speak: "Thank God you're safe."

He clapped me on the back and we started toward the white van. I half-expected him to launch into a lecture about getting mixed up with the Reagan administration. Tony's a liberal Democrat and I'm about as conservative as Republicans get, at least when it comes to our country's defense against foreign threats. But he skipped the I-told-you-so routine and just hugged me harder. Mike, who's the political neutral in the family, was all sympathy and curiosity.

"We've been glued to the TV."

"How's mom?" I asked.

"Worried sick."

"You look tired," said Tony. "Are you feeling alright?"

I started to answer when I was interrupted by shouts. High up on the roof of the main terminal, a row of about fifty photographers peered down at us. They'd been recording our little family reunion through lenses that looked like canons. Believe me, being home again after what I'd been through the last month-and-a-half, there was no need for anyone to coax me to say "cheese."

Maybe my brothers were a little overwhelmed. There was no doubting their show of relief, but they seemed confused too. This all must have taken a toll on them. For the past several years, they had no idea what I'd been doing. I'd told them I was a freelancer, traveling to write articles, putting stories together for a possible book. For them to have to learn through the news that I'd been lying all this time, and then to have to sift through all the conflicting stories, they probably had no idea what to believe. But to see the love in their eyes despite everything … Christ, my heart went out to them.

We piled into the van along with two federal agents, and I took over with the questions, asking more about Mom and their families, work, anything to keep my brothers talking, anything to set them at ease. Every now and then I'd catch Tony eyeing me, like he was trying to put the pieces together, but mostly he just looked happy. And of course we weren't alone. They weren't about to get too personal in front of the agents. Probably they were waiting for some privacy.

I turned to one of the agents. "So what's the plan now?"

"We're taking you to the VA hospital. They'll want to keep you a couple weeks."

I hadn't even considered medical attention. I was a little banged up, but I'd worked myself back into shape. The only thing I thought needed looking at were the sores on my head, courtesy of Maggie the mat.

"Don't worry," said the agent. "You'll have round-the-clock security."

I wasn't worried. Some much deserved R and R and a private room sounded like just the thing.

A welcome party greeted our arrival at the hospital. Again I felt like a celebrity. The chief administrator and about seven other department heads rolled out the red carpet, while staff attendants offered coffee, anything we wanted. They treated Tony like royalty.

"You know Mike and I both have flights to catch," he said.

We spent a little time milling about with the doctors, then the three of us found a room where we could be alone.

I tried to fill in the blanks for them as best as I could, right up to the imprisonment.

"And you're sure you're all right?" Tony asked again.

"I've never been happier. I'm so glad to be back."

The time seemed to fly. An attendant knocked at the door and announced that my room was ready. The doctors wanted me to settle in and rest.

That's when something the agent from the van had neglected to say hit me like a slap in the face. My private room just happened to be in the psych ward.

"We need to keep you safe and secure," said the chief administrator.

If I'd been feeling the first signs of exhaustion from the trip, I was now wide awake again.

"Sorry, boys," I said. "That's out of the question."

One of the agents approached at the sound of my raised voice. I looked around for Gary. My brothers stayed by my side.

"Try to understand," said the administrator.

I understood too well. This felt like that fucking Mike Wallace interview all over again, only this time I was wise and wasn't budging.

"Sam, you need to be kept—"

I crossed my arms and the administrator retreated a step.

"Think about what happened on the plane," said the agent beside me. "You were threatened."

He calmly explained that the security team had gone over the plans to the hospital and concluded the psych ward was the only location where they could guarantee my protection. It had nothing to do with sanity. My brothers agreed. They were concerned about the press and didn't want me being harassed. The longer I listened, the more I thought I'd overreacted. It was the fatigue. The image of a real mattress and clean sheets called to me.

When I apologized for getting worked up, a collective sigh passed around the room. The administrator smiled again.

"Even when you leave your floor, you'll have an escort," he said.

The agent nodded agreement, but he wasn't smiling. He couldn't have looked more serious.

# TWO

I woke the next morning to the sound of blinds going up. It was the nurse practitioner from the night before. She greeted me with a cheery hello and set up shop by the bed, picking up where she'd left off. Apparently I'd started quite a bug collection. The open sores on my head were so infected, it seemed every bug in Nicaragua had taken up residence, hired housekeeping and started a family. Now it was her job to apply alcohol swabs to my scalp every hour and soak my lame leg in a foul smelling brew. That was in addition to the pills that came with breakfast; enough penicillin, I was told, to cure cancer.

About half way through the treatment, the doctor stopped by. He was glad to see me up and joking with the nurse.

"I still can't believe you've come from six weeks in a prison," he said. "Other than the scalp infection, you're in better shape than most people I see on the outside."

We laughed, and I told him about my workout routine with the bunks.

"You know," he said, "it's probably not much fancier than the bunks, but we do have a gym here at the hospital. Feel free to use it any time you like."

I thanked him, and he said another reason he'd stopped by was to tell me they'd scheduled a small interview session with the other doctors.

"If you're up to it," he said.

"No problem."

It gave me an excuse to shower and shave. Besides, I'd been poked and soaked enough and was eager to explore the hospital.

An hour later, the chief administrator knocked at my door. The agents standing guard were different from the night before and must have clocked in early that morning. One followed us while the other stayed behind.

We left the psych ward and took an elevator down a floor. Along the way, the administrator pointed out the gym and the community room where I could go if I needed to smoke.

"Smoking in the room is prohibited," he said, putting emphasis on the word "prohibited" in case I got the wrong impression and thought he approved.

A moment later we walked into a conference room. Seated at a long rectangular table was my doctor from breakfast and a couple others I recognized from the welcome reception the night before. There were other doctors as well, all wearing ties under white lab coats, and two men in suits who didn't introduce themselves. They had lab coats as well, but weren't wearing them. Rather, they sat with the white coats folded in their laps like napkins.

"Good morning," I said, taking a seat opposite them.

"There's water if you need it," said the administrator, motioning to a silver pitcher and glasses in the center of the table.

That's when I noticed that each of the doctors had a notepad and pen except for the two at the end, the ones not wearing lab coats. Something smelled, and I'd just showered, so I knew it wasn't me.

I shook my head, folded my hands on the table, and studied each doctor. Something told me it wasn't going to be a friendly gathering.

Were they C.I.A.? N.S.A.? F.B.I.? Remember, this was long before 9/11. There was no communication among the agencies then, and with the Iran-Contra scandal running full boil, each department was investigating the other. The F.B.I. wanted to take down the C.I.A. C.I.A. was trying to cover its ass, and the N.S.A. was looking to protect the president. I might have been free, but I'd landed myself smack-dab in the frying pan of an information war.

After a short speech by the lead doctor, another doctor started to speak without introducing himself. Right away I cut him off and asked his position at the hospital. Turned out he was the head psychiatrist.

I shot a withering glance at my doctor, who looked embarrassed, and then nodded for the shrink to continue. He cleared his throat and flipped some pages of his notepad, which were already covered in scribble.

"Mr. Hall," he began, "help us understand, why were you down in Nicaragua?"

I had to bite my tongue to keep from asking the medical relevance of that question. Instead, I turned my gaze to the two suits at the end of the table.

"Who are these gentlemen?" I said.

After a long pause, the administrator pushed his chair back and stood, forcing a smile: "Doctors, perhaps we should postpone this to another day."

Some of the men bolted from the room. A few looked bothered. I guessed they were the ones who'd orchestrated the little pow-wow. Who knew if all of them were even doctors.

I was so furious that I went straight back to my room, guard in tow, and changed into sweats to hit the gym. It wasn't that I had a problem co-operating, just that I had no patience for the cloak-and-dagger bullshit. If they wanted information, they'd have to ask me to my face and not use a bunch of doctors for cover. And as far as the doctors were concerned, it bothered me that they'd agreed to play a part in the charade. They could justify my stay in the psych ward on safety grounds, but that didn't explain the shrink at the conference room asking about my mission. Something wasn't right. I was probably being watched. Most likely the phone was tapped.

Normally working out relaxes me. Not that day. When the nurse came to swab my head, I was still pretty steamed. She soaked my leg and left my pills on the nightstand in a little paper cup.

"What are these?" I asked.

"Your antibiotic."

"Yeah, but what about this one?"

I held up the second pill and she blinked.

"Maybe you should send the Doc in," I said.

She left in a hurry. That's when I got my second surprise of the day. Turned out they'd been giving me medication for bi-polar disorder. I nearly hit the roof.

"What the hell for?"

The doctor tried to remain calm.

"I didn't O.K. this," I said.

"Your brother …"

"What about my brother?"

"There was concern that …"

Was the whole world against me?

The doctor started again: "Given the circumstances, Congressman Hall felt it would be best if …"

I fell silent.

I could still see my brothers at the airport waiting for me—the look in their eyes as we clung to each other. I could get high and mighty over the spying and doctors, but not my brother. The news smarted, but only for a second. Tony wasn't some hack of a journalist with an agenda to make me look nuts. He was family with only my well being at heart, and I'd been lying to him for years. That I'd done so in service of my country exonerated me in theory, but not in feeling. To dwell on any sense of betrayal then would have denied his love.

"I'm not taking this anymore," I said and put the pill back in the cup.

"Of course if that's your decision, but perhaps we should—"

"I don't want you to tell my brother."

"That you've stopped taking the medication?"

"No that you told me he was behind it. If you talk to him, say I blamed you guys, or the government, whatever you like. See?"

He agreed.

I went to bed that night thinking about my brothers and about sacrifice. People might look at me and say I'd sacrificed for my country. I've said it myself, not to garner praise, mind you, but just because the phrase is used so often, it's a simple way of implying a lot. But what had I ever really given up? Money? Accolades? If approbation's what I needed, I'd picked the wrong line of work in covert ops. No, as far as I could tell, the only thing I'd given up was feeling sorry for myself. The fact that my service required lying to my family didn't lessen the right of my actions, it just meant I had to be understanding of theirs and love my brother even more. At that moment I did.

* * *

I never found out who the two men were at the conference room meeting or what department they were with. The next day a group of several N.S.A. agents came knocking at my hospital door. Right away they identified themselves, and the debriefing session kicked off with a mutual dose of respect.

I recounted my capture and the prison conditions. They were especially interested in whether I'd remained at one location or moved around. Unfortunately, the only times the Sandinistas took me off the compound, I'd been blindfolded. The men showed no emotion, but I knew they were disappointed. Really they wanted any descriptions that would help draw a bullseye on that compound.

There was one bit of information I thought would brighten their moods. On the way to the prison interrogation rooms, the guards would make me walk with my chin on my chest. If I raised my head too much to see around, Juan would whack my leg with a thick four-foot-long plank. On one particular evening, however, I did manage a glance up and noticed a group of officers, accompanied by a very blond, crew-cut bruiser, wearing a completely different uniform. No question, he was Soviet, and in the instant his cold eyes met mine I could tell he had a special interest in me.

I remembered getting back to my cell that day, how my mind returned to my high-board event at the Rome Olympics. Two Russian divers had impressed me, blond like the officer in the hallway, but these two oozed goodwill and a joy for life. Without their Eastern European warm-up suits they could have passed for a pair of California beach boys. When I claimed my medal, they were among the first to shake my hand. Those big Russian bear-hug handshakes helped me see past the politics, past the Soviet insignias and fed my youthful One-World idealism. How much I'd changed. Sitting there in the cell after the encounter with the Russian officer in the hallway, all I could think was how I'd crush his windpipe if given the opportunity.

As expected, the agents considered my sighting of the Russian at the prison a blond bombshell. Since the Red Army was still playing footsy with Fidel in Cuba, the government had been looking for any hint of Soviet involvement in Nicaragua. I'd given them a lead.

After the debriefing that second day in the hospital, I settled into a routine. If I was being watched, I didn't care. All that mattered was getting healthy and getting out of the hospital as soon as possible.

I'd hit the gym at least twice a day. My phone was ringing off the hook. Radio stations, TV stations, magazines all wanted to send writers and photographers to interview me. Publishers wanted to buy my life story. I even got a call from a film producer, offering ten grand for the movie rights. Said he'd produced the movie *Silkwood* with Cher. I'd never taken money for putting my life on the line, so I wasn't up on the going rate. But ten grand seemed low. How do you measure a man's life that way? I told him to get lost.

If I wanted company, all I had to do was go to the community room for a smoke or check out the cafeteria. I couldn't walk down the hall without people calling me over to shake hands and congratulate me. A lot of the vets in the psych ward were recovering drug addicts, and I'd tell them about my own struggle and quitting cold turkey. They treated me like a hero, reminded me why I'd gone down to Nicaragua in the first place. In between the limelight of the hospital halls and the media attention, I tried to take stock of my life.

My mother was well and still a steady source of love and advice. I'd led a life of privilege before heading off to fight in Israel and Africa. My deceased father had been a successful real estate developer as well as a popular mayor of Dayton. After he died my brothers and I decided to sell his company and follow our separate inspirations. Tony wanted to morph his Peace Corps experience into a political career which he later did as the world hunger expert in Congress. Mike's dream was to improve the state's education system as a teacher and administrator.

My goal was admittedly more worldly. I went to work for Foreman Industries as a Project Manager and found myself in charge of over 800 great men and women, who built factories for General Motors and Ford. Our biggest accomplishment was putting up the Ford Batavia plant outside Cincinnati. It was an engineering marvel, forty-seven acres under one roof. Unfortunately the owners of Foreman Industries made a series of business blunders and the company eventually collapsed. Just before it happened I saw the handwriting on the track hoe and quit. After that I went to work for a Dayton developer and department store mogul named Arthur Beerman. He was my Godfather and helped sow my seed of love for Israel, a respect that later sent me to the Middle East to begin my counterterrorism career.

I didn't have any money worries, even though I'd spent thousands of dollars buying arms and equipment for my military adventures. Between the bundle from my Foreman Industries severance perks and my inheritance trust fund, I could certainly put food on the table. But what then?

I had no idea where to settle or what to do. I had solid evidence of my family's continued love, but I'd refrained from calling any of my closest friends on account of the phones possibly being tapped. The few friends I did talk to acknowledged being harassed by reporters. Sometimes I'd see people I vaguely knew on TV, mere acquaintances in cases, describing crazy pranks I'd pulled when I was younger, dares they'd only heard about and not actually witnessed. My dad used to say, "Son, you can take all your real friends and their luggage and stick them in the back of a Volkswagen bug." I'd had plenty of buddies, rich and not so rich, liberal and conservative, white, black, yellow, and brown, but I knew who my real friends were.

At any rate, after two weeks of supplying the government with as many whats, whys, and wherefores as I could, and absorbing enough alcohol into my scalp that my hair was in danger of developing cirrhosis, I was ready to end my VA vacation. I told the doctors to pass my bed on to somebody who needed it and signed my release.

I planned to hail a cab and check into a Miami hotel for a few days to sort out my options. But as I stepped out into the Florida warmth that February morning I discovered alternate plans waiting curbside.

Surrounded by a dozen reporters and photographers was a shiny new red Cadillac. The passenger door swung open and out leaned my friend of forty-plus years, Harry Holden, a much-divorced bachelor from my home-town of Dayton. Our families had been close and we'd grown up tempting trouble together. He'd amassed a fortune in mergers and acquisitions, as well as playing the stock market on the side. He was the consummate wheeler-dealer, so smooth I'd always sworn he could scoop jellyfish off the beach and sell them to surgeons as breast implants. Now he was a millionaire several times over and owned a mansion in Ft. Lauderdale, which I'd used as a temporary haven during my Stateside time in the recent past. He slapped the white leather seats and shouted, "Let's roll."

I pushed through the barking crowd and climbed in. Hadn't even got the door shut when he floored it. Reporters dove out of the way. He just laughed.

"You look O.K. to me," he said.

"Thanks."

"I bet you could come in first and third in a jerk-off contest."

"What can I say?"

He winked. We were driving like he'd just broken me out of jail. Sinking back into that plush leather seat, I felt like he had.

We drove for about twenty minutes, not nearly enough time to catch up, when Harry veered into a drive and screeched to a stop.

"You remember this, don't you?" he said.

I sat forward and looked about. We were parked in front of what used to be the old McFadden-Deauville Hotel. Every Christmas without fail Harry's family and mine would come here from Ohio. Those were the best three weeks of the year, swimming from the beaches, surfing the waves. And the history of the joint … The Rat Pack were regulars. The Beatles played their second ever U.S. concert here in the Napoleon Ballroom. The owners had later sunk a bunch of dough into renovating the place and changed the name. Now it was just called the Deauville. But as Harry and I sat looking at the façade, a smile worked its way across my face.

"Wow, does this bring back memories," I said.

Harry clapped me on the shoulder and nodded: "Come on, I've got a surprise for you."

With that he urged me out of the car and up the entrance steps. We slipped through the glittering lobby and down a corridor to the poolside bar. There, sitting on a high stool talking to a pretty brunette was my other best bachelor buddy, Jimmie Bonbright.

Years ago Jimmie had moved from Ohio to St. Pete. We'd met at the Dayton country Club back in the sixties. Like Harry he had a nose for good fortune. He'd compounded his inheritance from his father's beer distributing business and come to Florida to suck the juices from the good life. Now he leapt up from his barstool and wrapped me in the biggest bear hug this side of Glacier Park.

"Sam, you friggin' mother," he boomed near the top of his lungs. "I'll bet Ronnie and Nancy are overjoyed to see you back in the States."

Jimmie banished the brunette and the bar manager showed us to a private table, roped off for the occasion. To top that he assigned us a personal bouncer in case any press had followed from the hospital. We started stoking the memories of family and friends with round after round of margaritas. And, of course, we talked about women as befitted our serial husband status. Combined we'd accounted for ten divorces.

They didn't seem in any rush to press me about my treatment in Nicaragua. I guess they felt I'd talk about it when I was ready, and for the moment, it was nice to just sit back and listen to them debating who had paid out more alimony over the years.

My mind drifted back to memories of the hotel the way it used to be. The original had boasted the world's largest salt-water swimming pool with high boards. It was here that I'd first learned to dive. The original owner, Bernard McFadden, was a famous health nut back in the fifties. Pictures in the lobby had showed him jumping over a tennis net at the ripe age of eighty, sky diving when he was pushing ninety, spreading the gospel of the strenuous life far and wide. I wanted to lead a life like his: intense, physical, risky. So far so good, and I intended to keep driving myself, like the poet recommended, to go full-throttle "into that good night."

But as the margaritas flowed and the evening wore on, I found myself still casting back, reflecting on a time of my life that seemed to have been forced to a close. Thanks to the media attention, my covert cover was blown around the world. Two weeks of lying in a hospital bed, and still I couldn't think of a way to be useful to my country again. I wasn't happy with the politicians at that point anyway, but again, this was all to be expected. "Plausible deniability," that's what they call it. I'd put my butt on the line in Honduras and El Salvador only to be counted a clown by the media pundits and undefended by the political establishment. Seemed like destiny had ordered me a major slow-down.

Setting my drink on the table, I told Harry and Jimmie that the time had come for me to leave off the breakneck life.

"I need to try my hand back in the private sector," I said.

Harry scooped up the pitcher to refill my glass.

"Maybe get back into the development business," he said.

Jimmie agreed.

"Something that doesn't involve getting shot at for a change."

Since construction seemed a solid bet, they offered to set up a venture partnership for the three of us and supply most of the capital themselves. Both of them thought the business would do better in Pompano than Miami where investment land was scarce and the market saturated. I could be head honcho with discretion to run things. Their reward if all went well would be to anchor me in Florida for future nights on the town and maybe some extra pocket change in the bargain.

Long ago my father had warned me: "You can't afford partners." By which he meant that no matter how close you are to a potential business associate, and I trusted Harry and Jimmie like brothers, misunderstandings have a way of cropping up. Dad had sure managed to do more than alright for himself without entangling alliances. I could do the same.

"Sorry fellas, I need to go this one alone," I said.

I'd been a success at real estate development before. Doing it again would certainly be easier than taking down terrorists.

Harry and Jimmie were understanding, but Harry made another offer: a seven figure loan to get me off the ground. Then Jimmie tried to trump Harry by offering to co-sign whenever I needed to approach a lending institution for future projects.

"They might be leery of loaning to a lunatic international spy," he said.

They both knew I was no credit risk. Most recently Harry had backed me on my last Free Lancer mission in Africa. I knew I could pay them back, and their help would allow me to keep my inheritance trust fund intact.

By the time the party ended that night it was agreed that I was back in the construction business.

"Not only that," said Harry. "You're coming to stay with me."

"I would have offered my place, but it's getting a face lift," said Jimmy. "Figured you'd prefer some peace and quiet."

"Like I'm going to get that with him."

I'd stayed with Harry in the past. He lived on a mansion-studded street just off Los Olas Boulevard in Ft. Lauderdale. It was a five-million dollar, 12,000 square-foot bachelor barracks: the kind of house you get lost in. Just what I needed.

"Welcome back," said Jimmy.

Harry and I drove home in quiet. I'd barely said anything about my incarceration all night. Usually he hounded me for details, pumping me for information. But that night he gave me the gift of space, and in the privacy of his sprawling home I'd have even more space—time to reflect, time to adjust. Thanks to him and Jimmy, I now had some direction. I should have been more excited. It was late.

We entered the house through the garage and came into the kitchen. The phone was ringing. Harry switched on the lights. We heard the answering machine kick in, but whoever it was hung up.

"How 'bout a nightcap?" said Harry.

Then the phone rang again. While he looked for the receiver, I headed for the john. I heard him answer. Something about the tone of his voice stopped me.

"Uh-huh," he said. "Who wants to know?"

I looked back over my shoulder. He waved me over and handed me the phone. The cheer had gone out of his expression.

"Mr. Hall?" came a deep voice.

"Speaking."

"This is FBI special agent Ed Dunnigan. Would it be possible for my partner and I to come out there tomorrow to speak with you?"

"Sure," I said.

I set up a meeting for ten thirty the next morning and hung up.

"How'd they know you were here?" said Harry.

We looked at each other, and he turned for the liquor cabinet.

If I was going to get a new business off the ground, the last thing I needed was to be the center of a government investigation. What else could they want aside from more information about Nicaragua? I racked my brain trying to remember all the details of my debriefing sessions at the hospital. If the room had been bugged, what was said that could be used against me? The one thing I kept coming back to was the fact that if any of the agencies wanted to paint me a fall guy, all they had to do was charge me with illegally crossing international borders.

So much for peace. That night all the Jack Daniels in Dade County wouldn't have cured my insomnia.

# THREE

The next morning Harry and I were debating in the reception hall what the FBI might want from me when at ten thirty sharp Dunnigan and Espy thumbed the main entrance doorbell. They were dressed the part of intrepid investigators. Dark suits, sunglasses, and the apparently mandated wingtip shoes. Once Harry ushered them inside they introduced themselves. Harry asked if they wanted to talk out by one of the pools. Dunnigan drained that idea with a quick comeback.

"It would be better if the three of us talked inside. Sound travels over water and I'd rather keep this conversation between the three of us."

Harry didn't need a third reference to "the three of us" to do the math. He excused himself and got lost somewhere in the expanse of his mansion. Actually, Dunnigan's request saved me the trouble of asking Harry to leave. There was always the possibility that something would be said in front of the agents that might link Harry too closely to me and I didn't want him mixed up in anything he might come to regret. A couple of my other friends had written me in Nicaragua that they were being hounded with questions about their connection to me.

Once the two agents were satisfied there were no moles hiding behind the furniture, they, got right down to business. They started asking about my Central American connections. A lot of their questions were repeats of the ones I'd been asked at the VA hospital and I began to suspect the agents were leading up to something else entirely. Then Dunnigan said something that made me certain.

"Sam, can we talk off the record?

"Sure."

Espy closed his notebook and Dunnigan wound his way toward what was on his mind.

"Sam, we think you know several people who might have information about the drug trade. Does the name Correlli mean anything to you?"

A bell rang right away. In those short Stateside stretches that broke up my globetrotting during the previous five years, I'd taken advantage of Harry's hospitality and enjoyed the nightlife around Miami and Ft. Lauderdale. Drinking and kibitzing and spending at just about every beach bar around put me in the middle of the "in" crowd. And scattered among the local wealthy and wannabes were a number of truly creepy characters who were part of the New Jersey Diaspora, hoods who'd headed down Interstate 95 from up north to make a mark among the local losers. Correlli was such a specimen. He was always bragging about how many influential people he knew who were constantly breaking the law, dealing in drugs, scrubbing money, buying automatic weapons, running guns, and assorted lesser laxities. Apparently, the braggart had broadened his audience to include at least one FBI informant and now I was somehow supposed to expand on his probable exaggerations so the feds could feed their database on South Florida crime figures. I told the two agents that though I'd met and exchanged drivel with Correlli, it hadn't ever amounted to much more and that I could only repeat the names he'd dropped in my presence. I said I'd always worked with the white hats and didn't know much about the criminal element. That was true and I couldn't be in any trouble on that score. I'd always had the coldest contempt for underworld types and tried to avoid them like the plague they were. And that wasn't easy since the South Florida bars I bankrolled with my patronage were swarming with them.

After a couple more questions the agents seemed satisfied. In fact, I thought they were about to leave when Dunnigan dropped the other wingtip.

"Sam, we also came out here to ask a favor. We know about your work for another agency. And we know how they treated you. But we want you to consider a proposition about some work we think you're perfectly suited for. (Pause here for maximum impact). We want you to help us fight drugs."

For a minute I thought Dunnigan was talking about doing some "Just say No!" TV spots for Nancy. But Espy cleared that up fast.

"It's not the users we're talking about, Sam. They're not a big priority with our division. We're talking about the Florida drug lords, the mafia in the States, and the cartels in South America. I don't have to tell you we're always trying to disrupt their operations. There would be risks, of course. but we'd always be there to cover for you."

If the two emissaries from the fed heard me gulp they didn't let on. They just stood mute and let their proposal sink in and stimulate the old adrenaline rush. My face must have signaled the desired effect because Dunnigan broke the thirty seconds of silence.

"Your reputation as somebody who's been mixed up in Central America could be a big asset, Sam. The dealers would assume that you got around in the drug circles down there. There would be risks for you, of course. But the Bureau would always be there to see to it that you got maximum protection."

Despite the seductive sound of that word "risks" which Dunnigan had enticingly mentioned twice now, it occurred to me about this time that, given my situation, I would be nuts to get involved in another diversion from what most people consider a normal life. For once my brain beat back my bent.

"Very flattering, gentlemen, but I'm afraid I'm not your man. I'm getting a new business up and running and it doesn't involve getting shot at."

But Dunnigan wasn't about to accept my first answer.

"If it's a matter of money, Sam, we can fix that. You'd be getting 20 to 30 percent of the gross receipts from cocaine busts. It could amount to millions in a matter of months. And, of course, there's always a confiscated Lexus or Lincoln to be had. Or a boat or an airplane. We could write you an agreement"

Now I was beginning to get pissed off. These two birddogs had obviously skipped their homework. Any job I did for the government wasn't motivated by money or a legal piece of paper. I never had a contract or took any shekels from the government. Surely, I thought, the CIA could have told these two as much. But, of course, these were the days before we all learned that the CIA and the FBI weren't on speaking terms. So I had to explain my position.

"It's not a matter of money. I do what I do for a different kind of reward. And besides, I've never had financial troubles. It's a matter of settling down for a while. And having a little bit of fun. I just got out of a stinking prison, for God's sake."

Now it was Espy's turn to cajole.

"Well, we'd cover your expenses at the very least. You wouldn't want to finance the kind of role we've got in mind for you out of your own pocket. This involves throwing around hundreds every night of the week. That's one of the reasons the Bureau thinks you're a good fit for the work they've got in mind for you. You're well known all over the area already as a guy who likes to party and spends up a storm to have a good time. And you've got a ready made reputation that's a little on the shady side. Soldiers of fortune aren't thought of as saints, you know. And one who's been screwing around in Central America might just be a sinner with a yen for some drug-generated pocket change."

Then Dunnigan broke in.

"You'd have to have a lot of training, like learning the dealer's lingo, how to measure cocaine, all about the methods of the various cartels, everything you'd need to know to pull off a 'cutout' role. We'd line you up with some experts from the Bureau to school you in the trade. And the more you learn the less the danger, of course."

Espy did the follow-up.

"And you know all the risk would be for a worthy cause. You've seen the way drugs destroy people with all kinds of potential. In fact, you know it first hand from being addicted once yourself. Your role would be dangerous but you'd have the satisfaction of helping take some of the traffickers off the streets."

I was beginning to think the Bureau had sniffed out my psychology pretty well after all. This was the agents' fourth reference to danger or risk so apparently Dunnigan and Espy had been told how to stir my sauce. And apparently too they'd managed to find out that I was a recovered addict, something that only a few of my closest friends knew. What they couldn't know was the depth of my contempt for drug lords and all of their minions. It'd taken me many months and a enormous effort to kick my habit in the mid-seventies. I'd gone cold turkey and driven myself to run up and down Colorado mountains for six weeks to reclaim my body. And I couldn't see a TV or newspaper reference now to the drug problem without a surge of anger surfacing. If the report included a story of some poor individual addict my blood boil would be balanced by my heart hurt. There was no doubt that helping disrupt the drug trade would match or surpass the satisfaction I derived from my earlier causes. Still, it made no sense now to neglect a startup business and a life that was beginning to burgeon for a tilt at another windmill, no matter how just the fight or enticing the excitement. So I tried to put a cap on the conversation.

"I'm really sorry. As intriguing as your proposition sounds, I'm not ready to put all my plans in limbo just yet. I owe it to my family to spend some quality time with them."

Espy delivered the parting shot.

"Think about it for a few days, Sam. If you change your mind, give us a call at the Miami office."

As soon as the front door closed behind Dunnigan and Espy, Harry reappeared and asked me what all the secrecy was about. I told him every-thing the agents had said and he got more excited than I'd seen him in a while.

"Wow! And you thought you might have been in some kind of trouble. But this is another great opportunity, Sam. You know you'd love working undercover for the Bureau. Think of the romance of it. Spending the government's money to do the stuff you love to do anyway."

"But what about the business?"

Come on Sam, you're an experienced builder. You know how to del-egate. In fact, I can recommend a guy up in Jacksonville who'd make you a great superintendent. He's the kind you can give free reign and never lose any sleep over it. Hiring him would buy you the time to build condos *and* put away slime balls. Consider the possibilities. Your average drug kingpin would think from force of habit that your business was a front. Something to make you seem to the feds like a solid citizen."

Even though I knew Harry read too many three-dollar thrillers, I let him have his say. He was a very bright man and I counted on him for good advice. But he'd had his own bout with drugs. That was probably why he seemed so enthusiastic about my taking the FBI up on their proposal. That and the fact that despite his living a life that compared well to Donald Trump's, he loved to get a little vicarious verve from my adventures. So I'd have to weigh his words well now. And there was no shortage of words to weigh.

"And this house would be the perfect place to meet your FBI contacts. You could take the training in one of the rooms upstairs. They're big enough to hold a couple of dozen agents, with room left over to store half of J. Edgar's pink tutus."

Harry's logic was beginning to get to me. Tycoon by day and trafficker-trapper by night *would* have advantages. If the business went well I'd gener-ate funds for future adventures while I was enjoying a buzz or two on the government in the present. And Harry was right about the house. It had a garage big enough to accommodate five full sized sedans or two-and-a half Hummers, but it was hidden from prying public behind the house. Even the bathrooms were big enough to host a small convention. In fact, a wag who once took a solo tour of the place during one of Harry's many parties came back to the other guests an hour later and announced he'd discovered a lost Southeast Asian tribe living in one of the upstairs back bedrooms.

And the more I thought about it, the more I had to admit I had the right stuff to be the darling of the FBI's dreams. First there was my less-than-enviable reputation that Dunnigan had so impolitely mentioned. Lots of news organizations world wide were still featuring my face on their front pages and TV screens and many of them had branded me a mercenary and international troublemaker. Not only that but there was that pick-axe job Mike Wallace had done on me. By the time he got through with me, his viewers probably thought I was mixed up in drug trafficking and/or gun running or that at least I was spaced out on something myself. My ranking in the public's mind at this point ran the gamut from Z to Z-minus and I was rapidly becoming infamous for being infamous. The most flattering thing I'd been called in the mainstream press was an "eccentric millionaire." But all that negative publicity only made me more suited for the FBI's purposes.

Beyond my credentials as a crackpot loose cannon. I also had some standing at the venues around town where drug dealers and higher-ups in the trade took their pleasure. There wasn't a singles' bar or strip joint or casino in the vicinity where I hadn't been an intermittent but highly visible scene-maker, lots of times with Harry who was also known at the beach as rich and unattached, and as an even bigger spender. The whole crowd in town that thought they counted knew me, everybody who was anybody in the metro area north and south on Route A1A. So even though I'd been clean for nearly twenty years the local drug buyers and sellers would have no trouble taking me for a player in the trade or a journeyman junkie. One more plus from the Bureau's point of view. In the few minutes I'd mulled over my assets as an potential undercover operator, I was already anxious to start knocking a few narco heads together.

"I think I'll call those two back."

"Now you're talking like the old Sam. Here's the phone book."

My call reached the local FBI office before Dunnigan and Espy had a chance to report back in. I told the receptionist to page them when they arrived and they were back at the mansion in half-an-hour. Harry had long since retreated to his inner sanctum when Dunnigan opened the conversation by bragging that he'd already figured things out.

"I knew you'd change your mind, Sam. There's too much at stake in this for you to turn us down. How far are you willing to go to help us?"

"All the way. I hate drugs and anybody who's remotely connected to the hooking end of the trade. You guys sure know how to induce a guilt trip. I'll take the assignment, but as I said, I don't want any part of the take from any arrests you make. Covering my expenses will be enough. No blood money for me."

Espy sealed the deal.

"Agreed. On Monday morning a special agent from headquarters will contact you to set up the time and place to meet. His name is Vic Fowler.

He'll be your backup and control officer when you're working the bars and the clubs. And he'll bring in some help to get you up to speed on the racket and how to act and speak on the job."

"If it's also agreeable to the Bureau, we could use this place for the training and all the other contacts. It's pretty snoop-proof and Harry's offering it for the asking."

Espy liked the idea.

"That would be perfect. I checked out the big garage around back. I'll have Fowler get an automatic opener programmed for one of the doors so he can drive in and out without much notice. In the meantime, we'll check out Correlli and make sure he's not working with any other agencies. We wouldn't want to step on a DEA investigation. If he's not on their payroll we'll get a read on the names he's throwing around."

I knew there was a keen rivalry between the various government snoop groups so Espy's concern about a potential entanglement with the drug enforcement people came as no surprise. But his remark raised a question in my mind. My CIA contacts had left me high and dry more than once after I did their bidding. I wanted to make sure the FBI wouldn't leave me down and damp if I got accused of some drug crime by another branch of government or by the press. So I asked and Dunnigan tried to clear up my concerns.

"Everything you do for us will be backed up by us. Fowler will teach you all you need to know about how we get convictions, both here and overseas. And you'll never have to testify in open court against any of the targets we bring in. Your talking will be strictly in front of grand juries. And if worse comes to worst, we'll keep a spot open for you in the Witness Protection Program and get you a new ID."

I got a double dose of reassurance from Dunnigan's answer. I hadn't thought things through to their logical conclusion. If I cooperated with the feds in making drug cases, naturally I'd have to tell a court about everything I did leading to an arrest. That might be the riskiest part of my role. But these two agents were so cool and collected that I felt I could trust them. They showed none of that cloak and dagger swagger I'd come to dislike in some of the CIA representatives I'd dealt with when I did some work for the NSA.

Before Dunnigan and Espy left we talked over the first step I was to take in my new role. Since I hadn't paid much attention to specifics during Corelli's talkathons, I was told to make contact with him and see if I could get some of the names of the people he was always bragging about knowing. Any such success would trigger a bit of research by the FBI to endorse or exclude trying to build a case against them. If my sources proved productive, I'd be provided all the protection I needed right away.

After the agents left I looked up Correlli in my phone book, called, and left a message. He called back a couple of hours later and I asked him to meet me at the Ocean Manor Lounge in Ft. Lauderdale around nine that night. When I arrived early for the appointment the place was packed with the usual Friday night suspects—a few young swinging single social elites of both sexes, a mass of middle-aged serial divorcees on the remake, one or two pricey prostitutes, a muster of mostly male, affluent retirees, a small group of baby boomer businessmen. Probably a couple of mafia members and admitted wannabes too. And the demographic I'd long since grown to despise, the species I called the lily-livered lounge lizard. They were always blowing smoke about how tough they were but nowhere could they be found if a fight actually broke out. Or they would try to impress you with their fantasy fortune but never buy themselves or anyone else a drink. You could always spot them when the kitchen staff appeared around seven in the evening with the complimentary appetizers. There were usually a half-dozen freeloaders milling around the buffet table making short work of the chicken wings and pizza pieces, or in the case of the Ocean Manor, the artichoke hearts and sirloin cubes. I'd often spotted Correlli making a dash for dinner when the clatter of dishes dented the din made by the other patrons. He was the kind of low-life bar flea I usually took pains to avoid. Now here I was sitting behind the mahogany making progress with a Glenn Close look-alike and losing my concentration wondering when or whether the budgetless gourmet would show up.

When he did I said goodbye to the Glenn clone and led Correlli and the two cocktails I bought us to a crowded corner of the bar where the decibel level would frustrate potential eavesdroppers.

"Listen, Roberto, I know you know lots of important people, people with connections. I'm starting a construction business and I want to make a big investment in some property over in Pompano. But to make it work I'll need a major infusion of cash. Do you have the ear of anybody who could float me a loan of, say, five hundred thousand?"

"Are ya kiddin' me Sammy? I know lots a high rollers. They love me like a brother. But five-hundred large, Sammy? Fugheddaboutit ! Besides, I ain't never known you to be short of big bucks. Rumor around here is you made a fortune on guns and drugs down in South America. You surely ain't hurtin' for nothin.'"

I must have had trouble hiding my mixed pleasure and pain at the news that I'd indeed been connected in local lore to the international drug trade.

On the one hand, that reputation promised to smooth my see-sawing back and forth between upright Pompano entrepreneur and Miami miscreant. On the other hand, being tagged a gun runner wouldn't get me invited inside the best social circles or impress the local ladies, not to mention reassure my family that its black sheep had finally been shorn. But right now my job was to keep Correlli talking.

"Well Roberto, I took a big hit on the stock market last month. My liquidity isn't great right now. But I do have around a-hundred-and-fifty-thousand to play with. If I could double that somehow I'd be on my way to the big bundle I need. But being out of the country the last five years has put me out of touch with the major players. And I know you travel in those circles."

"I sure do, Sammy boy. And if ya got that much to play with I might put ya in touch with a friend of a friend, if you catch my meanin.' This guy's a go-between who goes between himself and the really big fish. That's the route I always take when I'm ready to make a big investment and need a little extra to swing the deal."

I had a tough time suppressing a gigantic guffaw right in the punk's face. Big investment my auntie's ass. I knew on rock-ribbed authority that Correlli didn't have two buffalo nickels to rub together in hopes they'd hit it off and make a herd. But I wasn't standing at this bar to do a financial audit.

"Who's this go-between?"

"Name's Little Jimmy Gleason. Lives over in Hollywood but he's here most weekends. I ain't seen 'im yet tonight. But if ya want I'll set up a meet for next Saturday night here."

My contact with Gleason arranged, I spent the next couple of hours cruising the bars looking for Miss Right and maybe another lizard with some information I could use. No luck. The women wouldn't stop talking and the men wouldn't start. So I went home and spent the rest of the weekend doing some rehearsing for my upcoming turn as a creepy character looking for a dark deal.

At eight o'clock Monday morning I met the man who was to become like a brother to me over the next five years. That was the appointed time for Vic Fowler of the FBI's Miami office to make his appearance. And quite an appearance it was. Harry and I were sitting in the reception hall when right on schedule we heard one of the garage doors opening and quickly closing and then a knock at the hidden side entry to the reception hall. Harry and I both went to the door to greet Fowler, a six-footer who couldn't have weighed more than a hundred-and-fifty pounds. He looked to be in his late fifties and he flashed a wide smile that put us at ease right away. His shake advertised a surprising physical power but his face told me he had a high intelligence and I'd later learn he also had an uncanny understanding of my psychological makeup.

Within thirty minutes Fowler and I were in the designated upstairs den-turned-classroom. It was time for me to enroll in Covert Cutout 101. But I wasn't looking forward to these "classroom" sessions. In all my student days, I'd never cracked the academic honor roll, though I did deserve a summa in summer vacation. Anxious is my middle name so now I was chafing to get on with the business of catching crooks and I thought Fowler's instructions would be the bore before the action. In advance of the lesson I told Fowler about my appointment on the upcoming Friday with Gleason and got an immediate surprise.

"When you meet with Gleason, Sam, don't try to act or talk any differently than you normally would. There's no need to play the role of an international criminal. The bad guys have probably had you researched already and they'll be expecting you to be Sam Hall, not Al Pacino playing Sam Hall. Any deviation from the norm will arouse suspicion."

Maybe these lessons would be worthwhile after all. Fowler had probably already saved my butt. In my play acting over the weekend I'd been practicing a new identity somewhere between Bogart in *Casablanca* and DeNiro in *Taxi Driver*. But as Fowler pointed out in what I would come to appreciate as his understated way, that kind of phony façade would no doubt earn me a Razzie followed by a rat-a-tat-tat.

Fowler followed up with more advice for my meeting with Gleason.

"Remember Sam, when you're working 'cutout', there's no such thing as small talk. What might seem like a target's off-the-cuff remark about the weather could be significant. Routine conversations often lead to a broadening of an investigation. Always keep your ears open. You never know how many dirtbags your attention to detail can trip up. And remember too that you should be inquisitive without obviously playing dumb so you can pick up as much information as possible. Get the target to spell out as much as he's willing to spell out. And keep in mind during conversations what the tape library you're building will sound like in court. You want to get the right material for an indictment."

As I was to later learn, Fowler's favorite designation for a drug distributor was "dirt bag." It was clear that his work with the Bureau had bred in him a fierce hatred of all things connected with the trade. I began to wonder if he, like me, had friends who'd fallen victim to some scum of a dealer. But probing his mental makeup would have to wait till later. The pointers were coming at me to fast and furious now.

"Sam, you'll need to know a lot about who and what you're going to be dealing with. I'll go through a structural chart of the Organized Crime setup in the States and abroad. Here's a printout of the material I want you to get familiar with."

Fowler handed me the paper and proceeded to walk me through a dirt bag dictionary.

"First of all, 'Mafia' isn't the term of art these days. Since the sixties the official designation has been Organized Crime. A New York mobster back then named Columbo brought a civil suit and stopped the press from using 'Mafia' after that. Organized Crime is modeled on the Roman army, with a pyramid of ranks and a rigid chain of command. At the bottom are the associates or connected guys. On the streets these lower echelon types are called half-a-hood or half-ass wise guy. You need to know these names in order to work smoothly with the punks who can ease you on up the ladder toward the leadership. Above the half-hoods you've got the legions, the soldiers who do most of the dirty work. They're known by different names like 'button men' or 'wise guys' or good fellows or in Italian *amici nostril* which means 'friends of ours.' Then above that layer there are the 'captains of ten' or the '*cappdeconi.*' Then another rung up from them are the 'under bosses.' The Italian word for them is '*consiglieri.*' They're the royal gatekeepers for the boss or the '*don.*' The boss we're dealing with in Florida is Santos Trafficante."

My wrist did a major pulse pound when Fowler mentioned Trafficante. He was a legend in his own slime, a super hero to the pushers who dealt addiction and sometimes death to untold numbers of victims from Miami's poorest population to the upper strata of the city's society. If the dealers and the pimps they propped up were pieces of shit, Trafficante was the origin of the feces. I was always especially enraged at the animals that promoted prostitution and its degradation of women. And Trafficante was ultimately responsible for operating Miami's well-oiled slut machine. What a pleasure it would be to put a crimp in his crime club. But I'd have to learn my lessons from Fowler well to get the chance. And about now I was having doubts about being able to stay the course. After the agent's elaborate explanation of the organization's flow chart, I wondered whether I could keep all this stuff straight. But that question was crowded out by a couple of more basic ones, like can I pull off the whole assignment and what have I got myself into? But there was no time for many second thoughts. The lessons were still coming non-stop. If I wanted to stay alive more than five minutes on the job, I'd have to pay rapt attention.

For up to six hours twice a week for a month and intermittently after that, Fowler poured out professional secrets I'd need to know. For example, he gave me a graphic lesson in weighing and analyzing coke. He put three big boxes of baking soda on the floor and made me demonstrate a testing technique over and over again. He fed me all the measurements I'd need to know to set up a buy. He not only left me papers full of details but he also gave me mini-lectures on the way coke is packaged.

"An '8-ball' means an eighth-of-an-ounce of cocaine. Thirty-eight grams equals one ounce. A pound-and-a-tenth makes seventeen-and-a-half ounces or 500 grams. A kilo is two-point-two pounds or a 100 grams. When you weigh cocaine, remember that the plastic packet weighs fifteen grams, so if you're buying, let's say, three kilos, consider that the kilo weight also includes the fifteen grams of the packet. Sam, say you're doing your first buy with a new perp. You haven't done any business with him before. Let's say he thinks you're not savvy enough to insist on weighing each kilo. Say you're buying fifteen kilos. You forget that the plastic holding a kilo is fifteen grams and the perp could walk away from the transaction with the excess in his pocket and at another location he could jump on the missing grams eight times and wind up with a windfall of over 50,000 dollars. Good for him, Sam, but bad for you. You just got screwed over. And besides that, your *bona fides* as an experienced tradesman have taken a fatal hit."

If only my grade-school teachers had grabbed my attention like this FBI agent, I mightn't have spent so much time parked in the principal's office or tracked by the truant officer. Of course, I knew my life was on the line now, or soon would be. Funny how that realization will rivet your attention and stretch its span.

"Will I be carrying a piece when I make buys?"

"No Sam, no guns, unless there's a really dicey situation that demands an arsenal. And remember never to pick up a weapon that might be left at the scene. Not even by the barrel with a pen or pencil. That screws up the ballistic exam. If you come across a weapon, call your handler or the field team and they'll take care of it. And remember, only call the Bureau using a public pay phone. "

That first month with Vic, as I was invited to call him after our first day together, was consumed with additional information. Like the going rate for cocaine per kilo in the States and overseas and the names of mob moguls. Then there were all the instructions, such as how to communicate with FBI headquarters in Miami, which I was to do using my newly bestowed code name, "Compass." Vic said the boys at the Bureau had hit on that name because I was going to point them in the direction of the dirt bags. I was told how to tail a suspect without being spotted, how to approach an information source or a potential set-up, and how to buy and test drugs. My head was reeling from information/instruction overload and I was only sleeping about three hours a night in anticipation of the end of the month and my introduction to my first wise guy, Little Jimmy Gleason. Most of the month my stomach was fluttering to the wing-beat of more butterflies than there were Monarchs in Mexico at mating time. But I welcomed the old feeling, last felt when I was trying to avoid detection in Nicaragua. And I knew in my bones that I was born to do the kind of work I was about to start.

# FOUR

Finally, the evening of my hot date with Little Jimmy arrived. I was all nerves driving to the Ocean Manor but when I got there around seven there was no sign of Correlli or Gleason. To wash off my worry I ordered my usual Old Granddad with a splash and tried to relax by surveying the assembled females. Half-a-leering-hour later I was ready to give up on my two potential setups. But about that time I spotted Correlli leading a gangly, seemingly anorexic, sandy-haired man of about thirty my way. He certainly didn't look the imposing organized crime type. His dark blue suit and shirt unbuttoned to the breast bone played to type but he didn't have the required medallion or the chest hair to support it. Correlli did the introduction.

"Sammy, good to see ya. This here's Little Jimmy Gleason. He's been workin' with the big boys for two months now. Jimmy, Sam Hall."

Little Jimmie gave me the limpest handshake I'd had since I'd taken a ID bracelet off a dead terrorist's wrist in Lebanon. Then he motioned for Correlli to get lost and zeroed in on business.

" I hear you're interested in a little investment."

"Yeah, I've got a hundred-and-fifty thousand that I need to grow pretty quick. There's some property over in Pompano I want to develop to keep up appearances. I hear you can put me in touch with some big players in the trade."

"I don't like shits who never worked their way to the top like me. I was pushin' shit on the streets of Newark while fucks like you was rollin' in stash."

Not the friendliest come-on I'd ever experienced. I resisted the temptation to punch the punk in the mouth and played along.

"No need to take offense. I appreciate guys like you who started out as soldiers and made something of themselves. You've got my deepest respect." I tried not to gag.

"Yeah, sure I have. Let's get back to the business. What about all yer South American connections? I'd think ya'd be pretty set up already."

Vic Fowler had prepared me for this one.

"I can't go that route. Ever since I got captured down there I'm too hot for the Central Americans. They think the feds are laying in wait for any contact between us, and they're probably right. But I could deal with your boys without raising suspicion."

"Well, there's no way you're gonna deal with the big brass. Ya'll have ta go through a couple of the goodfellas like Tommy Andretti and Joey Aiello. If ya check out O.K. with them over a long haul, they might put ya in touch with one of the captains. I deal with them all the time. I guess since ya got in touch with me through Correlli ya got nothin' against dealing with Wops. Am I right?"

"You're right. I have absolutely no problem working with Italians. Hell, I once got an Olympic medal placed around my neck by one of them in Rome. And I've worked with every nationality all over the world."

"Good for ya, Sammy. I hate the grease-balls myself but ya gotta deal where ya gotta deal. But there's one other thing. I ain't doin' favors as a charity. There's got to be a vig in this for me."

Since I'd just passed one of Vic Fowler's vocabulary tests, I knew Gleason was claiming a cut of any profit I might make from a deal finessed through his connections.

"How does five percent sound Jimmy?"

"Don't fuck with me, Sam. I don't do business with fuckin' crooks. Who do ya think yer fuckin' with?

"O.K., O.K., Jimmy. Eight percent it is."

"That's more like it. And we'll talk bonuses when and if the stuff's delivered."

"Agreed. Can I meet with the two you mentioned soon. I want to seal my bid for that property before somebody comes along and turns it into another amusement park."

"Don't push me. The boys will have ta do sommore checkin' before any O.K. for a meet. I'll get word back to ya when I'm good and ready."

With that Gleason walked halfway around the bar and rejoined Correlli. When I left they were still standing in place, no doubt reviewing my performance. As I began the drive home I was feeling pretty self-satisfied that my first attempt at a big drug buy had passed muster. But it didn't take long to put things in a gloomier perspective. It was obviously going to be a lengthy process to get to any significant players in the trade. I couldn't see why it would take so long to set up a meeting with the next echelon of creeps. And the disappointing truth was that Correlli was blowing smoke when he sold Little Jimmy Gleason as a "middle man." That would be somebody who'd reached second base but Gleason seemed barely out of the batter's box. He was no more a high roller than Correlli and I wouldn't have been surprised if at this minute the two of them were scarfing down a freebie dinner together at the Ocean Manor appetizer spread. The most you could say about Gleason was that he apparently had a lot more ambition than Corelli ever showed. His insistence on a substantial coke cut revealed a resolve to hang lace curtains in his shanty.

The next morning I reported on the Gleason meeting with Vic. I told him I was really disappointed that the Irishman had turned out to be such a tiny fish, literally and figuratively. But Vic didn't see it my way.

"Nonsense, Sam. You've got your foot in the door. We'll run a check on Andretti and Aiello. They may be keeping just the gate we want to crash. And Gleason's physical appearance wouldn't sideline him. Remember, Meyer Lansky was only five-foot-three."

"But why the long wait before I meet the two wiseguys?"

"They'll be checking you out thoroughly, Sam. It's important for you to keep to your behavior pattern for the next month. Don't change a thing."

That was the kind of encouragement and explanation I really needed about now. For the next several weeks I was antsy as a picnic, anticipating what could be a crucial linkup with Andretti and Aiello. Vic let me know the hours of checking me out that the bosses would have set in motion would either establish trust on their part or the whole deal would be off and I might be in for an ID change and a new address.

The uncertainty was compounded one morning when Vic arrived for an instruction session.

"Have you seen the morning papers, Sam? Santos Trafficante is dead. Heart attack. I never thought he'd die a natural death."

"Shit ! Does that mean I'm off the case?"

"Hardly, Sam. There'll be a power struggle now between Santos Junior and some of the underbosses. We can use all of the information we can get on who's holding the aces."

Although it wasn't clear whether the next step in the operation would actually come to pass, Vic was almost certain it would, so he wanted to take full advantage of the time before the action started. Whatever the result of my crook credibility check, he wanted to run through a lesson on listening devices. Bureau Headquarters in Washington had informed him that I'd been granted special permission by the Attorney General's office to wear a wire in pursuit of legitimate targets. That told me that I'd been fast-tracked to active status and that, as I was to learn in all other instances, Vic Fowler played it by the book. He began by describing the undercover operator's various electronic options.

"There are a couple of ways to go as far as wearing a wire is concerned. When there's a high level of certainty that an undercover agent has been accepted by the mob, we usually fit him with a Nagra. It's basically a miniature, concealed backpack. It's not the most comfortable accessory to wear, but it gives us a clearer recording than some other devices. The bad news is that a savvy dirtbag can detect it by running his hand down your back when he's giving you a greeting. The agent has to improvise ways of denying his or her targets the opportunity for an impromptu pat down. But the Nagra will let us record any names the agent picks up so they don't have to be committed to memory."

That reference to "his or her" really caught my attention. Were there really women who did this kind of dangerous duty? I wondered what a woman that reckless would be like in altered circumstances. Maybe I could pat one down myself sometime and find out. But that was just a fleeting fancy. I was locked in otherwise on Vic's effort to provide me with a practical electronic education.

"Before an agent has got the confidence of his targets, we almost always fit them with a Kel device instead of a Nagra. It's a tiny transmitter, not a recorder. It sends short-range radio signals. If the agent is in a sticky situation, a field team that's always monitoring the conversation can come in like the cavalry. The problem with the Kel is that it's not always reliable. It's transcriptions can be broken up by concrete walls or passing cars or other kinds of interference."

I didn't want Fowler to think my frequent and fascinated silences signaled inattention so I interjected a question.

"If the Kel is so iffy, why not start with the Nagra?"

"Even the Corellis and the Gleasons are hip enough to give you a pat down at some unexpected moment. The bigger boys are far more sophisticated so the Nagra is saved for the cutout whose established the complete trust of the target. On the way to establishing that level of trust you'll find yourself getting patted down so often you'll feel like you're engaged. The thing we really worry about is the dirtbag who asks the agent to submit to a strip search. We've lost a cutout or two that way."

"So what else do I need to know about wearing the Kel?"

"Well, it's worn under your belt buckle. Sometimes a lot of sweat will cause it to give off a little electric charge that has to be gotten used to. If every time a dirtbag mentions a juicy name or makes a physical threat the agent has a convulsion from the shock, he won't last long in the business. But the good news is the burning sensation around the stomach area is proof the Kel is still in place. If a difficult situation arises when you're wearing a Kel, you need to lose it as soon as you can. If you're lucky enough to be within pitching distance of the Inter Coastal, the best thing to do is give the Kel a heave. If there's no ocean in sight, bury it beneath the top layer of junk in a not-too-convenient trash can if you get the opportunity. Or give it a fast flush down the nearest john."

"What happens if the Kel comes loose and falls on the floor?"

"You just 'accidentally' step on it and say something like 'Oh fuck, I don't think my insurance will cover another pacemaker.' Then you run like hell and don't look back."

By now I expected Vic to indulge in an occasional bit of levity to leaven the utter professionalism he exuded at all other times. The more I came to know him, the more respect and admiration I had for him. This was true of all of my FBI contacts, but especially true of Vic. We were destined to become the best of friends over the years. He would prove many times to be my lifeline, always there to back me up. The kind of closeness under the extreme pressure that we shared cemented our permanent friendship. But now I wanted to know what was in store for me.

"When do I start practicing with a wire?"

"Right away. There will be plenty of risk involved when you meet with Andretti and Aiello, even without a wire. When you're wearing one, the risk increases ten-fold. If you get any bad vibes when you're wearing a wire, get out of there fast. Your career with the Bureau might be over at that point but at least you'll be alive to pursue another field. And never get complacent when your wired. Some smart dirtbags are sophisticated enough to buy anti-transmission equipment, mail order spy gadgets that can alert them to a person strapped with a transmitter."

But at this point I was too absorbed in learning how to wear the two kinds of bugs to think much about consequences. I'd worry about the Orkin man later. First, Vic strapped me with a Nagra and we played hide and seek around Harry's grounds while I talked to myself and Vic monitored my monologue so he could quote it back to me. Next he fit me with a Kel and I'd get lost on the property so he could tape my transmissions. That way he could show me how walls and other obstructions beat the bug. I had to learn how to subtly keep a culprit out in the open if possible. I even practiced wearing the Kel at make-believe mob powwows with Vic playing drug lord. I prided myself on never setting off an electronic reaction in the tiny transmitter when Vic said something calculated to increase my blood pressure.

During those weeks of worrying about my impending performance, Vic kept playing professor, providing depth and detail. There were classes on how to recognize a stash house, search and seizure methods, even about forfeiture laws and minimum sentencing guidelines for criminal offenses related to drug and gun running. These learning sessions were stimulating enough in themselves to keep me fascinated. Vic had turned out to be a great guide through the intricacies of cutout codes and conduct. I was every bit as enthralled now as I was with the only classes I did A work in at Ohio State, Phys Ed and Human Sexuality. But it wasn't a football game or a roll in the hay I was looking forward to on the upcoming weekend. The only Big Ten that interested me now were the top drug dogs on the FBI's most wanted list.

Finally after what seemed like an eternity I got a Wednesday morning call from Gleason telling me to meet him on Friday night at Frankie and Johnnies lounge in Lauderdale. Andretti and Aiello would be there to check me out. In the hours leading up to the big meeting I ran through my lines with Vic, stewed over what to say and how to phrase it, how to ask questions to get a response that might bring out some relevant names. I already had regrets about my first dialogue with Gleason. Why hadn't I drawn him into a longer conversation? He might have let something slip. Maybe if I'd played it a little dumber I could have got something useful. But not dumb in the way I'd played it when Gleason asked for his vig. Why had I offered him five percent when Vic had clued me that the going rate was eight? That little improv had almost queered the whole deal. Now I was determined to draw Andretti and Aiello out if I got the chance. But carefully. Vic had always stressed how little verbal slipups could lead to self-incrimination. I vowed to do better than I had with Gleason.

When I walked into the bar that Friday night the pencil-necked Gleason was standing with the two tall, muscular "wiseguys." I realized immediately that I'd underdressed just as sure as if I'd worn fatigues for the occasion. Andretti and Aiello could have been models for a special organized crime issue of *Gentlemen's Quarterly*. They were both wearing expensive dark blue suits with navel-plunging wide-collared shirts. Each had a garish gold medallion that was making love to a mass of black chest hair. On each of their pinky fingers the required gold and diamonds dazzled. Blinding black shoes completed the ensemble.

Gleason's etiquette proved impeccable.

"Sam Hall, this here is Angelo Andretti and Joey Aeillo. These was the two guys I tol' ya about. Guys, this here is Sam Hall, the fortune soldier."

The social niceties proceeded as Angelo and Joey each embraced me like I was Michelle Pfeiffer. If I'd been her I could've sued for sexual harassment. While I was held in their hugs they helped themselves with their hands to my back and chest. Angelo tried to make amends for the grope.

"Sorry, Sammy. Ya can't be too careful these days ya know."

"I know that. I've been in your spot before. You could never be sure you were dealing with a legit dealer down in Honduras. Only way to do business down there was with a pat down"

The two hoods waved Little Jimmy away and led me to a corner table to begin what I hoped would be the negotiations. Once we were seated and shed of the waitress, Angelo leaned over the table toward me and started making small talk in the hushed way you might in a church, all the while making sure there was nobody within earshot. When he was satisfied we weren't likely to be disturbed for a while, he got right to the muffled point.

"Little Jimmy says ya got a few thousand ya want to grow. What kind of deal did ya have in mind?'

"Well, I was thinking if I could get my hands on some quality blow I might be able to turn it over for a decent profit. I've got some customers up in Jacksonville lined up. They'll pay top dollar for good shit. I want a hundred-and-fifty thousand worth of the stuff. I could plow the profits into a sweet real estate deal I've got going over in Pompano. With a few thousand extra, I could make the down payment."

Joey wasn't sold on my proposal. I could tell by his clenched teeth and his frown. He leaned across the table, looked me right in the eyes and loudly whispered,

"Fugheddaboutit, fuck ! What kinda fuckin' deal would it be if you was the only party to profit. Me and Angelo here would be awful fuckin' dumb to set you up out of the goodness of our hearts. What's our vig in all this?"

Angelo agreed that the two weren't stupid and told me so in no uncertain snarls.

"Listen, Sam. What do ya take us for? We didn't come down here tonight to get fuckin' insulted."

If I could have kicked myself hard enough under the table I would have. Vic had prepared me to begin negotiating by offering the wiseguys a substantial cut and I'd completely forgotten to attach that preamble to the proposition. And I wasn't expecting *their* expectation so early in the conversation. Now I had to scurry to reassure my new acquaintances that I was as deeply concerned about their financial portfolios as I was about mine.

"Sorry, boys. I got carried away. Sure there's something in it for you two. How about the supplier gets a hundred-and-fifty thousand for a shipment of top grade shit? That's half of my cash stash right now. Will you take the offer to your friends?"

I was relishing the rush I got from playing my role when Joey let me know I'd committed another major blunder.

"We ain't got no friends, Sam. We work with the big studs but we don't mix business and friendship, least of all with fuckin' amateurs like you. We came up through the ranks, man. Me and Angelo here started in the streets hawkin' to junkies till we got where we are today. Hell, we make more at the dog track on a weekend now than most guys make in a lifetime. Anybody fucks with us, they get their ass kicked good. Ya understand what I'm sayin'?"

I had to fight off the urge to ask Joey to put his money where his big mouth was but I had to stay focused on getting these two wiseguys to buy into the deal. They weren't in any hurry to cooperate, as Angelo let me know. He was obviously the more savvy of the two, a much cooler customer.

"And slow way down, Sam. We'll think about a deal in our own good time. We don't know enough about ya. All them newspaper and TV reports don't mean jackshit next to a little up close and personal. We need to get to know ya a little."

Joey was more direct.

"Yea, we don't know shit about ya. Not shit."

Then Angelo came to my rescue, sort of.

"Back off, Joey. We both know Sam needs some juice for the downstroke on a piece of property in Pompano and that he's got a Jacksonville connection. Or so he says. Let's just get acquainted from there. We got plenty of time to decide on a deal. Tell me Sam, what do you do to blow off steam? Do you gamble?"

"I love the dog track. And I've been known to bet a yard or two on a golf match."

"Angelo and me just won a couple a dimes at the track last night. Hell, we won five yards there last week."

"Don't bore the man with our balance sheet, Joey. Sam, have ya ever bet on jai alai?"

"A couple of times. But I don't know the game as well as I should. Maybe the two of you could give me some pointers some time."

"It's a sport worth knowin' somethin' about Sam. Easy to fix. A lot of variables, but they can be controlled."

Angelo seemed to be warming up to me.

"Listen, Joey, Sam seems like a straight-shooter to me. And the boss, man gave him a clean bill. If there's a decent vig in it for us, why shouldn't we give his proposition a think? Go ahead Sam, let's here the rest of your pitch. How many packets are you thinking about?"

About then I was really thinking what a damned shame it was not to be packing that Kel. When I was patted down the two hadn't come close to my belt buckle so I could be broadcasting now. What a pleasure it would be to collect the first incriminating chatter from these two pricks. To bring them down would be so satisfying, especially Joey, the cocky bastard!

"Well, first things first. What kind of vig are you getting these days? I know the rate in Central America but I'm out of touch here."

Joey had the figure at his fingertips.

"We get eight percent, rain or shine."

"Sounds fair to me. This is what I've got in mind. Five, maybe ten 'keys.'"

Angelo took charge of the negotiation at this point while Joey watched with great respect for his partner's expertise.

"Who is the tester, Sam?"

"I am."

"And what are ya lookin' for?"

"Ninety-five percent pure."

"How many times are ya jumpin' on it?"

"At least eight. My buyers in Jacksonville will sell the stuff on the streets and make a little something. Meanwhile the rest of us come out way on the plus side, me, you two, and the whole family."

Angelo put a sudden stop to the conversation.

"We'll call ya if we think we can do a deal. If we can, we'll set up another meet. Write down your phone number on this matchbook. That's it. It was real good talkin' to ya, Sam."

The next thing I knew Joey was trailing Angelo out the door and I was left to stew over my latest performance. Had I been wearing the Kel, would I have got enough to incriminate these two peddler/pushers? Would any of what they said have stood up in court, if it ever got that far? I knew I'd done a pretty good job of sounding knowledgeable and juggling the jargon Vic had taught me, like asking for ninety-five percent pure cocaine and "jumping on it eight times," or multiplying profits eight-fold.

The next day I debriefed Vic on what the two wiseguys had said and asked if it was the kind of thing that would have put them in deep shit.

"You got some pretty incriminating stuff, Sam, but it would have to be augmented by a lot of hard evidence to get a conviction. Maybe that will start piling up if you have another meeting."

But Vic was pleased with the way things had gone and thought it highly likely that a follow up call would be coming.

We didn't have to wait long for that word from the mob. Joey called the same afternoon to say that Angelo had been impressed with me and wanted another meeting at Dante's Steak House two days later. This time I was fitted with a Kel. Vic thought that since the first meeting had included an elaborate pat down it was unlikely that Angelo and Joey would get physical this second time.

That Friday night driving to Dante's I got a feel for what Vic had been trying to tell me about the Kel having a mind of its own. I was so worked up over my immanent meeting with the two wiseguys that I was sweating up a tsunami. All of a sudden I felt a jolt of juice under my belt and almost swerved off of 1A1. Not that the shock was that strong but the sudden surge surprised me out of my skin. It occurred to me that it would have been a lot more satisfying to have the device strapped a little lower on my torso. At least a short nearer the short hairs would have had some compensations.

When I got to the lounge Angelo had a different scenario in mind for our meeting. He told Joey to wait in the bar while he had a "walk-talk" with me in the parking lot. Once outside, Angelo spelled out the proposition he'd been authorized to pursue.

"We'll deliver ten kilos of 95, Sam. Ya come up with a-hundred-and-forty-five large. But for my trouble, I need another fat percentage point on the vig."

"Hang on, Angelo. You agreed to eight percent. What's going on here? If we're going to keep doing business, you'll have to be straight with me from the start."

Angelo leaned over and spat spittle in my ear while delivering his idea of a subtle response.

"Watch your fuckin' mouth fuck-face ! You mouth off like that again and I'll bust your fuckin' ass."

ZAP!. My sweat met the metal and I got another jolt of Kel juice in the gut.

Luckily, Angelo didn't notice my twitch.

"I'm tellin' ya the vig has changed. I got overhead and I got to give Little Jimmy a finder's fee and split the vig with Joey. Take it or leave it, I told ya the terms."

"I guess I'll have to take it. How do I know you'll deliver?"

"Ya fuckin' fag! Are ya tryin' to make light ofme? My word's golden, you fuck! Maybe I should crush your skull for doubtin' it."

ZAP.

"OK, Angelo, you're playing all the aces. But I want to know if we can do business on a regular basis. My buyers in Jacksonville may want to stay supplied."

"If this deal goes down O.K., Sam, we're talkin' the possibility of every-other-week deliveries. But if anything goes wrong anywhere along the way, yer a dead man. I'll track ya and I'll whack ya!"

Zap.

That "dead man" reference gave me a relatively weak stab to the stomach and I wondered whether I was already getting cooler at this work or if the Kel had begun to rust out from my monsoon of adrenaline-produced perspiration. But in any event I managed to seal the deal and agree to Angelo's delivery date of one month from that evening. When I got home I removed the Kel and worried that it might only have succeeded in Xeroxing its own zapping. If it'd slurred the sounds of Angelo incriminating himself I'd be in for my biggest disappointment since the gold eluded me at the Rome Olympics.

The next morning I showed Vic the stomach stigmata the Kel had inflicted and asked if he could tell whether the little bug had bitten Angelo. That's when he checked the transmitter and I got the good news that the Kel's acoustics had been perfect and that Angelo's every word would soon be on its way to an FBI file clerk. The savvy hood had been hoodwinked and he was now on record as a coke supplier, the first step in relocating him to a federal prison cell. Vic was pleased and I was proud of my first real success as a cutout. The fact that I'd done a decent job in my first assignment gave me a big boost.

# FIVE

Helping get the goods on Andretti and Aiello had revved up my engines for more. But before I could get back in action there were a few other things to take care of. Besides having to testify in front of a grand jury about my role in the dirtbags' undoing, Vic had another set of lessons lined up for me. I got drilled for the next couple of weeks in subjects like trafficking operations, cocaine packaging and distribution methods, drug trade negotiation techniques, money flashing, the legalities of arrest procedures, entrapment avoidance precautions used by dealers, taping, and writing policies, emergency tactics, special telephone numbers to call for information or backup, and the names of various dirtbags to be on the lookout for during my circuit of the Miami bars and lounges. On top of all that, Vic left me with a bundle of books for my bedtime browsing. I was never much of a reader, but now I was expected to at least skim tomes with titles like *Lucky Luciano*, *Valachi*, *Teresa*, *The Family*, and *The Sicilian Heritage*. During all this time I kept on kibitzing with lowlifes at the local bars. Vic thought this was the best strategy because even though the chances of the drug riffraff or Andretti and Aiello themselves out on bail connecting me to their indictments were less than fifty-fifty I'd arouse less attention if I just went on like before. If I suddenly dropped out of sight suspicions would surely grow. The tactic suited me since the added uncertainty about whether I'd be outed rounded off the rush. And besides, I was getting addicted to the life I was leading.

By early the next month things were working out well on another front.

My construction business was really taking off. I had pulled my permits, cleared the land, and broken ground for my first row of condos in Pompano. My father had trained me to be the best in the business and now that instruction was paying off again. And Steve Surovec, the site foreman Harry recommended, had turned out to be every bit as competent as advertised. In fact, he was so good the project was already weeks ahead of schedule and sales were surpassing expectations. I was running things in Pompano with one or two visits a week and Steve covered for me otherwise. The rest of my time was spent in Miami, conferring with Vic during the day, and hitting the bars and lounges till the early hours of the morning. It was shaping up to be a good life, combining the kick that came from the business startup with the intoxication of the undercover work. As the weeks fled by, I made a number of real estate buys. And I did three drug deals with a couple of new characters named Charley and Vito. We were conferring on a by-weekly basis and I was gaining more and more of their confidence. Vic was counting on them to grease my gradual acceptance by more sterling representatives of the mob's social register.

My invaluable training never stopped, however, but it did change one day when Vic announced that he would be strictly working backup for me the next few months and that the information/instruction side of the equation would be turned over to a special agent working out of his office. He said the agent would be Hispanic and that I would be contacted Monday morning. When I got the call I was surprised to hear a female voice on the line. She said her name was Gloria Guerrero and she asked if we could meet at Harry's in two hours to start the training. Believe me I was ready to begin instantaneously because I was already under the spell of that breathy voice. When its owner appeared outside Harry's door I discovered that the voice fit its frame. Agent Guerrero was a long-haired, longer-legged brunette beauty who, it would turn out, was a ten-year veteran of the Bureau. At first sight, I questioned whether I could keep my mind off of her and on the teaching she had been sent to impart since she pushed all my bachelor buttons. But as soon as the first session started I discovered that she was as no-nonsense a professional as Dunnigan, Espy, and especially Vic.

Guerrero's assignment over the next two months was to enlighten me about international drug trafficking. She described the workings of Columbian organized crime, pointed out the differences between the Cali and Medellin cartels, provided biographical sketches of drug lords like Pablo Escobar, Jorge Ochoa, Jose Santacruz Londono, Gilberto Orejuela and his brother Miguel. I learned about the alliances formed between the South American cartels and the Japanese Yakulza and various European distributors. Guerrero explained how the cartels would adjust if the FBI or DEA located a shipment, changing shippers, using different routes, or other anticipated deceptions. One day she iced my blood with a warning.

"Sam, so far you've been dealing with low-level Florida hoods. If they found out what you've been doing, you'd be a dead man. But if you were informing on the Columbians themselves, or on the Asians, it wouldn't just be you. Your whole family would be wiped out, even your brother the Congressman. The Columbians especially have no qualms about killing anyone they deem a threat and adding relatives to the list of victims to make a point to prospective imitators."

If Guerrero was trying to engage my full attention, that kind of counseling was well calculated to turn the trick. But once again, I didn't have time to reflect much on the situation. Guerrero was fast feeding me more morsels. She began an exposition on Jamaican gangs, a subject about which, I later learned, she was the nation's foremost expert. In fact, Vic later told me that she knew more about foreign traffickers in general than any government agent in Florida. For hours she tutored me on the going rates for coke from South America, which at the time averaged around 10,000 dollars for two-and-a-half pounds of 90 percent pure uncut. She also offered lots of practical pearls, like how to carry large cash caches across security checkpoints at international airports. For example, I would need to know that 50,000 dollars in one hundred-dollar bills would equal three-and-one-half inches of thickness. If the wad were covered with a damp cloth, no security scope could detect what it was.

The good part of another day was spent speculating about what seemed like every exotic encampment from Belize to Brazil as possible sites where growers and distributors might be meshing their machinations. Thanks to Guerrero, I also learned that my old tormentors, the Sandinistas, were involved in the trade, as was Manuel Noriega's Panama. Most often the minor leaguers like Nicaragua and Panama were aligned in some way with the Big Show, which was Columbia. And it was in connection with the Columbians that Guerrero planted the word narcoterrorism in my vocabulary. The term was tied up, like it sounded, with the financing of terrorist operations through the narcotics trade. Unholy alliances had formed between the fanatics trying to frighten nations into changing political policies and the drug lords with their dirty profits.

By the time my several weeks of classroom work with the Bureau beauty were up, I'd also committed to memory, as much as possible, information on the connection between drugs and the Shining Path in Cambodia, the Burmese Communist party, the Shan United Army in China as well as the old tongs and triads there. Just before I said goodbye to Guerrero for the last time she made my week with a compliment sure to swell my pride. She said the extra instruction the Bureau was providing proved that they thought well of me, that I had done a good job so far, and that they wanted me to learn all I could to expand my contribution in the future.

At the beginning of the next week I met with Vic again and more training followed, this time with FBI manuals of procedure. Though he wasn't nearly so visually stimulating as Gloria Guerrero, the lessons didn't lessen in intensity and interest when he took over again.

In mid week Harry suggested a Saturday night break from the books, including *Counter-Terrorist*, since on the following Monday I was due to begin a month-long publicity tour to launch its publication. Jimmie had called from St. Pete to recommend a gala fund raiser and dance scheduled for Saturday night at the posh Yacht Club there. Since I'd always fancied myself a dancer who could show Michael Flatley a hoof or two, I gladly agreed to join my two best buddies in what I hoped would be a relaxing interlude between my construction project and my next meeting with Charley and Vito. So, promptly at nine-o'clock on the appointed evening, the three brave bachelors, suitably spiffed up for the occasion, made a self-conscious entrance into the grand ballroom. Right away we laid claim to a table strategically situated to maximize ogling opportunities. Drinks began to disappear and soon we were joined by a couple of dried up ex-debutants who wanted to talk about which Florida colleges offered the most rewarding social connections for their no doubt equally ding batty daughters. Jimmie's reflexes proved the most rapid and he excused himself, leaving Harry to endure the blonde's babbling and me to swallow the redhead's stream of quasi-consciousness.

After five minutes of mind-numbing chit-chat I started to survey the room in hopes of locating an escape route. On the second scan I spotted a striking, slender, thirty-something, blonde woman walking our way toward a nearby table. Our glances met and I got a subtle smile that told me this was someone I wanted to meet. In fact if I'd been wearing my Kel I'd have gotten a ZAP. She had all of the physical features that pulled my draw string, petite, perfect legs, and gorgeous hair. But at this point in my life I was looking for more than looks. There was something about the way this woman presented herself to the world that promised intelligent understanding of the kind I needed just now. After all, I'd not only gone through nearly two months in prison but had also been disavowed at the hands of the government I'd served so faithfully. Not to mention the not so little ridicule from a skeptical segment of the press. Adding to the fact that my recent spate of hobnobbing with some of the most repulsive reptiles in South Florida, I found myself more than a little open to the idea of spending some time with a bright, thoughtful woman. So I watched with growing curiosity as my new discovery reached her table and took up a conversation with her companions. She had a fascinating way of amplifying her thoughts with that subtle smile and her hands would take intermittent flights to punctuate a point. At the same time, I was observing all this, I was trying without success to keep up with the paltry patter of the red-headed nitwit at my side.

After a few minutes the woman who was quickly capturing all my attention must have felt my gripped gaze. She turned toward me and gave me a look that locked onto mine, and we stayed shackled for several seconds until she turned away in obvious embarrassment. Another half-minute more of steady staring rewarded me with another return rivet, this time accompanied by an even more inviting smile. It was now or never to follow up on the seeming possibilities, so I made a couple of polite excuses to my insignificant other, walked over to the table in question, and began a relationship that was to brighten my life ever after that and better me as a person.

I've often reviewed that Yacht Club evening in the context of a quote I'd heard not long before. One of the writers I'd hired to tell my story in *Counter-Terrorist*, who would become a good friend and the transcriber of my experiences for this book as well, was an admitted but recovering college professor with a rabid research interest in the novelist Theodore Dreiser. We'd had a number of discussions over the years, but especially during the work on my first book, about one similarity between ourselves and Dreiser. It seems that he was always in search of the ideal woman for him, or as the professor put it, the "impossible she." I sure couldn't argue that I wasn't like that. All my life I'd been engaged in what the unimaginative call "womanizing" because they don't understand the depth of the desire or the intensity of the emotion involved. Leading up to that June night at the St. Petersburg Yacht Club I'd been "in love" with a succession of women, including three wives, and the inevitable broken connections would always afflict me with an ache that never substantially subsided. But that first smile from the beauty at the nearby table somehow promised a different order of enthrallment. And here is where the Dreiser quote sums up this particular woman's irresistible appeal far better than I could. According to my friend the writer, Dreiser talked about how you can be captivated by the "show of soul in some passing eye." Those words had ratcheted my heart rate up when they were quoted to me a couple of years earlier. I'd experienced that sort of lightning link through a look a very few times, but never in my youth when they it might have been expected, if you listened to the conventional romantic wisdom. No, this "show of soul" stuff seemed to be reserved for later years, when there was sufficient soul to shine through. Those few times I'd seen it in a passing eye" I'd made the mistake of letting it pass. But I didn't intend to hesitate this time.

When I reached this woman's table, I was uncharacteristically unable to turn my thoughts into words. In fact, I was totally tongue-tied. Of course, that may have been for the best. Normally I would have exercised my morbidly obese ego and said something like, "Hello there, I'm Sam Hall the famous counter-terrorist. You might have seen me on *the* evening news and "60 Minutes." Or even worse, "How do you like the Yacht Club Doll-Face? Want to do something nautical?" Instead I stammered, "My name's Sam. Would you like to dance?" So I was surprised when I found myself moments later drifting back and forth across the ballroom floor, my arms filled with one of the most attractive women I'd ever met. As we did dance after dance we began building biographies of each other. I learned that her name was Melinda, that she was going through a painful period in her life involving a messy divorce, aren't they all, and that she shared a lot of my interests. What surprised me the most was her revelation that she was in the construction business, on a small scale, and the way she talked about the projects she was involved in told me that she was not only beautiful but brainy. Most admirable of all though was her avid interest in all kinds of charitable causes from national wildlife protection to the local food pantries for the poor. I was able to score quite a few points with her when I told her my brother Tony was the Ohio Congressman known as the government's most articulate advocate for the world's hungry. When the evening ended with the last sentimental strain from the orchestra seemingly mere seconds after I'd met Melinda, we made hurried plans to get together the next day for an early picnic on the beach. On the way home from the Yacht Club, Harry and Jimmie diverted themselves by making jokes about my bent for getting bewitched. But later that night back at Jimmie's, I bored my buddies with every detail I'd learned about my new love, trying to hold her in my head until I could be with her again the next morning.

I'd been looking forward to the limelight the looming book tour would generate, but now I hated whoever set it up. Those four weeks would create a gaping gap that might be fatal to my chances to win Melinda, and I felt like canceling the whole trip. But at Sunday's picnic I was reassured that she seemed to feel at least a fraction of my own feeling and that she would look forward to my phone calls from the road. Our conversation that morning ran the gamut from gardening to guns to God. When we said goodbye and she let me kiss her, I not only knew the initial impact of her physicality would build to a pitch of passion. I was also sure I'd finally found my mind-mate.

On the post-picnic Sunday afternoon drive back to Miami through "Alligator Alley," Harry, whose eyes were still coated with the glaze created during his evening-long conversation with the two mindless debutants from the lurch I'd left him in to approach Melinda, admitted that despite the hard time he'd given me over the weekend, he yearned himself to someday find his own "impossible she." And I knew the same was true for Jimmie. And probably for all single men except the ones hankering for an "impossible he."

The first days of the *Counter-Terrorist* publicity tour went by in a blur of bookstores and television studios. During each TV interview I tried to make the point that it was only a matter of time before there would be a terrorist attack on American soil, a prediction that proved prescient, but one that a succession of American presidents remained oblivious to. On one memorable occasion at an outdoor display in Manhattan where hundreds of potential buyers browsed the colorful empty covers of the still undistributed final product, I made my pitch to the browsers that we needed to be on guard against the looming terrorist threat. I only wish now I'd been a lot more persuasive.

Each night my spirits were lifted by wonderful telephone conversations with Melinda. She was excited about interesting me in a particularly promising piece of property for development in St. Petersburg. It seemed just the sort of deal I was seeking at the time so I looked forward to getting back to Florida for more than one reason. But then I started receiving a series of far less welcome calls. My role as an Iran-Contra figure was being revealed not only by my book but also in Congressional hearings. Now several left-wing fanatics who were unhinged by Reagan's foreign policy were phoning my hotel rooms with death threats against me. In Michigan at the beginning of the third week of the tour, I got what was in some ways an even more unnerving call. It was from a reporter at the *Detroit Free Press* telling me that the federal court in Miami had me listed as a defendant in a lawsuit brought by some outfit I'd never heard of called the Christic Institute. I was supposed to appear before a grand jury in three weeks and name some other people who'd participated with me in some kind of a murder plot. When I heard that word "murder" I lost all the curse-control I'd worked so hard at in preparation for my book discussion appearance on Pat Robertson's "700 Club." What the fuck was the Christic Institute and how in the hell could they link me with a murder? As soon as the reporter finished filling me in on his less than illuminating information, I pressed my fingers on the phone's cradle button and dialed my Miami lawyer, Carl Mears, to ask him if he could find out what was going on.

Nine hours later, around midnight, he called back with the scary scoop, an allegation that I was supposedly involved in a convoluted assassination plot.

It seemed that the Christic Institute was a Washington D.C. interfaith legal foundation that fronted for a gaggle of left-wing loonies led by somebody named Dan Sheehan. They'd done an extended investigation that was actually sanctioned by the U.S. Attorney's office in Miami. And they'd come up with a number of explosive claims. According to the Christics, the Contras in Nicaragua were into narcotics smuggling from Costa Rica to Colombia, using dirt airstrips and small boats to move cocaine and other contraband drugs that eventually wound up juicing junkies on the streets of America. The motivation behind all this skullduggery was supposed to be the financing of the Contra war against the Sandinistas. The Institute lawyers also thought they had evidence that the Contra leaders were getting additional financial support from major narcotics traffickers and that U. S. government funds supposedly earmarked by the Reagan administration for the Contras actually went to drug lords. The lefties even thought the C.I.A. was helping smuggle drugs into the U.S. in exchange for the drug kingpins' help in arming the Contras. All of these branches of conjecture were attached to the trunk of the Institute's lawsuit on behalf of a couple of American journalists named Martha Honey and Tony Avirgan. These two had been injured in a 1984 assassination attempt against the Contra leader, Eden Pastora, in Nicaragua. The bomb involved had spared Pastora but killed eight people and injured the two reporters. The Christics had filed suit trying to tie twenty-nine people, including me, into a vast right-wing conspiracy that'd helped supply the assassins with the C-4 explosives, the idea being to blame the Sandinista government for the blast.

At about this point in Barrister Mears's dissertation I broke in to ask how in the hell I fit into this Christic crew's paranoid take on the Central American situation. That's when I was told that, according to the labyrinthine lawsuit that the Institute filed in Miami, they knew for a fact that I'd met with one Steven Carr, who'd since apparently died, and three other guys I'd never heard of, at the Miami International Airport Howard Johnson motel on June third in 1984. At that meeting, according to the imaginative Institute lawyers, I agreed to blow up the U.S. Embassy in Costa Rica and shoot our ambassador, Lewis Tambs, making it look like the Sandinistas were responsible. Through this ingenious plot, I would help heap negative press on the Nicaraguan government and ease Ronald Reagan's takeover of Central America. The whole notion was absurd, of course, but I could see my immediate future screwed up by the need to defend myself against these trumped up charges, even though Carl Mears assured me the Institute case was headed nowhere. Apparently its instigator, Dan Sheehan, was known far and wide as a conspiracy concocter, a guy who, whenever he added two plus two would always come up with 666.

The next day I fielded more questions from reporters who'd got wind of the Christic lawsuit and I tried to pump them for whatever they knew about the situation. One of them had a tantalizing take on why I'd become a target for the left wing in general and the Christics in particular.

"Sam, you're living in Miami and that's where the Institute's investigation has been sanctioned by the U.S. Attorney's office. And we all know that you've had dealings with General Singlaub and General Secord, not to mention Oliver North and his errand boy Rob Owen. Plus you've got a book coming out and you've been all over TV and the papers. Right on all counts? Do you see? They're getting press because you're getting press. They're using you."

After I let loose with another chain of colorful expletives, I braced myself for another ten days of book signings before I could get home to assess my situation.

As the date for my court appearance crept closer back in Miami, Melinda and I got nearer to each other with nightly phone talks. I discovered, in those weeks, what a substantial person she was, full of wise counsel and tender giving. She was a real contrast to the bar scene Barbie dolls I was unfortunately use to. And I was getting more and more seriously involved with her.

When I was called to the Miami courthouse at the time of the Christic trial I learned all the details surrounding my supposed conspiratorial law breaking. The Institute had constructed an elaborate evidence diary that showed me meeting with the other two men and hatching the plot to pulverize the embassy. The only problem with this scenario was that it couldn't have happened because I wasn't there. All I had to do to convince the court of that fact was to produce my passport and other documentation which showed that I was flying from Israel to Africa at the time of the alleged meeting. The Institute lawyers might have been able to convince the judge that Ronald Reagan had personally taught me how to use spy telescopes but teleportation was another matter. When I was able to show how slipshod the Christics' research had been, the embassy blowup and ambassador assassination part of their case crumbled.

But that didn't stop them from pounding me with questions about my contacts with certain people they'd targeted as cogs in what they thought was a secret, parallel government operating deep in the bowels of the White

House. In particular, they wanted me to finger two figures I'd mentioned in *Counter-Terrorist*, Admiral William Hamilton and General John Singlaub. I'd already given the feds two depositions in which I'd told them all I could, but I'd reserved the right to keep six documents and the sensitive answers to some thirty-three questions to myself. Most of those documents and questions dealt with who had sent me on my mission to Nicaragua, who I'd reported to, and who had paid my way. Now the Christic Institute took me in front of a different judge from the one hearing their main case.

While the first trial was still in session, I was ordered by the new judge, Magistrate William Turnoff, to hand over every official document I had pertaining to Hamilton and Singlaub, not to mention any other relevant names I knew and documents I might have. Of course I refused and took the fifth amendment. When Judge Turnoff asked me on what grounds I was invoking my right I answered on the advice of counsel that it was to keep from implicating myself in a violation of the U.S. Neutrality Act. To have done otherwise would have been a betrayal of everything I believed in and fought to uphold for so long. I'd done my designated job in the jungle with honor and love for my country and I wasn't about to turn on the anti-communist heroes who'd sent me there. On the other hand, I was willing to tell the Christic creeps anything they wanted to know about some of the sleazier political operatives involved. I'd already passed a polygraph a month before that proved my Central American activities had been undertaken at the government's behest, and never on my own. During that exam I'd also revealed that Rob Owen, the errand-running stooge of Colonel Oliver North, had twice assured me I'd never be prosecuted for anything I did for the cause in Honduras or El Salvador, or Nicaragua. Not only that, but Owen swore I'd be given a presidential pardon. I didn't believe that bull at the time, and I certainly didn't believe it now. My dad's homely advice came to mind in the context of Owen's oath. "Hold a promise in one hand and a piece of poop in the other and check to see what you've got the most of." In this case that poop palm was also crammed with thousands of dollars in attorney fees for depositions and court appearances that didn't show any sign of ending soon.

But the Christic lawyers didn't ask me about Owen or North. And what was more concerning was the fact that the judge wasn't buying my prin-cipled rationale for taking the fifth. He saw it as simple stubbornness and ruled that I was in contempt and would have to go to jail the next Monday and stay there with the cell keys in my pocket until I agreed to cooperate. As soon as I turned over the requested information, I could go. But I refused again to play ball as the worried but proud Melinda, who'd come over from

St. Pete for the sentencing, looked on. Before I left the courtroom for what might be my last weekend of freedom for a while, my lawyer arranged with me that if in the unlikely event I changed my mind and wanted out of jail during the next week, I would call him and repeat the code word "tierra" three times. If he or his secretary heard those words, based on his home island of Tierra Verde, he would see to it that the court's questions were answered and the desired documents delivered. Once my immediate fate was sealed, I went back to Harry's with Melinda to wait for the federal marshals to show up for my escorted trip to the Miami criminal coop.

While tossing and turning that Friday night I hatched a scheme so whacky it even seemed out of character for me. If I were going to spend time locked up, why not do it someplace where I could be of use to the Bureau. If Judge Turnoff in the second Christic case could trump up a trafficking charge and have me sent up for a short stay at a federal bunk and bread instead of a local keep, I might be able to pick up some "actionable intelligence" about the Florida mob. On Saturday morning, I decided to run my idea past Harry before telling Vic. After breakfast Melinda, who'd stayed over at Harry's after my court appearance, took my suggestion that she have a swim in the pool while I stayed at the table with Harry and filled him in on my stroke of genius.

"Listen, Harry, I've told you before that I sometimes worry even after all this time about the government making trouble for me over the Nicaragua caper. Spying down there might still buy me prison time in the U.S. But what if I could get Vic to convince Judge Turnoff to see that I got slapped with a charge of withholding information about dope trafficking in Central America. And if he could arrange to have me sent to a federal facility I might be able to get some juicy gossip about some bad bigwigs."

Harry wasn't having any of it.

"Are you out of your mind? It's one thing to spend a little time in the local lockup and another thing entirely to get sent up a lousy river for God knows how long. You've got a business to run and you're planning to ask Melinda to marry you, for God's sake ! You can't put that on hold and hope to keep her."

But I'd talked myself into my brilliant plan overnight and I wasn't listening.

"It'd be the perfect set-up. Especially if I could get sent to the tough slammer in Illinois and maybe get bunked with an inmate who was a Trafficante intimate. Sure there'd be rough times for a couple of weeks, but getting the goods on a major player would sure make lemonade out those lemons."

Then I added a note that should have told me I was getting way too big for my undercover undies.

"I've already begun to build a reputation around town as a real player in the trade, Harry. I could come back from a prison stretch an even bigger banana."

Harry was not pleased.

"Enough with the lemons and bananas. You've already got yourself into this cutout work up to your eyeballs. Give your crazy idea a rest. Think of Melinda."

But there was no way Harry could talk me out of at least running my proposition by Vic. I called him fifteen minutes after Harry gave up talking some sense into me. I wasn't surprised when Vic seemed kind of intrigued by my idea.

"It *might* be an opportunity to pick up some incriminating material, Sam. A situation like this doesn't come along very often. It's a natural. Soldier of fortune turned drug middleman is assigned to a cell with a fellow tradesman. Couldn't be more believable. But Sam, remember, this Christic business isn't an FBI case. It's a civil action RICO case in federal court. The chances of your being sent to the federal pen over it are slim to none. And there's no way I or anybody else in the Bureau could influence Judge Turnoff. The Bureau has no clout in your kind of situation, and even if we did it would be unethical to use it. And besides, I thought you were considering getting married. Haven't you got enough on your plate with the cutout work?"

Vic wasn't having any more luck than Harry trying to talk me out of my idea.

"Well, if there's no way to jack the Christic case into a suitable sentence, what about arranging for me to be arrested on a phony felony. Something stemming from dealings with the Miami mafia?"

"You mean you'd accept a prison term to collect information for the Bureau? That's above and beyond, Sam. There's no way I could let you do that. And besides, I'd rather have you on the outside working for *me*. I like you and you've been a big help."

I knew Vic's complement was partly smoke blowing. He was trying to talk me down from the cloud I was on thinking about the good I could do by going to prison whether the rap was real or not. And about the precious poop I might be able to get on the Trafficante crowd through a target who was already serving time. That could save the Bureau a couple of dozen cows' worth of shoe leather. I was ready to do the Bureau's bidding by cozying up to the creep whose cell I might share in Illinois, or wherever they wanted to send me. My family wouldn't understand the government's friendly frame-up, of course. So far my brothers and mother didn't know a thing about my FBI work and I wasn't relishing the prospect of putting them through more adverse publicity. After all, they'd watched me a few years earlier paraded before the cameras and called a spacey spy. But if I lived to tell this new tale they'd be proud of what I did. And if I didn't survive, hopefully Vic could put their minds at ease by telling them the truth. Of course, I'd also have to explain everything to Melinda before putting the plot in motion.

I was getting more and more carried away with my own bravado and I pressed my case again on Vic.

"Couldn't you just try my idea out at the office? Come, on Vic, you admitted yourself that opportunities like this don't knock every day."

I must have been wearing him down because he agreed that he'd mention my idea the next week at headquarters.

"You've got a little time to think this over, Sam. You'll probably be in the city jail for at least a week. We can get word to you about options. And it may be that something will come up where you won't have to go to jail in the Christic case at all. At that point, if headquarters buys into your idea, we can have another charge filed and get you convicted on that."

So when Vic left, we parted with the understanding that I was ready to play a new mole role and would wait in the Miami jail for some specific instructions.

I spent Sunday afternoon filling in Melinda on all of my mysterious activities of the past months. I'd asked Vic a couple of weeks earlier if it was O.K. to let her know what I'd been doing during all of my dubiously accounted for absences. Vic didn't hesitate giving me the O.K. when I assured him that Melinda was totally trustworthy. Now I was trying to console her as best I could about my situation, including my possibly going to prison for a spell. Actually, she wasn't all that surprised by my confession. She knew she'd hooked up with someone headed for a different drummer's destination and figured I'd been up to something dangerous.

My looming absence from Melinda's life wasn't the only trouble taking a toll on her. Her husband wasn't cooperating in their divorce negotiations (do husbands ever?) and her business partner was dumping a lot of his responsibility on her. I encouraged her to keep fighting for her spousal rights and reminded her I'd be waiting in the wings, even if they were the east and west wings at Sing Sing. And then I proposed a less romantic merger. I asked her if she were willing to dissolve her business partnership and join me in my construction firm. The idea made perfect sense since Melinda was a financial wizard and a terrific manager. She'd also met and hit it off with my site foreman, Steve, so she seemed to be the perfect person to keep one blue eye on things if and when I served time in the slammer. She agreed that my idea made some sense and promised to work out a split with both her husband and her business partner. When we went our separate ways that night toward one of Harry's big bedrooms, we were agreed on our future together and expected a separation of unknown duration starting in the morning.

But bright and early Monday we got the news that Judge King had thrown out the whole original Christic case as frivolous. Apparently he'd concluded that Dan Sheehan and his scheme chasers were dotty from misconnecting all the dots. So instead of having bread and water on Dade County for dinner that night, I treated myself and Melinda to a thick steak at Dante's followed by dancing at another club.

On Tuesday morning Vic appeared and gave me good news and bad news from headquarters. The good news was that the Bureau thought I was really doing a fine job as a cutout cruising the South Florida bar scene. The bad news was it was apparently so fine they didn't want me to stop, least of all to chill my chops in a federal pen.

# SIX

With the Christic Institute lawsuit out of my hair I went back to business as usual, building condos by day around Pompano and hanging around South Miami and Ft. Lauderdale lounges at night. Melinda and I agreed that we'd put off marrying until my FBI work was completed. She didn't know all there was to know about my undercover assignments but she accepted my word that my work was yielding satisfying results. One typical case climaxed on a June evening a year later at the Yesterday bar. I arrived in a good mood. I'd just shot a seventy eight at a beautiful Miami golf course and then stopped at the construction sight to discover sales three weeks ahead of schedule. While kibitzing about baseball with a group of male and female patrons at the Yesterday we were joined by a particularly loathsome specimen of local low life, Two-Tone Clementi. Two-Tone got his moniker from his mug, half of which had been nearly blown away by an explosion. Rumor was that he'd been constructing a car bomb years back and earned an A in Chemistry and an F in Electrical Engineering. Later on he obviously brought his grades into synch, since he'd served time out in California for turning a Mercedes into metal spaghetti.

Clementi's looks hadn't dented his self-image. He was a highly gregarious creep, and now he slid into the conversation as if he'd been invited to. Of all the scum I had to suffer in my cutout capacity, Clementi ranked among the rankest. And just now he was indulging in one of his least endearing pastimes, feeling up the female clientele. He had one hand on a blonde's breast and the other cupping a drink as he blathered about the misfortunes of the baseball Devil Rays. He inevitably got away with this sort of behavior since he looked so menacing that the women were too frightened of him to object and the men were no less leery in more ways than one. I'd long wanted to "operate" on Clementi's face to bring it some balance but I also had higher alternative hopes that called for friendly relations. A few nights earlier at Dante's, Clementi had taken me aside intending to "run something past" me. I said "Sure Johnny, let's grab a table" and he started his *sotto voce* spiel while looking over his shoulder and all around the room for snoops.

"Sam, I need three-hundred large. I gotta finance a little deal in Santiago. I can triple your end of it inside two months max."

"Sounds intriguing Johnny. But is it too good to be true?"

"Naw, Sammy, it's a sure thing. Has to do with makin' guns."

It turned out that Clementi had, or thought he had, a way to mass produce a replica of the Ingram Model 10 nine-millimeter. The Model 10 was a wonder of the gun running trade, a concealable weapon with more firepower than a Glock nine-millimeter semi-automatic pistol and nearly as much firepower as a bulky AK-47. The Israelis had long since demonstrated the gun's effectiveness. A soldier would strap one on his back under a jacket and patrol with a buddy close behind. At the first sign of trouble the partner would reach under the soldier's vest and produce the show stopper. Clementi claimed that with my 300,000 dollar investment, he could produce 5,000 to 20,000 guns a month. But I nearly sprayed my drink when he named the angel who could set him up in the manufacturing business.

"Sam, I've been paying Pinochet under the table."

"Jesus, Johnny. You're telling me that you paid hush money to the President of Chile?"

"Yes. Not so loud."

"But if you're "in" with the president of Chile, why do you need three-hundred large from me?"

"Shit, Sam, that was six years ago. After that I fucked up and got busted on a trumped charge and did three at a level two in California. I'm just tryin' to get back on my feet and I need help."

So, I thought, that sojourn in the slammer would have something to do with the mangled Mercedes. I wouldn't help this prick if my life depended on it but I proceeded to make him think I was interested in tripling three-hundred large. That convinced him to drop the names of two of his alleged partners in the Pinochet scam, not to mention half a dozen others whose pockets the Chilean president was supposedly currently lining. At this point

I feigned a ballooning bladder and headed for the john. Inside a locked stall, I employed the low tech method I'd been taught to use when I wasn't wearing a wire. I took out a pen and paper and wrote down the names I'd memorized as Two-Tone recited them. Then it was back into his ugly presence.

At this point he was really getting loose and the names came tumbling out faster than I could keep up. I cut him off and ordered a Heineken to recharge my bladder but the best I could do was commit a half dozen names to memory and reject the rest for a later day. About midway through Two-Tone's soliloquy he started talking about rocket launchers and grenades and a name that brought me to full attention.

"Shit, Sam, I can mass produce those babies and sell 'em in a blink to the Ochoa boys."

"How well do you know the Ochoa brothers?"

"Me and his right hand are like 'this.'" Here he held up two fingers rapped around each other. Then he clued me in on how I fit in his future.

"Sam, I know your rep. I know ya spent a lot a time in Central America. Ya know what it's like down there. Every swingin' dick is crooked. Fuck, I've even got contacts with some ex-U.S. government types."

Now that peeked my interest too.

"Who are they?"

"I can't tell ya Sam. Sorry, but I was told not to tell. I got integrity ya know."

I suppressed a belly laugh and asked if he knew the names of three ex-CIA officers who were "painted gray" by the agency and let go, Theodore Shackley, Tom Clines, and Robert Quientero. A surprised smile broke over one of his two faces but he clammed up, temporarily. I made a bee line for the head to release more Heineken and scribble more names.

Then came another torrent of talk that revealed Two-Tone's plans for operating an arms distribution center and manufacturing plant in Malta and a big explosives warehouse on Madagascar. There were additional names dropped like Howard Herndon and Mitch Warbell who'd both served time for trafficking fifteen years earlier and were apparently at it again. He also bragged that he'd bribed a corrupt Mexican police chief while putting together a subsidiary drug deal. Plus he asked me if I'd ever heard of somebody called Edwin Williams and he seemed especially proud to call him a friend. I couldn't recall any such name but since Two-Tone thought so much of him I filed him under "check this out" in my already crowded brain. But the lowlight of the evening for me came when my double-faced "friend" announced that he expected one of his top customers to be Yasser Arafat, my old enemy from my days fighting for the Israelis. It would give me such pleasure to take down Two-Tone. I had enough on him now to do that, but I needed to string him along until I could tape him at some later meeting. So I told him I wanted to think about the investment and set up another get together for the following weekend.

Back at Harry's the next day Vic was juiced over my list of names. He was especially intrigued by Two-Tone's linking Edwin Williams with his gun manufacturing scheme. Williams was serving hard time at one of the country's roughest and toughest federal prisons in Illinois. Just how he intended to combine busting rocks with peddling arms left a lot to the imagination. I'd never seen Vic so anxious to get back to headquarters with the morning news.

Within twenty-four hours I got a call from him. He said there were some things in the works regarding Two-Tone and that the Bureau wanted me to introduce him to an agent posing as a moneyman who would be interested in one of those opportunities to triple an investment. That didn't sit well with me because I was looking forward to toppling Two-Tone on my own. But Vic insisted I needed to spend full time on a couple of other cases I was working in an ongoing attempt to get closer to the Trafficante higher ups. He also pointed out that I was due to give testimony at a Federal Grand Jury in a couple of weeks. I had to reluctantly agree that my regular case load represented the first priority. As For Clementi, Vic told me to keep stalling him, which I did for a couple of weeks.

Halfway through the stall Vic brought the agent I was to work with, a bald and burly six-and-a-half footer named "Curly" Anderson, to Harry's. It turned out that the enticing tidbit that spurred the plan I was to help set in motion by bringing Curly and Two-Tone together was the one about the Mexican police chief. It didn't take me long to figure out that Curly wasn't FBI. The DEA operated big time in Mexico so it looked like the Bureau would be working all the other names I'd relayed while passing off the Mexican part of the investigation and the take down of Two-Tone to the drug agency. This sort of deal was rare in 1991 because of the jealousy between the FBI and the DEA that didn't make for much cooperation. But now Curly and I were getting acquainted and rehearsing for our little weekend drama, which began with a call to Two-Tone telling him I was going to introduce him to a friend I'd done some business with in the past, one who was a real moneyman interested in making an investment. But this friend was strictly interested in the drug trade, not arms dealing.

The ruse didn't start off all that well since Clementi assured me that if I was setting him up, I'd get mine in short order. In fact he threatened to, "cut your fuckin' head off" and, "snuff" my girlfriend and my kids if anything happened to him. That kind of threat had become routine, but Two-Tone's tirade did impress on me how vulnerable working with a new agent of unknown talent made me.

Finally a Friday night found my new friend and I waiting for Clementi at the Ocean Manor bar. Within minutes half a familiar face was smiling at us. I made the introduction.

"Johnny, this is Curly Anderson, an old friend of mine. He was an advisor like me in Central America and we worked a couple of gigs together in Africa."

As Curly offered a hand to shake, Two-Tone grabbed it and wound his other arm around the agent's upper torso for a pat down, which proved an amusing sight since Clementi was all of five-foot-eight. Equally amusing was the fact that I was the one wearing the wire and Clementi had never bothered to question my creep credentials from the night we first met. Since there was little to be gained now by beating around the bush, I got right to the point. That way I wouldn't have to spend any more time than necessary in the scumbag's company.

"Johnny, I trust Curly here like a brother and he's interested in the investment. He's got the kind of money that could make for a profitable permanent arrangement."

After half-an-hour of enticement, Two-Tone wanted to see some green. He and I walked out to my car and I opened the trunk to reveal a hidden compartment and a bundle of paper that did a flawless imitation of around 50,000 in cash. That made half of Clementi's mouth salivate and I knew then the deal was going down. And in fact, within a few months Two-Tone was residing in a federal facility with a number of his erstwhile associates for neighbors. Apparently the DEA had also convinced the Mexican authorities to switch the offending police chief to the other side of the cell door.

The news that Two-Tone Clementi was looking at another long stretch in a federal lockup normally would've made my month but at this point in my cutout career it couldn't do much to banish my blues. I'd been swimming in a moral cesspool with Clementi and his ilk for so long now I wasn't sure I could ever climb out with my own integrity intact. And my next encounter with the Florida flotsam didn't do a lot to lift my spirits. On a rainy Thursday close to closing time I was sitting at the bar in Dante's when Louie Caldoni showed up. Caldoni was a two-bit dealer and part-time pimp who'd been sucking up to mid-level operators like Clementi for years without making much of a mark for himself. He was a burly bruiser who must have been burlier at some point because his suits fit him like sacks. When he perched on the stool next to me on this night and flashed his cheap pinky ring I wanted to walk out of the place. But I'd just ordered a nightcap on the Bureau's budget so I decided to stay even though it meant listening to Caldoni's claptrap.

"Sam, did ya hear Two-Tone got twenty breakin' rocks at Joliet? Damn, ya can't do business anymore without the feds fuckin' with ya. Seems like they're stickin' their noses in everybody's business these days."

"Yeah Louie, you're right. It's not like the old times is it? Back in the sixties you could buy off a badge with two or three large and the feds would never be the wiser. There's a lot more coordination between the Bureau and the cops now."

"Say Sam, speakin' of cops the word's out on the street there's a couple guys lookin' for a third party to pull off something' big. I don't know just what they've got in mind but I heard there's a good vig in it. Would ya be interested?"

Since I was between cases at the time I decided to play along, even though the odds of Caldoni being on to "something big" were longer than a Bill Clinton speech.

"I might be. Who are these guys?"

"Names are Tuti and Shiavonne. They've only been in town a couple a days. Word is they work for Junior."

I doubted if Caldoni knew what he was talking about but the mention of Santos Junior peeked my interest. The Trafficante family fight was still hot and heavy though Santos Junior was close to closing the deal and ending up on top. More than one of his rivals for the honor had turned up floating in the Atlantic in recent months.

"When can I talk to these guys and what's in this for you Louie?"

"I don't know about a meet Sam. I'll try ta set one up for ya. As fer me I thought I might pick up a part a the vig. Does that sound like a doable deal Sam? I think these guys already know about ya from yer book and all. The guy I was talkin' to says they mentioned yer name. There'd be no wasted time checkin' you out. What about the vig?"

"Depends on how big a vig we're talkin' about and what kind of job these guys need done. I don't play games for peanuts. Let's talk about a split after the meet."

"O.K., Sam. Ya got a rep around town as a straight shooter. I trust ya to be fair. I'll see ya here tamarra afternoon around five with some info about a meet."

The next day I talked myself into and then out of and then back into wearing a wire to the meeting with Caldoni's contacts. I'd made it a practice never to wear one to an initial intro for fear of a prolonged pat down or a short one that just proved lucky. I wondered if I should check with the Bureau before I decided. But Caldoni had seemed sure the night before that the two hoods I'd be meeting wouldn't have any qualms about me. So I made up my own mind and taped a tiny recorder to the calf of my left leg. It was ready to listen by the time Caldoni's call came. I arranged to meet him and his contacts the next night around ten at the Monarch Club. That put a crimp in my plan to join Melinda for the weekend in St. Pete so I had to call her and disappoint her for the hundredth time. She was the biggest reason for getting out of this miserable cutout business. Not that I didn't have a hundred lesser reasons. But right now I couldn't pass up the chance to dig up more dirt on the Trafficante family.

At the appointed hour the next night I was sitting at the bar and kibitzing with a young couple from Jacksonville. We were just getting into an engrossing conversation about surfing off Australia's beaches when the three scumbags sauntered up to the bar. Without a word the blotch-faced smaller of the three who turned out to be Tuti motioned in the direction of an empty table and then with another wave signaled Caldoni to get lost. I made my excuses to the surfers and followed the two. When we sat down Tuti introduced his pony-tailed pinky-ringed slimemate without bothering to ID himself.

"Sam, this here's Vito Shiavonne. We'd like ta talk about a deal ya might be interested in."

Shiavonne just sat there with a sour look on his face. Caldoni was right. There wouldn't be any wasted time with preliminaries. These two were nothing if not efficient. Now I was expecting a proposition about a coke buy. The only question was how big a buy. But as Tuti began to detail the deal I got a sense that I was in for a surprise.

"Sam, there's this cop up in Detroit that's been workin' fer the family fer three er four years now greasin' the skids for buyers and sellers. Name's Khaki John. He's been a real help to the northern operation keepin' book on what the Detroit fuzz is up to and even sometimes what we can expect from the feds. But he's gettin' too big fer his britches, Sam. Keeps uppin' his vigs. Thinks we can't do without 'im. Plus word on the street up there is he's been talkin' too much. Even threatenin' to roll over if he ain't cut a bigger piece of the pie."

"That's all very interesting, but where do I come in?"

My question prompted Shiavonne to break his sullen silence.

"We need somebody that ain't connected to us to whack him, Sam. We thought you might be interested. And from what we hear yer good with a gun. There'd be a nice fee in it fer ya. We're O.K.'d to offer a hit contract that pays twenty grand."

My heart picked up its pace and I almost puked all over Shiavonne. This was the first time I'd been asked to kill somebody and I felt sick inside and a little faint for a few seconds. When I recovered myself I had to douse my desire to grab Shiavonne by the throat and crack his head as hard as I could against Tuti's. There was no way I'd ever pull the trigger on anybody but terrorist enemies of America and even then only on foreign soil. Trafficante would have to find another sucker to cool his crooked cop. I couldn't wait to tell Vic what'd just happened but I knew he would want me to play along at least until he could alert the Detroit PD so they could get a full ID on this "Khaki John" before Tuti and Shiavonne found somebody willing to earn their 20,000.

"I don't know , boys. It's a question of whether I want to buy the bother. Let me think it over for twenty-four hours. I could use the twenty large but I don't know if killing somebody is worth forty large."

Tuti rubber-stamped my request with the kind of caveat I was use to from dealing with his ilk.

"Just don't string us along, Sam. We don't take ta bein' strung along if ya catch my meanin'"

I assured the two punks I'd have an answer for them by ten the next night at the same bar. Then I went right home and put in a call to Vic. I was still feeling sick to my stomach and disgusted at what I'd become, one of the mob's top candidates to pull off a contract killing. Vic tried without much success to salve my spirits. He reminded me again about why I'd volunteered for a cutout role in the first place. Then he said he'd get in touch with an agent in Detroit so the PD there could get started sifting the streets for somebody who could put the moniker "Khaki John" with a face on the force. He told me to tell the hoods I'd been mulling their offer but decided against it since I'd never killed a non-combatant and didn't want to start now. That had the benefit of being the simple truth and if they didn't believe it and couldn't understand my ethics they could go to the library and check out my book. Before he hung up though, Vic said he viewed Tuti's and Shiavonne's proposition as solid evidence I was making great strides convincing the local dirtbags I was one of them and the family that they could trust me with what they considered sensitive stuff. That pleased me quite a bit but it didn't make dealing with those dirtbags any more appealing.

The next night I told Trafficante's errand boys I wouldn't join their hit parade and they seemed to accept it with what passed for good graces among goodfellows. Vic told me that same night that he'd got my information passed on to the Detroit PD but he didn't tell me what was going on up there. He didn't have to. I was sure that Khaki John would've already got a knock on his door and an invitation to spend a vacation at the state's expense. And he was probably adding a few names to the slimeball social register so the clean cops could pick them off one by one.

Between 1988 and 1992 I'd established evidence against a number of wiseguys who were connected with the Trafficante club, the very slimeballs who bore the ultimate responsibility for hooking innocent kids all over Florida and the Southeast on coke and heroin. And used the dirtbags to get valuable information for the Bureau. I'd handed hot scoop to Vic on the location of a stash house just 300 meters from the Miami airport. And most satisfying of all, I'd been able to use my contacts to learn the location of a huge "kitchen" in the Selba mountains 20 miles south of Bogotá. A hood named Henderson had personally eyeballed the operation, close to a town called Villa Vadow. It was doing an estimated billion dollars of business a year processing poppy seeds on a farm high in the foothills. The setup was sweet for the cooks. A 1,500 square foot grass strip practically invisible to international drug enforcement. Just to get to Villa Vadow you had to drive through a long tunnel super slippery from water cascading down its walls. And the tunnel was always filled with gas fumes pumped in by the cartel to make getting there a health hazard for intruders. The "kitchen" was run by a married couple who alternated weeks as supervisor. There was a concealed airstrip in the surrounding jungle. The trip from the jungle to Miami was less then an hour's flight on a DC-3. Henderson said he could point out all the major Miami and Tampa dealers who were using the Selba site for supplies. He never knew his bragging brought the Columbian government troops in force to shut down the operation.

* * *

I told Vic one day that I thought all this time playing the role of cutout "Compass" was sending my morals south. That concerned him. He was afraid my worry would take my mind off the details of one of my drug deals and increase the odds of a fatal false step. He tried to reassure me that my work was well worth it and reminded me that I could quit any time. Then he tried to lighten things up a little with a joke, but one that carried a not so subtle message for me.

"Sam, there were these two old guys in their nineties named Sal and Sol who both loved baseball. All they talked about was baseball and they went to every minor and major league game they could get to at their age. Day and night they went over statistics, compared the old-timers to today's players, scoured the newspapers for word of big trades. One day, Sol says to Sal, 'I wonder if there's baseball in Heaven.' Sal says, 'Oh God, I sure hope so. There has to be.' So they decided that whoever died first would come back as soon as possible and whisper in the other's ear whether there was baseball in Heaven. Sure enough one spring morning just before opening day Sol has a heart attack and dies. At the funeral Sal is praying over the casket of his old friend when all of a sudden the hair on the back of his neck stands up as he hears in the distance a soft melodic voice that says, 'Sal, I've got great news and not so great news. The great news is that there's definitely high quality baseball in Heaven and everybody plays. The not so great news is that you're pitching tomorrow.'" Vic let his little rib-tickler sink in before he said, "Sam, be careful out there. I don't want you pitching on my watch."

That little story reminded me of how lucky I'd been during all my FBI case work. And how lucky I was to have had Vic as my handler. Despite the many pat downs and the constant threats I'd managed so far to come through unscathed, at least physically. And there was no denying the thrills I'd banked along the way. But I found it tougher and tougher to look in the morning mirror without my own image morphing into an Angelo Andretti or a Two-Tone Clementi. When I shaved these days I could almost picture a pinky ring enhancing the hand that held the razor. Melinda complained a few times about my talking like a hood. Luckily she hadn't seen me act like one, which I did more often than I like to remember. I was making physical threats all the time now. And sometimes having to follow through. And lying through my teeth. Cozying up to killers. Snitching on people, even the creeps I was helping take down, doesn't do a lot for your self-image either. For a while now I'd been thinking about how bad I'd feel when Vic retired, which was due to happen in less than a year. At that point I'd have to endure this scum storm without my male emotional anchor. Maybe it would be best to hang up my listening device when Vic called it quits. One Saturday night with Melinda an incident occurred that made up my mind for me.

She had come over to Miami for the weekend to be with me. We were drinking and dancing at Frankie and Johnnies on Friday night and enjoying each other's company for the first time in a couple of weeks. As we sat at the bar talking to another couple between sets, I heard a deep voice ask Melinda to dance. She turned down the invitation right away and I didn't think enough about it to even turn around and check Arthur Murray out. But fifteen minutes later the same voice was saying to Melinda, "Come on, baby, show me your stuff." This time I did turn around and stared daggers at a forty-something piece of flotsam holding a cocktail glass in a hand that featured an enormous pinky ring. For Melinda's sake I decided at that point to employ what passed for diplomacy with me those days. I got up within an inch of his face and said, "What is it about 'no' you don't understand, you piece of shit? This woman is with me and she's already turned you down politely. What's your problem?"

I was trying to be cool and Melinda was trying to help.

"Honey, it's O.K. Just drop it. Everything's all right."

But the pinky punk wouldn't cooperate. Instead he swung his cocktail glass for my face but missed and splashed my silk jacket's shoulder and Melinda new satin dress. This did not please me. After I head butted his nose into an altered shape I grabbed his windpipe with my right hand and his family's future in my left. His face turned bright red as he fought for air while two bystanders tried without success to pry my hands off his throat and his privates. Melinda was crying and begging me to stop so I finally let go and the bystanders caught the dancing queen before he hit the floor. As the Good Samaritans held him up I snarled, "Next time I'll snap your neck." It was only afterward I realized I'd been within an inch of killing the poor bastard and that my wild rage had painted a graphic picture of what I was becoming.

The next day I told Melinda that September would bring a double retirement and we set a wedding date for a month after that.

# SEVEN

My last hurrah with the Bureau began innocently enough. It all began during a stakeout one evening at a South Beach bar that had lately become a wiseguy hangout. There'd been a lot of suspicious comings and goings there in recent days and Vic thought I might pick up something worthwhile. So that's how I found myself, in the middle of a late Thursday afternoon cocktail hour, walking into a dark lounge called the Sea Urchin Club. Once my eyes adjusted to the transition from the sunny outside to inside lounge light I could make out a jazz pianist caressing his keyboard and half whispering the lyrics to, "My Funny Valentine." What looked to be a female patron sat on the piano and sang along with him. She wasn't half bad at it. There were over a 100 people crammed into the place with the usual percentage of freeloaders picking at the hors d'oeuvres on a big table in one corner. I made my way to the two-deep standing-room-only bar through a thick knot of patrons and ordered an Old Granddad with a splash. My intention was to tap into the talk around me to see what I could pick up. The place had the ambience that promised a productive evening of eavesdropping. Lots of silk shirts, pinky rings, and gold chains.

A sixtyish woman talking to a friend spotted me and introduced herself. She said her name was Marcy and she'd only been in Miami for a month. Lots like her came south from the Midwest after losing or unloading their latest husband and paying a plastic surgeon to set back their odometers.

This one was bending my ear to the breaking point when a drunk sitting two stools down the bar arrested all my attention by growling something in between piano sets.

"Frankie, ya tell him he better or I'll cut his fuckin' head off, ya hear me. Ya tell that prick I'll chop him into bits just like I had done to his friend."

After that outburst I knew Vic had chosen fertile ground for my evening's endeavors. I crushed a little closer in hopes of hearing a few names but the growler's companion had calmed him down and a few minutes later the two left the lounge and consigned me to the not-so-tender mercies of Marcy. She'd glued herself to my backside when I'd pushed through a couple of patrons to better gather the growler's gossip. Now I was trapped among a swarm of barflies and resigned to at least a few more minutes of suffering. So I resolved to make the most of my predicament by doing a visual survey of the crowd. While I was watching for potential targets moving between the bar and a back area where there were a few secluded booths, and half listening to Marcy complain about her ex-husbands, three bruisers worked their way through the mass of bodies and positioned themselves behind me. The next thing I knew one of them bumped me and spilled my drink all over Marcy's silk dress. When I turned around and told the jerk to, "watch it, bozo" and, "apologize to the lady" he declared a war of words.

"What the fuck did you say, asshole?"

"I said watch it Jerk-off. You hard of hearing?"

"Fuck ya!"

About this time I noticed the two gentlemen behind my new acquaintance. Their faces were totally expressionless and their combined shoulder span roughly approximated that of the Miami Dolphins defensive line. But as usual my mouth was a whole lot bigger than my brain.

"I hope your talkin' to your two girlfriends, Buffalo Breath. Because if you're talkin' to me, you're in big trouble."

That barb seemed to have no effect on the two backups who remained outwardly emotionless, but it didn't sit well with the main man.

"Fuck ya, asshole. Ya wanna do somethin' about it. Ya wanna go outside. Ya wanna walk? Let's walk."

Well, I was being pretty stupid, but not that stupid. I knew better than to go outside for a fight with a stranger. You could never tell how big an army he might be able to activate on short notice. And this guy's reserves included at least two cold-blooded palookas big enough to make a platoon. If our dustup was going to end in a fistfight, it would be within the friendly confines of the Sea Urchin Club. So instead of responding to my drink-spiller's request, I slowly removed my Rolex and put it my pocket. Then sluggishly, sleeve by sleeve, I took off my jacket, folded it into a neat square, and gave it to Marcy's care. Next I confronted my provoker and his two sidekicks, Num and Nummer.

"My friends, you and I aren't goin' outside at all. We're gonna settle this right now, right here. And I'm gonna make a little wager with you that I will wind up whipping all three of your asses and when I do I'm gonna spend the rest of a pleasurable evening drinkin' with Marcy here on your money. If I should be wrong and you should beat me, it will be no great disaster since everybody in here expects you to win. On the other hand, if you lose, you lose a lot of respect from whoever mistakenly thinks you're hot shit. Let's get with it."

That's when the bully said, "Ya've got one big set of cojones on ya for sure, Sam" and grinned from molar to molar. Then he yelled to the barkeep, "Hey Oswaldo, this guy's money's no good tonight."

With that he threw his arms around me like a long lost bro and Marcy and the rest of the onlookers relaxed in relief. After he let loose of me he yelled over toward one of the booths in the back.

"Hey, Harrington, you were right. He didn't back down."

I looked over his shoulder and who should be walking our way with outstretched arms but an old Ohio State fraternity brother, Dave Harrington.

"Dave, you prick. You set me up, didn't you?"

"That I did, Sam. And you nearly laid into Carlos here. Not to mention Benito and Cesar. You old son-of-a-bitch. Come on, let's get caught up on the past thirty years."

I said my goodbyes to Marcy and followed Harrington back to the booth where he'd been watching the fun. Carlos and his two confederates formed a phalanx 10 feet from the table, drinks in hand. For the rest of the evening, Harrington staked me to an endless flow of Bacardi and Coca Cola while he abstained and outlined his successes since we'd last played tennis together on the campus courts at Ohio State. He was looking prosperous with his imported suit and Cuban cigars and there was a reason. He let me know that he was the Number Two man in penny stock sales with a big Miami brokerage house that had offices all around the country. To hear Harrington tell it, he was the firm's golden boy, destined one day to inherit the mantle of CEO. I had no trouble believing it, since he'd been known from his student days as a major league brain who could also parlay his sports connections into financial rewards. He was a good enough tennis player back in Columbus to have tried out for the pro circuit, and once he even beat Arthur Ashe, although inconsistency cost him a place on the tour.

For the rest of the evening, the Sea Urchin Club rocked to the rafters, but by closing time my head was spinning from the rum and all the recollections of college days. So I gathered myself up, made a lunch date with the strictly sober Harrington for the following day, and weaved my way on foot over to the nearest fleabag hotel for the night.

When I arrived at the Shady Lady for lunch with Harrington the next day, he was slurping a martini and that surprised me a little given his striking sobriety amid the previous night's revelries. At any rate, we continued to bring ourselves up to date on thirty years' worth of separate lives. I quickly discovered that my review was mostly redundant. Harrington knew nearly everything about me, at least from the last ten or twelve years. He'd studied all the media accounts of my involvement in the Iran-Contra affair and he even produced a dog-eared copy of *Counter-Terrorist* for me to autograph. He knew all about my stand against the Christic Institute and about my success in the Pompano development business. I was afraid that in a minute he was going to ask me how my undercover FBI work was going.

On the other hand I'd lost complete track of Harrington in the intervening years. After a time as a tennis coach he'd worked his way up the ladder of a Columbus investment firm after graduation, which was three years later than mine, and made a reputation as a penny stock wizard. He'd married and had a couple of kids but ditched his wife just before their eighth anniversary because his sexual passion for her had slowly slackened to a seven-year inch. Then he'd come down to Florida and carried on a wild life for nearly a decade doing drugs and trying on his own to kick the habit. Finally he'd gone into rehab and straightened up and for the past twelve years he'd been flying right as one of Miami's most successful brokers. Or so he said.

When we'd finished rehashing our résumés Harrington ordered a hamburger and hit me with a proposition.

"Sam, I got some big deals going right now, and not just deals to do with the stock market. I'd love to have you working with me on them, especially as legal partners if you're interested. I'm making in the high six figures, Sam, and I won't be happy till I build them to seven. I'm no empty suit living from vig to vig. And you know your way around the construction business. We could parlay your knowledge and mine into a money machine. Think of the women we could corral, Sam, real barn burners. I've been thinking of calling you for the past few years but I've always hesitated because your reputation intimidated me. But when I saw you at the Urchin last night, I decided it was kismet. The two of us could make an unbeatable team."

Under other circumstances I would have been sorely tempted to take Harrington up on his proposal. There was no question, and there never had been since his student days that he was a brilliant operator, one with a 154

IQ. Back at Ohio State he'd once played chess against twenty guys at the same time and won hands down. But the more he bragged about his wealth and his connections and his interests in so many unrelated businesses, the more convinced I became that he was as drug dirty as your average don. There were at least three other good reasons to be suspicious too, and their names were Carlos, Benito, and Cesar. With friends like those you probably earned lots of enemies in law enforcement. Another clue that Harrington was hip deep in the trade was the lingo he used at that lunch. Terms like, "empty suit" for mafia wannabe and, "barn burner" for beautiful woman not to mention "vig" were part of the unmistakable vocabulary of the ring's English. If my hunch was right, Harrington's avid interest in my activities over the past several years surely had uncovered my associations with all the local scum who'd succeeded in rubbing off on me. Was his partnership proposal just a ruse to drag me into his own drug cabal? If so, our meeting last night was a different kind of kismet than Harrington had in mind. I decided to find out by feeding him a few leading lines.

"Dave, you know I don't need the money. I'm headed toward an eight-figure net worth myself. But I love to dabble while the development money multiplies. I've got a couple of minor deals going that will net me close to a million. I can't talk much about them because they're not exactly legal. I've been doing them on the side for extra pocket change."

I didn't have to say another word to hook Harrington. He started detailing all his drug dealings and naming enough names to clog every federal slammer between Miami and Seattle. Names like Carollo and Capeci and Russo and Balistarri and Tessio and Tocco. About then I was kicking myself for not wearing a wire. But if I played my hand with skill, there would be plenty of time for that. Now I just listened as Harrington went on and on about his ambition to become a mover and shaker in the trade. At one point he got all starry-eyed about John Gotti.

"I met him, Sam, just after he'd rubbed out Paul Castellano in '85. Gotti's a beautiful man, built like a fortress and just as tough to take down. And the clothes ! He was really wearing it! The feds are investigating him now, Sam, but he'll never get indicted. He's way too savvy. Meeting him was the most exciting thing that ever happened to me. I want that kind of power for myself, Sam. And I'll bet you have the same yen. Think of the women we could bag. Real barn burners. Way better than those Ohio State coeds, eh buddy? Gotti must get pussy by the truck load. And I'm on my way to his kind of status, Sam. I've done business with guys who work for Carlos Marcello in New Orleans and Sam Giancanno in Chicago, just to name a few of the top brass."

Harrington gave no sign of running out of gangster rapture so I just let him do all the talking.

"Sam, the Italian name for what I do is *campiere*. I'm an estate guard, a representative of the mob. A *campiere* usually gets his position from drying a couple of scalps. But I've never really whacked anybody myself. I'm hired to exercise my brain, not pull a trigger. I got my designation to give me more clout in the organization. Right now I'm working for Junior Trafficante who's trying to hold off a takeover by Vince Loscalzo and Frank Diecidue."

If Harrington thought I'd be impressed with his Trafficante tie-in, he had a couple more thinks coming. They'd still been big up until the late eighties, although their heyday was in the sixties when the CIA contracted the Florida mob to kill Fidel Castro and when they'd been rumored to be involved with Marcello in the Kennedy assassination. But I knew from Vic and my other FBI handlers that after Santos Senior's death in '87, the Trafficante family had been headed downhill. In fact I'd helped head it in that direction. By now they were having lots of internal squabbles over leadership and the Bureau was still very much interested in the civil war between Junior and his rivals. Whoever won that tag team match might be capable of getting the gang to shoot straight again.

Harrington finished his pitch for a partnership and I gave him the impression that I was quite taken with it and would get back to him soon. When I left him he was punching cell phone numbers to call a cab.

Back at Harry's the next day, Vic was enthused about using Harrington to keep tabs on the Trafficante family feud. He told me to stick to him like super glue for the next couple of months and pick up any intel I could. I didn't share Vic's eagerness. Harrington had proved to be an insufferable blowhard, one more piece of shit in an seemingly unending shower of shame. What's more I was feeling down because Vic's retirement from the Bureau was getting closer. But also up since I'd decided to quit too. Anyway, Harrington was in my sights now and I knew I had to bust him. I also began to realize about then that I'd got so good, or more likely so lucky at what I was doing for the Bureau that it no longer paid off in shivery sensations. So I prepared to meet Harrington again with a grim determination that was new to me. And I steeled myself for six more months of slumming.

The next day Vic arrived again at Harry's with word that everything Harrington had told me about his day job had been horse manure. The Bureau's overnight checking had established that there was no Dave Harrington working for any Miami brokerage firm. But there was one such who'd been sacked six months prior for lying to investors. Obviously my old fraternity friend had scammed me and no doubt a whole lot of others. Vic didn't have to remind me of my next move. I needed to convince Harrington that I was the best buddy he'd ever had or ever would have. So I introduced him to Harry and all of my other Miami friends. Soon we were making the scene at the clubs where discerning wiseguys dropped in.

One day a couple of weeks into Operation Harrington, just after I'd met with Melinda and we'd made plans to develop a new seashore yacht club in Largo, Harry dropped a surprise on me. It seemed that the pseudo stock baron had given my real buddy an irresistible line of malarkey and sold him 47,000 dollars worth (Ha!) of "hot" penny stocks. I don't know whether I was more enraged at the scammer or the scammee. The first recipient of my wrath though was Harry who I'd told about Harrington before introducing them. I couldn't believe someone as bright as Harry could fall for such an obvious con job. But then I remembered what a charmer Harrington could be when he decided to turn it on, as I'd first learned back at Ohio State. He'd used his gifts then to seduce about half the coeds on campus. Anyway, Harry cooled me down further with an abject apology for being so stupid and reminded me that he sometimes spent more than 47,000 on gas for his two boats alone in a month. So now I reserved the rest of my wrath for Harrington and resolved to let him have it when we met next. Luckily however, Vic showed up and suggested a better plan. I was to play along with Harrington and see if I could get him to put some of the particulars of his deal with Harry on paper. That evening I tried just that at Dante's Steak House.

"Dave, Harry wanted me to ask if you'd get him a transaction receipt for that stock deal you two did a few days ago. Something about needing to give it to his accountant for safe keeping."

"Sure, Sam. I'll get some copies made at Hastings and Arnold tomorrow. I meant to give Harry a receipt when we dealt. Can't let down the SEC. I just forgot about it."

I couldn't wait to see what kind of an excuse Harrington would come up with to explain why he couldn't deliver the receipt. Hastings and Arnold was the firm that'd fired him. Certainly he was too smart to try forging one of their documents. But sure enough the next day at the Sea Urchin he handed me an official looking paper and told me to give it to Harry. When I brought it back to the big house that evening Vic was waiting with Harry and we all had a good laugh at the legal language and the wax seal that supposedly authenticated Harrington's wheeling and dealing. But then Vic put the situation in a professional perspective.

"Now we have him where we want him, boys. We could get him arrested right now by the sheriff's office. The FBI couldn't touch him for cheating you, Harry, but the locals could. However, I can't advise you to press charges because the court would throw out the case for collusion. Besides, we want Harrington swimming along with the bigger fish so Sam can help fry them."

Vic added that I was to play along with Harrington, assure him I accepted him as a legitimate stock broker, and if the hoax he'd pull on Harry ever came to light, to laugh it off as a good joke on Harry who had more money than God anyway so there'd be no hard feelings. Meantime, Vic alerted the Sheriff's office to hold off on arresting Harrington no matter what they heard or found out. Then Harry and I both gave a deputy depositions laying out the details of the stock scam.

Just a month before Vic was to hang up his gumshoes for good with me following in his bare footsteps, I made the big breakthrough I'd been hoping for. It all went down one rainy afternoon when I got a phone call from Harrington asking me to join him at his favorite strip club, The Guzzly Bare. I hadn't seen him in a week and I could tell something was wrong when I spotted him. He was in a back booth sitting alone and staring straight through a silicone-stuffed blonde nude making lust to a pole on stage. He looked terrible. He'd been drinking up a deluge and he was a disheveled mess. When he saw me he motioned me into the plush-leathered booth and started sucking up with slurred speech.

"Shit down, Sham. Letch have a drink. I want ta be with my besht friend."

He seemed depressed but in a talkative mood so I was glad I'd come prepared to take notes. He flagged down a waitress wearing next to nothing and ordered my Old Granddad for me and what must have been his own tenth bourbon and branch. I wondered how many "lines" he'd done that day. But I felt lower than dirt myself, drinking near noon and watching topless tramps in this smut hut that smelled like somebody had spent twenty years flooding the floor with piss. Then he turned back to me.

"I've jusht want ta shay how much I reshpect ya, friend. I look up ta ya like a big brother."

I could tell he wanted to air out some things and hoped my notes would pick up some quotable material.

"I've been down lately, Sham. I jusht want to get shome things off my chessht."

And off his chest came a sleazy slough of admissions from embezzlement to money laundering to drug running. He even owned up to screwing Harry out of that 47,000. He was naming names of legionnaires and wiseguys and captains of ten and lots of other Trafficante traffickers. After a while I was memorizing all the names. It was like I was Harrington's priest and this back booth in one of the tackiest skin marts in town was the most convenient confessional. But there was no seal to guarantee the confidentiality of this pseudo sacrament.

It never ceased to amaze me how often the dirtbags I'd been dealing with over the last five years felt forced to spill the names of all the creeps they were associated with. Somehow they needed to brag about their connections even though they must have known about the danger of doing it. Their whole self image seemed to be tied up in who they knew and they just had to share their good fortune with others. It was a fatal flaw the Bureau would exploit again and again without the dirtbags ever wising up to their own complicity in their downfall.

As I sat letting Harrington drone on I was thinking how great it was going to be getting out of this cesspool I'd been drowning in for five years. What a pocket of puss this part of my life had become, a pathetic parade of con and hit men, drug and gun runners, pimps and prostitutes. I was weary of checking under my car for bombs before every trip and squinting with each turn of the ignition key. And once in motion doing more looking out the rearview mirror than through the windshield. Tired of the fights and the threats, both received and given. Tired of playing the role that made me feel no better than the scum I was pursuing. And really tired at this moment of having to deal with Dave Harrington. As it was I was going to have to go slow in distancing myself from him after I called it quits. I couldn't afford to arouse suspicion by dropping him too soon. It was satisfying that he was incriminating himself now beyond exculpation. And taking others down with him. Even without my prompting. But every sentence he uttered deepened my own sickness.

It was comforting to know that I was on the edge of a complete turn around though, a 180, spinning about face. Marrying Melinda would start the spin. I'd proposed to her a few months back and she'd surprised me by saying yes. I didn't think she would because she knew getting mixed up with me was a real gamble. I loved her so much. The proof was my willingness to make one more visit to the altar. After I broke up with my third wife I was surer than ever that I'd never stop wanting women but even surer that I couldn't be faithful to one. Which gave me a guilt trip about promising fidelity knowing it would be almost impossible to achieve. I felt like borrowing a lipstick, finding a public john, and scribbling on the mirror, "Stop me before I marry again." But I knew Melinda was different from all the other women I'd known. What really sealed the deal though was our agreement that we would never question each other's right to pursue our individual dreams. Melinda granted me maximum freedom to court danger wherever or whenever I wanted to. In fact, she often urged me on in my FBI work even though she had to fear for me and for herself. And we'd made the best of business partners, turning every project into a source of pride and big profits.

And then there was my friendship with Vic. Over the past five years we'd bonded like brothers. He'd been my most treasured and trusted friend through thick and thin. Whenever I needed a backup in a sticky situation or just a bit of moral support he was always there for me. During all that undercover work the most nerve-wracking moments were those I spent working on a drug deal out of Vic's view, sometimes with a wire but never a net. Now in just a few days we would be able to put our relationship on a new basis, purely personal as opposed to professional. But I'd never forget how I met Vic, through the FBI, the most scrupulously conscientious government agency I'd ever dealt with.

Harrington jarred me out of my daydream by grabbing my hand and hitting me with a surprising question.

"Sam, do ya think God'll ever forgive me for all the dirty rotten things I've done?"

I slid my butt across the booth's slick fake leather façade and stood next to him. I put my hand on his shoulder and administered an insincere absolution.

"It'll be all right, Dave. There's a little good in all of us. Have another drink. You need it."

Harrington waived the waitress over and I slid back to my listening post. With another bourbon and branch to brace him, my former fraternity pal turned dirtbag resumed naming names as my numb mind continued to take notes. I kept nodding encouragement when he started bragging about his friendship with Big Tony Gallanti. So much for contrition. Gallanti's was a name Vic needed to piece together a couple of puzzles he wanted to complete as a last contribution to the Bureau's drug war. And the more Harrington talked, the juicier the details about Gallanti's operation got. I was feeling good about what I was hearing and hoping just a few more minutes of Harrington's company was all I'd have to endure. But then I remembered Vic's admonition to be as thorough as possible in acquiring intel because even with a lot of grounds against them, organized crime types were seldom arrested. And if arrested they were rarely indicted. And if they were indicted rarely brought to trial. And if they were brought to trial they were rarely imprisoned. And if they were imprisoned they were usually quickly released. So it was best to bring an Everest of evidence to the hunt if you expected to catch your quarry.

When Harrington had finished unintentionally implicating Gallanti in about fifty felonies, I excused myself and headed for the head. Inside a stall I wrote as many of the names Dave was throwing out that I could remember and then I returned to sit once more opposite Harrington, who'd ordered himself another drink.

Now he began mouthing off about how he was positioning himself to be a big shot with the Trafficante mob once they crowned a new kingpin. He said he was working his way up the ring's ladder and hoped his climb would take him to the highest possible rung. Next he was off on the virtues of John Gotti again and I was beginning to think I'd reached the point of diminishing returns as far as this so called conversation was concerned. But I didn't have to make excuses or even say goodbye. In the middle of a sentence glorifying Gotti, Harrington trembled his glass of bourbon and branch to his lips, then took a belt and buckled. His head hit the table hard but the impact didn't seem to bring him back to reality. He was still out after I'd given the waitress my credit card and signed for the drinks, the least I could do for Harrington short of shouting *kudos* for his cooperation.

The next day at Harry's I met with Vic who'd read my typed report on everything Harrington had said at the Guzzly Bare. Vic was in a buoyant mood because of all the connections he was now able to make to construct a case against several of his most elusive targets, not to mention Harrington himself. My own mood was far less upbeat. Even though the end of my undercover snooping was just days away, I couldn't suppress the stink from the sewer hopping I'd done. So I decided to ask for a little help from further upstairs than FBI headquarters in Washington. I wrote to my Dayton pastor, Ron Julian. I'd been neglecting my religion for years and I felt a tremendous need now for some kind of spiritual support. I hadn't seen or talked to Pastor Ron in a long time but I knew if anyone could convince me that God still had some ennobling use for me, it would be him. Within the week I had an encouraging call from him, followed by a thoughtful letter that put my life in perspective.

> *Dear Sam,*
>
> *Monday morning as I was having my devotions before leaving for a conference in Cincinnati, it was so good to contact you by phone and share with you some things that were going through my mind. I talked about when Helen and I were with Tony at the Prayer Breakfast in 1983 in D.C. and how we talked and prayed concerning the fact that God often gives us a special focus in life. As we come to salvation and allow God to guide that inner focus to become His,*

                                                       

*and therefore spiritual, we enjoy it more than ever. We see that happen in Tony with "food for the hungry." As I look back over your life I see an unusual ability to be a risk taker. This can expose you to danger but it is rooted in a desire to share 'faith' in leading others. You believe that it can be done. This is often misunderstood and causes you to feel alone. But you know that most things can not be done alone and therefore you are able to gather others around you in reaching the desired goal. Please read the following scriptures. Ask God to make them clear but don't think you can completely understand them at the present. I am trusting that something good will happen in your soul as you realize how much God loves and understands you and that He has made you the way you are. He wants to cause this truth to bring you closer to Him. Now for the scriptures.*
*First Timothy: chapter one, verses twelve through seventeen.*
*(Life of Samson) Judges: chapters thirteen through sixteen.*
*(Life of Paul) Second Corinthians: chapter ten through chapter thirteen.*

*Enclosed is a picture Helen took of Ron Ballard and me on the twelve acre site in Trotwood where we want to put up a church building.*

> *Joyfully in Jesus,*
> *Ron*

I read Ron's letter over and over, especially the part about the possibility of "something good happening" in my soul. What he wrote clearly implied that I'd find a way through an as yet unfound new source to gain God's favor. That wonderful thought bucked me up a bit since I felt farther from God than I ever had thanks to my intimate interaction with Harrington and his ilk. And I hoped I'd soon be shown a less dehumanizing way to serve God's interests.

At the end of the week Melinda, Jimmie, and my three kids; Kelly, David, and Samantha, all joined Harry and me at the Miami mansion for a private celebration of Vic's and my retirement. I still felt depressed since the impact of my decision hadn't sunk in yet. The only other less than ecstatic person at the party was Harry. All the intrigue of the past five years had hooked him worse than cocaine ever could have. He kept asking if I didn't think I'd miss the non-stop action. But I said I'd had enough and that I'd always wanted Vic and me to go out on a high note. Jimmie was happy I'd be moving to St. Petersburg so Harry wouldn't be able to monopolize my free time like he'd been doing. My kids were still worried about my safety but were overjoyed I was getting out. It seemed to me that Melinda was the happiest of the lot. We were both relieved to have this chapter of our lives behind us, and were ready to start our new lives as Mr. and Mrs. Hall.

A week before the wedding I got a call from Vic with some jolting news. He'd just heard from a buddy in the Bureau that Dave Harrington was dead. It seemed that the Miami sheriff's department had acted on a tip and fished the floating body out of the Inter Coastal. Apparently the coroner didn't waste much time considering suicide or accidental drowning since Harrington's wrists and ankles were wired together. Vic thought he'd probably run afoul of someone high up in the Trafficante governing group because the ties attached to his extremities before his ocean plunge shouted contract killing. The mob didn't go in much these days for old fashioned cement shoes.

I didn't know how to feel about Harrington's death. On the one hand I was tempted to a tear or two for the poor son-of-a-bitch. What a waste of a first class brain. And he'd poured out what was left of his soul to me at the Guzzly Bare. I wanted to think he deserved better than to wind up dozing with the dolphins. On the other hand, more than half of his slurred soliloquy that last night at the bar had been bragging about how big he was in the dirtiest business in America. When I thought about all the victims of that enterprise, from ghetto kids on crack to affluent Hollywood actors doing coke lines in limousines, I had a hard time not hoping Harrington was at the moment meeting Satan face to face.

The next week I found myself sitting around the office at the new construction site in Largo with nothing much to do. Retirement already seemed like a drag. Melinda was such a marvelous manager and Steve Surovec such a fine foreman that I was having a tough time keeping myself busy. And now on top of that my kids were being assigned duties that would normally be mine. One cloudy morning as I sat playing roulette with the TV remote I landed on the Weather Channel where a gorgeous blonde stood pointing to a map of Florida. Well, as the saying more or less goes, I might be getting married but I wasn't going blind, so I decided to watch for a while. It turned out that the blonde was tracking a huge tropical storm with the name Andrew and it was due to slam the coast of Florida in two days. It also happened that I'd always loved big storms. When I was a kid, growing up in Ohio, I had prayed for mammoth winter snowfalls, and crazy summer storms. I loved the crashing sound of thunder, accompanied by the dazzling lightning displays. What a thrill it would be to walk the shoreline in the middle of one of nature's biggest blowouts. I decided to tell Melinda I needed a short sabbatical and drive over to the Atlantic close to the spot where the storm was predicted to make landfall. I wasn't surprised when Melinda agreed that I should take a couple of days off. She knew I was still struggling to banish the blues and besides, she always seconded whatever I decided to do.

The next day, the fifteenth of August in 1992, I pointed my Jaguar toward South Beach just below Miami and headed through Alligator Alley in a drenching downpour. When I finally pulled up by a shoreline access across from a row of boarded up cottages, a terrific 70 mile per hour blast blew a blinding sheet of rain against the windshield. But the local announcer on the radio predicted the brunt of what was now being billed as a "category five" hurricane wouldn't hit for about twelve hours. So I headed back into town through a cloud of flying palm fronds and found one of the partially boarded up but still open restaurants. After a few hours of small talk with the owner and a scattering of patrons I was ready to go back to the battered beach. When I got there again the wind was even fiercer than before and I had to push the resistant driver's-side door open with all my muscle to step out into the fury. It took me a good five minutes to fight my way the 50 yards to the beach and when I got there the low tide was looking damned high. There was only a thin strip of walkable beach flush against a reedy dune, but wide enough for a wanderer intent only on losing himself in God's gusts. I began making my way north while getting buffeted sideways against the dune and soaked through and through. During an hour-and-a-half's struggle in that direction the only other human beings I saw were a TV reporter and her cameraman filming what threatened to be their own final minutes. But there was a flood of faces washing over my mind. Corelli, Little Jimmy Gleason, Andretti, Aiello, Dice Jackson, Lou, Harrington. Also though, there were Vic and Harry and Jimmie and my mother and my kids and most of all Melinda. I wanted desperately to restrict mental admittance to the latter group, but my thoughts couldn't expel the procession of dealers and junkies and pimps who'd sullied my last five years. By the time I'd walked some distance north the tide forced me up on the dune and I'd have to stay on it for the return south to the car.

As I started to struggle back south I decided to pray for God to wash away the bad memories. And if He could figure out what to do with a fifty-something adrenaline addict, I prayed too that I'd be lead toward some sort of saving service for the greater good. A mission that might bring me to-gether with ordinary folks, not lawbreaking losers like drug dealers. If the Lord would only use this still strengthening hurricane to blow the collected filth from my brain and being, maybe I could figure out on my own how to turn my life around and become a better person. Someone who wouldn't lose sight of the souls he'd pledged to help. Like I'd lately just about forgotten the poor victims of the drug trade in my ego-driven pursuit of cheap macho thrills. Even back in Israel and Africa and Central America I'd never given more than passing thought to the victims of the acts I'd undertaken on behalf of equally callous politicians.

About halfway back to my car, at the mid-point of my prayerful plea for the wisdom to understand how I might turn my life around, I had a kind of revelation. I suddenly remembered the Pope praying for that Turk who'd tried to assassinate him about ten years earlier. At the time I couldn't figure out where the Holy Father had found the forgiveness to offer a guy who'd just fired a couple of bullets into him. It was one thing to try to understand your run-of-the-mill murderer but when you were an intended victim how could you ever come by such compassion? And yet John Paul's response was not only to pray for Mehmet Ali Agca but to plea for clemency. It was the kind of thing Jesus would have done, but a mere man, even a holy man? What could have been in it for the Pope?

Now it occurred to me here on this Florida beach that maybe part of the Pope's wisdom back in 1981 had been to recognize that there really was good in every human being like I'd insincerely said to Harrington, even the most sinful. And maybe that was a way for the Pope to affirm his own human value in the face of his shortcomings. And it occurred to me that the first step for me to reestablish my own worth could be to forgive or at least try to understand the very people who'd dirtied my world and dulled my conscience for the past five years. Who knew, after all, what personal demons had turned Dave Harrington from a genial frat friend into a hollow-eyed hood? Or what had sapped the no-doubt early potential for worldly worth of a Corelli or a Gleason or a Dice Jackson? There was no way to forgive their deeds, of course, but one way to loosen their grip on my mind might be to lessen their power as figures of pure evil.

It was a rain-drenched, wind-blown thought that couldn't have crossed my mind when I was face to face with them. In my few lucid moments over the years I'd recognized that even the simplest seeming souls were really pretty complicated, but most often I'd suppressed that idea to make reality seem more like a war. Since I was a teenager I'd been putting the people in my life in white hats and black hats to appease my enormous appetite for the dramatic. Then my military training, starting at Culver Academy and stretching through my Air Force experience and counter-terrorist activities and spying and especially my FBI cutout work had encouraged me to divide the world between the virtuous and the villainous. And all this time I'd been wearing a white hat, of course. But walking by the stormy Atlantic that August day, it dawned on me anew that all the hats were really shades of gray and that mine had been darkening for a good while. I knew I needed a lot of my Maker's grace to begin the brightening, so I revved up my petition again. As I struggled south I told God how tired, how whipped I was and how filthy I felt. How ashamed I was of acting like the very men I was trying to put behind bars. How I needed help and guidance to make my remaining time on earth an expiation.

I sat down on the dune a couple of 100 yards from my car and waited for an answer. But I couldn't read any message on the maelstrom.

# EIGHT

Andrew's anger was peaking when I decided to get out of the wild wind's way and head for home. All through the four-hour drive across the state I kept up a steady appeal to God for guidance. I'd felt cleansed by my walk on the storm-tossed beach, but also empty. The puss had been purged from my life but I had no plan. If God would just point me toward a path. By the time I pulled into my driveway in St. Pete, there'd still been no parting of the clouds to reveal a beckoning finger. And that night no revelation roused me from my sleep cradled in Melinda's arms.

During breakfast at seven the next morning the two of us watched the TV reports describing the hurricane's devastation. A few hours earlier the brunt of the blast had hit Homestead, about 200 miles from our house, but the whole Atlantic Coast was a mess. The loss of life was mounting by the minute, eventually totaling sixty-five, and the damage estimates had already reached the tens-of-billions. Over a-hundred-thousand houses were said to be destroyed and a couple-of hundred-thousand people were supposedly homeless. In Homestead itself, ninety-nine percent of the city's many mobile homes had apparently been blown to bits or at least severely damaged by the 150 M.P.H. wind gusts.

Melinda and I were watching an old man being interviewed about his terrifying experience in the storm when she said, "I hope those poor people over there are getting the help they need."

That's when I decided that I had to provide some of it. Hell, I could sure pass out coffee and sandwiches and blankets as well as next guy or gal and maybe I could lend a hand in other ways. I ran the idea past Melinda and she bought it no questions asked. In fact she wondered if she could come along to try to do some good. But I reminded her that she was needed just now at the project site in Largo, where the construction and financing were reaching a critical stage.

It occurred to me about now that I couldn't just roll into Homestead with a load of doughnuts and start distributing. The TV had been stressing the need to keep the town clear of sightseers and I'd sure be taken for one if I arrived in a green Jag and had no ID tag. The TV had also stressed the role the Red Cross would have to play in the relief effort so it looked like the best way to be of use would be in their harness.

With Melinda's kiss warm on my lips, I cut out for Clearwater, where the nearest Red Cross office could be found. There I submitted a dossier and was told that normally I'd have to take several hours of classes before being assigned to disaster relief but since help was desperately needed now I could do some cramming later. So I soon found myself assigned to service as a volunteer in Homestead. With my newly minted Red Cross ID card secured, I headed back home to pack for what I thought would be a couple of days' duty distributing meals and medicine.

When I got back to the Atlantic coast, destruction was evident everywhere. Trees and power lines were down and roofs were stripped and streets were littered with palm fronds and shingles and pieces of furniture and other household debris. But the sun-drenched day was totally tranquil, without so much as a puff of wind. I stopped beside a freshwater lake and marveled at the dead calm. The stillness of the water was eerie. Later I learned that this was often the aftermath of stupendous storms. A quiet so complete you couldn't be sure it was real and not just a post-hurricane hallucination.

Further south on the outskirts of Homestead I began to see neighborhoods decimated with houses sheered off at their foundations and shade trees shaved to stumps. And a few places that had been spared for no apparent reason. I went straight to the Mayor's office and introduced myself. His Honor went over my qualifications and decided I'd make a better building inspector than a doughnut dispenser so he directed me over to the Planning and Zoning offices and from there I headed to see the City Manager who sent me to the highly stressed chief building inspector, Ed Kline. It turned out that the chief didn't have any Indians. Kline was the only full time construction snoop in Homestead. Since he was overwhelmed he was overjoyed to see me and took me on right away as his helper. He had me pose for a quick ID snapshot and then he gave me a town map, a list of addresses to judge, and a set of forms to fill out. With my new building inspector's credentials completed, my job would be to condemn or condone homes for the county. I was supposed to report directly to Ed. The assignment didn't thrill me since it seemed like just another government gig that wouldn't involve helping people directly. But it sure couldn't be too hard since there weren't all that many homes still standing in Homestead to inspect.

Before I started my duties I wanted to get a close up look at the heart of the city so I walked a couple of blocks and stopped at one of the many tents set up by the Red Cross. I talked there to a middle-aged man named Paul at a makeshift desk and told him I'd volunteered to inspect houses but wanted to see downtown before I started. He introduced me to an attractive brunette named Marge who gave me a quick tour. On my walk with her I discovered that the storm had turned the town's name ironic overnight. Not a home had held steady in Homestead. There were missing roofs and shattered windows and tree trunks driven through walls and dead animals and birds everywhere. A huge percentage of the houses here too were sheered off to the foundation. And the smell of death rode the air. Block-long lines of human survivors waited patiently to tell their stories to Red Cross workers and claim some comforts from the piled up provisions the agency had assembled. I told Marge I'd never seen such devastation even though I'd been in a few war zones.

An hour later, driving down the flotsam-filled streets on my first inspection tour proved to be a real test of tires. My typical tour of a neighborhood involved parking the car and walking to the nearest house, inspecting it and either condemning or sparing it, then checking the next house and the next while describing a rough grid enclosing a number of structures, if you could still call some of them that. Locating the houses intact enough to be inspected turned out to be tough because most of their numbers had been blown miles west by the incredible wind. Once I got the hang of it though, I could figure out which places were which. The first half-dozen sites were easy to judge because there were no residents around to second guess my calls. Of those six homes only one was in any condition to consider exempting from the wrecking ball.

It was when I got to the seventh house on my list that the true toll of the tragedy hit me head-on. As I approached the cul-de-sac where one lonely tri-level with a missing wing now stood among a dozen stripped foundations, I spotted a knot of five folks standing in the shard-scattered front yard. When I joined them I met the homeowners and their six or seven-year old daughter along with a social worker and a nurse. The husband and wife were waiting for me to inspect their place in the hope that I'd find it fit to fix. And if I didn't, the social worker and the nurse were there to console and medicate them and their daughter. The father fought back tears as he explained the family's predicament.

"We've lost everything that was in the house, even the stove and the refrigerator. The only thing we have left is the part of the house that's still standing. We didn't have hurricane insurance. We bought this place with all of our savings and hurricane insurance is so expensive. Please don't condemn the place. It's all we have now."

His wife and daughter started to cry openly and I put my arms around the three of them and hugged them tight for a full minute before walking through the front door to start my inspection. Once inside, my worst fear proved well founded. Every wall in the house was close to coming down around me and the ceilings sagged dangerously. No way the place could be saved. Now that fine family outside would have to be told the devastating truth. Before I could face them, I sat down in the middle of one of their wrecked rooms and tried to get my own emotions under control. I wanted to think of some way to soften the blow but couldn't. I had to deliver my verdict directly, and it would be one of the hardest things I ever had to do. I went out into the junk-strewn yard and faced the father.

"I'm really sorry. I'm afraid I've got bad news for you. There's no way your place can be salvaged. I'll have to condemn it. Is there any way I can help you get through this?"

With that the wife collapsed into the nurse's arms. While the nurse coaxed the wife to take some vile looking liquid medicine, the social worker tried to calm the crying man. That left the beautiful little girl to me. She looked badly bewildered and she was sobbing softly. I cradled her in my arms and told her how sorry I was but that she'd soon be happy in another house, even though I wasn't sure I was telling the truth. Without insurance who knew whether these three wouldn't find themselves living on the street before their luck looked up.

Once the nurse and social worker had the three victims sedated it was time for me to go off to the next inspection. Before I could break away though, I gave the father three of the ten one-hundred-dollar bills I had in my wallet. He refused them at first but when I insisted that he take them for the sake of his wife and daughter he finally agreed. As I drove off, I thought of all the times I'd thrown hundred-dollar bills around at bars and strip joints and race tracks in the past, and not just during the days when my FBI cutout work had supposedly justified the indulgence. Those diversions had never salved my sense that something was missing from my life. What I'd missed was obviously the feeling I felt simply giving a small gift to that flattened family. It was such an insignificant gesture compared to the selfless giving I was about to observe in the other Red Cross volunteers I'd meet, but I've come to think it was my initial inkling of the answer to my prayers for God's guidance. Whoever said giving trumped getting was one great guru.

Over the next three weeks my role as assistant damage-determiner for Homestead had me hopping from neighborhood to neighborhood. There were daily scenes of men and women and children slouched in lawn chairs in front of their destroyed houses, worrying and waiting for me or Ed Kline or some insurance rep to approach. Even though the Twentieth Special Forces Group had set up 24/7 patrols to thwart thieves, some homeowners were showcasing shotguns to add emphasis. Some had no dry clothes and/or no money. Most were suffering from post-traumatic stress so I made sure I always had a nurse or a social worker at my side when I went inspecting. The town's mail carriers became a source of "actionable intelligence" in this environment. They were the only ones who knew for sure who'd left the area and who'd stayed and which ones were in the worst shape. There were also civil affairs units roaming the streets looking for lost and suffering animals. Combined civilian and military agency crews were sweating to remove debris. Army Humvees hovered everywhere, their loudspeakers directing citizens in English and Spanish to free food and tent facilities.

The pace of the work was so exhilarating but exhausting the first week that I enlisted my son David, my son-in-law Jeff, and my step-son Ashley, the three foremen on our latest Largo project, to spend a week's sabbatical as additions to the inspector's staff. Even then we were still so overburdened we could've used a lot more bodies. But the compensation I culled from helping out in the town's time of need added spice to the dash. Especially since, after my encounter with that forlorn family the first day out, I'd made a practice of contributing a little money to stricken survivors. And I tried, whenever a break allowed, to assist in other ways. Like serving in the food lines or encouraging townsfolk to talk out their trauma. More than once the boys and I did our best to counsel men and women who were seriously considering suicide. They couldn't figure out how or why they'd survived and weren't sure they were all that glad they had. Working with them took a toll on all the relief workers, myself included. But despite the strain, midway through my stay I knew I'd found the calling that it'd been beckoning that day I walked the Andrew-battered beach south of Miami trying to distance my demons. That walk seemed like years earlier though it'd only been a couple of weeks back. I knew now though that the wind and rain that day had started the cleansing process that this work in Homestead was completing. I counted my prayers answered and my future on a firmer foundation.

At the end of my third week in Homestead the regular building inspector seemed reasonably sure that he could now handle his work load on his own. He thanked the boys and me three or four times for our help and hoped we'd visit Homestead again under happier circumstances. Our goodbyes came at the right time since David, Jeff, and Ashley were needed back at the building site in Largo and I was anxious to tell Melinda all about my recent experience and new sense of direction. And I was ready to sign up for those Red Cross classes. So on a sunny Saturday morning I put Hurricane Andrew, along with Homestead in my rearview mirror and headed toward my new life beckoning through my clear windshield.

# NINE

Back in St. Pete I asked Melinda a question I'd been mulling over on the drive from Homestead. The development business, it appeared, was going to make us rich beyond our wildest dreams no matter whether I was around or not and consequently I was spending more and more time away from the construction sites. Why not close the business and retire? That way Melinda could relax by the pool instead of worrying through each new project and I could follow my burgeoning bliss. But Melinda wasn't buying it. She reminded me that she loved the business and so did the boys. She wanted to do at least a couple more projects before hanging up her cement mixer. I couldn't argue with her reasoning so I took another tack. We'd been donating a lot to charity over the years but I told Melinda now I wanted to grow our giving to match what we'd make in the future. And even cut our current worth for worthy causes. She didn't hesitate in giving me the O.K. to line up charities as I saw fit. Even though her goal had always been to build the business into a half-billion dollar enterprise by 2010, she was no more interested in piling up a personal treasure than I was. Only in seeing to it that the boys and my daughters got enough inheritance to launch themselves but not so much it'd cloud their moral compasses.

While I waited for my next chance to help out in an emergency I decided to get myself ready for what I was pretty sure would be an eventual terrorist attack on the U. S. I spent much of the rest of 1992 re-sharpening my rusting counterterrorism and first-responder skills at a couple of Florida schools. I learned to give CPR and how to use AED heart defibrillators and I took some Hazmat training. I studied the roles of FEMA and the FBI during terrorist attacks and brushed up on the methods of terrorist cells around the world and the status of their current operations. I was taught about the motives of terrorists and how they organized themselves. I was also given information about WMD (as the politicians have come to call weapons of mass destruction) or B-NICE (the antiterrorism insiders acronym for biological, nuclear, incendiary, chemical, and explosive). My curriculum also included Hazmat's ways of combating chemical and biological attacks with cholera, plague and anthrax spores as well as sarin gas.

In November of 1994 Hurricane Gordon hit the Atlantic Coast and I couldn't resist volunteering for the cleanup crew. Once again I drove to the predicted landfall site in advance so I could experience anew the rush from being buffeted by the center of the storm. And at the scene of the devastation in Vero Beach, I was able to use my recent classroom studies to help organize a reasonably effective response. I got so good at guessing where later storms would hit I could pack the car and be on hand to help before any agencies had time to get set up. I like to think my efficiency saved a few lives during June, 1995's Hurricane Allison in the Florida Panhandle, Erin at Vero Beach in August of the same year, and Opal in Pensacola that October.

✳ ✳ ✳

Late '98 drew me back to Central America. This time it wasn't to spy on the people. I'd long since put politics on the back burner and fired up the front one with my zeal for volunteering. On this trip south my goal was to help counter the chaos left behind by Hurricane Mitch. Massive mudslides were devastating parts of the countries down south thanks to the big storm. Melinda and I were watching the news one night and saw a moving story about one battered village in Honduras where men were digging frantically to unearth women and children. The death toll throughout the country was in the thousands and rising by the hour. Damage estimates already put the cost in the billions and hundreds-of-thousands of houses had been crushed to kindling by the rushing wall of mud. Watching the news footage reminded me of how much I'd liked the Hondurans I'd met doing Reagan's Iran-Contra bidding a decade earlier. And since nothing Mitch had done to Florida could match the disaster down there, I knew where my priorities pointed.

A couple of hours post-newscast I had my small travel bag bulging and my flight ticketed to Tegucigalpa. Shortly after that I found myself sitting in a storm-spared government office getting instructions from a bureaucrat who was an old friend I'd met in Honduras during my Central American adventure in the eighties. This time I worked on the outskirts of the city in mud over my boot tops. I passed out blankets and space heaters and fuel and water for four days. My nights were spent sleeping under a lean-to propped against a mud-encrusted palm tree. All this while the Honduran military operated what passed down there for earth-moving equipment. There were collapsed buildings everywhere and huge rocks and tree trunks clogging the streets. Out in the countryside a lot of the banana plantations were ruined. The people's lives were uprooted too, of course. A lot of them were still stunned and incoherent. My Spanish vocabulary went a little ways beyond "salsa" and "siesta" but I couldn't understand much of what they said to me. It didn't take a linguist, though, to figure out how much they were suffering and I found myself tasting my own tears more than once.

* * *

The following spring Hurricane Floyd hit Florida with a wallop and I headed to Cape Canaveral for the cleanup. But in the fall a far worse disaster drew me to Mexico where a huge earthquake had punctured the Pacific Coast and done damage south as far as Guatemala and north beyond Mexico City. I made it to the capitol within forty-eight hours of the temblor and took my place on a disassembly line taking down part of a tall building. As we passed rocks from man to man the military was everywhere trying to restore order and search for possible victims in piles of rubble. They used a lot of K-9 units and one of the handlers who spoke a little English told me he'd just come from an area to the south where the damage was greater and the search for casualties more intense. He said the post-traumatic stress syndrome I'd witnessed all around me wasn't limited to humans. It seems that every time a dog came up empty on a survivor search it would have to be consoled and given some time off.

The next day I joined another stone gang cleaning up the fallen façade of a hotel. Across the street there was a high-rise that didn't sustain any damage but, looking at it as I wrestled with the rocks, I couldn't help thinking of Juan Botella. Juan was a wonderful Mexican high school diver I first saw in action when he put on a display of his skills for my coaches at Ohio State where he wanted to enroll. To call him sensational in that exhibition would sell him short. He did dives that some of our seniors could never match. After he signed his letter of intent and came to Columbus, we dove against each other in warm-ups a lot and sometimes in competitions and though I always managed to best him, it was just barely. We talked sometimes and that's how I learned his father was the top architect in Mexico City. Juan told me his dad was a perfectionist who wouldn't accept anything less than top honors for his buildings or for his boy's diving. In fact Juan felt he was being driven too hard and that the pressure from home might prove too much for him. When we competed against each other in the 1960 Olympics I had to settle for the silver when my left foot brushed the board. And it was Juan who finished third that day. No sooner was my medal around my neck than my dad grabbed me and hugged me and said he couldn't be prouder, the way a good parent should. I wondered and worried how Juan had fared bringing home the bronze. Not long after I got what I've always thought must have been the grim answer. Juan jumped to his death from the top of one of his father's prize-winning buildings in Mexico City. Now, thirty-nine years later, I imagined that the high-rise across the street might be the same spot where Juan executed his final dive. Since the first day I'd heard about that tragedy, I have made sure that I shower my kids with all of the positive feed back that I could.

✳ ✳ ✳

All during those last years of the nineties Melinda and I kept on making money faster than we could find charities to fund. She had such good business sense that I could keep up my volunteer work without disrupting things in the slightest. And that was a good thing because I was rapidly losing interest in the business. I'd been at it off and on for forty years and it'd been good to me financially and at times in other rewarding ways. But truth to tell, I've always had a really low boring point. Never could concentrate on any one thing for long. Now there weren't enough hurricanes or mudslides to keep me going. I was happier than I'd ever been, knowing I was contributing something to the world that most others couldn't or wouldn't. Still, I'd turned sixty and there were a lot of things to do before the final buzzer. And so began a frenzied quest for fresh pursuits.

I'd kept in top physical shape after my counter-terrorist days by working out at various gyms. During my FBI cutout stint I hung around a spa in Miami whenever I could and did the same in St. Petersburg in more recent years. I even did my best to get in some iron pumping on the road to the latest hurricane or earthquake. In '97 just after my sixtieth birthday my old buddy Harry suggested I try the Senior Olympics and they kept me interested for a couple of years. I began to train for the swim competition in the morning and then lifted weights in the afternoon. Toward evening I'd head for the local high school and prep for track events including the shot-put and the discus and the javelin and the hammer throw and the high and broad jumps. Back at Ohio State in the late fifties I'd done pretty well at the decathlon before I gave it up to focus on diving. Now for diversion from my geezer games training, I did some shooting and some sky-diving with my son-in-law Jeff.

I did really well against my fellow greybeards at various senior meets across the country. I came in first or second in most of the track events on two bad knees that qualified me as a disabled vet. And I won most of the swim meets so that got me outstanding senior athlete of the year awards twice. I even set two world records in triathlon relays at the world senior championships in Utah. But in between competitions I had to fill the empty space giving other hobby horses their head.

When I was in Rome to dive at the 1960 Olympics I spent some spare time soaking up as much European culture as I could at churches and museums. I came away from that experience with an avid interest in sculpture and now, nearly forty years later, I decided to try my hand at it myself. I'd never been very good at drawing but I thought maybe I could work with clay. One day around the 1st of December in '97 I noted in a local magazine an article about a St. Petersburg sculptor. So I called him and asked if he could take me on as a student. He told me he didn't give lessons but I made him an offer he couldn't refuse. Fifty dollars an hour with Christmas coming up for his three kids convinced him to cooperate. Every day after that for six weeks I attacked alabaster or Italian crystal or marble with the best instructor available and managed to create a couple of funky figures. But I got restless again and asked around about the best places to study sculpture in Italy. Before you could say Francoise Auguste René Rodin I was getting instructions and chipping away at alabaster in European studios. I stayed and studied for awhile and got enthused enough to spend a small fortune shipping marble and alabaster back to Florida for future figures. But I'll never forget the time over there, especially the two weeks working alongside master sculptors in Pietrosanta. That's where Michelangelo used some divine inspiration to outdo art.

After my study in Italy I worked sporadically at sculpting figures when I could find the time. Melinda would get annoyed when I'd destroy some of my better creations. I tossed a lot of the things I'd made but didn't like into the Inter Coastal waterway where they're still giving shelter to sharks. Most of the stuff looked like the work of a clumsy adolescent though I was proud of a couple of items I crafted. But the whole process started to bore me and I began looking for other ways to pass the time between volunteering gigs.

To keep me occupied during those off hours, Melinda bought me a new baby grand. So I hired an instructor and started back on the piano lessons I'd left off when I was a kid. My parents had made me play the piano then so it was fairly easy to be retrained. At first reacquainting myself with the keyboard gave me some satisfaction but before long I wanted to butcher my teacher who kept nagging "I see that you haven't been practicing your scales and chords." After a week of suppressing the urge to punch him in his ivories I quit the lessons and went back to playing by ear once or twice a year. I'd always been able to listen to music on the radio or a CD and sit down and burn the tune on the keyboard. I could sit there for hours and copy what the best pianists were playing, but not without eventually boring myself to tears.

* * *

In the late summer of 2001 I happened to be in our attorney's office joshing with one of the partners in the firm. I knew he was on the board of trustees at St. Petersburg Community College and on a lark I asked him if they needed any teachers in a subject I'd be interested in teaching. Before I knew what hit me he'd set up an interview for me David Pucket, the guy in charge of hiring. That interview plus a couple of follow-ups netted me an offer that sounded pretty sweet. Pucket said the college had set up a program for first responders to disasters including terrorist attacks and that they were looking for someone well qualified to teach it. The students would come from surrounding-area police departments. He also said there'd be some military types who'd probably enroll. The course sounded right up my alley. I was supposed to stress just the kinds of things I'd trained so hard to gain expertise in. But I wasn't really sure I wanted to be a professor. The academic life was just about as far removed from the one I'd led as it could get. Still, I'd only have to trade my fatigues for a cap and gown for a couple of hours once in a while. Maybe that wouldn't be so bad. On the other hand I remembered how my book writer had put down his fellow professors. He'd described to me in detail how some campus dispute would have them talking like teed-off tigers but when the time came to act they morphed into puling pussycats. He'd called colleges a "hotbed of cold feet" and at the time he'd even shown me a flag he'd designed for his profession. It featured a chicken lying prone on a field of yellow beneath a motto that said "Tread on me."

When I told David Pucket on the phone I'd have to think about his offer he gave me the weekend to decide. He said I wouldn't have any other duties besides teaching the course, that I'd have no committee assignments and no faculty meetings to attend. That was a real enticement because I'd also remembered that my writer friend had told me what he called a weary whopper about an Oxford don who was asked if he had his druthers where he'd like to die and he answered he'd prefer an Oxford faculty meeting since he'd never notice the change. But by Sunday night Melinda had me convinced that I should take the job, that I'd probably enjoy it. On Monday morning I told David I'd audit the session of the course that was being given the next day so I could get a feel for what was going down. I was impressed with the teachers and the class and thought I might be in my element after all. The students, who were all marines, paid rapt attention and I knew when I took over I'd find myself hamming it up with stories from my counterterrorism and storm-chasing days.

# TEN

My first day in front of a class was scheduled for mid-September. I spent my mornings the week after my interview relaxing with nine holes of golf and the afternoons doing odd jobs around the house and at the Largo job site. All that putting and puttering was boring me silly but new adventures would have to wait. I'd received a notice a week earlier from the St. Petersburg municipal court to report for jury duty at eight in the morning on the eleventh. I got to the courthouse with two or three minutes to spare only to find myself crowded together with about 300 others in a big antechamber. There must have been a wave of warrants issued by the county since my quick calculation broke the swarm into as many as two-dozen juries give or take a few rejects. I'd long ago learned in the military to "hurry up and wait," so I started staring blankly at "Good Morning America" on the TV set suspended from the ceiling and silently cursing this waste of my time. If I had known what others were about to go through at that very hour I would have been deeply ashamed of my unimportant impatience.

At 7:59 A.M. American Airlines flight 11 with ninety-two passengers and crew on board left Boston's Logan Airport for Los Angeles.

At 8:01 A.M. United Airlines flight 93 carrying forty-five people departed Newark Airport for San Francisco.

At 8:10 A.M. American flight 77 lifted off from Washington's Dulles Airport with sixty-four souls on their way to Los Angeles.

At 8:14 A.M. United flight 175 and sixty-five people were airborne out of Boston also headed for Los Angeles.

After forty-five minutes sharing frustrations with the waiting would-be jurists, someone close by suddenly said, "Look at that!" I instinctively glanced at the TV screen and couldn't comprehend what I was seeing. One by one in rapid succession heads were raised and eyes riveted on the screen and audible gasps and murmurs were spreading across the room. At first I thought the courthouse keepers of the remote had switched channels to some sci-fi network but within seconds I realized that what I was seeing and would see in my fitful sleep for months to come was all too real. I'd been to New York many times and I knew that the north tower of the World Trade Center had just been hit by a commercial airliner. But the infamy of what I would shortly recognize as an obvious attack didn't begin to register until a tall middle-aged man made a comment above the muted babble.

"Listen, you're not looking at an accident. I'm a pilot and I know. There's no way that could have happened accidentally."

Now the folks in the room were riveted to the tube and trying to make some sense of the garbled rehash of reporters. Were we under attack or had some depressed pilot skipped his Prozac and decided to take thousands of people with him to a better world? A couple of women and a man ran outside. Through a window I saw them on the street looking wildly in all directions. The TV screen kept flashing photos of the plane hitting the tower. I was still having a hard time crediting what I was seeing with my own eyes. Finally my shock gave way to wonder for what had to be an incalculable loss of life. The thought of those poor souls jumping from the tower windows was the hardest to take. Maybe because I couldn't bear the TV image searing my sight at the moment, my mind flashed back instead and dredged up those old newsreels I'd seen of the Hindenburg crashing in the thirties. That awful explosion and then the fire that revealed the ribs of the dirigible before they collapsed in on themselves. And that unforgettable voiceover: "Oh, the humanity!"

By now most of the potential jury panels were leaving the building by the dozens and I began my own wooden walk for the door just as a quavering female voice came out of a loudspeaker.

"Due to circumstances beyond control, citizen's services will not be needed today. Those waiting to learn of possible jury duty are dismissed."

On the dazed drive home I hit the radio "on" button and must have got an ABC affiliate because Peter Jennings was describing the damage to the second tower. I didn't face the fact just then that ruled out any "psychotic suicide." Instead I was fixated on the "circumstances beyond control" of those poor New Yorkers' right now. There had to be hundreds trapped in offices and hallways and elevators. Most of them knowing they were about to die and thinking of their wives and husbands and children and mothers and fathers and grandparents. What a terrible way to go to God ! And those loved ones waiting for word back home or wherever and knowing deep down the chances of coming out of those twin infernos alive would be microscopic to nil.

Back at the house Melinda was watching the attack replaying for what must have been the thousandth time on TV. She was crying and I comforted her as best I could. By this time my own shock had subsided and I needed to scratch my itch to do something, anything. I had to purge my first urge which was to plant a toe-tag on the mastermind behind the attack. I knew from my counterterrorism work in Israel and Africa during the late eighties that Islamic fundamentalism was breeding a generation of degenerates bent on bullying the West through terror. And by the time the "holy" warriors had blown a hole in the hull of the Cole killing our sailors in 1998 it was pretty clear that there had to be a diabolically clever chairman of the horde. Only someone really brilliant would've been able to mount the master plot I'd seen carried through on the municipal court's TV screen. If I could have got my hands on his windpipe I'd have sent him to his own seventy virgins, but he wasn't likely to show his face for a while let alone his neck. Besides that, reaping revenge for the trade tower attacks would be the job of the military's special forces and they weren't recruiting senior citizens.

The day after I got home I had a phone call from one of Vic Fowler's friends who worked at the sheriff's office asking me to apply for a sky marshal's job. I'd already been wondering how long it would be before Washington would put out an all-points petition for airplane police. They'd really be needed now to secure the skies in the wake of the New York attack. And apparently I wasn't too old to make a contribution after all. But it didn't take long for the first of the flattery to wear off so I could turn back the temptation. On the one hand the idea of foiling fanatics in midair made for the kind of derring-do I was always dreaming about. And saving citizens from a fate like the one that awaited those poor victims on 9/11 would be a noble mission. On the other hand the chances of seeing much action in the foreseeable future were not especially promising. The terrorists would be thinking long and hard about using the same tactics for their next plot. Better from their warped point of view to search out softer targets. That meant a sky marshal would likely be logging lots of frequent flyer miles sitting in coach and reduced to reading puff pieces in airline magazines from the seat pouch in front of him. Important work but it wouldn't bring *my* tray to its upright position. I knew there was something I could do to help the country that didn't involve an endlessly boring round of boarding and browsing.

My third thought told me I could be more useful right now through service to the city of New York. I was perfectly positioned through my training to help out in the cleanup effort that would have to be undertaken. But I wasn't sure I wouldn't be in the way of the first responders who were probably already swarming the site. I had to try so I called a few friends in New York and was assured by a couple of authorities there that they could use all the help they could get from experienced destruction workers. As soon as I heard that encouraging word I told the once more agreeable Melinda I'd decided to go to New York to help out. Then I spent a couple of days waiting for the airlines to begin flying again, making a rolling reservation at a hotel close to the twisted towers, the Holiday Inn in Chinatown, and packing my gear. I also grabbed my Red Cross badges and other credentials I'd picked up over the years from emergency responders I'd worked for. Melinda packed my bag and put me on a plane headed for New York at noon on September fourteenth.

In the city that afternoon the faces of pedestrians showed the shock and strain of the past few days. The usually buoyant New Yorkers seemed to slouch along the sidewalks. The most energized city in the world looked to be grinding to a halt. I went straight to the Incident Command Center behind the security barricades and showed the deputy in charge my Red Cross credentials. The deputy didn't take more than a few minutes to issue me another badge courtesy of New York's Office of Emergency Management. When I got to the footprint of Trade Center in Lower Manhattan I took my first sweeping look at the sight. I could hardly control my rage. Those once proud towers reduced to rubble and all the precious lives lost. I said a silent prayer for the thousands of dead. And in that moment I knew that just as the towers had fallen the cowards who felled them would also fall. But mere death was too good for them. I wanted the perpetrators and the planners of the attack to burn forever somewhere near the center of the seventh circle of hell.

Once I showed my credentials, I was waved through security. As I passed the Command Center I approached a fire department supervisor directing a crew at the south tower. My first question was what kind of help he needed most and I was told the first order of business was the search for human remains. And if God still worked wonders maybe a few survivors. The big cranes scooping up glass and girders and other objects would probe the higher heaps and expose the hell holes beneath. Then it was the job of the searchers to sift through the smaller debris, much of it still hot metal that had melted and solidified again. And crawl into crevasses in hopes of finding something human. The supervisor's deputy said I might not be able to hold up at my age under the physical and psychological pressure and that I might want to consider some other role. I told him I wanted to start searching right away and within fifteen minutes I looked the part in face mask and helmet and goggles and surgical gloves. Half-an-hour later my three-week, indescribably fearful but wonderfully fulfilling job as digger at Ground Zero began.

# ELEVEN

"Quiet, quiet!" Quincy, the Bedford-Stuyvesant firefighter beside me, thought he'd heard the sound of someone crying. One by one the generators and hoses and other equipment shut down and only the neighboring sound of the big cranes rifling through the remnants of the north tower scraped the stillness. The other diggers and I stood motionless listening for sounds of life. Then we began yelling "Is anyone there? Can you hear us? Is anyone there?" Nothing. Quincy pointed to the place where the prayers of some victim's loved one might now be answered. There was what looked to be a small passageway under a mound of metal that could hold the right response to our own prayers too. Since I was thinner than the average digger and spent a lot of time rock climbing I'd volunteered to be one of the mission's tunnel rats to go in with alternating cleanup teams. Our job was to negotiate crawl spaces in the debris and, tethered to a rope, drop down holes in search of sounds or the smell of human remains. Inching through horizontal pathways below the debris. Trying to avoid hot metal. Praying for a discovery. This probe, like too many others, proved fruitless. My half-hour of fevered rummaging uncovered only shards of steel and a few battered objects from some office.

That's when the rescue dog made his appearance. We had to be sure the sound Quincy thought he heard was just a hopeful hallucination. And that I hadn't missed something in my quick descent beneath the rubble. The team leader wanted to make sure with a canine assessment of the evidence.

So Bob Schnelle got called over from the north tower ruins with his beautiful German shepherd Atlas. The knot of diggers at the vaguely encouraging spot dispersed at Bob's direction.

"Doing a live find, doing a live find! Let Atlas do his job."

I remembered the wonderful work the K-9 units did locating buried survivors during that earthquake in Mexico and now I hoped that Atlas would prove again that "man's best friend" wasn't just an empty cliché. But hard as he tried he couldn't produce what wasn't there. Quincy broke down and cried when Atlas and his handler headed off to answer another call and the generators roared back to life and the sizzle of the hose water hitting hot steel could be heard again. That's when we forgot our frustration and renewed our frantic digging.

Similar incidents happened hourly during my first few days at the dig. And there were worse conclusions to our searches of course. From day one when I took my place with the other responders at Ground Zero I saw sights more harrowing than I'd seen in the aftermath of military battles or other terrorist attacks. I'd been in Beirut shortly after the barracks blasts that took the lives of 241 marines and I'd seen the grisly results of the carnage first hand. And I cried at the burial ceremonies. (Don't ask me how I came to be in Lebanon at the time or under whose auspices I was there). But not even that experience could compare with crawling all day through small openings in this rubble or down one of these still smoking holes only to come across a bundle of bloody body parts, a cheek or a thumb or a foot or an elbow or an inner thigh. Rarely did we find a body intact. The fact that we were issued pink plastic bags about the size that a supermarket would dole out for taking home a loaf of bread said it all about the expectation of the project planners.

I'm not ashamed to admit that I was seriously scared every time I tunneled beneath the fragments or explored a promising hole. I couldn't take my mind off the real chance that some of the steel poised above me might collapse and crush me at any minute. And then there was the anxiety around what the next awful discovery in the debris might be. My knees always jerked like Jell-o and I upchucked more than once and my briefs were seldom dry. It took an enormous effort to hide my fright so as not to spook the other diggers. But I knew they were all feeling the same shame because they never judged someone who couldn't take the horror any more and opted out.

On a typical search I'd crawl on my belly or, when one of the big cranes lifted a girder to reveal a deep depression, rappel down little metal mountains that sometimes still smoldered. As careful as I would be to keep from being scorched, a couple of times every hour I'd pick up or brush against some scalding object. And as often as not some body part from a victim would be bonded to its surface. As the first week flew by the acrid, metallic, rubbery stench worsened because the field of flesh started to decompose. The smoke rising from the scattered shards made seeing tough most of the time and it turned the diggers black like Kentucky coal miners. But no John L. Lewis here to bargain for our betterment. This hellish routine ground on most of the time in sixteen-hours-on and eight-hours-off segments. My shift began at four in the morning. Sometimes I'd be so exhausted in the middle of my duty I'd collapse on one of the cots set up around the seven block area for the searchers. All the workers took short naps in this way or they would drag themselves to the cruise ship in the harbor where other cots called. Or sometimes if the fatigue was especially enervating we would drop down right on a concrete slab from the Trade Center façade for a moment's rest. But a nap never lasted more than an hour or two because the task at hand was too troubling. After the shift was over I'd creep back to the Holiday for six or seven hours of malignant dreams.

Toward the end of the first week there were signs the city was coming back to life. At the disaster site the mountain of debris was slowly shrinking as the cranes and forklifts kept pouring load after load into the beds of waiting dump trucks. Streets outside the seven-block area began to bustle with activity. Thick dust coated everything within blocks of the sight but the people were determined to stay positive. There were sad posters taped to surfaces all over the city. With photos of loved ones and captions that read, "Missing … Please notify" Then there were more upbeat messages. Like the guy who'd written with his finger in the dust of a still stranded Buick's trunk, "I survived … Moe." Display boards had popped up everywhere, including some pinned with encouraging words for the diggers from grateful groups and individuals including lots of children. Every night scores of citizens held candlelight vigils to comfort one another. Everyone in their own way proving that compassion and not commerce was the real core of the Big Apple.

My seventh day at the site was a particularly rough one. I'd found what was left of a child's toy among some broken and twisted office equipment. I had to stop and try to clear my mind and staunch my tears so I took a break and headed for the heart of the city to buy a breakfast I knew I couldn't eat. On the way I paused for some reason by a spot just outside the barricades where lots of folks had posted messages. I started reading at random and came across a couple of encouragement letters addressed to the diggers and tunnel rats. They'd been written by two girls from the same elementary school, probably at the suggestion of their teacher. Their simple sincerity and promise of prayers hit my heart hard. In the midst of this death and destruction and the depression I felt from finding the child's toy, these young children had taken the time to remind all the firemen and police and volunteers that we were loved and admired for the job we were doing. I took out a piece of paper and wrote down the children's names and when I was advised later in the day to take a break I composed a long letter to the two.

*September 21, 2001*

*Megan 6th Grade*
*Alexandra 4th Grade*

*Dear Precious Megan and Alexandra:*
*Oh my, how do I begin to describe what you did for me today ! I am sitting on a cold muddy sidewalk with my back against a charred portion of what once was a Greek Orthodox church at "Ground Zero," 200 feet from where Building One of the twin towers stood.*
*My throbbing legs are sprawled out in front of me, my helmet is off and my head is tilted back against the charred wall while I willingly let the rain wash away the tears on my cheeks.*
*It seems that I have been crying more of late, but down here at "Ground Zero" it's nothing unusual. There are thousands of brave men here and all will admit to the shedding of tears. They say the more you cry, the tougher it makes you. If that is true, I must be one of the strongest men in the world.*
*I am wishing that the rain would pick up a little harder so it would wash away the terrible smell of smoldering fires and other things …*
*In my left hand, clutched to my chest are your two wonderful letters. With my right, I am trying to write you on the back of Alexandra's letter of thanks, but it's too difficult in the rain and because my hand is shaking too much that it is difficult to decipher my own handwriting. I want so much to explain to you how grateful I am, but my hand keeps shaking so …*
*I have been working on this disaster as a volunteer for the past week, sometimes twelve to fourteen hours each day from two-thirty in the morning until I feel that I am being ineffective. My stitches itch, my body is racked with so much pain, throbbing legs, broken heart that I just want to go home and give up and quit! But then, something came over me, like a second wind. Alexandra, Megan, I am convinced it had to do with your two letters let me explain as best I can:*

*About an hour ago, a group of us came out of the smoldering Hell of ash, steel, and rubble of World Trade center #2 carrying another unidentified person on a gurney. All of us, as has been the case all week, were depressed of not being able to find anyone alive. We knew, all too well, that time was running out. We were all in need of rest, so we separated to be alone, to catch our breath, to rest, and to nourish ourselves. We would get ready to enter Hell again later, when needed.*

*Not knowing why or where I was going, I simply put one foot in front of the other and slowly started walking. I lost all sense of time. Sometime later, not knowing rhyme nor reason, I found myself on the opposite side of the disaster area, near a small harbor staring at a huge poster board covered with letters from boys and girls from all over the United States.*

*I do not know how long I had been standing there, but it must have been a long time for I noticed the rain had subsided and dawn was upon us. I stepped closer to the poster board because I couldn't read the letters as my eyes ached so much that I thought I must have been crying again, and the bile taste in my mouth made me wonder if I had been sick again. I stepped up between two firemen, and started reading the posted letters. All of a sudden, I started feeling different a smile perhaps a whimper of amusement from the depths of my ash covered throat. I kept reading, and reading, and reading. I felt like I was being cleansed—the more I read, the cleaner I felt. What a wonderful experience, showered by beautiful words from beautiful boys and girls who really care.*

*So I decided to pick two and the first one I chose was yours, Alexandra. The reason I chose it is because I associate your beautiful name with one of the loveliest spots in the world Alexandria, Egypt. It is situated on the beautiful shore of the deep blue Mediterranean. It brings forth visions of sandy beaches, palm trees, and soft summer breezes. The second letter I chose was yours, Megan, because of your eloquent penmanship, and also because it took my breath away for it suddenly hit me that I haven't, for the past seven days, thought about my own granddaughter named Megan Oh my God, my grandchildren, and my grown children. I hadn't thought about all of them at all!*

*Do you understand what you have done for me? Instead of thinking about death, smoldering ruins, unfound bodies, because of your letters, I am now thinking about soft summer breezes, and the pleasant sound of children laughing.*

*I crawled out of Hell, and found you two. Do you see what your letters have done for me? They have picked me up, dusted me off, said, "Good work Sam, hang in there, we love you." Like the song says, "you are the wind beneath my wings." Just think Alexandra, Megan, how many others are feeling the great joy I feel for the letters of your classmates.*

*I am so thankful for what you have done for me, that it changed the way I think. Earlier in the darkened sky, while gazing up at the void where the twin towers used to stand so majestically, my heart was broken ... yet now, gazing upward, I can find our hope.*

*I am crying again, but that's O.K. I am weeping with joy ... Thank you Alexandra, than you Megan, thank you, lord ...*

*All right kids, I am setting aside and blocking out the pain, the anguish, the exhaustion, and my sick heart. I am feeling better thanks to you. It is time to regroup ! The heavy machinery is moving again, and pretty soon another hole will be opened, and we'll be going back in. Maybe this time, we'll be lucky. I need to get ready so I have to feed this sixty-four year old body with some nourishment, stock up with some additional water, and get another packet of surgical gloves.*

*I have made a decision, since you brought me such joy and happiness; maybe you two are my good luck charms ... I am taking letters with me. In reality, this attempt will be done as a team. The three of us: Sam, Alexandra, and Megan. But don't worry, we won't be alone: New York's finest will be with us.*

*The request has gone out, there is no time left, I will have to finish this letter after the attempt, so here's the game plan: Listen up ! It's time to become numb and listless, void and senseless, time to become a cold professional.*

*Your letters are in my pocket. Alexandra, you will be my eyes, the light on my helmet, and the flashlight in my left hand. Don't worry, I change out the batteries every day with new ones. Megan, you will be my ears. We will be listening for any distant sobbing, scraping, tapping, or meek cries for help. Your mothers will be our hearts in this attempt. Your fathers will be the strength in our legs. Your grandparents will be our backbone, and your classmates will be our cheerleaders cheering us on, the whole populace of your town will be the trenching tool in my hand.*

*HEAVENLY FATHER, RICHLY BLESS THIS ATTEMPT ...*

I had to leave the letter off at that point because a search team was forming and they needed help. I thought God would forgive me for stretching the truth in my message to the little girls about the possibility of finding anybody alive from now on. I just couldn't let them lose their belief in miracles. I meant to close out the letter right after my next probe of the ruins but by then I was too exhausted to finish it. It would have to wait till the next day when I was scheduled for a quick flight back to Florida, at the suggestion of one of the medical tent doctors, for a day of rest and some patching up before coming back.

Around three the next morning I dragged myself as usual the two blocks to the harbor where a moored cruise ship had been leased by the New York FEMA office. It was a great place to get a hot meal of steak and eggs to fuel the coming day's deeds. On the weary walk from the securely barricaded Ground Zero to the ship in the harbor there were pastors and preachers and Red Cross volunteers and Salvation Army officers on every street corner. And psychologists too. They'd massed to minister to the diggers and anyone else in need during the most trying time the city had ever experienced. Several of my fellow searchers said they really appreciated the encouragement and counseling and kindness these urban angels offered. I know I appreciated them. And their prayers too. I was constantly asking them for guidance.

That night on the flight to Tampa, after the attendants made their final pass through the cabin, I pulled down my dinner tray and finished the letter Alexandra and Megan.

*Although I didn't find anyone alive that morning, there is some good news to report. Two days after the attempt, I walked over to the poster board that displayed all the letters from your classmates at your school. And guess what? They were all gone ! Word had obviously spread about the good fortune you two brought me, and the other letters are now being carried around in others' pockets. Many of the brave men and women here wanted me to thank your fellow classmates for their support. Tell your school and all the schools around you that the brave men working in the disaster area send their love and thanks.*

*As for me, I get to go home for awhile to rest up before I go back. This is standard procedure. We are now only allowed to work nine shifts in a row because the work is so hard. If we were there longer, we may tend to lose the needed efficiency in doing our job.*

*Alexandra, Megan, there is something I want you to do for me. I*

*want you to write to me and tell me something about yourselves and
your families. What are your hobbies? Tell me about your school. Tell
me what interests you have, such as sports, music, etc. Tell me about
Scotia. I imagine it is beautiful. And most important, SEND ME
YOUR PICTURES.*

*Know that I love you and will pray for you everyday from now
on. The three of us are a team forever. God brought us together. I
want you to make a promise to me that you will go hug your mother,
your father, and especially your grandparents. Their hearts are broken
for what happened on September 11, 2001. Sit in on your parents'
knees, and ask them to explain why this nation is so great. Then hug
them tight and give them a kiss. Tell them for me, since they live in
the great state of New York, how proud we, the volunteers are of your
governor, and especially of the leadership of Mayor Giuliani. When
people say the police, EMS, and New York Fire Department are the
best "New York's finest," they are true heroes, all!*

*One final request: our great nation is going into war against the
terrorists. I don't want you to worry, as our U.S. military (Just like
New York's finest) is the best in the world. I want you to pray for our
men and women in the military. And I want you two girls, along
with your classmates to write to them overseas. Give them the same
words of thanks, but go one step further. Include your picture and
across the top of your letter say, "pick me up, fold me up, and put me
in you pocket." Then tell them you want to bring them comfort and
joy, and that you are their good luck charm.*

*Alexandra, Megan, I'm telling you everything is going to be all
right. How wonderful and strong this nation is because of true "little
heroes" like you.*

*Filled with such emotion, your friend,*
*—Sam N. Hall*

I never claimed to be a writer. If I were one I wouldn't have to pay for
somebody else to write this book for me. I know I probably broke more
grammar rules in my letter to Alexandra and Megan than there are grammar
rules. And lots of cynics out there will think my sentiments are corny but I
couldn't care less about them. Because like it or not, I'm damn proud of
what I wrote if not how well I wrote it. It's tough to tell somebody else what
you feel so deep in your gut you can count the cramps. And I knew I couldn't
reach down as far as I wanted to but I thought somehow that Alexandra and
Megan would get the message.

The next morning back home I had my secretary Annie type up the finished letters and put them in unsealed envelopes. Then I called the girls' principal at thier school and told her what was in the letters. I wanted to make sure I wasn't doing anything taboo in writing Alexandra and Megan. Or running the risk of upsetting them. Maybe the principal, would think they couldn't handle the graphic and depressing detail. But I got a quick O.K. over the phone from her, so I put the two unsealed envelopes addressed to the girls inside a bigger one with a note telling the principal to use her discretion about giving the girls their letters. I mailed everything off, still not sure if the girls would ever read the words I'd wrenched out of my heart and soul. My worries would vanish a week later back in New York when I got a call from Annie telling me that there were three letters waiting for me in the office. After that I wrote to and got letters from Alexandra and Megan on a regular basis.

✳ ✳ ✳

One afternoon during my four-day reprieve in Florida I got some post-traumatic treatment along with some clean stitches to replace the ones the medics had sewn into my lacerated left arm at Ground Zero. And I got an HIV test too. Handling all those bloody body parts might have been the most dangerous part of the tunnel rats' routine. I also had a long phone session with my minister Ron Julian. He told me that God surely approved of my latest offering. I knew he was right and that God had guided me to Ground Zero. In spite of all the horror and heartache, I knew I was doing the right thing.

One memorable morning back in New York just after I'd emerged from another "rescue" dig I headed for a break and a cold glass of water at the cruise ship. I was exhausted as usual, soaked in sweat and covered with grime, scratched and scraped, black and blue and bloody. Halfway to the harbor a man stopped me and introduced himself. His name didn't mean anything to me at the time and I quickly forgot it. But he asked me all about what was going on at the site and what my job was and how I was holding up. Then he told me he was a volunteer chaplain with the Salvation Army and offered to pray with me. So we stood on that street corner reciting the Lord's prayer together as streams of dirty diggers and curious pedestrians passed by. A couple of months later back in Florida I got a letter from this sympathetic stranger asking how I was doing. He'd also enclosed an article about Ground Zero from the November 2001 issue of *Christianity Today* that mentioned me. Most of what he had to say was flattering except the part about me being the only tunnel rat he'd met who was older than he was. I found out from the magazine his name was Gordon MacDonald and he was a noted scholar and speaker as well as a damn good prayer leader. I kept in touch with him and once told him I wanted to follow in his footsteps as a chaplain and later I did.

One exhausting afternoon while I walked with a group of searchers around the remains of Building Seven, which was where the secret service office with all its classified papers got incinerated, we literally ran into Rudy Giuliani and Governor Pataki with a line of their lackeys. The mayor obviously made me out as the oldest of the bedraggled bunch and asked, "How are you holding up trooper? Are you getting enough to eat and drink?" I lied and said I was fine and fed but he reached over and grabbed the face mask hanging from my neck then gave it a look. And said "Hey this is filthy. You'd better replace it." I told him I would. I didn't tell him that the new mask would be just as inefficient fifteen minutes after I got back on the job. The mayor and the governor and all their hangers-on shook our hands and asked us where we were from and thanked us for our efforts. We appreciated Rudy's efforts too. We'd seen him a number of times checking on the progress at Ground Zero.

Any time a digger ventured out of the restricted area he'd be recognized of course and thanked by pedestrians and cabbies and doormen. One day I walked over to the Soho district for lunch after I'd picked up some of the developed photos I'd snapped at the dig. While I sat at the bar picking at a sandwich and checking my pictures, a guy standing behind me and evidently peering over my shoulder said, "My God ! Those are shots of Ground Zero aren't they?" Suddenly I was surrounded by curious customers who wanted to see the shots and ask me questions. One of them wanted to know why I volunteered to do such dangerous work and I said without thinking but truthfully, "Because so few others will." That became my standard response to the question of why I volunteered in general. Anyway, then someone shouted to the barkeep, "Give this man whatever he wants. He's a worker at Ground Zero." So I got my coffee cup refilled for free. About then I could have used a gallon of Old Granddad with a thimble of splash but drinking on the dig was a sure fire way to get yourself badly burned or worse. It was common for New Yorkers to wear their curiosity on their sleeves about the project and they expressed their gratitude to the workers over and over again.

Another morning after a horrific day of fighting fatigue I decided to vary my eating routine and headed to the Marriott a couple of blocks from the dig site. The hotel, which would eventually have to be torn down, had been converted into the Red Cross headquarters and a place to provide food and rest for the workers. Sitting behind a big breakfast there I felt faint and almost landed face first in my scrambled eggs. About then one of the other diggers who was a native New Yorker and a stockbroker asked if he and his friend who was a fireman at the site could join me. When the two pulled up their chairs the stockbroker began to recall the day of the disaster.

"I was just coming out of the Fulton Street Subway when I heard the explosion. I looked up and saw the smoke. People started running and some were trampling others. It was awful. Mass hysteria."

He choked up and I could see the tears in his eyes.

"The flames were shooting out of the front of the tower. Just as I came around a corner I saw the second plane hit. There were dozens of people jumping out of windows on the eightieth floor. Bodies were landing on the roof of the Plaza. That's the sight I can't get out of my mind. My wife says I talk about it in my sleep."

Then the fireman described what it was like the morning of the tragedy.

"We were answerin' the first alarm at eight forty five. Me and five other firefighters got as far as the thirty-first floor of the north tower carrying hoses but we were ordered out. When we got back down to the lobby it looked like it'd snowed."

He paused at that point and sipped his coffee. He was obviously having a hard time emptying his emotions.

"I remember lookin' over my shoulder and sayin' to the fireman next to me 'where's the other tower?'"

That's all the two of them said to me that morning but when the three of us got up to return to the site I could picture better than ever what the terror of that day must have been like.

My own worst time came in the middle of my third week. I was crawling on my stomach through a dark narrow still smoldering tunnel so hot I couldn't breathe through my mask or see through my protective goggles for all the sweat. So I had to get the equipment off my face or stop breathing altogether. I wanted to lose my helmet too but without its searchlight there'd be no chance the crawl through this cauldron would be worthwhile. I kept saying to myself oh shit, oh shit, will I get out of here alive? This tunnel was hotter and narrower and scarier than most I'd maneuvered. But trying to turn around here could get me stuck and suffocated before the team above could pull me out so I kept inching forward. To this day I wish I hadn't. As I snaked ahead past a slight bend in the tunnel my helmet light exposed a sight so horrific it burned into my brain and it'll be there as long as I live. Fifteen feet ahead of me in a little grotto created by the rubble was a fireman bunched into a ball with a large shaft of steel sticking out of his upper torso. His head was thrust backward and his mouth was contorted in agony. I lay there for several minutes shaking and crying before I could size up the situation. What should I do now? I took a few more minutes to compose myself and then decided there was nothing to do but turn around in this nearly circular space and crawl back through the tunnel and report my find. Turning around though would bring me within inches of that harpooned figure and it took me a few more minutes to accept the closeness. Then as I crawled nearer the fireman I saw that the steel rod, before it pierced his body, had ripped open his rubber jacket. At first I thought his knees were just jammed against his chest under the jacket but then I saw, Oh my God, I saw that they were actually *in* his chest. That's when I threw up and couldn't stop and if I'd had my face mask on I might've choked to death.

On the slither back to the opening above I kept gasping and gulping the bad air and trying to ignore the smell of the puke that saturated my jersey. The more I thought of that fireman's face the faster I crawled. My voice was shaking when I made my report to the team leader but I managed to get the spot marked where I'd found the fireman. It would take a couple of cranes and dozens of searchers three days of relentless probing to free him. Now, at least, his family could come closer to what those who've never lost a loved one call "closure." God rest his soul. As for me, I'll be trying to forget the time I spent with him in that terrible tunnel to my dying day.

I must have looked as bad as I felt when I reported in about the fireman because the team leader urged me to take a break. So I hobbled over to a group of diggers' cots set up next to one of the few still-standing office buildings inside the barricades. The cots were lined up under an improvised walkway protected by a wooden overhang attached to the forty-story structure. Every now and then one of the building's cracked windows that hadn't fallen out would change its mind and crash against the overhang. Sleep was always hard to come by anyway while we were working the site because our minds would still be racing whether we were crawling a crease in the rubble or curling up on a cot. The intermittent crash of glass didn't help. Just now I had my eyes closed but my mind was working overtime rerunning the past hour's events. Suddenly a window that must've come from the fortieth floor rattled the overhang with a terrific crash and jarred me bolt upright. So, exhausted or not, I decided to drag myself the fifteen blocks back to my room the Holiday Inn.

As I wrestled my gear off in the hotel room I switched on the TV. A shot of the smoking ruins I'd just left dominated the screen. But what really riveted my attention was the crawl across the bottom of the picture. It broke the news that traces of anthrax had been found in a Florida commercial building. I'd known for a couple of days about the poisoning of postal workers on the east coast and empathized with their families but this Florida incident rattled me worse than the glass hitting the overhang half-an-hour before. I called Melinda right away to see if everything was O.K. at home and got a reassuring answer. After we'd talked awhile and I'd told her a couple of dozen times how much I loved her we hung up and I began turning a new idea over in my mind.

That Florida anthrax incident was way too close for comfort. What if a terrorist attack had hit St. Petersburg? What if Melinda and the kids were within the bulls eye circle? What would I do if I were off somewhere in another city or another country? I'd never forgive myself for not providing protection. I'd been too busy this past week to think about that possibility. But now I saw that I had to act on two fronts, New York and Florida. And all that night I tossed and turned in the only comfortable bed I'd seen in a week. By 4:00 A.M. and time to head back to Ground Zero I'd hatched a pretty good plan for a shelter back home that would be as terror-proof as I could make it. And whenever I had a free minute away from the dig after that I cast and recast my plan to safeguard my family.

By the end of the third week at Ground Zero it was obvious to everybody but me that I was way too worn out to be much more use. I tried to put in another day at the dig but by then even I couldn't convince myself I wasn't just getting in the way of the workers. And besides, armies of fireman from other states were arriving at the site by the hour. I knew if I admitted how weary I was and went home my small contribution wouldn't be missed. And I didn't need to force feed the feeling I felt right now with another week or month of the tunnel rat routine. I couldn't have been more fulfilled. And I knew in my heart I was a better person for my experience in New York. For the rest of my days the 9/11 tragedy will torture my memory. But I'll always remember its amazing aftermath too. The cast of characters at the dig who showed such courage. The posters promising prayers for the diggers. The people on the street who extended encouragement. And the great city's rebirth that dovetailed with the personal peace that went with my own continuing renewal.

Heading for the hotel to arrange for a flight home I was about to pass what looked to be a makeshift shrine near the dig site. I was drawn to the little structure. I said a prayer of thanks there to God. I was so physically beat I wasn't even aware what religion I was patronizing with my presence. But it didn't matter. It could have been Baptist or Buddhist or Catholic or Mormon or Moslem. God would get my message one way or the other. God gets around.

# TWELVE

The day after I got home from New York I called a family conference. I wanted to run my shelter idea past Melinda and especially David and my two daughters Samantha and Kelly who'd followed their brothers to the St. Petersburg area to be close to me. The idea was to get the whole family's input. When they were all assembled I told them I wanted to build a post-9/11 haven safe from a worst-case-scenario terrorist attack for the family and all the in-laws. Everybody thought the shelter was a great idea. And Melinda knew what I'd been through at Ground Zero so she wasn't too surprised by my plan.

"Sam, you know I've never once denied you or complained when you wanted to do your thing."

She was right about that and I loved her for it. What other wife would let her husband time after time tilt with the world's windmills and never arch an eyebrow? Or give away wads of what was as much her money as his? No, I had to admit Melinda was a real gem. I dreaded more than anything in life being tied down to one house or one town or one lifestyle or not being able to act right away on any itch that said, "scratch me." What a plus to have a loving wife who understood.

Now that I had the whole family on my page I could plan the "Hall Compound" in earnest. In the worst case scenario there would be no water. I knew from my counterterrorism classes taught by HazMat experts in Alabama that it was possible to buy a couple of common cleaning chemicals in fifty-five gallon containers at a hardware store, mix the ingredients, and pour the solution into one particular aquifer that feeds seven states. A witches' brew like that in the drinking water could kill millions in just a couple of days. Tom Ridge later addressed that vulnerability. Or the terrorists could go for the electricity grid. The rolling blackouts our own neglect of the system had spawned in recent years proved how easy the terrorists would have it on that score. And if either of those or a slew of other scripts unfolded, the supermarkets would sell out in a flash. So there'd be no way to restock standard groceries. And there'd be no sanitation either.

Of course the evil-doers could also serve up a chemical cocktail or a biological blend. So the compound would have to be prepared to counteract Ebola, sarin, plague, cholera, typhoid, diplococcic, bacilli, sarcinae, spirochetes, as well as anthrax and a host of other toxic agents. Luckily in this context I could call on my counterterrorism courses with the British SAS and the Israeli Mossad.

After a week of work on the plans for the compound, I was ready to roll. I first went searching for a piece of property that we could easily reach from our current home in case of crisis. I needed a house with at least 4,000 feet of living space and suitability for sixteen people to populate. It had to be secluded and located on open water and accessible by car or boat. And since my father didn't raise any financial fools, I wanted something that would bring a princely profit in the bargain, if I ever sold it. Within a week I'd signed a six-hundred-thousand-dollar contract to practically steal a huge Inter Coastal spread that met my specs and I closed on it inside of six weeks. Since I already owned or rented a lot of earth-moving equipment, getting protective barriers constructed presented no problem. While a handful of workers got the place ready to move in I decided to give each of my kids a specific assignment in order to speed up the procurement process.

Samantha, my youngest, worked in St. Petersburg as a pharmaceutical rep so it made sense to task her with stocking the medicine cabinet. I knew you could buy everything from anthrax antidotes to zebra zits overseas with no questions asked and Samantha was a whiz on the internet. So I gave her a list of our needs and an unlimited budget. The first priority though was enough CIPRO for sixteen since the anthrax killer was still walking the streets. That order was filled within two weeks from Europe.

By the end of two months I had a mountain of medicines and a bill to match. I even paid a physician-advisor to produce a book to guide me through the correct dosages to administer according to the weight and age of the victim. Then I bought a Sunbeam Postal Scale from Office Depot so if need be I could dole out doses in precise amounts. I'd never mastered math but

*Sam at Ground Zero following 9/11.*

these calculations could kill if I didn't get them exactly right. I learned that in a bacteriological attack, for example, my grandson Christian who weighed sixty pounds would need 0.29 teaspoon which is 0.024 ounces or 0.70 grams or 10.73 grains of Terramycin Soluble Powder-343. I also learned that combining mild silver protein with some of the dosages works against nearly all bacteriological agents. I bought medicines too for bubonic plague, diplococcic, staphylococci, bacilli, sarinae, spirifla, and cholera. I even tried to get my hands on some small pox serum but couldn't. I had a reasonable comfort level about smallpox though since some of my other formulas mixed with the silver protein would work well. And by itself the silver protein fights viral, fungal, bacterial and spirochetal invaders. By the time the Hall Compound was ready for the family it had an impressive collection of medical manuals and I could cure everything from vaginitis to West Nile virus, or at least reduce the chances of infection.

Kelly, my older daughter, was dubbed the Martha Stewart of the compound. It was her job to fill the shelves with a year's supply of food for all of us. Pretty soon the cans of meats and vegetables and fruits started piling up faster than they could be stored. Most canned goods had a shelf life up to five years but my master plan called for replacing the stuff after twelve months and donating the last year's supply to the local charities that fed the poor. Kelly saw to it that there were kitchen utensils of every kind and cooking vats and other cauldrons for sterilizing. She bought plenty of Sterno plus charcoal candles, plastic bags, and paper plates by the case. Then she piled up hundreds of pounds of bleach and bags and bags of water purification tablets. I even had her pick up a supply of hybrid seeds to plant in case we were confined to the compound for the long haul. For entertainment Kelly set up a pretty impressive library of novels and had several large screen TVs installed. There were video games for the grandkids and even a year's supply of hard candy for their good behavior treats.

I put my son David in charge of security and transportation for the shelter. He took a little time off as supervisor of our commercial job sites to install the shelter generators and bury a bunch of fifty-five gallon drums of fuel. I couldn't help with the fuel drums because for months after my stretch at Ground Zero I couldn't even use a trowel in the garden for fear I'd unearth a body part. But David was a wonderful organizer. He saw to it that our emergency water needs would be met with fifty five-gallon containers and a dozen sixty-gallon military bladders. Then there were the portable toilets and the hanging bladders for showers and flashlight batteries by the gross and Visqueen to cordon off parts of the house if need be and yards and yards of duct tape. David picked up battery operated two-way communica-

*Sam at Ground Zero following 9/11.*

tion gear and shortwave radios. We had gasmasks with a supply of extra filters for all sixteen of us. The kids' masks came all the way from Israel where they knew a thing or two about fending off terrorists. David saw to it too that each male had a chemical suit for probes outside the shelter and even a radioactive-fallout detector. And he laid in lots of weapons and thousands of rounds of ammo. I was determined that no enemy would overrun this bunker. I even had David buy body bags for burials but we didn't tell the others about those.

I suppose I could forgive a reader for wondering why anyone would want to go through all this trouble and incur all this expense, I figure supplies alone for the compound cost over fifty-grand, just to prepare for an attack that might never come. And a shrink would probably say all that time rifling through the rubble at Ground Zero and finding fragments of people had turned me paranoid. But a paranoid is somebody that puts ten and ten together and gets twenty-five. At worst I was a little neurotic. I knew ten and ten were only twenty but I was still a little nervous about it. And when it came to my family no amount of man hours or money could come close to compensating for their loss should another 9/11 type plot focus on Florida.

Way before Ground Zero I'd seen what terrorism could do, even or maybe especially to the innocent. Living in Israel in the eighties I'd seen human flesh scraped off walls after a suicide bomber in Tel Aviv blew up a restaurant. A sight like that rivets your mind on your loved ones and how best to keep them out of harm's way in case of an attack. That's not fear. It's facing facts. I knew too from watching the Israelis' struggle against Hezbollah that once a terrorist organization declares itself against a society it's total war. No distinctions are drawn between soldier and civilian. To the terrorist, even a baby is a threat because it will grow up to be a soldier. The mother is a threat too because she will bear the baby who will become a soldier. The pediatrician is an even bigger threat because he could deliver a division in a matter of months. Now, after 9/11, all Americans were going to have to learn these lessons.

There's a tendency for Americans to think of terrorists as irrational. But that's a dangerous distortion. To pull off an attack like 9/11 you have to be captive to a calling but more than that you need to be methodical and systematic and thorough. The research and planning that goes into even a relatively simple terrorist plot can be intricate. Winning this war would be no muscle match, This was a chess game and the terrorists' first move had wiped the board clean of our poor pawns at the World Trade Center. It would take strategic thinking and not just about military means. Probably over generations to challenge and then checkmate the fanatics. And truth to tell maybe a few more horrendous hits to sharpen our synapses. Meanwhile American families would endure endangerment. But I'd do what I could to reduce the risk to mine.

At any rate the work crew put the finishing touches on the Inter Coastal house turned survival shelter in early February of 2002 and the family gathered for a trial run at the place the second weekend of the month. Everything seemed ship shape and super secure and we shared stories about how we'd contributed to turning the house into a world class counterterrorism compound. Our only regret was that the average American family couldn't afford a fort like ours, though I was determined to spread the word about some steps they could take to be more prepared against the terror threat that looked likely to grow. But my family's weekend at the Hall Compound convinced us we were perfectly positioned for any eventuality. We all went back to our permanent places knowing the retreat was ready.

About that time Melinda took a call for me from Tom DeLay, the then Republican Majority Whip in the Congress. Turned out he wanted me to be a co-chair with him on the House's Business Advisory Council. The council was supposed to bring together lots of high-powered business types to thrash out ideas on government reform. I couldn't say no since serving would be a feather in my fedora and pile prestige on our construction business. And I'd have a chance to see Tony from time to time in Washington. So now I was making intermittent trips to Capitol Hill and listening to experts spout ideas about the best way to stimulate the economy, how to get debt reduction, what to do about the social security system, what level of tax reduction was possible, and how to cut down on government waste and inefficiency. And on every flight I passed the time trying to figure out who on board were the sky marshals.

All during this time I was still suffering a degree of post-traumatic stress from my Ground Zero grind. That syndrome made sitting through meetings in Washington even tougher than it would normally have been for somebody as restless as me. I still had nightmares and daytime visions of bloody body parts, but good memories too. Especially of the heroic firefighting men and women I'd met. In fact they were still so inspiring to me that I cut out a poem about them from the St. Petersburg paper and pasted it above my desk at home and made a copy for my temporary office in Washington. The poem was written by a woman named Sue Ikerd in memory of the firefighters who died at the World Trade Center and the lines I liked best said, "They were on their way to Heaven when they hurried up the stairs,/Not only were they heroes, they were angels unaware." The more I thought about their sacrifice the more I knew I had to be a part of their profession. And lately there'd been stories in all the papers about a series of devastating forest fires in the west. What if I volunteered to fight the fires out there? I could save homes from fires and their owners from the kind of heart hurt I'd seen after the Florida hurricanes. And keep the forests from being devastated too. The hurricanes and Ground Zero had already purged my soul of all its drug war damage. Being close to nature in the western woods could go a long way to restoring me physically too. And of course there'd be the ever enticing danger.

I knew the idea of fighting forest fires in my mid-sixties would lead most mature minds to call me a lunatic only fit for locking up. After all, I was a Congressional advisor on Medicare and still dreaming like a little boy about a future as an action hero. But I couldn't help it if I'd been wired weird. Besides, a lot of those mature minds were leading uptight lives they'd trade if they could for something spicier. Whatever the reasons for their repressions, I was determined to check into my chances of supporting Smokey the Bear soon with my own helmet and hose. But a new disaster put my latest dream on hold for a while.

# THIRTEEN

On a bright and beautiful Florida February morning in 2003 my son David, my son-in-law Jeff, and I'd just reached the seventh green at the country club. Such Saturday threesomes equaled my entertainment for the week these days. Between trips to Washington to promote other people's businesses and returns to take care of my own, I didn't have much time for other relaxation. That's why I was so annoyed when the cell phone's ring in my ear and vibes in my shirt pocket broke my concentration on a par putt. When I pushed the right button and put the right end of the piece against my ear my daughter Kelly's agitated voice told me something big was happening again.

"Dad, you won't believe this! The TV is showing the space shuttle breaking apart. All the astronauts are dead."

After I calmed Kelly down, David, Jeff, and I fast-walked straight to the clubhouse to watch a rerun of the horror on one of the sets there. The pictures hit me hard because I'd always been a big fan of the space program. I'd met some of the astronauts over the years through my connections, including one of my greatest heroes, John Glenn. I'd even thought long and hard about volunteering for astronaut training in the early days of the program but I knew the gimpy knees that got me mustered out of the Air Force would have done me in again. So now I had to take some action to show my respect for the courage of the Columbia crew and my sympathy for their families.

The next day I called the sheriff's office in Lufkin, Texas to inquire about the hunt for Columbia debris. The person I talked to in the office said that volunteers were already beginning the search and that any help I could give would be appreciated. She said that most of the debris was thought to be distributed around a couple of northern Texas counties near the Louisiana line and that the most important ICP (Incident Command Post) was in Sabrina County. Ten minutes later I had my ticket to Houston booked and when I boarded and we were airborne I couldn't help staring out my window and wondering what the Columbia crew felt as they anticipated the oncoming earth in those final minutes. I hoped the abundant courage they'd shown throughout their training and prior missions served them well in the end.

After I deplaned in Houston I rented a car and headed North to Lufkin but the nearest motel I could find was more than 50 miles away. I checked in and before first light the next morning went straight to the Sabrina County command post. I arrived around five and got handed a cup of coffee and told breakfast would be served in an hour. As I waited my fellow volunteers began streaming into the improvised camp. By the time breakfast was ready the huge hall was swarming with nearly 300 volunteer searchers. They seemed to be from every walk of life and every ethnicity. There were doctors and truck drivers, Wal-Mart workers and Wall Street types, retirees and unemployed. Anyone who wanted to help was being accepted at that point, though by the end of the week only those with prior search and rescue experience were wanted. By then you had to have a badge that pegged you as a Red Cross knight or a professional firefighter or a National Guardsman or a Forestry Service worker or somebody with similar status.

It was obvious from the first meeting run by the County Emergency Director, with advice from NASA professionals, that this mission would be meticulously organized. He showed great leadership and organizational skills and he had exceptional charisma. When he talked everyone listened intently. That first day a routine was established that never varied. It started with a prayer for a successful search and then an astronaut from Houston read several letters from the shuttle crew's spouses and kids and extended family members thanking the volunteers in advance for their efforts. Later in the week two or three astronauts would be on hand to inspire the searchers. Some of the speeches they gave and some of the letters from the crew's loved ones brought tears to the eyes. Six of the seven Columbia astronauts' bodies had been found and there was an urgency to find the last body for burial.

After the first day's opening ritual each of the volunteers was assigned to a team of twenty with an identifying number. I was assigned to Team Four led by a U.S. Forestry Service Officer. Then each team got herded on to a big bus to take it to different search areas the leaders had decided on. The idea of the separate searches was to grind out an overall grid. Each team would walk its own smaller grid and the resulting pattern would almost literally leave no stone unturned. Each searcher was given a map for orientation to the area he or she was working. Each day we would begin the search at the spot we'd left at the end of the previous day's hunt. We'd know that spot because it'd been marked with fluorescent tape of different colors hung from branches or bushes. The drill involved always walking to the left of the line marked with tape while the searcher on the far left marked a new line so as not to miss a foot of ground. Each walker had a partner on his or her right to coordinate and communicate with. Each team would fan out with each searcher 10 feet apart and all walking slowly in as straight a line as possible. And then turning around and walking an area a little more to the left. Back and forth. Back and forth. Five miles north and then 5 south. And the next day starting all over again.

A NASA expert walked with each group to help identify badly charred pieces of debris. There was always an FBI agent with us too. He or she made sure we didn't touch any item, for security reasons and for our own safety. A special discovery team with anti-contamination gear would be called in to handle any discovered debris.

The search wasn't as mentally exhausting as the digging at Ground Zero but still it was grueling. The Texas terrain was thick with thorn bushes that ripped through clothes and skin if you brushed against them. Some places were pocked with fairly deep gorges that had to be stumbled through. And there were patches of old and fresh snow for avoiding lest you slip and slide a few 100 feet. The early mornings froze you to the marrow but five minutes of fighting through a field of thorn bushes would start you shedding layers of clothes. And you couldn't lose a layer without first freeing your backpack which was weighty with communication gear and your lunch and a day's supply of water. Tough and tedious going.

But the first day of searching produced the most important find of the entire project and made the rest of my Texas time anti-climactic. My partner that day was a NASA employee who worked on the shuttle docking system. He was one of a growing group from the space agency who'd volunteered to help. We were about 3 miles into our day's walking, looking for any significant debris but especially for several shuttle items we'd been shown pictures of early that morning. These were pieces that would help the NASA engineers put together a picture of what went wrong at crucial points in the fatal flight. Suddenly over our walkie-talkies we heard three excited voices off to our left, "HAZMAT requested!" Shouts and cheers erupted from all the team members because we all knew what that two-word exclamation meant. The body of the seventh astronaut had been found. Everybody took off running to the spot and got there at the same time the HAZMAT specialist did. And gathered around a grisly scene. The astronaut's charred body was naked and only one-third intact. It had apparently been dragged several feet and partially devoured by animals. Even with all I'd been through at Ground Zero the sight iced my blood. I knew of course that the astronaut was long past any possible suffering before he came to be in this forsaken field. And I took some solace in the knowledge that our discovery would be a comfort to the family and that they could now plan a proper burial. But death in any of its disclosures is disconcerting. And in this case it had taken a hero who had briefly touched the face of God a few short days ago. I said a silent prayer for the astronaut and joined the rest of the onlookers as they took up the task searching for debris once again.

The rest of my week with the searchers was absorbed with walking and untangling myself from thorn bushes and slipping in mud. And more walking and untangling and slipping. And now and then alerting the anti-contamination crew of a find. Small pieces of landing gear or cockpit plastic or insulation foam.

One day in the middle of the week my walking partner, the NASA engineer, made a discouraging point.

"If we had 2000 searchers and we walked these grids 24/7 for ten years we'd still only come up with around 15 percent of the shuttle. At least 85 percent will probably never be found."

That was enough to convince me I'd done my duty as fully as possible and after two more days I packed up my things and drove back to Florida. A few weeks later the chairman of the Columbia Accident Investigation Board, Admiral Hal Gehman, announced that as many as 5,000 searchers were still combing the Texas countryside for debris. All in all some 28,000 large and small pieces of the capsule had been recovered to that point. The admiral also thought more would be found once all the snow melted and the farmers began their spring plowing.

# FOURTEEN

Once again through my volunteer work I'd met some of America's most dedicated citizens and several had become good friends. That'd been enough to make all that walking and the scouring of those bleak Texas fields worthwhile. But what to do next? Business still bustled at the construction sites but that wasn't nearly enough to fill my cup. I needed something more substantial for soul stoking. So I decided the time had come to act on my insistent urge to join in the wonderful work of firefighting. Within a week I was filling out U.S. Forestry Service application forms for the romantic sounding job category "Wildland Firefighter" (Helitack Helishot). To qualify you had to be able to rappel down a rope from a hovering helicopter. The fact that the position also carried the less romantic designation GS-0462-05 didn't dampen my enthusiasm a bit. I just hoped my disaster relief references would trump my status as a sixty-six year old. I knew it said somewhere in the government's guidelines that they weren't supposed to discriminate according to age. Neither are other employers but every senior citizen that's applied for a job knows better. And the government's destroyed more forests writing their regulations than a couple of centuries of fires so I knew somewhere they could find a subsection to keep me out. My hopes were mixed when I mailed my application because I'd appended it with a DD 214 claim that certified my disabled veteran status. On the one hand that might give brownie points but on the other hand two gimpy knees might make the deciders think more than twice about whether I could do the work.

I knew the feds would take their time about coming up with a decision even if every bureaucrat up the chain of timeserving chuckled his way through my application and told his wife that night about the old coot who wanted to be a GS-0462-05. So the wait gave me time reinforce the regimen I'd added to my already rigorous exercise routine over the past few months. To get my red card that would qualify me to join the smoke eaters out west I'd have to pass the punishing pack test. That meant making a 3 mile trek at 4 miles-per-hour in 45 minutes with a 45 pound load on my back. A trek like that would require a trot and not just a walk like the ones that'd tested me in Texas. But I was hell bent to someday be a Helitack Helishot so I'd started training months before I mailed my application. Of course with those two bad knees, not to mention one leg that'd been shot twice and the other that'd been operated on four times, the progress had been slow to say the least. At first I couldn't handle twenty-five pounds but after a couple of months I was hauling forty and hating/loving every minute of the hardship and pain. By the time I heard back from the forest feds I was jogging the 3 mile route in a few seconds under forty-five minutes and feeling quite proud of myself. What I wasn't thinking of then though was the decisive difference between training in Florida at 6 feet above sea level and fighting fires in the thin air 9,000 feet up on an Idaho or an Oregon mountain.

After two months of anticipation and disappointment with no response to my application letter in sight I decided to play a couple of cards I had hidden up my sleeve. One was my Red Cross ID. With it I could go to any disaster area in the U.S. or even overseas as a highly trained damage assessment specialist. The damage I was qualified to assess included structural stuff of any kind. And didn't forest fires sometimes damage structures? Sometimes too a wildfire in the woods could injure or kill a firefighter or a homeowner who couldn't beat the blaze to a safe site. And my credentials included first responder medical treatment and loss of life counseling. Then too I'd met most of the Incident Commanders chasing hurricanes and at the Mexican earthquake and the Honduran mud slides and at Ground Zero and most recently in Texas looking for shuttle parts. After all, the disaster detail was a small fraternity and I was sure I could turn my contacts into a ticket to the western wildfire scene.

I'd been interested in firefighting in the west for as long as I could remember. When I was a kid I had gone on a few vacations out west and I fell in love with the mountains and the animals I'd see on the way, especially the antelope in Wyoming, and the elk in Oregon, and the bears in the National Parks. Ever after that when I'd hear about a forest fire I'd get depressed and somehow diminished by the loss of a portion of that paradise. Maybe the

*Sam fighting forest fires on the border in Idaho, 2004.*

sense of loss loomed larger because I shared a streak of wildness with the animals and the land. I'd always wanted to return to the West. At any rate, early on I'd developed a strong longing to join the men and women who were tasked with saving God's gift of trees and rivers and all the untamed. Especially when I found out how dangerous the job was!

Between reading books about forest fires and talking to firefighters over the years I tried to learn all I could. From one point of view wild land firefighters weren't much different from city firemen. The uniforms were different of course because the forest fighter's had to be lightweight and flexible to allow for digging containment lines and chain-sawing trees without generating the body heat a city fireman's bulky getup would. Heavy clothing would slow down a woodland firefighter and maybe cause heat-stroke from the combination of body warmth and the tremendous temperatures. Both professions were highly trained in some of the same skills though. In lots of ways wild land firefighters were just glorified ditch diggers and lumberjacks. But they did their digging and jacking to protect some of our most sacred national treasures. And it wasn't only the forests and the animals. There were also the man-made structures that meant so much to many who'd struggled so hard to build and maintain them. It took a lot of training to be a professional firefighter whether you rode a red truck in the city or chose a chainsaw in the woods. And terrific discipline to face a fire with your fear in check.

I found out too that ninety-five percent of the blazes that burn our woodlands are caused by lightning. The rest of the time it's usually arson. An arsonist has always ranked right down there with a terrorist in my book of bad guys. In fact in some ways a fire bug is worse than a lot of terrorists. At least a terrorist who flies a plane into a building or walks into a restaurant strapped with a stick of explosive has to call up some corrupted courage. What kind of strength of will does it take to strike a match and run? Anyway, all fire, whether it's a flickering flame on a birthday cake or a 200 foot high, mile-wide wall of flame roaring up a canyon, comes down to a chemical reaction pure and simple. It's a naturally occurring consequence of energy release in the form of heat and light when oxygen combines with a combustible material at the right high temperature, which in the case of wood is about 617 degrees Fahrenheit.

My firefighter friends always talked about "fuel" by which they meant combustible material working together with oxygen and heat to form a "fire triangle." Take away one of the sides of any triangle and it collapses. Remove the fuel or oxygen or heat and a fire fizzles. That's the firefighters job. To take away at least one of the sides of the triangle. For example, when a crew digs a deep trench around a fire its access to fuel is cut off. When air support drops water on a fire it reduces the heat. Or better yet retardant which is a soupy substance that coats the fuel and keeps it from catching. So the firefighter's always jousting with geometry, always trying to take apart the triangle.

But it's a tough job. Big fires feed themselves. They can create their own weather that generates more oxygen. Sometimes fires can spawn hurricane force winds that a thousand firefighters couldn't do a damn thing about. And when you see a forest fire on TV or in a newspaper photo your eyes play tricks on you. The trees and the shrubs aren't really burning, their being converted into gas. Of course that's just a technicality that firefighting wonks talk about. The forest is just as charred whether you think the trees burned or they morphed into gas. But if you care about the chemistry, sit in front of your fireplace and watch the logs "burn." You'll see a space between the logs and the flame. That's the visible part of the process that changed a log into gas.

It turned out that I never took the 45 pound pack test. And it's a good thing. After months of working out and wearing out a local running track I still couldn't handle more than forty pounds. What I could handle was the politics of the game. I got on the phone to a friend of a friend I'd made digging at Ground Zero. The friend was a fireman in the New York City Department who knew some folks in the Forestry Service out west. And my first call to one of the fireman's friends got me the cell phone number of a higher-up in the agency who suggested I round up my Red Cross credentials and report to the Incident Command Post outside of McCammon, Idaho just south of the Sawthooths where the Harkness fire had been blazing for a couple of days. So I flew into Boise on July twenty-third and rented a car and drove through some barren high desert until I got to some gorgeous green back country up in the mountains. A couple hours of driving later I took the AAA's tip and checked into a dingy motel that should have been called the Norman Bates Sleephole in a little town about 60 miles from the fire site. That sort of strategy would get to be routine when I was chasing fires. Sometimes I'd be lucky to find a bed within a 100 miles of the action deep in the boondocks. That was because the other firefighters had already seen to it that the closer motels all had their, "No Vacancy" signs prominently displayed.

Anyway near McCammon I got myself checked in at the Bates and unpacked and bedded down for twenty winks. Way before dawn the next morning I grabbed my pristine new gear and threw it in my rented Subaru and headed for the ICP with the help of a government map that didn't do justice to the terrain. But then no map could ever match the mountains in the west. The landscape couldn't make up its mind. There were soaring mountains and deep valleys and glimpses of Snake River tributaries. It gave me the same feeling I'd always got out west. Like I was renewed in spirit and ready to take on anything life had to offer.

What life offered that morning was the chance to help contain the so-called Harkness fire which was a small one by western standards. When I got to the Command Post I found out that I'd be working with about a 100 men who were battling two fires that they were trying to keep from joining.

The Forestry Service supervisor gave me a dubious look when I reported in. But when I dropped the name of his superior and said I wanted to get right to fighting fire he pointed me toward a pile of equipment and told me to suit up. A quarter-of-an-hour later I was weighed down with forty-three pounds of fire-proof personal gear including cleansing and medical and survivor kits plus extra sweatshirts and fire hood and cameras and radio equipment and heavy trenching tools and a couple of gallons of water and enough food for twenty-four hours. Then an idle fire truck took me up country to the containment line at a secondary fire where I was inducted unceremoniously into an Oregon crew and put to work cutting down trees and dumping dirt on smoldering stumps. I soon found out the work was as tough or tougher physically than the Ground Zero digging. Every 20 feet or so there was something smoking or entirely engulfed and it would have to be hosed or dumped with dirt. And when I accidentally touched a couple of innocent looking trees I found out they could sear flesh.

Everywhere there were dead animals, mostly small ones like birds and squirrels, some badly burned and others apparently choked by smoke. The bigger animals like deer and elk could take care of themselves by outrunning a fire. But the sight of all these smaller scorched creatures made me sick to my stomach and sorrier than ever that nature worked this way. There were black flies everywhere feasting on the animal carcasses and on our own. The flies were big enough to father pheasants and their bite was worse than the burning bark's.

As we were sawing and snuffing, one of the Oregon line crew members filled me in on the scope of the Harkness fire by shouting over the din of chainsaws. He told me the main fire had started two days earlier with a lightning strike and was about 5 miles away in the center of a 5,000 acre burn. There was no way the crews could get close to it until it wore itself out. Our job was to keep it from jumping beyond the containment line of felled trees and wide trenches on this 7,000 foot high ridge. The day before helicopters had lowered a big pump and miles of hose to a spot by a small pond in a clearing. One of the crews played the hoses on the stubborn hot spots while the rest of us did the dousing with dirt and the digging. The work was exhausting but my main worry was washed away. I'd told Melinda before I left for the west that my big concern was whether I would hold up my fellow firefighters because of my age and relative lack of conditioning. But by mid-afternoon I was still stomping stumps and digging ditches at the same frenetic pace as my new buddies.

That was about the time I spotted the injured deer. He was a yearling and all of a sudden he stumbled out of the woods by Harkness Creek and stood watching our crew tending to the hot spots. I kept an eye on him as I worked at widening a trench and wondered if his mother had been lost to the flames. He was burned badly himself. His right flank was singed with an oblong mark about eighteen inches wide and ten inches high. A little later when the crew was taking its afternoon break I told the guys I was going to try to catch the young deer so he or she could get some treatment back at the camp. One of the crew whose name was Jim said he thought the two of us might be able to catch the deer since it looked like it wanted somebody to rescue it. It was just standing in the clearing looking sick and pathetic. But when Jim and I got close it hobbled just out of range and kept doing that until we lost it in the woods and the break time was over. Even though it was out of sight I couldn't get it out of my mind and I told Jim I'd look for it again the next day.

Along toward dusk the day's work wound down and the crew prepared to put the equipment to bed. So far so good in keeping the main fire at bay. I'd been planning to drive back to the Bates Motel that night but when I stopped moving I just about collapsed from fatigue. That's when it hit me that I'd been operating on pure adrenaline all day and couldn't make a move now without asking for agony. Besides that I felt so sick I was afraid I was going to live. I had a splitting headache and I kept fighting the urge to upchuck. The Bates seemed more like 6,000 miles away than 60 and when I told the Incident Commander how bad I felt he pointed to a pile of sleeping bags under a fir tree and told me to make myself at home. I could barely lift the bag and getting into it was torture. I barely kept from throwing up but the second I got situated in the sack I was into the soundest sleep I'd had in years.

The next morning I could barely make it out of the bag. That's when I came to appreciate the super strength and incredible conditioning of my crewmates. While these guys were already up and going over their gear and bragging about who could eat the biggest breakfast, I was still trying to muster the muscle to stand up. But I made it to the morning briefing on time. My first briefing would be like most of the others I would sit in on every fire fighting morning over the next two years. The leaders of the different parts of the overall operation like the hose crews and the trenchers and the support groups would talk about how we did the day before and what our tasks would be that day. We'd hear about safety issues and about how much damage the fire had done so far, which was always too much. And we were told to keep a close eye on the daily weather watch report including wind direction and gust strength. The briefing on this morning lasted for about forty-five minutes and that gave me a chance to stir up a little wind for my own sagging sails. When I got out on the containment line it only took me around an hour to catch up with the crew's bantering and joking that was part of the camaraderie and humor that they needed to stay sane on their dangerous duty. But their work ethic exceeded any I'd ever encountered. I knew I'd never feel threatened by anything out here battling blazes because I was with the best, real professionals. And what a privilege to be accepted by them. On this morning I was limping and probably still a little green around the gills but they hailed me like a hero as I joined up for a day's trenching.

Around noon the burned deer showed up again and this time it looked dazed and confused. But at least it'd made it through the night. Jim and I watched it while we worked for about an hour. It started for one side of the ridge and then another but wound up back near the containment line. Which was working well. The main fire had just about burned itself out and our secondary smolder was looking much less likely to hook up with another hot spot to ignite the big blaze. That gave Jim and me the chance to try again for a capture when the crew took another break. This time we got within a couple of feet of the yearling as we trailed it along Harkness Creek but at the last second it would bolt away a dozen or so yards ahead. After half-an-hour we had to give up and rejoin the crew.

That night I felt a little better physically than the one before but not chipper enough to drive the 60 miles back to the Bates. So Norman could use the money he saved on sheets to buy a new bread knife.

The next morning we got the official word that the Harkness fire was totally contained and we could take a break and then head out for the next threatened forest. But before I drove to the motel to check out I went back to the creek bed near the containment area and did another search for the deer. I walked up and down the creek for over an hour but there was no sign. Then I retraced my steps in the hope that I'd just missed the animal but that didn't do any good. Then I checked deep in the woods for three hours getting more and more frustrated. I'd always been a sucker for an animal in trouble. When I finally walked out of the woods it was nearly dark so I headed for the car to hunt for another motel. I found one about 30 miles west and spent the next couple of days in a frustrated attempt to locate the yearling.

My next stop on the firefighting circuit was north of the Harkness near Stanley on the Continental Divide between Idaho and Montana. A much bigger fire was reported to be out of control up there. More gorgeous scenery flashed by the northbound blue highway my map displayed. Since I'd learned my lesson about the lack of motel space in the back country close to the firefighting action, I stopped at a dingy dump about 50 miles south of Stanley. I checked in and discovered my room here made the Bates back at the Harkness look like the Ritz. It didn't even have a phone. But I had my cell with me to put in place the plan I'd hatched during the drive up here. So I called the *Idaho State Journal* which was the paper I'd noticed on the newsstands in the area though I'd never had time to read it. The operator at the paper put me in touch with a reporter named Zach Wesley and I told him I wanted to put up a reward of 1,000 dollars for anyone who could catch the wounded yearling alive and get it treated by a vet. I told Zach I'd also pay the rehabilitation cost. And that I didn't want my name published.

I told the motel clerk I'd be back that evening and headed the car north again. In a little while I ran out of pavement and found myself on Forest Service dirt ruts not much wider than the wandering lines on the map and with potholes deep enough to annihilate an axle. All the while I was marveling at how the fire support detail must've struggled to get their heavy equipment over these so-called "roads." But I finally bounced up to the ICP and dismounted to rest my bruised butt and report for duty. That's when I began to take in the seriousness of the situation here and the scope of the operation. There were upwards of 2,000 firefighters on the job as opposed to the 100 or so at the Harkness. The camp surrounding the ICP was organized so well by the Forestry Service support groups that it seemed like a small city. There were rows of tents for sleeping and mobile showers and over a 100 portable potties. The treatment and trauma centers had more medicine and machines than the Mayo Clinic. There were catering trucks unloading piles of provisions in front of huge mess tents. I'd learn in the next few days that the big tents were also used for morning planning and safety meetings that doled out duties and warned about wind changes and other dangers.

The big fire near Stanley was named the Black Wall/Black Frog by the Native Americans fighting it. There were 12,000 acres of forest in flames and waves of helicopters were dumping water and retardant on the hottest spots.

*Animal Rescue on the Alaska border, 2004.*

By my second day at the Black Wall/Black Frog fire the news about my posting a reward for the deer saver was all over the camp despite my trying to stay anonymous. That's why the Incident Commander approached me and asked if I'd join a crew assigned to rounding up stray and abandoned animals to take them to safety. Which sounded like a great gig to me so I said sure. Later that day I found myself helping a couple of Native Americans named Peace Eagle and Still Water herd everything from horses to house pets out of the fire's path, We'd get out in front of the fire and relocate animals or we'd find them after they'd been slightly burned. Or badly burned and then we'd have put them out of their misery which was the worst part of the work. When you love animals like I do it's gut grinding to have to shoot one. But I must have done a pretty good job because nearly every fire I volunteered for after that day I got asked to do some of the same kind of animal rescue and relocation work. And pretty soon I was doing a lot more rescuing and relocating than actual firefighting.

Each morning at an Incident Commander's briefing, right after he'd described the wind conditions, he'd assign a few men to the animal crew and if I volunteered I'd be sent out alone or with one of the teams to round up cattle and sheep and goats and whatever livestock or wild animals were trapped or threatened by the fanning flames. In fact by the end of the week at the Black Wall/Black Frog fire I'd moved so many animals around I felt like a bronco-busting cowhand. I even got pretty good with a lasso. I'd had a little experience rounding up horses years ago in Ohio but getting them to go your way with a fire nearby took more patience. In fact all the animals we moved were super sensitive to fire and wired like they were injected with half the caffeine in Brazil. The horses were the most skittish of all the animals. The roar of a fire in a nearby mountain was enough to spook them. And if there was a lot of smoke and most of all if there were burning cinders flying through the air it was worse. Trying to get a handle on horses in conditions like that was like trying to catch a hummingbird with a hairnet. And if you were on horseback yourself the difficulty doubled.

I did a lot of roundups on horseback at those fires in Idaho and later in Montana. The riding took me back to the time when I was nine or ten and my dad the mayor bought my brothers and me a show horse. We took turns training on it so dad could enter us in jumping contests for trophies. I'd felt really silly dressed up in a derby and jodhpurs and carrying a crop when I wanted to wallow in mud like my friends. I really loved that horse though and especially being astride him so I put up with playing Little Lord Fauntleroy for my dad. Then almost fifty years later trying to win one for the Gipper against the Contras I got blown off a horse by a landmine in

Central America. It was 1982 in El Salvador. I was faking the role of a freelance journalist interested in communist insurgents who were fighting against U.S. trained troops. My cover included an expensive camera and a press pass that would've bought my way into a Kremlin cocktail party. When the CIA's insurgent contact fell for the ruse the group sent a couple of shady characters to pick me up at a San Salvador hotel and they told me to pack for a three day trek into the jungle. The next morning I was blindfolded and plunked on a horse for the ride to the rebel camp site. On the way back one of the horses up ahead stepped on a land mine and blew me off mine. The insurgent on the horse ahead was killed but luckily my fall didn't even dislodge my blindfold. If I'd been a few feet further along the trail that day I might be moldering in a mountain grave somewhere in El Salvador right now.

Getting blown off my mount in Central America tended to make me horse shy for a while. But two years afterward I was astraddle a saddle again fighting terrorists behind enemy lines in Mozambique and I rode a broken down nag in retreat for six-and-a-half hours straight to get over the border. That time my pants were packed with Kotex to make a comforting cushion between my butt and my briefs. One of the other freedom fighters swore by the pads as protection against butt burn and coaxed me to try them. But they didn't work as well as they apparently do in the nether regions of the other gender's geography. My hemorrhoids had hemorrhoids for a month after my marathon ride. On the other hand, I knew that pathetic plug over in Africa was the reason I was still breathing God's good air. So I had another reason for wanting to see to it that the horses here in Idaho and Montana stayed out of harm's way.

Most of the time the animals we relocated were domestics. We'd run across a lot of stranded smaller animals like fawns and other forest dwellers that weighed in at less than fifty pounds. Their small legs couldn't carry them fast enough to outrun fierce fires that could top speeds of 35 miles-an-hour. Sometimes what happened in a forest fire taught a sad lesson in survival. Over and over we'd find suckling fawns that had been abandoned by a doe to save her own hide. One day at the Black Wall/Black Frog fire we found a two-week old fawn standing stunned and alone by a smoke shrouded pond beneath a roaring mountain blaze. I couldn't stand the sight of the poor abandoned animal so I told my crew members I'd try to catch it. When I walked over to it the fawn didn't move and let me pick it right up and carry it home to the base camp slung over my horse's withers. Back at camp a woman who'd had a baby a few months earlier gave me one of the nursing bottles she'd kept so I could feed the fawn. It was worth all the kidding I got from the crew about being a lovely mother when I was able to turn the healthy fawn over to a Forestry Service officer for transplantation in a safer environment.

Speaking of women there were a few who I met on line crews in the west, but only a few. Most of the females in the Forest Service were administrators or rarely smokejumpers or part of a three-person fire truck crew. The big fire trucks would roll over the roads in front of a fire. The crews would head for homes and other structures that'd already been prepared for the fire's arrival with newly dug or bulldozed containment lines. Sometimes the lines would be dug on both sides of the road. The idea was to keep the fire from jumping the road and continuing on its way. The fire trucks carried anywhere from 2,500 to 4,000 gallons of water. Their three person crews would soak structures and the driveways and the nearby trees. And they'd flood the containment lines too. I rode a truck as a crew member more than once out west and almost always one of my mates was a woman. And they did great work. I've never understood the attitude that says a woman has no place in a battlefield foxhole or on a forest fire line crew. I've seen some amazing accomplishments by women in the Olympics and in the Israeli army and though I've never fought in military engagements or on forest fire containment lines with them I surely wouldn't object to it. If a guy in his upper sixties can handle fire fighting's most dangerous duty it's a safe bet a woman can.

The work of saving animals was just as exhausting as the time spent on the containment lines. One night after a draining day relocating some sheep at the Black Wall/Black Frog fire our crew dragged back to base camp for a hot meal. We'd been herding and lifting a couple of 100 sheep that weighed 125 pounds each into big stake trucks for almost sixteen hours. And catching the sheep to load them was a chore in itself since they were severely spooked and the roundup was pure turmoil. The smoke was so thick that day it darkened the sky to such an extent that the bats came out of their caves at high noon to join the flies harassing our heads. Dinner at the mess tent in the evening around ten took more effort. I had to shovel the food into my mouth with one hand because the other one was busy holding up my head.

I went to my pup tent that night practically sleeping while I staggered. But when I got into my bag I couldn't drop off to save myself. Eight hours later I was still tossing and turning my aching body. I'd sometimes had sleepless nights like this after sixteen straight hours of trenching at containment lines. Those times I'd spent the night cursing some prick named Pulaski who'd invented the trenching tool back in 1910. The ones we were using

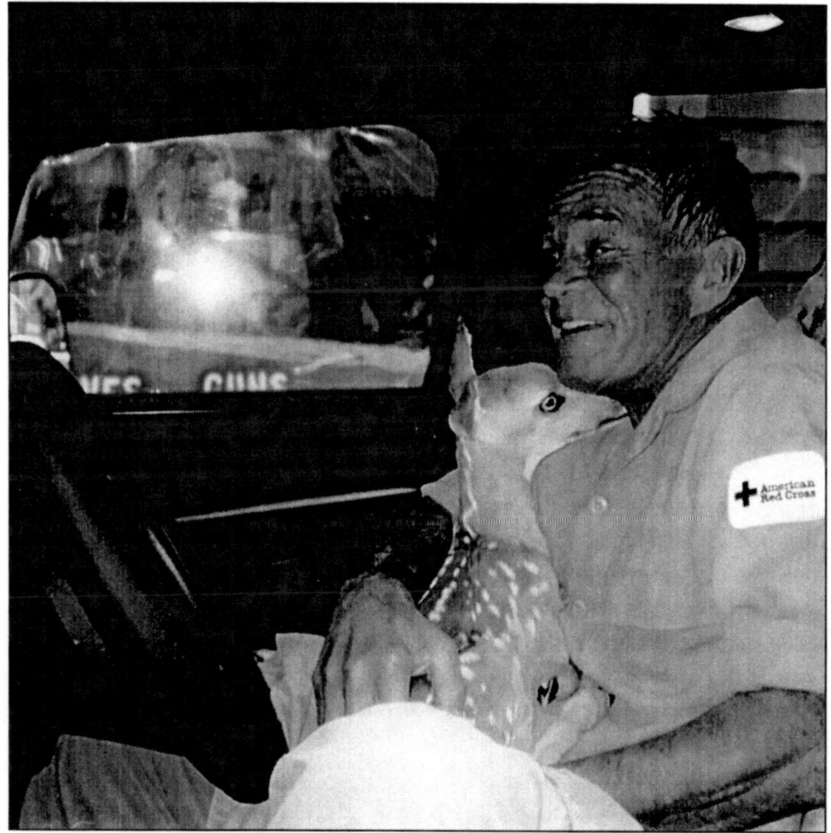

*Animal Rescue on the Alaska border, 2004.*

had a business end with an axe on one side and a grub hoe on the other. I could see mine swinging up and down and up and down through those sleepless nights. Now my wrath was reserved for those ranchers who'd waited so long before the idea of moving their stock away from the fire zone occurred to them. We were called in at the last minute to help them load up. But most of all I focused my anger on those other ranchers who'd pulled out of their places and left their animals behind to face the fire. Half of the sheep I'd rounded up and loaded this day had been abandoned. Some had cracked and bleeding skin brought on by the low humidity so we knew they'd been neglected for a good while.

During our rescue efforts I spotted what I thought was a wolf walking slowly near a stand of birch. When I crept closer I could tell that it was a coyote, and that its right front leg was badly burned. I was working with a game official of the state, and he darted the coyote. I reached for my two-way radio and was patched thru to the on sight BLM (Bureau of Land Management). After the coyote had been tranquilized he was relatively easy to handle. That is as long as he was drugged and roped! Within ten minutes we had him in an animal travel cage and he was taken to one of the local vets for rehab. That was the kind of capture and release that made my work so rewarding. And though I didn't know it at the time, it was the kind of experience that was slowly making my mind up to specialize in animal welfare volunteering.

What made matters more physically miserable on this particular night was the added irritation of the sniffles I'd caught that day from one of the other crew members. Colds and the flu were always being passed from one firefighter to another and this nose wiper had hit at the most inopportune time. Plus the rocks under my tent's thin canvass floor managed to dent my sleeping bag and find the sorest spots on my body. That bag was so uncomfortable anyway it made Maggie my lumpy mat cum mistress at the Sandinista prison in Nicaragua seem like a cloud full of down feathers. And there was literally no level ground at this base camp. When you sacked out you had to decide whether you wanted all your blood to flood to your head or flow to your feet. So I kept squirming the bag from one position to another. And I'd shoveled in too much food at dinner. Now it was combining with the industrial strength coffee and the wood smoke to reignite the intermittent heartburn that plagued me during all my firefighting gigs. The portable potties were only a dozen yards away but I'd brought an empty water bottle from the mess so I could roll over when the spirit and my bladder moved me. At one point I peed in the bottle and must've dozed for a few seconds because the next thing I knew my underwear was soaked and when I checked the bottle the cap was missing. But I was too beat to do anything but squirm the rest of the night away in my own piss. And thank the Deity I didn't have diarrhea.

That night was far from unusual for this volunteer firefighter. A lot of times after a day of drudgery I'd stumble back to camp and spend the night twisting and turning enough to shame Saint Vitus. But when I did fall asleep there was no more rerunning the day's digging or counting the sheep I'd helped load. Just dreamless oblivion. Whatever the nights were like though, the days never failed to deliver more pure happiness than I'd ever known.

# FIFTEEN

It was at the Black Wall/Black Frog fire too that a Forest Service Supervisor doubled my duty by assigning me part of the time to a detail that helped homeowners prepare for the raging fires that were roaring their way. Five of us would head for a threatened smattering of houses or other structures in the fire's path and clear a zone around them by chain sawing trees and raking brush and wetting down or pre-soaking everything in sight with hoses and an ingenious portable sprinkler system. Like GIs when they cleared zones in Vietnam or in any war so they could see the enemy making its advance. But in this war against forest fires there was never a chance for a truce and you were always on the defensive.

One day in Idaho we were working a threatened scattering of mountain homes that we thought had been evacuated days earlier. We'd just finished clearing the trees and brush around a tiny frame house and were starting to hose it down when what I used to think of as an old lady came through the front door onto her miniature deck and called to us. Turned out she wanted to thank us for our efforts to save her place. When Joe, the Native American firefighter next to me asked her why she hadn't been evacuated she said she wouldn't hear of it. She'd been living in the little place for thirty years and her husband had died there and no fire was going to chase her out. She reminded me of that guy with the unlikely name of Harry Truman who insisted on staying in his home near Mt. St. Helens and paid for his stubbornness with his life when the mountain exploded. Joe apologized to the woman for denuding her property but she just smiled and thanked us again, this time for clearing the yard so she could plant a bigger and better garden the next spring. She showed the kind of attitude I always admired in people. So much so that I made it a point to go back the next day and check on her. I was glad to find out then that the fire had spared her house though it did do a number on the small shed out back.

After the Black Wall/Black Frog fire I headed to the Crystal fire near the Oknogan and Wenatchee National Forests in Montana. A terrible tragedy had happened there just three days before. I learned about it while I was riding in a four person fire truck. One of the firemen named Ben had tears in his eyes as he told me the story. A team of twenty men had gone up in a Chinook chopper and two of them volunteered for a really dangerous job. They were lowered with their chainsaws by rope into a dense stand of trees to make a swath for a helicopter landing pad. While they were working on the pad the fire shifted and they were trapped. They couldn't outrun the flames and they were burned alive. One of the helicopter crews saw the whole horrible thing happen. After Ben finished the story there was total somber silence in the truck and the muted mood lasted for a good fifteen minutes.

Just before I was scheduled to fly home to Florida I went over east of Eureka, Montana where the Trapper and Wedge fire was consuming thousands of acres of prime timberland not far from Glacier National Park. Forest fires have such romantic names. The Wolf Creek fire, the Fox fire, the King Creek Fire, the Eagle fire, the Deer Creek fire, the Porcupine fire, the Billy Creek fire. But there's nothing romantic about the flames themselves. And especially when they threaten lives and treasured structures. Anyway at Trapper and Wedge an incident sent a shiver up my spine despite the fact that we were fighting an inferno that was producing wind blasts that hit 2,000 degrees Fahrenheit. We were hosing down a line of pines on a ridge when all of a sudden there was a tremendous explosion and at the same time all the experienced smoke-eaters yelled, "COVER!" I was the last one down since my reaction time wasn't fine tuned like the others' and I almost got felled by a fireball from the huge pine that exploded and sent burning bark bullets in every direction. I stayed down for a full minute before I dared to stand up and brush myself off and get back to work. For the rest of the day I was leery of even brushing up against a tree for fear of igniting it and causing another explosion.

By this time I was getting used to the firefighter's routine. We were in the field from eight in the morning until eight at night. After the work, and on the good days when the fire too, had wound down we'd stagger back to the bus that took us to camp and get there by about nine. Back at camp the first order of business was to get out of the fireproof uniforms we'd been issued that morning. Then they'd been yellow but by now they were pitch black and every day we'd need new ones. Next we'd have to sharpen the tools that'd been blunted during the day's dangerous drudgery. That meant dinner was served around ten. After the twelve hours of exertion and my ultimate exhaustion we started shoveling again only this time our tools were knives and forks and spoons. Mountains of food seemed to disappear like magic into one gigantic maw. The menus were packed with protein which was the firefighter's fuel. Steaks and roast beef and pot roast and pork. After a really rough day rounding up cattle my appetite would be so strong I'd never question whether the steak on my plate was a distant relative of a steer I'd just saved from the forest flames. Whether they were close cousins or complete strangers the camp cooks and my huge hunger managed to make the grub at the makeshift mess hall taste like haute cuisine from the culinary capitols of Europe.

The woods that burned in the Trapper and Wedge fire were so dry that the voracious black flies at the containment lines were feasting more than ever on the firefighters to suck moisture out of them. But the firefighters weren't as vulnerable to bugs as the trees were. For the past five years the bark beetles had infested the western forests and sucked sap and helped turn some of our most splendid scenery into smoking cinders.

Whenever I was alert enough at night to focus my attention I loved to listen to my fellow firefighters talk about their experiences. Especially the Native Americans. They were super story tellers. On one beautiful moonlit night in Montana a dozen of us were sitting around the camp when "Chief" Collins, a big Blackfoot, told about his ancestors who'd helped fight one of the biggest Idaho fires the last century. It was in 1910 and the fire had raged for weeks with no relief from the weather in sight. At that point the people in Wallace, Idaho, which was the closest town to the fire, decided dynamite was needed to bring rain. The theory back then was that since thunder and lightning produced precipitation then surely enough explosions would detonate a downpour. So for sixty straight hours the townsfolk set off charges but the newspaper had to report the next day that only a drop or two of wet stuff fell from the sky. As "Chief" said though, with all our technology today we still can't do much to squelch a really big blaze.

At the Wedge fire I met a couple of members of the famed Missoula Smoke Jumpers. They were wonderful professionals who made dangerous jumps into remote areas that couldn't be reached any other way. These storied heroes had made the crucial difference in putting out more than one western forest fire. So I was surprised and thrilled when they asked me to stop in and visit them if I ever got over to Missoula. Needless to say the first chance I got during a week off in August I drove over and they showed me all around their training camp. I was most interested in the "three thumps." Those were the three phases of the smoke jumpers' early landing training. First they performed from a high platform in full gear including helmets but without a chute. The idea was to teach them the safest way to land, which was to hit the ground on their backs or butts after they'd shaped themselves as much as possible like a ball on the way down with their heads protected by holding on to their helmets with both hands. Once they touched terra firma the drill called for rolling over a couple of times to break the fall instead of their backs. There was a definite method to it every bit as precise as my high diving technique Once they mastered the platform jump the recruits learned to hit the ground from higher up with the help of a landing simulator. That was a device that pulled the potential parachutists along a cable and then dropped them so they could use the same landing style they did when they jumped from the platform. The rationale this time though was to gradually introduce the rookies to the longer drop and harder impact. Then the final phase involved and even higher leap from a fifty-foot jump tower. The novices were harnessed in a contraption that acted like a parachute as the rookies got swung from side to side by a pulley before it dropped them. If all the tests were passed, then in another week the soon-to-be smoke jumpers would walk out the door of a C-130 for the first time.

After I'd been shown the ins and outs of becoming a smoke jumper, my two new Montana friends tantalized me with an offer to join them in their rock climbing and rappelling routines. Need I say that I grabbed at the chance? Of course I wanted to do some tower jumping with them but I knew the state code nixed any practice leaps from a tower unless you had resident status. Instead I spent a week having a blast climbing cliffs and dangling down vertical rock walls with a couple of real American heroes during their off hours. I managed to scrape and scratch my body in the few places that hadn't been bruised over the past few weeks, but the thrill of walking while roped down the sheer face of beautiful cliffs made the week worthwhile. Then it was back to chasing burning trees across the great northwest.

After a couple of more weeks of containing and corralling in Idaho and Montana my body was aching and my mind was numb. I wasn't even sure which state was which anymore. But one morning toward the middle of my northwest stay I figured I had to be either at the Wedge fire or the Roberts fire. For the past four days I'd been working the containment lines and clearing debris and cutting trees and moving animals. I got confirmation of my coordinates later in the morning while we were making a defensive stand in a gorgeous meadow. Walking a nearby road I saw a singed road sign that said "Canada 25 miles" and I knew we must be in the extreme north of Montana in or near Glacier National Park. That would account for the scenery which was even more spectacular than usual in the state. Soaring granite peaks topped by glaciers and gorgeous green valleys. Whatever fire I was fighting had been a big one and though the weather was a little cooler and the fire was seemingly licked there were westerly winds predicted that threatened to blow the sleeping giant back to life.

We'd been trying for the better part of a week to beat back the flames from the few buildings in the vicinity. Most of the structures were wrapped in expensive "aluminum foil" fire blankets and others were doused with retardants from helicopters high above. I saw lots of examples of neighbors helping neighbors in their frantic effort to save each others' homes. They'd been told to evacuate their property but the fire and smoke weren't leaving and the ranchers had a right to protect their places and they told us they'd stay and take their chances. Most of the residents of the area had been long since evacuated but the few that were left behind were helping us firefighters or patrolling the roads.

In the middle of the week I was so worn out I had to take a big break so I invited Melinda to come out and join me for a little R & R in the Grand Tetons. She came right away when she heard the fatigue in my voice and we rented a cabin and did a little sightseeing the first day. But I was so beat I wound up sleeping around the clock. Pretty soon the routine got established that I would stay in the cabin and rest while Melinda did a little exploring on her own. In the process she fell in love with the little town of Jackson Hole and every day she shopped while I dropped off to sleep back in the cabin. During the time I wasn't falling asleep we had a great time sightseeing and catching up on our lives. She told me the business was still going like gangbusters and she filled me in on a new project she was planning with my kids.

One day we decided to drive over to Yellowstone and rent a cabin there. We spent the next couple of days reacquainting ourselves with the landscapes and watching the animals. One sunny early morning while we were driving through the park and watching a heard of elk grazing in a meadow we got hung up in a stalled line of about fifty stopped cars and campers. After we'd waited ten minutes without any sign the logjam would break up, I got out of the car and walked up the line to investigate the holdup. When

I came around a bend in the road, there up ahead were fifty or sixty buffalo standing without a care in the world right in the middle of the two lanes. The drivers and passengers halfway down the line of stopped cars were snapping pictures like paparazzi but the people in the cars closer to the animals had already augmented their albums. They were fuming from exhausted patience and they were about ready to snap without their cameras. I've never been known as Mr. Relaxation myself so I started fast jogging back to the rental car with a plan of attack already hatching. I'd seen the signs all over the park telling tourists to stay away from the animals but this was an intolerable situation. When I reached our car which was now at the halfway point of a line of about a 100 vehicles I told Melinda what was up and that I thought I had the solution. I told her to get behind the wheel and reached into the back seat and grabbed the two metal cups we used for coffee breaks and headed back toward the buffalo. When the big beasts were in sight I started banging the cups together while I walked straight for them. They must have been thinking, "Who is this clown with the coffee cups coming our way?" or more likely, "Get ready to charge this chump!"

The tourists weren't as shy about expressing their opinions though. The closer I got to the buffalo the more the people in the stopped vehicles voiced their disbelief. One woman screamed, "You're a damned fool!" and a man yelled, "You're out of your fucking mind!" Of course that was just the sort of spur calculated to keep me walking and banging even though my stomach was doing the Watusi. A couple of guys got out of their cars to take photos of my impending serial impalement on the herd's horns. By the time I reached the pickup truck that was first in line I was no more than 6 or 7 feet from the animals. They started to shuffle their feet and a big black bull was staring at me with one evil eye. About that time I remembered I was wearing my bright red Red Cross rain pull-over. I wondered if buffalo reacted to red like Spanish bulls because instead of a cape all I had were a couple of coffee cups for my dance of death. That's when I told the driver of the pickup beside me that if the big bull started to charge I'd jump in the bed of his truck. He didn't seem too happy with my plan. Maybe his insurance didn't cover acts of God's country buffalo.

But I clanged my cups harder than ever as I inched forward and yelled toward the line of vehicles to start creeping ahead and not to stop for anything. A couple of the buffalo started to move off the road but the black bull just stood and stared at me with a look that told me he had murder on his mind. I knew from my visits as a teenager to farms around Dayton that every bull back there had a different personality though most were mean. I'd also been told a story by an Ohio farmer about cows' individual identities. It seems each of his would want to have her teats pulled one certain way during the milking. He'd even have to sit on the stool at a specific angle with a particular cow or risk getting kicked or swatted with a tail. Different herds he'd had went so far as to demand the music in his barns be classical or soft rock or old standards. The farmer didn't say if a cow could mimic a migraine to bar a bull but it sounded like she could. And now this buffalo bull was looking at me like his whole harem had just faked a collective headache and I'd coached them to do it. But I kept creeping toward him and clanging those cups till he looked away and finally trotted off the road taking his whole entourage with him. At that point my sigh of relief could be heard all the way back at the park entrance but I played it cool and gestured the line of vehicles forward. I got a lot of high fives and, "way to goes" and old fashioned plain, "thank yous" out the passing car windows until Melinda pulled up and I jumped in the passenger seat beside her. I told her I felt like General George Patton just after he'd shot that mule blocking the bridge to his tanks but she said I was damn lucky the apt analogy wasn't to General George Custer facing a wave of red warriors and yelling, "Bring ''em on!"

After Melinda flew back to Florida at the end of the week I headed north to Montana and joined a crew fighting another fire near the Canadian border. A few days into a grueling battle with a blaze close to a small town our crew was getting an early morning briefing called by the Incident Commander. By this time I'd been through lots of meetings like this one. A commander or some other leader would use the time to fill the crews in on what would be expected of them during the day's activities and coordinate a plan for fighting the fire. There'd be lots of instructions about containment strategies and safety precautions and weather reports. But on this morning when the meeting broke up it occurred to me that at none of these briefings had there been a single prayer uttered, at least out loud. I'd been so busy and beat out here on the fire lines that I'd hardly noticed or thought about it before, Now I remembered that during the daily briefings before the shuttle searches in Texas there'd always been a chaplain leading a prayer. But not here. So I got right on the cell phone with Pastor Julian back in Dayton. I told him about the situation and that I wanted him to write a special prayer that would fit the firefighters.

Since lots of the crew members were Native Americans from different western tribes I told Ron I didn't want the prayer to mention Jesus. Those tribesmen were terrific firefighters and a couple became good friends so I didn't want my prayer to offend them. But when I told Ron to leave out Jesus he didn't understand and he gave me a little lecture. He said the Lord had led me to see the need and I shouldn't shun Him in a prayer of all places. But when I insisted that I knew He'd understand my concern for the crew members from the reservations he said he'd think about it and to call him back later. When I did he told me he'd thought better of my request to downplay the Christian element in the prayer and that he'd written one for me. This is how it went.

> *God, we pause to acknowledge your presence with us today and ask that you will increase our awareness during this time of challenge. As we work as a team, please grant us the wisdom to use the knowledge and experience we share to preserve human life and the natural resources that surround us. Protect us and give us courage and strength. As we do our best, individually and as a team, use us for good and help us to accept the end result, which we leave to your higher power and purpose. In the name of our Lord, we pray. Amen.*

I thought the prayer was really appropriate. I wrote it down and thanked Ron two or three times and told him I'd stop in to see him as soon as I got back east.

The next morning I asked the Incident Commander if I could lead the crews in the prayer once he'd finished his daily briefing. He said sure and from that day on I gathered groups together to recite the prayer before we all headed out to the containment lines. I found out later that those prayers made me eligible to call myself a chaplain. No formal swearing in necessary and no long hours studying theology. Just the willingness to lead prayers when there was no clergyman present. What always affected me the most though was when one of the Native Americans would thank me for helping them face a fire. Pastor Ron had done a good job in making the prayer apply to all creeds.

I went home in the middle of September to take my mandatory fourteen days away from the containment lines. I got myself ready for the next round of firefighting by doing some cardio-vascular training in between taking care of a few business matters. By this time I'd coached my secretary/assistant Annie to prepare me a printout of all the national forest fire info at the end of each workday. And I made it a practice to get to the office by five each morning to check out the previous day's fire facts. That's how I learned in late October about a monster blaze in the California mountains above San Bernardino. When Annie got into the office later that morning I had her book me a flight to Los Angeles. Late the same night I checked into a hotel there and the next morning got myself assigned to a strike team which was a unit of special fire trucks loaded with 2,500 gallons of water each. They're the kind of equipment that's used to fight fires in places where there aren't any fire plugs to tap into. The big trucks carried crews of three.

The California fire of 2003 turned out to be the biggest on record in the state. The rig I rode was assigned to an uncontrolled blaze at the edge of the San Bernardino National Forest, just above the Top of the Rim High School near Lake Arrowhead. Our strike team was to link up with five others while six backup units stood ready. I was supposed to meet the team at eight in the morning but I was up five and raring to go. After fidgeting around for an hour I couldn't take the wait anymore so I got on part of my firefighting gear and headed to the rendezvous site. Halfway there I decided to gas up and get myself a big cup of coffee at a Shell station. Not that I needed the caffeine. I just wanted the cup for company on the long trek up the mountain road to the fifty-seven hundred foot summit. As I was getting in my rental car with my coffee a small sedan came screeching to a halt beside me and a hysterical sixtyish blue-haired woman jumped out and started screaming at me. From what I could make out her house was on fire and I was elected to be her savior. Anyway I told her to get in my car and she did and she calmed down a little. That's when I learned her name was Victoria and it wasn't her house but her boyfriend's that was in danger because the place next door was on fire. And that the boyfriend was an invalid who wasn't answering his phone. So I got Victoria to give directions and peeled rented rubber out of the station.

All the roads for miles were closed but I had my special pass on the windshield so it would be no sweat to beat the blockade. I didn't have time for figuring out how my new passenger had managed to get from wherever she lived to the gas station. But I did stop a few seconds. That was to tell a highway patrolman to get one of the backup twenty-five-hundred -gallon trucks to the address Victoria was shouting in his ear. Then I practically pushed the gas pedal through the floorboard while Victoria pointed and yelled directions. We flew down suburban streets and then a dirt road while she filled me in on a few facts despite her panic and tears. It seemed her boyfriend Bill was slightly handicapped and a problem drinker and the night before there'd been a big blowup between the two of them over some minor matter. Victoria thought Bill was probably passed out now and not even aware that a house a hundred yards away had already burned to the ground according to the TV news. Either that or his own place had gone up in flames and Bill was dead.

When we came to a still standing wooden house on Palm Avenue Victoria yelled, "This is it!" and I hit the brakes hard. Sure enough the house next door was nothing but a few charred support beams and a stone fireplace. And flames were already torching the tops of trees next door and licking at the grasses and brush on Bill's property. I jumped out of the car and ran from burning patch to burning patch stomping out flames even though I was pretty sure I was only delaying disaster. But after a few minutes of a stomping routine that could have landed me an understudy spot in *Oklahoma*, all of the flames seemed to be out. About then I yelled at Victoria to try rousting Bill while I grabbed his garden hose and started wetting down the house from roof to foundation. By the time I had the front of the place soaked Victoria was pulling Bill out the front door. He was stone sober by this time and scared shitless since he'd seen the fire next door and couldn't reach Victoria or anybody else.

I rang up the ICP on my cell phone and told the commander to call off the big tanker truck because the fires in the immediate area seemed to be burned out. Victoria was thanking me over and over and hugging me and calling me Bill's guardian angel but Bill was still too scared to say much. I told him he was damn lucky he wasn't toast and that he shouldn't drink while the big fire up on the mountain was threatening the homes down here. And that he should treat Victoria better and not fight with her anymore because she'd just saved his life. He said he'd learned his lesson and would do what I asked. I told him and Victoria I'd be by to check up on them from time to time while I was in the area.

Then I drove up the highway to the Top of the Rim High School where the strike team I was assigned to was assembling. All the way there I marveled at how God had used me to help save Bill Kruger's life. And how the blessing was as much mine as his. I never felt more hyper or happier and I thought, *I live for this kind of rush.* If only God stayed by my side out here I could save California surer than Arnold ever could.

When I got up on the mountain that day I found out that God wasn't about to make things easy. I was two hours late getting there from Bill's house and the winds had just changed direction for the first time. As soon as I joined a crew working to establish a firebreak I could hear the mountain roaring in the distance. We couldn't see it but we could hear, and smell it. The sound and smell of sudden death. Scary. That day and the next four I thought a lot about the Malcolm X quote where he talked about the plight of the blacks in this country and said, "We didn't land on Plymouth Rock. Plymouth Rock landed on us." Because all that time we didn't attack any fires. The fires attacked us. The Santa Ana winds decided over and over again that week to change direction and they had us retreating more often than the Italian army. We would set a goal, like establishing a containment line across a ridge, only to have the winds shift and blow a shaft of roaring flames right at us before we could do much more than try to dig a trench that dented the ground a couple of inches. Then we'd be beaten back to another position where the same thing would happen again.

Now the flames were headed toward Bear Lake and the crews were busy trying to hold them off. But the C-130s overhead dropping the red-dyed fertilizer-fire retardant called Phos-Check weren't able to slow the blaze. Neither were the dozens of helicopters spewing 400 gallons of water on each pass. We kept losing ground to the fire until it finally jumped one of our defense lines and took off toward the forest around the posh Lake Arrowhead community. That evening we lost 350 homes but fortunately no lives. Finally one morning after we'd been hosing and trenching for thirty hours in a row Mother Nature took pity on us and sent us a strong breeze from the Pacific that sent the humidity up twelve percent and the temperature down twenty-five degrees. And then came a marvelous mist. Nature's retardant. At last the crews on the ground and the C-130 and helicopter pilots and the rest of the administrative and support staff were able to relax. And make plans to head for home to regroup for the next big fire. I drove back to LAX and caught a plane back to Tampa and the next morning kissed Melinda for the first time in over a month.

# SIXTEEN

God blessed me more in 2003 than ever before and for sure more than I deserved. Between the firefighting trips out west there were so many good things coming my way I couldn't keep up. Melinda and the kids were building the business into a mega market. Despite the national economic slump we couldn't build condos fast enough to dent the demand. Our profits were out of sight. Then in the spring I got to fly back to Ohio to see an eight-foot tall tribute to my dad unveiled in downtown Dayton. That was how the folks back there decided to show their appreciation for one of their most popular mayors. When I saw the concrete column with a big bronze plate picturing my dad's face overlooking a four block area now called "Dave Hall Plaza," I really got choked up. To think that dad was now keeping carved company with other famous Daytonians like the first-in flight Wright Brothers and their friend the talented African American poet Paul Lawrence Dunbar. That gave my spine a spasm. And since I'd done a little sculpting myself, I could appreciate how well the artist had bound dad's face in bronze. The size of the column fit dad's stature too. In my eyes he always stood at least 8 feet tall as a husband and father and a public servant. And especially as a mentor to me.

Later in the spring I got the great word that my brother Mike had been named Educator of the Year in Ohio. He'd been a terrific teacher and a principal for thirty years in Cincinnati. Mike was always the brainiest of the brothers Hall. And that's a rave review when you consider how much my baby bro Tony's accomplished in Congress. Between Mike and Tony they've got three honorary Ph.D.s. The only Ph.D. I'd ever qualified for was a "Phool for Danger." There was something in the Hall genes that'd just missed me. That was demonstrated again in the autumn of 2003 when Tony was sworn in by Colin Powell in Washington as George W. Bush's Ambassador for World Hunger at the United Nations. My shirt buttons almost popped from pride when I watched the swearing in ceremony.

I didn't do so bad myself in '03 for black sheep brother. And since it wouldn't have been like me not to toot my own tuba I told anybody who'd listen about my being named Businessman of the Year for Florida and getting the Congressional Gold Medal Award which was the highest honor given by the House to a businessman and being asked to serve on a special Congressional business task force by Speaker Dennis Hastert. Not to mention, but I did and do, breaking bread with President Bush, and a hundred or so others, in the White House and attending a black tie blowout hosted by Vice-President Cheney. All this for the construction business I'd mostly neglected to chase fires. Truth be told, Melinda should've been the one being honored. But it was better for her figure that she wasn't. Every award came with a big banquet in Washington. I ate so much rubber chicken in 2003 I bounced when I burped.

However the highlight of the year for me came about because of my interest in golf. I'd always played well but in the previous couple of years I'd decided on an earnest improvement effort to maybe qualify for some senior tour. I thought I could bring down my twelve handicap, which meant I could every once in a while shoot a round in the mid-70s, by hiring a golf pro and I even bought my own private course for the lessons. Early in 2001 Melinda and I had bought a seven acre parcel that was attached to two existing golf courses. I'd just finished building one-hundred-and-eighty new condos and I plowed part of the profits into the courses. I did manage to improve my golf game a bit and went on a few amateur tours, some with players a lot younger but when they kept beating me I lost interest. In the process, though, I made a lot of great friends on the fairways and crossing tees with them gave me a bright idea. That was to establish a new annual St. Petersburg golf tournament named for my late nephew, Matthew Hall, who died of cancer when he was only sixteen. The tournament would also be dedicated to my fourteen-year-old insulin dependent granddaughter Corri. That first year, 2003, the drives and the divots brought in 2,200 dollars for the Leukemia and Lymphoma Society and the Juvenile Diabetes Foundation and for the local arts community. The goal for the next year's tournament would be another 50,000 and hopes were high that in years to come it would generate millions for crucial causes.

Of course I knew all the great developments in my life were straight from the hand of the Almighty. I used to ask God what on earth he wanted me to do, but not anymore. After 9/11, and the volunteer work at Ground Zero, I knew what I was put here to do. My job was to work for the benefit of others, even if it meant putting my life on the line. I thought of it as a role in more ways than one after a talk with Ron Julian just after I got back from rummaging through the rubble in New York. He was interested in the turns my life had taken and he told me, "Sam, the Lord has written a play for you and all you have to do is follow the script." Ron knew me better than anybody so his advice meant a lot more to me than most. And I knew I needed guidance like his since my life sure hadn't been a model of morality over the years. I'd once seen a billboard outside a Baptist church that said it all; "It's always good to follow in the footsteps of a pastor who follows in the footprints of the Master." And Ron was great at sharing Scripture when it fit my situation. Like Psalm 90:12 that asks, "Teach us to count our days that we may gain a wise heart" or Hebrews where it says, "Let us consider how to provoke one another to love and do good deeds." I wanted to do as many good deeds as I could in the time left to me here. I have in no uncertain terms done hurtful and sinful things in my past. I feel incredibly blessed that God is always willing to give sinners a second chance. I continue growing in my faith, as I play the part that God has written for me. I will be the first to admit, as those who are closest to me will attest, that I am not pious, but I am lucky enough, now, to feel the hand of God in my work. I hope that I'll be remembered as someone who wore the light grey hat of a pretty good guy, because God knows I'll never be remembered as somebody who wore the white collar of a Holy guy.

One wintry afternoon I got a call from Harry who I hadn't heard from in months. He said he and Jimmie each had new serious squeezes and he wanted to know if Melinda and I would join the four of them for dinner at the Captain Kosmakos restaurant and entertainment bar the next evening around seven. I said sure since I missed my old trouble-making mates and I knew Melinda would want to check out their new love interests. When we got to the Kosmakos the live music was in full swing and Harry and Jimmie and their two companions were already nursing drinks at a window table. One eye-sweep of the women told me neither friend had lost his taste. Harry introduced Mary who was about the thirteenth beauty with that name he'd been hot for over the years. She was a stunning petite blonde in her early twenties with short curls and gorgeous blue eyes. Then Jimmie did the honors for Dean which was short for Geraldine. She was a taller, pretty brunette in her mid-thirties and she was built like Wonder Woman. As soon as we were all seated together the conversation took off with Harry and Jimmie filling us in on their latest life stories. But they suddenly went silent when the cocktail waitress showed up and I ordered an Old Granddad and a margarita for Melinda. What stopped their palaver cold was the waitress, a blonde bombshell who'd introduced herself as Janice. I could tell by their survey of her assets that no matter how sold they were on Mary and Dean they'd never be able to leash their libidos. I'd been just like them before I met Melinda, falling in and out of lust with reckless abandon. My email address in those days should've been moveon.orgasm. But I'd finally formed the perfect partnership, a ménage a trios featuring me, Melinda, and the joy of being able to pursue my whims as they came to me.

Once the gabbing gained momentum again Harry and Jimmie and their lady friends wanted to hear all about my firefighting experiences. I told them about the Harkness yearling and the California devastation and how impressed I was by the Indians I'd met. When I finished Harry had a suggestion that hadn't entered my mind.

"Why don't you do another book, Sam. A lot of people would be interested in your adventures."

"No, never again. Reliving my life on paper was too tough the first time. And all the work of putting the memories and the details together. No thanks."

But Melinda surprised me by agreeing with Harry. She said she thought the rough journals I'd kept for my kids over the past couple of decades could be turned into a book without too much sweat. And what really opened me up to the idea was her suggestion that my story might induce some others to do volunteer work. And especially to inspire so called "senior citizens" to see that they could still contribute to vital causes. That would make any agony in assembling the material well worth the while. And Harry had another idea that might make building a book easier.

"Why don't you get in touch with the guy who wrote *Counter-Terrorist* for you? That was a big seller wasn't it? Maybe he'd help you with a new book."

After Melinda and I left the restaurant that night we talked over the possibility of putting my story on paper. I was still resistant to the idea because the more time I spent working on a book the less I'd have for fighting fires and other adventures. But Melinda kept encouraging me. She said she thought I could manage to do volunteer work while I fed the facts of my life to someone who could turn them into a narrative. So after about a week of stewing I decided to call my *Counter-Terrorist* scribe who'd been a professor at an Ohio university when we'd worked together. I didn't have a clue when I dialed the phone if he was still alive or, if he was, whether he'd be up for another collaboration. Our lives had uncrossed and I hadn't talked to him in more than ten years. But as soon as he picked up the phone he greeted me like a long lost brother and we traded over a decade of details that filled in all the blanks. He'd retired from the university and spent his recent days teaching in Poland and Portugal. But he said his calendar was open and he'd enjoy doing another book with me. His only bad news had to do with Felicia Lewis, the woman who'd been his research assistant taping my recollections for *Counter-Terrorist*. She was a little blonde beauty and we'd both been in love with her at the time. These days, it turned out, she was running a yoga business in North Carolina and wouldn't have time to help out. We made an arrangement, though, that I'd start sending the information from my journals to him and he'd turn it into a book. So now I had a major project on my hands at the very time I'd get turned on by a new adventure.

# SEVENTEEN

When President George W. Bush was stewing over going into Iraq I was paying close attention. In fact, Iraq neared the top of my personal watch list. I'd first learned about Saddam Hussein's cruel rule when I fought beside the Israelis against terrorists bankrolled by the Iraqi dictator during the mid-eighties. There were rumors back then about Saddam's torture chambers and the mass graves. And about all his lavish palaces. Then in 1991 I'd cheered from the sidelines during Desert Storm and especially when our troops cleaned the tyrant's clock in such short order. That war happened as my FBI work was winding down and if it hadn't been won so fast I'd have found a way to get back to the Middle East to help out in any way I could. Back then I was one of the many who thought President Bush made a big mistake not sending our troops sweeping on into Baghdad to bring back Saddam's puss on a platter. But our coalition partners had apparently nixed that idea. So in 2002 when the dictator's dance around the UN started I was hoping we'd get another chance to free the Iraqis from the their house of horrors. And I knew if Saddam didn't directly sponsor the sorry nineteen who flew those planes on 9/11, he sure as hell fired off a few rifle rounds to celebrate. So when all the talking failed and W. finally decided we'd take on the Iraqis again I thought he had no other choice. The UN sanctions would have eventually run out and Saddam could have started brewing bacteria and building filthy bombs to have his henchmen smuggle into New York or Chicago or LA.

In fact I'd have backed any decision the president made to go to war or not or anything else he wanted to do or not do. I felt a kind of kinship with Bush the Younger because before Laura cut off his tab at the tavern and he got born again he was on his way to becoming the black sheep in a prominent political family. And I came from a political family too, though one not anywhere near as famous. My dad the mayor's other two sons were a Congressman turned UN bigwig and an honored educator. When I compared my past with theirs I knew my fleece was dark as dirt. That was one reason I'd tried so hard in the last few years to make up for some of the things I'd done to bring shame to my relatives. I suppose I could take some comfort in the fact that every political family seemed to have one maverick messing up its midst. There was Ron Reagan and Billy Carter and Roger Clinton. And as far as I knew, maybe George Washington had a brother selling schnapps on Sunday. But using anybody else's life as an excuse for my own less than perfect existence had worn thin a long time ago.

Anyway when I watched Operation Iraqi Freedom play out on TV my response was more mixed than it was during the Gulf War. I was comparatively callous about the battlefield victims and the "collateral damage" back in 1991. All the violence I'd seen from Israel and Africa to the drug turf of south Florida had numbed me more than I could conceive. But by the time the invasion happened I'd changed for the better, thanks to Pastor Ron and my renewed religious faith. So watching the bunker busters fall on Baghdad I was suitably shocked and awed by the shock and awe but I couldn't help wondering how many innocent Iraqis were getting incinerated in the process.

When Saddam's statue fell I said a prayer that the Iraqi people would find the fruits of freedom sweet. But they soon soured. The aftermath turned out to be far worse than the war. My heart went out first to our troops whose lives were being shattered or ended in numbers we could never imagine after the stunning success of the invasion. I'd seen too many broken and bleeding bodies after battles and in VA hospitals and viewed too many flag-draped coffins returning from other wars to watch and read about the insurgency in Iraq with anything but growing grief. And I knew that though the TV and the papers downplayed the suffering of the Iraqis, they had to be going through more horrors than any humans should have to bear. I knew too that if our troops were physically or psychologically wounded they'd have the best of care from our great military medics. The same couldn't be said for the Iraqi civilians. So as the insurgency dragged on deadly day after deadly day I got more and more concerned. In October the equal drag on my conscience got heavier than lead. For over a month I'd thought about volunteering for some kind of humanitarian work in the Middle East, but I kept my thoughts to myself. I knew God would guide me to make the best decision about how and when to help over there. Then one morning, after a night of prayer, I told Melinda that I'd made up my mind to volunteer my services. She told me she was proud that I wanted to contribute and that if I went over she'd pray every day for my safety.

Within a few minutes of our conversation I called my old friend and boss, Kathleen George, at the Clearwater Red Cross office to volunteer. It didn't take her long to remind me that there were a lot of bureaucratic hurdles to negotiate before I could get assigned over in Iraq. She referred me to the AFES in Washington. AFES was the shorthand signature of the Armed Forces Emergency Services Reserve Corps. That's the outfit that supplies staff technically trained to assist the people assigned to emergency service units stationed in the U. S. and in other countries. The Reserve Corps personnel see to it that there's a smooth flow of services and sometimes they get assigned to military exercises and operations. When I got the right person on the phone in Washington and explained my background as an active affiliate of a local Red Cross unit and that I wanted to go to Iraq, he said I sounded qualified for special status. He meant I could probably select my level of commitment based on when I was available, where I wanted to go and what I wanted to do there. He also told me the assignment locations ranged from 50 miles from home to anywhere in the world. The length of assignments ran between fifteen to one-hundred-and-eighty days every calendar year and the maximum hitch didn't have to be served consecutively. All I needed to do was to fill out some forms and give some references.

When I got the application in the mail I filled it out and steeled myself for the inevitable wait. But in case AFES didn't work out I also made plans to ogle other organizations I knew were doing relief work in Iraq. In fact I spent the week filling out about fifty forms, though I was pretty sure I'd soon be on the ground in Iraq working for the Red Cross. For the next couple of weeks I kept in touch with the Washington office and each time I did I was assured that everything was going great. Then one morning I was watching Fox News when a news flash flattened my hopes for a fast deployment. The HQ of the International Red Cross in Baghdad had been blown up overnight. I knew that would mean a reassessment of the organization's commitment and sure enough two weeks later, during which I'd heard nothing from them, all the agency's offices and warehouses in Iraq were shut down and all their personnel were heading home. For over a week I was depressed as hell. I'd come so close only to be denied at the last minute. But even at my lowest point I knew I'd get over to Iraq some way soon. It was that confidence in my destiny that Pastor Ron planted in me with his talk about the script God had written for me. All I'd have to do was wait for a sign.

The sign smote in an unexpected place. A week after the Red Cross pullout I was waiting in the dentist's office for my biennial checkup. The dentist is a good friend named Sandra Lilo and when she led me into the exam room we got to talking about the mess in Iraq and I let her know about my Red Cross disappointment. I didn't have the gloom and doom out of my soon-to-be-scanned mouth before Sandra's supplied the sentences that were to mark another turning point in my life.

"Sam, later on today I've got a patient named Jerry Harfoot coming in. He's a high ranking officer in the Salvation Army. From what I understand, they're involved in Iraq. Would you like me to ask him if they could use you?"

Of course I told Sandra to not only ask but to put in a few good words for me too. I didn't know much about the Salvation Army. I'd seen some of their volunteers working at post-hurricane relief sites. And like everybody else I'd watched their "soldiers" in those funky uniforms shaking bells and stuffing bills into red tin containers outside the mall at Christmas time. And I knew if you had old clothes or furniture you wanted to get rid of you could call the Army to collect them. Oh, and if you pressed me I might be able to hum a few tunes from *Guys and Dolls*. But that was it. In fact I was really surprised to hear that the Army was on the scene in Iraq. I'd always thought they were a strictly U.S. based operation. But if they were over there maybe I could catch on with them. God works in mysterious ways and I guessed a sign from Heaven could light up a dental office as easy as a church.

That same night Dr. Lilo called me at home with the good news that Jerry Harfoot wanted to talk to me. So the next morning I called him and told him I'd prepared a packet overnight that would introduce me and my qualifications. He was very encouraging and asked me to fax my material to him right away. As soon as he got it and looked it over he called and told me to fax an introductory letter to Kevin Smith at the Army's office in Tampa. So I got right on that and stressed my background in the construction business since my overnight research had turned up info that the Army was helping rebuild Iraqi infrastructure. And that they were doing the same in Afghanistan. So I asked to be assigned to either country in case for some reason Iraq was a no go. Smith called me an hour later impressed with my credentials. He asked me to make an appointment with another officer who helped run the Florida Division of the Army. That's when I learned I'd come full circle. The other officer was Jerry Harfoot.

Harfoot set up a meeting with me for the next morning and when it began I asked why he hadn't just called me the day before without the preliminaries.

"We had to find out it you were serious, Sam. Not everybody wants to go to Iraq these days. And you know all organizations have their rules."

I couldn't argue with that but I had to suppress a groan when Harfoot said he needed to give me a little background on the Salvation Army. I was my usual impatient self and all I wanted to know was what time that afternoon I should board the plane to Baghdad and start helping rebuild Iraq. Now I had to sit still while Harfoot started a lecture about the Army and who knew how long he'd go on. He started with a biography of somebody named William Booth who for all I knew might've been a backup shortstop for the 1940 Cincinnati Reds.

"Sam, William Booth started the Salvation Army preaching the gospel to a small congregation of the destitute on the streets of London in 1865. And he did it with the dedication of a professional soldier fighting an implacable enemy."

I could see the excitement in Officer Harfoot's eyes but I still wasn't sure I needed a history lecture. What I thought didn't matter though. I could see I was in for a long lesson come what may.

"Booth's spirit was so infectious he began drawing followers and their numbers kept growing until they decided to form a legal entity around their ranks thirteen years later. That's when they organized themselves along military lines."

At this point Harfoot got up from his desk and pointed to a picture on the wall.

"This is William Booth. Before we talk about Iraq, I want you to know a little more about him."

That didn't sound good but Harfoot was so enthusiastic about his subject that I suddenly caught myself leaning forward in my chair to listen closer to his words about the organization I hoped to be representing soon in Iraq. That called for knowing as much as possible to make sure I didn't do anything counter to the Army's culture. In fact I felt stupid and ashamed for resisting Harfoot's enthusiasm from the first. Now he was really revving up his subject.

"Sam, when William Booth walked the streets of London preaching to the poor and the homeless and the hungry, he abandoned the idea of a formal church with a pulpit. He wasn't content to wait for the people to come to him, he took his message to the people. When his renown as a charismatic preacher spread throughout London he began to attract men and women who wanted to follow in his footsteps. Of course, his fervor led to disagreement with church leaders in London who preferred the traditional methods. But that was to be expected. People who are entrenched in power are always threatened by a revolutionary. But rather than bend to opposition, Booth decided to leave the church and travel all over England leading evangelical meetings."

Now I could see that this Booth was somebody I could relate to. A maverick who heard his own drum roll. Officer Harfoot wasn't finished.

"William Booth's wife Catherine could be called the co-founder of the Army. She helped him organize the first group and she backed him in his ambition to create a great missionary force."

That reminded me of Melinda and how she'd encouraged me in everything I wanted to do. A wife could be a wonderful helpmate and I hoped I'd shown sufficient appreciation to mine along the way. But Harfoot had still more to brag about.

"In 1865 Booth was invited to hold a series of evangelistic meetings in the east end of London. He set up a tent in a Quaker graveyard and his services there were a great success. They grew steadily from week to week. In fact, they proved so successful he had to suspend the wandering he'd been doing all over England. His first converts were thieves, prostitutes, gamblers, and drunkards. He brought them hope and salvation and a lot of them mended their ways. His goal was to bring them to Christ and link them to a traditional church for continued guidance. But he got frustrated because the traditional churches wouldn't accept his converts. So Booth kept preaching to them but now he added a challenge to them to go out and save others like themselves. And they did. They began preaching and singing in the streets as a living testimony to the power of God to change lives."

By now Officer Harfoot had me asking for more. In spite of my earlier skittishness listening to his lecture I had to admit I'd always been interested in history and especially the stories of great men and women who changed the world with their works.

"Sam, in 1867 Booth's new organization had ten full-time workers. But by 1874 there were a 1000 volunteers and 42 evangelists serving under what was then called the "The Christian Mission." And since the organization was now in need of a structure, Booth and Catherine organized it with Booth at the head as general superintendent. But his followers began calling him "General." And then someone started referring to his organization as the "Hallelujah Army." Finally in 1878 Booth settled on the name "Salvation Army." From that time on his converts were known as "Soldiers of Christ" or "Salvationists." By 1886 President Grover Cleveland officially endorsed the Army's activities and it spread all over the country and then to Canada, Australia, France, Switzerland, India, South Africa, and Germany. Even to Iceland!"

Officer Harwood was so enthused about the Army's history that at this big climax I wouldn't have been surprised if a whole brass band and a chorus of singing "Salvationists" had marched right through the room. But he was coming to the part I was waiting for now, the part about current Army operations.

"Sam, as of this moment there are more than 9,000 Salvation Army operations spread to every corner of the world."

I was hoping that pretty soon Harfoot would get to the corner of the world that was on my mind all the time now. But first he handed me the Army's mission statement and told me to read it.

"The Salvation Army, an international movement, is an evangelical part of the universal Christian church. Its message is based on the Bible. Its ministry is motivated by the love of God. Its mission is to preach the Gospel of Jesus Christ and to meet human needs in His name without discrimination."

By this time I was pretty ashamed of myself for living 67 years without knowing the extent of the Army's good works. And especially the part that I wanted to help with, the part about meeting human needs. That's what I wanted to do in a place where right then the needs were about as dire as any on earth. When I finished reading the Army mission statement Officer Harfoot just sat looking at me and let the ideas sink in. After a good minute-and-a-half his lips formed the words I'd been waiting for.

"Now let's talk about Iraq. I just came back from there two months ago. I was teamed with another officer just south of Baghdad at a distribution center. We handed out cooking fuel and space heaters free of charge. The needs of those people are so great."

I asked him if the duty was tough over there and he said it definitely was and that if he had it to do over again he wouldn't because he'd never felt so at risk in his life. I appreciated him being that honest with me. He wasn't trying to sugarcoat the deal in order to get a new recruit. So I asked him what the living conditions were like and he said he'd lived in a small house that the Army had rented and that there were a lot of problems with intermittent electricity and noise at all hours from the street.

Far from turning me off by those revelations, I was getting more enthusiastic by the minute. Especially since Harfoot had mentioned risk. I was so juiced at the prospect of joining the Army Officer Harfoot described and getting in on the Iraq action that my only other question was "Where do I sign up?" That's when the bureaucratic boondoggle started in earnest. Harfoot gave me the name of a Major Pat Kiddo at the international office in Washington and a blank application form to fill out and send to her. So I went right home and raced through the form and got together a clean copy of my résumé. Then I called Major Kiddo in DC and told her how anxious I was to volunteer and a little more about my background. She said to fax her my material right away and she'd look it over and call me back. So I sent it five minutes later and included among my reference letters one from a hotshot scholar who'd once been a Salvation Army volunteer. That was Gordon MacDonald who I'd first met at Ground Zero in New York where he was working as a roving shrink, passing out coffee and doughnuts and talking to us diggers and leading us in prayer. After that we'd become friends and written to each other now and then. I knew he'd put in a good word for me as an Iraq volunteer and that his word would mean something to the Salvation Army brass because they surely must have respected him a lot.

Two hours later the major called back and said she'd found my material "very interesting to say the least." She said I'd contacted her at a crucial time because the Army was looking for somebody with a construction background to help pilot their projects in and around a town I'd never heard of in Iraq, Al Amarah. I tried not to sound as hyper as I was so I said as cool as I could "I'd be interested in the job!" That's when I learned that if I could be ready to roll in six weeks I'd be considered for a four person team scheduled to leave for Al Amarah in December. I just about jumped out of the chair to grab my suitcase but Major Kiddo wanted to tell me about the operation in Iraq so I tried to calm myself down to listen. But she didn't get two sentences out of her mouth before she told me she had to take another phone call that she thought might be from her London-based boss who was in India at the moment. She'd already faxed my material to him so she hung up and promised to call right back. Fifteen minutes later she did. It *had* been her boss on the other line and he was very excited about my application and wanted to expedite a decision on me by sending an officer to the house the next day for an interview. He'd reminded the Major that time was running out in the selection process because the team had a lot of Stateside planning and work to do before leaving and he wanted to move fast. The planning involved a series of briefings in Washington on December 9th followed by a flight the same day for London where an official team meeting would take place on the morning of the 10th and then another flight to Kuwait that evening.

I said I'd be available any time for the interviewer and then Major Kiddo told me who the interviewer would be. Because of the time constraints in my case, after she'd called her boss in India she'd got in touch with a retired

Salvationist Colonel who'd been an Army Commissioner. She explained that the Army divided the U.S. into four regional sections with a commissioner for each. Since my case was special she wanted to put it on a fast track and she thought asking an ex-Commissioner to do the interviewing would speed things up. She said he'd agreed to call me within an hour to set a time for the next day. She also said it was an honor for me to be processed by such a high ranking person. In the meantime though she wanted me to hear about the way her office worked.

It was called SAWSO which stood for Salvation Army World Service Office and it was set up in 1977 to work out long term solutions to poverty in less developed countries where the Army was active. The idea was to help people help themselves through programs that improved living conditions and raised their skill levels and increased their productivity and self-confidence. SAWSO had spent twenty-five years spurring community participation which Major Kiddo said was critical in finding specific solutions that lasted. She had a small staff in Alexandria, Virginia that worked through the international network. All tolled the Army had 50,000 officers and professional staff and other employees working in developing countries. SAWSO'S job was to help the organization find out what the root causes of local problems were and work with community leaders to find fixes and keep programs going once they were set up. The organization created programs for training locals in planning and management and leadership and community development too.

Then Major Kiddo got to the part I was waiting to hear about. She said that the SAWSO office in London had called its Washington counterpart offering their cooperation in the Iraq effort. In Iraq SAWSO was distributing food and clothes but that came under the heading of relief work. Soon there'd be a transition to development by way of health services and income generation projects for the war victims. This work was all part of the worldwide Army effort that SAWSO was the funnel for. In its history it'd channeled more than a hundred-million-dollars in goods and services to developing countries around the world. These operations were directed by a board of trustees made up of senior leaders of the Army in the U.S. Then Major Kiddo recited the Salvation Army motto which was; "Serving the many one by one with Heart to God and hand to man."

By now I was primed to join the Major in a chorus of "I've Got a Horse Right Here" or some other stirring tune from *Guys and Dolls*. But she curbed my craving long enough to get me to hang up the phone so the Commissioner could call me. And he did and we set the interview for the next afternoon.

When the bell rang I opened the front door to the tall, uniformed Commissioner who turned out to be another soldier full of ardor for the Army. We talked for an hour about the volunteering I'd done in recent years and he said he'd see to it that my application was approved. That gave an extra thump or two to my heart rate and I tried not to crush the Commissioner's hand when I shook it. I didn't find out till later just how high up in the Army organization this man was and how honored I should have been that he'd taken the time to talk to me. In fact everybody I'd dealt with so far impressed me with their obvious love for the Army and their work in it. Being around people who were really religious in an obviously honest way always inspired me. Not the phony types who talked a good game but didn't follow through with any action. I remembered the time I asked my brother Tony of all the famous people he'd met when he was in Congress who'd impressed him the most. He didn't hesitate a nanosecond before he named Mother Theresa. He said you could actually feel holiness radiating from her and that God must've been present in the room watching over her. When he was telling me about meeting her I could see the tears welling up in his eyes. These Salvation Army officers may not have been in the same league with Mother Theresa but they did have a special something that made me feel their straight-on virtue. Just now I'd felt honored to be in the company of the Commissioner. Whatever the source of the spiritual strength he seemed to secrete, I wanted to tap into it myself.

The interview must have jelled well from the Commissioner's point of view because the next morning Major Kiddo called again and said that I'd scored high marks. A report had been sent to London and I was to be told something about my status by noon. But Major Kiddo was so confident I'd make the team that she said she'd overnight more paperwork to fill out and a schedule of immunization shots I'd need. Since we'd have to work fast she'd be in touch on a daily basis. The packet she was sending included a medical instruction sheet directing me to start taking pills for malaria right away and to arrange for typhoid and cholera and hepatitis A and B shots. There would be a form too for listing next of kin and other personal info the Salvation Army needed. And a list of job descriptions for projects they were overseeing in Iraq. Then the Major asked how soon I could get the processed packet back. I told her I had to be in Washington in two days for a meeting of the Congressional advisory board on small business that I'd been appointed to co-chair and that I'd come by her office and we'd go for a cup of coffee. She said she'd look forward to it.

I was so excited by all that'd happened in the last week and how quickly things were moving that I could've done handstands. I couldn't wait to tell

Melinda and the kids but then I remembered I'd have to tell my mother too and I wondered how I could do that without worrying her to death. I'd just have to say I was going to a safe zone and emphasize how important the Army's relief mission in Iraq was. Maybe that part about the safe zone was actually true. I wasn't sure at this point where in Iraq I was headed anyway, or whether Al Amarah was in the middle of the fighting or not. And I didn't care. I just wanted to get going.

Early the next morning Major Kiddo called.

"Congratulations, Sam. Cedric Hills in London phoned to tell me to welcome you aboard. Your application has been a Godsend for the Army since we don't have a lot of volunteers with your level of expertise in the building trades. You'll be heading with a team that will include three others to Al Amarah. It's in the British zone not too far from Basra. Your assignment will be as a contractor bidding on construction projects and supervising crews that will be repairing and building schools, clinics, hospitals, water treatment and sanitation plants, and roads. And one specific project involves completing a repair and remodeling job on a leper colony."

That last sentence really caught my ear. I hadn't heard about lepers since I was a kid. I didn't even know leprosy still existed. This Iraq assignment looked like it was going to be even more of an adventure than I'd thought.

Once I had my malaria pills started I went to the county health department for my first round of shots. When all my forms were filled out I headed for Washington and gave my small business input to the Congressional committee and then went out to Alexandria for an informal meeting with Major Kiddo. She turned out be a real professional and she was willing to answer all my questions and pump me up even more.

Back home in Florida I started the packing process and attended to last minute odds and ends. I managed to convince my mother that Al Amarah was peaceful as Patagonia and explained to Melinda all about the assignment. After I'd told her what I would be doing she relayed the news to the kids and I got an immediate visit from my daughter Kelly.

"Dad, Melinda says you're going to be working on a remodeling job at a leper colony."

"Yes, honey, doesn't that sound exciting? Think about how those people must be suffering with a war going on around them."

"No, it doesn't sound exciting. It sounds dangerous. Leprosy is contagious."

"There's nothing to worry about, Kelly. I called the CDC in Atlanta yesterday and talked to a doctor named Shinnick. He explained that there's nothing to be concerned about. You could have causal contact with a leper and there'd be no danger of getting infected. Only doctors and nurses need protective gear if they're in constant contact with lepers. And besides, Dr. Shinnick warned me that when I get over there I shouldn't French kiss anybody that's got a dripping nose."

At that point Kelly seemed not to appreciate my little joke since she said "Oh Dad, you're so disgusting" and stomped out of the room.

Once all my preparations were made there was nothing to do but hang around waiting for the ship out date. Except for a few planning meetings at the Salvation Army HQ building in Washington just south of the airport. I passed the rest of the time shaping up things at the office and playing a little golf, but the wait passed so slowly it was like watching nails rust in the sunshine. Finally the day came and I said goodbye to Melinda and the kids at the Tampa airport and flew to Washington to join the two other Americans who, along with a female Brit we'd meet late, would make up the four-person crew I'd be working with in Iraq. At the Washington meeting at Army HQ I met Bill and Don, two of my teammates. Bill was to be the titular team leader who would be in charge of accounting for the monies appropriated and spent and he was supposed to see to it that our Iraqi staff functioned without too many flub ups. Don was to be given some construction contracts to fulfill. He was from New Jersey and had wangled his assignment in Iraq through his sister who was a high ranking officer in the DC headquarters of the Salvation Army. My role would be main construction guy with control of forty-five hundred-laborers and skilled workers.

At the briefing we were warned that we weren't allowed to preach the Christian gospel in Iraq. Even if we were asked about our faith we were not supposed to say anything. And we were absolutely forbidden to pass out Christian tracts. I wasn't planning on doing any of those things but I thought it was interesting that the Army found it necessary to warn against them. And I couldn't figure out how the ban on Christian banter fit with the Army's status as a missionary organization. Apparently, they thought their project in Iraq to be so important that they were willing to let this slide. Maybe they thought that, in this case, actions would speak louder then words.

Once we'd been briefed the three of us boarded a British Airways 747 bound for Heathrow. That's where we picked up the fourth team member, the British woman whose name was Karen. She looked formidable enough to take care of herself in Iraq, or in any other dangerous venue. She was a yearly paid employee of the London branch of the Army and she was reputed to be a brilliant bean counter who was a computer and contract whiz to boot. Her job would be to run the Army's computers and also do some site work at Iraqi women's schools and give guidance at their sewing centers.

I was the only team member who wasn't an ordained minister. But it turned out that I did get a religious title. Even though the Washington leaders had warned us not to try proselytizing in Iraq, the international office of the Salvation Army classified anybody who worked for them overseas as "missionaries." That meant me too, but it was hard for me get my mind around that one. Of course a big part of my motivation was pure enough. I really wanted to help the Iraqis. But an equal part was my personal love of risk and adventure and I knew that didn't have anything to do with humanitarianism. Still, I couldn't wait to tell Harry and Jimmie and my other old drinking buddies that I was now in a far different missionary position than the one I'd sought so often during my swinging bachelor days. And since I hadn't had any alcohol in over a week I was feeling almost holy enough to merit my new title.

# EIGHTEEN

After a short Heathrow briefing it was on to Kuwait City via British Airways. There we were met by a Salvation Army major and six or seven Iraqis working in country for the Army. They took us right off to security headquarters to be photographed for Iraqi IDs and passes so we could cross over the border. All that took a couple of hours so it was early afternoon by the time we finally got into a Chevy Caprice with a Kuwaiti driver and formed a convoy that included two other Chevys, one carrying four guards with AK 47s and the other a local police car with armed officers. With all that protection there didn't seem to be much to worry about on the two-hour road trip to the Iraqi line. During the drive I broke conversation with Bill, Don, and Karen into bites by glancing out the window at the Kuwaiti countryside. I'd always thought Kuwait was a barren place, a lot like the Sahara sandbox, but the views out the van window changed my mind. There was deep green sod everywhere with gorgeous palm tees lining the beauti-fully maintained asphalt road. Even the median strips were kept like Martha Stewart gardens. And instead of the flat vistas I was expecting, the rolling hills reminded me of southern Ohio.

When we got to the Iraqi border we passed through the security check-point without a hitch. But then we got an inkling of what the situation was like in country. We were assigned an Iraqi security escort, three bruisers hanging on to the rails of a pickup bed with their automatic weapons promi-nently displayed. We were told the guards would be looking out for us at all times during our stay. That sounded ominous enough to give me that special tingle. We were also introduced to the Iraqi leader of the local workers who would make up my crews. He and I would be constant companions over the next few weeks. His name was Muntajeb Ibraheem. He was around forty-five and built like a bear and it didn't take more than a minute to figure out that he was an operator who would have to be watched. He blabbered in near perfect English that he knew practically everybody in Iraq personally, including Saddam. When he took a breath he joined the four of us Salvation Army types in our van and he didn't stop dropping names all through the four hour trip to our assignment location, Al Amarah. Except for a couple of times when he went into a tirade about the "fact" that the Air Force's "shock and awe" strategy early in the war had killed over a million Iraqi men, women, and children. I tried to set him straight twice on that score but it didn't seem to change his mind.

The rest of the time during the trip I tried to tune out his constant bragging by surveying the Iraqi countryside. The contrast with Kuwait was stark. Here there was no lush sod, only mud as far as the eye could see. I figured the soil must have been mostly clay because it acts like a barrier so that rain has a tough time soaking through it. That would account for all the muddy ditches and the number of soccer fields we passed by that were under several inches of water. It would take blazing sun days to dry out this quagmire. And the palm fronds hung limp here on the few visible trees, not neatly trimmed like they'd been in Kuwait. In Kuwait too there'd been cattle and camels grazing and flocks of well groomed sheep tended by prosperous looking shepherds. Here the few flocks looked "rode hard and put away wet" and their handlers appeared just as bedraggled. The whole scene was enough to send Little Mary Sunshine in search of a Prozac prescription.

Muntajeb was still braying when we reached Basra, the headquarters city of the British contingent that was such a big part of the Coalition forces. Basra was the first major city on our northward path toward Al Amarah. I was surprised at the city's size and how spread out it was. And like every other Iraqi city I'd be seeing, there were some wide streets but there were no working red or green lights so the traffic was pure chaos. In spite of how huge the city seemed there were very few buildings over two stories high. What hit me first was the smell of the place, something between a men's locker room and an outhouse. There was no percentage in stopping for water because none of it was running in the city. But we did stop for lunch in Basra with Muntajeb as our host. The lunch had the air of a party since it was our first in Iraq. It was served in a restaurant that belonged to a friend of Muntajeb and given what I learned later about my soon to be sidekick, he probably got a kickback for his patronage of the place. A six course meal of hometown lamb and chicken was served by a woman in a chador. That's when I found out there would be none of my favorite steaks in Iraq since there was no grass for cattle to graze on there. We washed down the lunch with bottled water. I'd be having lots of the latter in Iraq. Back in the States I was always bitching about the cost of bottled water but in Iraq I'd learn that it was a real blessing no matter what it cost.

The British were having a relatively easy time of it in this Shiite section of the country compared to what the American forces were facing in Baghdad and the perilous Sunni Triangle to the north. Up there the insurgency was gaining momentum and our troops were taking casualties daily. For the rest of my stay in Iraq I checked the TV daily for reports of U.S. losses and too often learned of their growing number. But according to Muntajeb, there'd been few if any casualties suffered by the British troops in their sector so far.

After lunch we headed north out of the city on Road Number Six, the infamous "Highway of Death." The stretch near Basra got it's ominous name during the Gulf War in 1991. When the Iraqi army was routed out of Kuwait back then they grabbed everything they could steal from the Kuwaitis and headed north toward Baghdad by way of Basra. But they never made it to the capitol because they were attacked from the air by U.S. fighters that destroyed every vehicle in sight. And as far as the U.S. military could tell, not a single Iraqi soldier on the highway had survived. There were still signs of that Gulf War death drive on Highway Six when we left the outskirts of Basra headed for Al Amarah on that cold December day. Burned and twisted tank torsos. Tons and tons of scrap metal strewn everywhere. And many of the former buildings still piles of rubble. This was definitely not a scene to shoot for an Iraqi travel brochure. But at least on this day there were no signs of current violence.

When we reached the province of Mayan where Al Amarah was located, Muntajeb told us what we'd be up against in the rebuilding process. It seemed the province was destitute. There was no running water for at least half the population. Electricity was even scarcer. Most of the food had to be lifted from the land in the form of a stray goat or sheep. There was no working infrastructure in any of the towns. There was chaos in the streets and corruption in the local government, all the result of the war. In Saddam's day the place had functioned well, if not freely. Now it was something short of the setup you'd want for a comfortable stay and productive working conditions.

Just before we entered Al Amarah itself we passed the British Provincial Authority base camp that I'd soon become very familiar with. I'd be going there on a daily basis to pick up or sign construction contracts and cash to pay the crews for completed work. The base was a series of low buildings spread out over open fields ringed by razor wire fencing to keep out terrorists. The buildings were dusty and dirty and there were hardly any power facilities. All the British military lived at this base camp. Toward the end of our guided tour we were shown where we would go to church, which was a small room in one of the inner buildings. This makeshift chapel consisted of a few folding chairs with hymn books sitting on them. No altar or icons.

When the skyline of Al Amarah finally filled the Chevy's windshield I said a silent prayer of thanks to God for bringing me to this place where I could be of some use to humanity. Like Basra, Al Amarah was spread out and there was the same chaos on the streets which were also reeking of open sewers. Again the buildings were all low but Muntajeb told us that at least half of them had electricity which made Al Amarah a paradise compared to a lot of places in the country. Muntajeb also said my new hometown had a population of around 300,000 which made it about the same size Dayton had been while I was growing up there.

It was around noon on Wednesday the 10th when we got to the safe house that we'd soon call home. The car ride to get there seemed endless, even though it actually only took three-and-a-half hours. The house wouldn't be ready for us until the team we were replacing left for the States in two days. But that first day in country we got a preview of the place. It was a two-story, five-bedroom building surrounded by an eight-foot high concrete wall in Al Amarah's version of an upscale neighborhood. In the part of the thick cement perimeter wall that faced the street there was a set of huge metal doors that swung out in welcome to the team's two vehicles, an innocuous white van and a vintage Honda. On the roof, of the building, a small court provided a place to hang dripping clothes on a line. And a vantage point that overlooked the city. Muntajeb said it would be ideal for watching the fireworks at wedding and birthday celebrations or pyrotechnics of a different kind if the insurgency heated up in this part of the country. Within the walls out in front of the house there was a big plywood shack where the guards lived and a huge generator to be used when the central power source in the city was offline. According to Muntajeb that would be at least half the time. And he added that the backup generator at the safe house only worked when it was in the mood. What he didn't tell us was that even when it was in the mood we probably wouldn't have fuel for running it. This in a country that was drowning in oil. Anyway, besides the bedrooms the house had three baths but only one shower. The toilets were said to work "sometimes" but you weren't allowed to put paper in them. That had to be flipped into a big smelly wastebasket in a corner. But there were advantages to the place. If the traffic ever thinned out it was only about ten minutes by car to the Civilian Provincial Authority where the Brits were running the reconstruction effort. The house cost the Salvation Army 800 dollars a month in rent paid to a local homeowner.

After we figured out the lay of the house we were introduced to the outgoing four-man team we were replacing. They were all died-in-the wool Salvationists and I was impressed with how much they seemed to know about the local situation. They gave us a lot of tips on what to anticipate in the way of snafus that might impede our work over the next month. All four of them professed to have enjoyed every minute of their maximum month's gig but I couldn't tell whether they were being straight or just trying to make us feel better about our situation. It was hard to imagine how anybody could be content in such a forlorn country. I'd only been in Iraq for a few hours but already the place reminded me of the terrible racist joke I'd heard in Florida from a journalist who'd been embedded with the troops over here for a while. It was about Ahkmed the Iraqi who'd gone to the U.S. and only been there a couple of months when he came down with a mysterious illness. He had constant headaches and nausea and he was spending most of his time throwing up. He went from doctor to doctor but none of them could diagnose his case let alone give him any help. Finally he found an Iraqi-American medico and as soon as he recited his symptoms the doc said his case was simple. He handed Ahkmed a bucket and said "Take dees pail into the next room and poop in it. When dee poop is in dee pail, pee on top of dee poop. Then when dee poop and the pee are mixed, put your head in the bucket and breathe deep of the fumes for ten minutes and then come back to this room." So Ahkmed did as he was told. He pooped and peed like he was supposed to and then breathed the fumes with his face forced deep into the bottom of the bucket for ten minutes. On the way back to the doctor's examining room he began to improve and by the time he got there he was feeling on top of the world. He thanked the physician over and over for the miracle cure and finally asked "Doctor, what was wrong with me?" The doc looked up from the insurance form he was filling out and said "You were just homesick."

After our tour of the safe house and the social niceties with the outgoing team we got down to a briefing that would clue us in on the procedures and rules we'd be working under. The two day overlap between our team's arrival and the outgoing team's departure was designed so this could happen. The team leader, who was a British Salvation Army officer, did the honors. He was thoroughly professional and a class act and he spent over an hour detailing the operation for us. He told us exactly what to expect over the next four weeks as far as working with the Provincial Authority and living in the safe house were concerned. And about procedures and rules and things to watch out for. He even spiced up the meeting with stories about his experiences and adventures dealing with the locals.

In the middle of the Brit's briefing Muntajeb left for a few minutes to talk with another Iraqi in a small adjoining room. I was surprised at that point that we weren't told to keep an eye on Muntajeb. I had a growing gut feeling that he was going to be trouble. But nothing was said about him. Instead we met our Iraqi house staff and some of the project personnel. The house staff had a certain pecking order. Muntajeb was in charge; then came a Mr. Mohammed who lived on a small farm of about forty acres where he raised a few sheep and nursed plants for landscaping jobs. We would later be invited to a picnic at his place where one of his goats provided the main course augmented by a lot of catered food trucked in from nearby markets. He was only around five-foot-six but he was built like a Bradley. And he had powerful hands that could crush a coconut. He claimed to be the forty-third generation descendent of the original Mohammed but I couldn't be sure he wasn't blowing smoke from the same source as Muntajeb.

A Mr. Aziz was next in the chain of authority, an Indian man who had some Iraqi blood. He was the first Iraqi that the SAWSO boss from London met with when the Salvation Army outreach to the country was being established. He then became an Army employee with the job of good will liaison. He was so tiny that if he stood next to Danny DeVito he'd make the actor look like Wilt the Stilt. Unlike the other two minor moghuls, Aziz was a Christian. Later on he would teach me a thing or two I hadn't known about the Bible, which he'd studied from cover to cover. He had a lot of respect for the Koran too. He became my escort when I traveled around Iraq and he also knew a lot of Iraqi history. He started giving me lessons about that during our tour of the safe house.

On top of their other duties, Muntajeb, Mohammed, and Aziz were supposed to function as our interpreters and guides. They would get us to where we had to go and smooth relations with the sheiks and mullahs we'd be dealing with. The three supervised the other employees too—engineers, cooks, cleaners, guards, and a couple of extra interpreters. There were also four permanent bodyguards with AK 47s and side arms. Some of the Iraqis on the work force, including one of the guards, were missing limbs that were shot off in the Gulf war or in Operation Iraqi Freedom or by Saddam himself. Most of them were very friendly and seemed to be enthusiastic about their assignments. But when the meetings finally finished I was worn out from shaking so many hands and spouting small talk and I was anxious to get started on the real work.

With the briefing and the intros accomplished, we all headed for our bedrooms to get a good night's rest before the grueling grind started in the morning. But before I could settle into the cot next to what would be my desk for the next six weeks, Muntajeb pressed an English translation of the Koran into my hand and asked me to read it as soon as I could. I promised him I would if I got any free time. I remembered what the Salvation Army officer in Washington had said about not passing out Christian tracts in Iraq. Apparently it didn't work the other way around. I started right in the next day reading the Koran at every scarce opportunity and I found it quite interesting. There was good advice contained in its pages like, "always be trustworthy," "help your fellow man," and "pray as much as possible." Stuff that no Christian cleric could object to. I wondered what parts of the Moslem good book the fundamentalists had perverted to justify jihad. But that first night at the compound I was so pooped from the trip and all the side-window sight seeing I didn't open the book. Instead I slipped it under my blanket and slept like a newborn.

# NINETEEN

On the morning of the eleventh of December 2003 the sixteen-hour per day work routine began promptly at four forty, when the soundest of sleeps was shattered by Muslim chants and prayers blaring from the compound's loudspeakers. Then at six we hit the ground sitting. There were meetings about everything from contract negotiations to storm sewer conditions and the palaver went on, and on, until two in the afternoon. The meetings were also set up to introduce the new Salvation Army team to all the Iraqi staff members we hadn't met the night before and to do a mock run through of the office routine. There was a special secretary to translate especially complicated Arabic documents. And there were three drivers, plus some custodial folks. They'd all be on duty full time. I was shocked when I found out how little they were being paid, namely a paltry two-dollars a day. That was a minimum wage with the accent on minimum, a figure calculated to shame even the Republicans back in the States. The Salvation Army set the pay scale and it was all they could afford. But apparently the Iraqi workers were happy to get the jobs because the Salvationists were winning so many contracts and providing so much work even if the pay was pathetic by American standards. When we processed IDs we found that some of the women workers had been certified teachers under Saddam and quite a few of the men were college educated. There was an eighty-seven-billion buck kitty in U.S. money to be tapped, but it was pitiful to think how far it didn't go in a country with problems on the scale of Iraq's. Because so many of the workers had been professionals before the war they hadn't had any experience with the kind of work they were doing now and I would be constantly making sure they had foremen who could get the best out of them. That would end up draining a lot of time since with just the street cleaning and drainage ditch crews alone I would be overseeing more than 4,000 Iraqi laborers.

All you had to do was look around the streets of Al Amarah to see the tremendous need created by the war damage and by the decay that resulted from the sanctions before the war. Not to mention the years of Saddam's diverting billions to support his lavish lifestyle. Whatever the ratio of resources to need, I was anxious to get started helping the people put their city back together again. And I was told that there would be no shortage of Iraqis who wanted to lay claim to the two-buck a day privilege of doing the grunt work. In fact, I was warned there would be an order coming down from HQ to take on another 8,000 of them which would triple the labor force under our team. They'd be part of the mob I'd oversee as they repaired or put up clinics and hospitals and schools. At the moment there were two small hospitals being built and thirteen schools with contracts let for twelve more classroom buildings. The land for the building sites was no problem. All the former Baath party properties had been confiscated by the new Iraqi government. This didn't strike me at the time as a planning mistake but later I figured out it wasn't such a good public relations ploy and might become a bone of contention. Many of the Sunnis were Baathists and they weren't especially pleased with the confiscation policy. But for the moment we had all the land we needed and could choose building sites at random.

As I was getting my mind around all this activity that first day on the job, Muntajeb showed me that he had more talents than translating and name dropping. He was doing a great job of lining up new work crews for the expected expansion of the labor pool. A steady stream of would-be employees filed up to the employment desks in the office. Muntajeb had already come up with plenty of laborers to fulfill the previous Salvation Army team's committed contracts and he was building a reserve force that could take over quickly to insure that future projects would match or exceed the pace of previous work.

My three main men, Muntajeb, Mohammed, and Aziz gave me a quick look-see at those job sites that were already up and running. And I arranged right away for a meeting with all of the Al Amarah bigwigs, the sheiks and the mullahs, so we could figure out what new projects needed priority status. The mullahs were like gods to the Iraqis so we had to show them the same respect the workers showed them. The workers would do whatever the mullahs wanted so it was essential to get on the good side of these clerics if we wanted to make sure the construction came off without any hitches. That meant a lot of bowing and scraping in their presence. Some of them seemed pretty self-important and it was tough dealing with that kind.

While we were inspecting the work at the job sites, Muntajeb gave me a quick class on Iraqi construction methods. He knew the Iraqi building system backward and forward since he'd had a part in it all his life. But their methods over there would make an American construction person shudder his steel-toed shoes loose. No sophisticated machinery. Just primitive hand tools, but in a way, that was an advantage because it made for lots of employment opportunities. I'd eventually find out the Iraqis have been building like this for 600 years so there was no use trying to change their ways. By the end of the day I'd figured out just what I'd inherited and what new projects needed to be pushed as priorities.

The next day, the 12th, the transition from the existing Army unit on the ground to our new crew was completed and we said our goodbyes to the team of volunteers heading back stateside. We were on our own now and on top of that my team would be short handed for a while. Don had come down sick with some energy sapping virus he'd probably picked up during an outbreak back in his New Jersey home town. It was clear he couldn't hold up his end of the construction planning and contracting like he was supposed to so those extra chores would fall into my lap. I was tempted to tell him to see an Iraqi doctor who'd lived in New Jersey and have a bucket handy but I resisted. Of course I said I'd take over Don's duties and I arranged for him, when he felt up to it, to do some computer work and keep a daily log of the places I'd visited and the contracts I was negotiating.

After I had him squared away I headed out to the British Provincial Authority compound outside of town and introduced myself to the base commander, a British Army Major named Isles, who would become a good friend over the next month. He'd been looking forward to my arrival because he'd seen my construction credentials in advance and couldn't wait to get me on board. When I told him during our first talk that I was a former Olympian the skids were greased for my future dealings with him because he'd had a yen to compete himself in his younger days. He'd been a talented wrestler then. In fact, we hit it off so well that he invited me come back to the HQ for dinner that evening and after that we got together socially there and at my safe house now and then. I think he appreciated the fact that I was a regular Joe who could throw back a glass of scotch with the best of the Brits and not what he thought to be a typical Salvation Army Bible thumper. That down to earth rep would help me wrap up contracts from his deputies who doled out Bush's billions for the reconstruction. Whenever I saw them on business they'd offer me a beer or two to smooth the negotiations. And I'd be invited to all the Brits' bashes for holidays and retirements and such. During that first dinner with the major he said he'd been impressed with Muntajeb's work for the Coalition, but he also let me know that he didn't think that my Iraqi aide/translator was the most trustworthy of characters. I filed that information way back in my brain, with my own suspicions. It worked its way to the front of my brain after a couple of weeks.

I'd asked Muntajeb, the night before, to set up a meeting with all of the local construction ramrods for noon that day and when they were all assembled I had John Berglund, the outgoing team leader, introduce me and I outlined what I expected over the next month. Everybody seemed willing to get with the program so things looked to be shaping up well. Then we had a series of planning meetings till nine that night followed by an armed escorted ride home to the safe house. Dinner was served at ten and that's when Bill, Don, Karen and I discovered that the head cook, a young Iraqi man with a wide smile, could throw together a rib-sticker of a lamb stew. We'd been promised three squares a day and we'd need to stoke up at least that often what with the work load. We had to trust the kitchen staff to make sure any veggies they served us were scrubbed till they ached. And we couldn't have any fruit unless it was peeled first. We'd been warned back in Washington never to let un-scrubbed vegetables or unpeeled fruits pass our lips in Iraq for fear of several unpleasant diseases.

When I got back up to my assigned quarter of the house everything was clean and shipshape thanks to the old Iraqi woman housekeeper who'd been introduced two days earlier. That first night in the bedroom I hadn't looked around at all, just flopped in the bed fully clothed and snored the night away. But now I got a reminder of how primitive things could be in the country when I turned on the tap in the bathroom to brush my teeth and produced a tiny trickle of brown, foul smelling liquid. That's when I remembered we'd been warned to use only bottled water for our dental duties. Not that anybody but an Iraqi would be tempted to let a drop of the local bilge touch a toothbrush. I wondered how the citizens of Al Amarah could possibly stay healthy when they couldn't afford bottled water.

My bedroom was about eight-feet-by-eight-feet small and the furnishings included a short thin cot, a wooden chair, four wool blankets and a tiny space heater. The cot was about the same size as my old mattress Maggie in the Sandinista prison but at least this one seemed maggot-free, which was a Godsend since there were no sheets. On the wall above the bed a light to read by amounted to the only amenity. The light deserved a laugh. Who would have time for leisurely reading with the work load that was already taking up all my waking hours? When I stripped off my clothes and lay down on the cot in my long johns I discovered that even with the electricity on it was way too cold in the room for minimal comfort. The only heat inside the house besides the bedside electric heater came from a couple of small camper stoves that were way overmatched by the elements. In fact I discovered that second night that the only way to sleep in the safe house was the way I'd done it the first night, with all of my clothes on, including socks and shoes. And even then I had to pile the four allocated blankets on top of my still shivering body. To top things off a cold wind whistled through the room and found the cot no matter where I moved it. Over the coming weeks I'd learn that Muntajeb was being a cock-eyed optimist when he predicted the safe house power would poop out only fifty-percent of the time. It usually went off at midnight so the morning hours were almost unbearable. It hovered around forty degrees and in that temperature the insulation in the best of Al Amarah's housing was less than adequate. But no matter how cold it got, the long days of grueling grind at the office and on the road made the hard cot comfortable when I staggered in at bedtime.

* * *

Bill and Don and Karen and I had other reasons to appreciate our digs. The safe house sat in what passed for an upper class part of town so we didn't have to suffer as much as Al Amarah's down-and-outers. A lot of Iraqis lived on the streets and had no possessions at all. Many more than you'd see in a big city in the U.S. And the streets were a slippery sea of the most irritating, clinging mud during the winter months. Even the monsoon season mud in Central America was never as bad as this stuff. This mud would stick to our boots and pants and an hour's scrubbing might or might not remove it. A lot of the Iraqis who were forced to struggle through the muddy mess in the streets nursed horrific wounds from the war or from Saddam's torture. Every time I passed these poor people sloshing along with nowhere to go my heart went out to them. And I vowed to do the best job I could to help get their country's infrastructure back in shape so they could be taken care of in a humane way.

The people in Al Amarah lived in luxury compared to the struggling souls in the suburbs. The houses in the outlying areas were made of scavenged wood topped with a coat of mud. Those hovels made the three little pigs places look like fortresses. The people had been living this way for hundreds of years but I couldn't wait to start putting up some structures to improve their lot. In fact I soon discovered that this work in Iraq would rank right up there with what I did at Ground Zero and my forest fire fighting, not only in the exertion and exhaustion involved but also in the exhilaration it delivered. I was convinced God wanted me in Al Amarah and that conviction kept me upbeat in spite of the already growing fatigue.

* * *

On the morning of the thirteenth the full folly of my quick offer to take over Don's duties hit me. Doing both jobs meant I'd have all the heavy construction supervising. That amounted to quite a burden since the labor ranks were huge and scheduled to multiply soon. There were carpenters and electricians and common laborers to oversee. I'd have the construction of more clinics, schools, roads, and other projects under my leadership. And the sanitation crews too. Those guys really had their work cut out for them. They were tasked with getting the canals to flow freely through the city, which was permeated by a horrendous smell because none of the waste treatment facilities were up and running.

Waste treatment would become one of our team's highest priorities. There was nothing like a regular trash pickup. People just threw their garbage into the streets in most neighborhoods. All the sewage emptied into the canals and rivers and they were full of feces. But that didn't stop the locals from washing in the river and even drinking from it. Maybe they thought the open water was more appealing than the brown trickle from their taps. Whichever source of water they chose meant that we'd have to make the reconstruction of clinics a high priority project. Only the very rich had sewage disposal service and even it was antiquated. Ninety-percent of the people in the immediate area around Al Amarah didn't have decent drinking water so our job was also to put up water treatment plants. Thanks to all the skilled Iraqi help, we could get a plant up and running in a week. We installed lift pumps on the banks of the Tigris River near where it joined the Euphrates to form the Biblical Garden of Eden. Then we built a couple of huge tanks to purify and run piped water for a few kilometers to the city stations that also had to be renovated because they'd been bombed by U.S. planes early in the war. The cost of this was two hundred-forty million dinar or a hundred-sixty thousand dollars. And that morning I bid on a big contract to do the same sort of building project in the city of Mashara, about thirty minutes to the northeast of Al Amarah.

The exchange rate on dinars to the dollar reminded me of those stories about Italians after World War II toting their lire around in wheelbarrows. Or the tale my writer friend told me. He was teaching in Poland three or four years after the fall of the Berlin wall when the exchange rate there was 127 thousand zlotys to the dollar. He said an American friend visited him and he took her to lunch. When they were finished he threw a million zloty note on the table and the woman almost proposed to him right then and there before she found out that he'd spent about four bucks on her. Anyway we won the Mashara contract and the next day work began on it.

One afternoon I got a sample of the bonuses attached to my job. I went out to a local elementary school with Muntajeb and we passed out pre-Christmas presents and treats to the kids. This was one of the regular Salvation Army practices and I loved doing it so much I asked to be included whenever another visit to the schools was scheduled. The Iraqi children were cuties, like kids everywhere, but there was a special light in their eyes that you seldom saw in American children when they got gifts at Christmas or any other time. I took some great pictures trying to catch that light with my camera. I made three or four more gift-giving visits to the school later and always got the same reaction from the kids.

That night we were called to a meeting of all the NGOs that had contracts with the Coalition for the rebuilding work and I was proud to learn there from the British Provincial Authority that the Salvation Army had the best track record of all the world wide groups working in Iraq. It was getting the lion's share of the agreements and controlling eighty-five percent of the work force around Al Amarah. I loved the responsibility and hoped I could keep the pace going. And I wished the process of job creation was as easy back in the States as it was here. If President Bush could pass out work at the rate I was doing it here in Iraq the American voters would be clamoring to abolish the two-term limit.

Meanwhile the members of our team tried to keep their spiritual lives on track. We prayed at every meal and sometimes I attended devotions with them in the morning. But I was so determined to outperform everybody that after the first week my schedule was hectic enough that I didn't have time to make every prayer call. I was hitting the road most days by 7:00 A.M. and didn't get back to the house until after nine at night. Then I'd have to fight sleep to fill out my daily report and after that was done stagger to dinner in the big dining room at the safe house. The cook was turning out to be a consistent winner with meals that pleased our palates and stuffed our stomachs. Usually the protein involved lamb or chicken. Every meal featured tomatoes with cucumbers so I started seeing them in my sleep. Dessert was always a super sweet pudding except when Muntajeb's wife came up with a cake, and of course I missed most my Old Granddad. Over in Iraq you were lucky to get a splash of hard water. Forget the hard liquor. And of course I couldn't drink at the safe house with my religious co-workers anyway.

✳ ✳ ✳

The 14th turned out to be a red letter day for the Iraqis. That's when we got the great news on Al Jazeera TV and CNN that the American troops had hung a "for rent" sign on Saddam's spider hole. Most of the Iraqi workers went wild with joy and they touched off a celebration that would take a couple of days to wind down. Their way of whooping it up was sort of like our 4th of July. Only they preferred real rifle rounds and rocket propelled grenades to our feeble fireworks. And they'd been prepping for this holiday for a while. Before the war every Iraqi had a weapon. Now every Iraqi had anywhere from three weapons to enough to make Wayne Lapierre euphoric. And they'd apparently never figured out that law of physics that claims what goes up must come down. So the Salvation Army troops had to stay inside during the fiesta for fear of getting hit with a salvo from the sky. As it was there were a lot of Iraqis admitted to the local clinics thanks to wounds from the falling ammo. Most of them were so grateful to the U.S. on that particular day though that they were willing to take a round or two on the noggin. After two days, the celebration finally wound down, and by then, 52 men, women, and children checked into hospitals wounded by falling bullets. But what a thrill to be in Iraq when Saddam gave up. Of course I knew Melinda would be ticked at me for not doing the capturing myself so I could collect the twenty-five-million-dollar grand prize.

One of the Iraqis who had a different reaction to Saddam's capture was Muntajeb. He'd jumped out of his chair and started screaming obscenities in English when the TV announcer broke the news. And he made it perfectly clear he thought Saddam was a coward for not fighting the Americans to his last breath. Or if he couldn't take a few GI's out with him, for not committing suicide "like a man." Muntajeb's face was flaming with the kind of uncontrolled anger I'd already seen him show when one of the Iraqi staff members made a minor mistake in typing a contract for him. Although that diatribe had been delivered in Arabic, there was no missing Muntajeb's white hot wrath. But what struck me about this latest tirade wasn't so much the fury as the fact that he seemed to side with Saddam against the Americans. Muntajeb would definitely warrant watching.

On the second morning of the celebration the city chiefs of the three main tribes that supplied 5,000 plus laborers came in to ask a favor. They wanted to get my permission to give the workers the rest of the day off after ten o'clock so they could join in the ongoing Al Amarah blowout over Saddam's capture. I had to sign a form in ink so their pay wouldn't be docked when they turned in their hours. Of course I gave them the O.K. right away and told them I wanted to attend too and I signed a proclamation for their temporary release. So the celebration revved up again and people were dancing in the streets with joy. Then the TV began showing those pictures of Saddam getting his medical exam which seemed to amuse all of the Iraqis except Muntajeb. He just stared at the screen and muttered something inaudible.

✳ ✳ ✳

On the sixteenth of that same December 2003, we got the word from the Provincial Authority that because of Saddam's capture we should prepare for a flood of returning refugees. We were only about 90 miles west of the Iran border and a lot of Bedouins and Marsh Arabs had fled over the line after the war started. They'd been coming home in dribs and drabs for a while now but with Saddam in the slammer there would likely be a big rush back into the area around Al Amarah. It was our job to have blankets and heaters and food ready for the influx, which according to Centcom might number in the thousands. In the next couple of days military intelligence would be able, through its satellite photos, to tell us the actual number of ex-pats streaming our way. Toward the end of my stay they actually started showing up in big numbers and the pace of the construction quickened.

On the seventeenth I made my first visit to the leper colony with an Iraqi doctor named Bahari. Muntajeb drove me out to the little hospital which was located a few miles from the Iranian border at the beginning of the marshlands that separated the two countries. The isolated, dilapidated building looked especially forlorn sitting in the muddy countryside. When we drove up we were greeted by the groundskeeper who directed us in to the reception area. The groundskeeper, who tripled as a cook and nurse, led us on a tour of the building. There were about fifteen patients of all ages being treated at the time. Old men with missing limbs. Several blind women. A boy without fingers and another with a missing eyeball. A couple of men who couldn't walk and had to crawl through the mud when they went outside. Truly searing sights. The groundskeeper told us that he lived in the compound himself so he could feed and care for the patients. And that life was a little better for them thanks to about 6,000 dollars worth of equipment and redecorating the Salvation Army had donated. The previous team had carried out the work that I'd been told I would be doing when I was in Washington and I was a little disappointed that my team had been beaten to the punch. Each patient now had a space heater and new blankets and the cook had some new utensils. Despite my nervous embarrassment and baseless concern about touching the lepers I shook their hands and engaged them with a steady stream of the fractured phrases I'd studied before going to Iraq. I managed to provoke a lot of precious smiles with my garbled gab and I was glad I'd overcome my hesitation and given them a small gift through

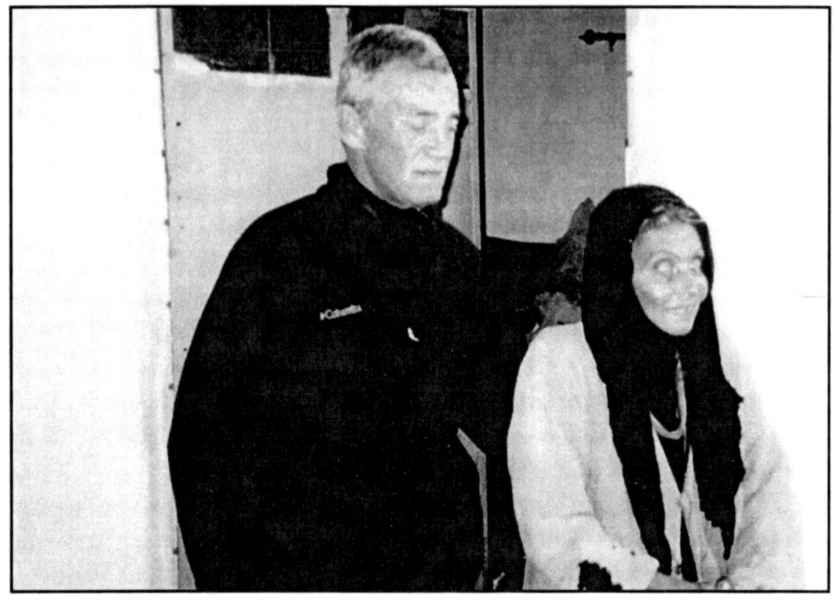

*Sam visits a leper colony in Iraq, Christmas 2003.*

my visit. Still, I couldn't beat back my stupid wish to wash my hands and burn my clothes. In fact, when we left the colony that day, Muntajeb produced a chemical salve and said I should rub it on my hands for safety's sake.

Before I left the States for Iraq my kids had asked me what I wanted for Christmas and I'd told them the best present they could possibly come up with would be 50 dollars each that I could spend for them on the lepers. So I'd put their money together with some of my own to buy the colony a new generator. With that basic perk they could have light and centralized heat in the hospital with no power interruptions, or at least fewer depending on the fuel supply. The generator would be an add-on to what the Salvationists had provided, but add-on or not, I made a promise to myself to come out here again on Christmas day and deliver the generator. All the while I was in that hospital I was thinking about how God had blessed me in my life and given some souls such a horrendous existence. I thought there must be a special place in heaven for folks who suffered so much.

Back in the van headed for Al Amarah Dr. Bahari filled me in on leprosy which was called in the medical textbooks Hansen's Disease. He said there wasn't much of it in Iraq but that efforts to wipe it out completely had failed. There were two kinds of leprosy, one relatively mild and another like the one we'd just seen. The cause was a slow-growing bacillus that attacks skin and the nerves and the mucous membranes. It was mainly found in

India and Nepal but there were even a few cases in the U.S., which really surprised me. Worldwide there were about two-million sufferers. The doctors weren't sure but the best guess had it that the disease was spread from one person to another through nose fluid. The only treatment was antibiotics and some of them worked so well that if a patient stuck with a regimen he or she could go into what amounted to remission. Up to this point the attempts to develop a vaccine had failed, though research was still going on around the clock in some places. When Dr. Bahari finished he lapsed into silence and I said a prayer for the lepers at the Amarah Hansen House and for the researchers trying to find a cure.

# TWENTY

By the end of that first week in Iraq I was on my own and had settled into the rigorous routine. In my role as general contractor I would go to the British civil authority in Al Amarah and be given a potential contract or several contracts to bid on. Then I'd bring it, or them, back to the compound and put together a bid, or bids, with the input of the three engineers and Muntajeb. The Salvationists paid me no salary for all this work and barely enough of a stipend to cover expenses. That suited me fine. I was happy just to be in Iraq. And I got some side bennies besides playing Santa to school kids and needy lepers. I had the fun of bidding for contracts against all the hotshot outside companies like Halliburton and Bechtel and I won my share since I had zero overhead. The Salvation Army got nothing in profit and only a five-percent handling and supervision fee.

I liked to visualize all those big execs at the private corporations tearing their hair out over us; a bunch of Christmas bell-ringers sucking up all those contracts that could have been theirs. Of course they were too busy bringing in the billions from their no bid boondoggle in the oilfields to worry about us collecting a few crumbs. But that didn't stop the big boys from bidding on the same smaller contracts we were winning. So there was a lot of satisfaction in beating them out. They had a big problem with their bids because they needed to pay their construction supervisors and laborers an arm and a leg, sometimes literally, to work in such an obvious danger zone. There was always the risk of a kidnapping or worse. So my low balling bids for relatively small projects like building or rebuilding schools and clinics had the Halliburton and Bechtel subsidiaries on the defensive and within a few days of getting to Iraq I was on an unbelievable roll, piling up new contracts faster than I could sign them. And that was no doubt why at the twice-weekly contractors' meetings I often had offers from Halliburton and Bechtel subsidiaries. These inducements always dangled around a 1,000 dollars a day and that wasn't including bonuses and vacations and R&R opportunities. In any other circumstances it would've been tough to turn down that kind of deal. But I always cut the seducers off at the pass because I was so proud of representing the Salvation Army and no amount of money could make me switch loyalties. That wasn't what I was about. The big shot execs couldn't know why I was over there and how much I loved my role. All this fun in a danger zone and working for a great philanthropic organization at the same time ! I wouldn't have traded places with a corporation contractor for five-million a week. It was hard not to remind myself of the irony that I was using tax payer money to take profits from Dick Cheney's Halliburton. Maybe that's why I was under such heavy guard, but I loved the wheeling and dealing. I kept emailing Melinda to tell her that her husband was beating the major corporations at their own game.

On a typical hectic day in Iraq I'd have fifteen schools plus three clinics, a hospital, and a library all under construction at the same time. But I wasn't only the contract bidder for the Army. My secondary roles had me playing building inspector and paymaster. Once I had a contract approved I would round up a driver and a bodyguard and head for the British Provincial Authority compound. I'd meet there with Major Isles and pick up U.S. dollars to pay my Iraqi sub-contractors, the ones that Muntajeb rounded up for me. Then I'd head back to the safe house where they'd be waiting for their cash. There were no such things as bank checks or credit cards so I was always carrying big bundles of up to 80 or 90 thousand dollars in large bills in my many-pocketed Banana Republic vest, a lot more loot than I'd toted around as an FBI cutout in Miami. After a while I couldn't help wondering if the next trip to the base would tempt one of my rotating Iraqi guards with an AK-47 to stick the barrel in my back and take off with a sweet slice of that eighty-seven billion John Kerry voted for before he voted against. But evidently all my armed attendants were straight shooters in more ways than one.

As chief building inspector I'd approve or disapprove of the work going forward on the projects. Usually I'd approve because the jobs were passably done and there was no percentage in starting over anyway because the workmanship would be the same. When I approved I put an official stamp and my signature on the original contract and then headed for the next construction site either in Al Amarah or somewhere else in the province. The trips around the area were made over the objections of Muntajeb and Mr. Mohammed. They tried to tell me I couldn't travel out of town because it was too dangerous but I was writing contracts for work all over the province and it was my job to personally eyeball everything. So I told them I'd check on the outlying projects by myself. And I began to wonder why the two of them were so worried about my safety when they didn't seem to be concerned about anybody else's. For some reason they didn't want me meeting the provincial sheiks and mullahs on my own. By then I'd begun to feel certain that my doubts, especially about Muntajeb's trustworthiness, were justified in spades. He was always trying to dictate how the Army should do business and my feeling was growing that he was up to no good. The fact that he actually did seem to know everybody in town didn't do anything to allay my suspicions. To top it all off I'd caught him in a series of little lies within days of our arrival in Al Amarah. I believed that he and Mohammed were both phony to the core. Within hours of meeting the staff I'd known I could trust Mr. Aziz with my life but I wouldn't turn my back on either Muntajeb or Mohammed.

The job creation crews were always a source of frustration for me. There were several thousand of them assigned to street cleanup every day. They were supposed to rake and shovel out the sanitation lines and sweep the streets. They were broken into twenty-man teams in different neighborhoods with each team sent to certain streets. They got the same going rate as the other laborers, namely two-dollars a day per man. The problem was that I had to take time out from pursuing contracts to drive the streets checking on their progress. Usually I'd catch a couple of crews kibitzing instead of cleaning so I'd have to have Muntajeb chew them out. Sometimes we'd double back just after one of my translated scoldings only to find them back on the slack. The goof offs were a surprisingly small percentage of the work crews, but the force was so big that the freeloading fraction took a lot of checking up on. When we found chronic slouches they'd have to be sent home for the rest of the day. And if there were enough of them the whole operation would have to be halted for a while. And that's when Muntajeb's blood would boil because he wasn't getting his full pay if the crews weren't working. The city was divided into six sections so he had six foremen and as many sub-foremen and they had to be paid whether the work was getting done or not. Whenever we came across a procrastinating crew Muntajeb would go ballistic. But I couldn't concern myself with his problems. The British had told me to be hard-nosed about making sure the crews were doing their jobs because if the goofing off got contagious the whole reconstruction program might come to a screeching stop.

During that second week on the job we won a contract to build 100 units of American style condos at 2,000 dollars each. They were one-story floor plans all connected by walkways. Each place was to be four-meters-by-five-meters with four-fifths of the living space taken up by the bathroom and the kitchen. These units were needed for the influx of refugees from Iran and other parts of Iraq due to flood Al Amarah in the next couple of months. The estimates called for a little fewer than 100 returnees a week so they would need around the same number of new housing units every thirty days. We had a lot of enthusiastic Iraqi engineers and translators who'd been in the construction business before the war and they were anxious to do the work. We estimated that we could put up the units for 1,500 dollars each. The units were rough brick work with a poured slab. The foundation would be no more than three inches of concrete or asphalt with a rebar driven into the ground. The roofs would be bricked. The houses wouldn't have running water and there'd be no heat. The amenities included a metal door and one window. They wouldn't be wired for electricity and a hole in the floor would have to pass for a john to squat over. There was no such thing in Al Amarah as central heating or air conditioning. No such thing as a ceiling fan. An archaic electrical system produced a little heat part of the time. But these units were being built for returning refugees who fled to Iran before the war and they definitely wouldn't be too choosy. They were starting to come back in droves now.

The spreadsheets we worked with in planning projects like this were half in English and half in Arabic. I took over all the presentations of contracts since I'd discovered I couldn't trust anybody else to develop them correctly and so I knew best how to explain them. With this latest contract I couldn't believe we were able to build that many houses for such a cheap price but when you're paying two dollars a day to workers you can make miracles happen. The Salvation Army had never done anything on this scale before but they gave me a free hand and told me to go for it. It was great fun despite the grind. I had a lot of confidence by now in Muntajeb's crews. The workmanship left a lot to be desired from an American perspective but the Iraqis seemed more than satisfied so who was I to complain?

A couple of days later we got the work started on the condos. Watching the laborers put up the units was an education in reverse. They poured formed supports by hand and used buckets passed from man to man. There were no pumps. It was like watching a process done by prehistoric beings. But after they applied a coat of stucco 5/8 inches thick over the framing the whole thing would hang together well enough. Actually, when the project was finished I was proud of the results.

When all of the contracting and building activity got to its most frenetic point during our second week in Iraq, Karen got so frustrated by the paperwork load I was piling on her that she yelled at me and used a few British expressions usually not uttered in mixed company. Then she apologized half the afternoon. I said I was sorry too and I really was because Karen was really a whiz at her work. But the contracts were feeding on themselves and nobody could keep up with them. We were racking up all kinds of projects, schools, family housing, tech centers. We were also putting together a package that contracted us to produce a 100 more housing units a month like the ones we were putting up just then. Apparently the Coalition deciders liked our work so much they wanted more of the same. At the rate we were winning work we'd have crews going at it around the clock.

Friday in Iraq is the equivalent of our Sunday. The only day of rest since there was no such thing as a full weekend. Which was fine with me because the day off was a big bore. There was nothing to do except hang out at the British base or bury myself in paper work at the safe house or join a game of street soccer with the neighborhood kids. I bought the kids a couple of new soccer balls at one point and they thanked me with cookies their mothers had baked. All other activity came to a halt in the city on Fridays except for small shops selling milk and soft drinks No mall walkers here. About nine on a particular Friday morning Muntajeb asked if I'd like to go to breakfast with him. I said sure, thinking we'd head out for some scrambled eggs and coffee. But he led me instead to the house of one of his friends. When we walked into a dining room full of people they all stood up as if a military drill instructor had given them the order. Muntajeb explained later that it was the custom for the headman of a tribe to receive similar treatment. That explained why I'd get the same embarrassing fanfare from my contract workers. At any rate the breakfast was a bit different than what you might expect at your neighborhood Waffle House. One of the women brought a big bowl full of meat and grease to the table. Then the ten of us dipped hunks of coarse bread into the bowl and chowed down on the meat and dripping grease. Sloppy eating but quite tasty. After we were finished though, Muntajeb took me on a tour of the kitchen and there on a counter was a big boiling pot and five cow skulls. The meat we'd just scarfed came from the jaws and cheeks of the former milkers. As it turned out the breakfast my mouth thought was so watering had approximately the same effect on my stomach and I spent the rest of the morning seated on the sometimes flushable throne back at the safe house.

A couple of times I decided to take my life in my hands and eat street food in some of the outlying villages. It was usually a greasy piece of meat that gave me the runs for the rest of the day. Each time I grazed at the public trough I regretted it because it took me what seemed like a week, though it was only a few hours, to get over the effects. But I was smarter about drinking water. Wherever I went I made sure I had bottled water or canned coke with me.

The more I learned about Iraq's social setup the more curious I got. It was a really backward country by American standards. For instance, anybody who wasn't married had to live with their parents till a marriage was agreed to and finalized. And there weren't any exceptions to the rule. Meaning a forty-five-year-old old man would have to live with mom and pop. That arrangement sounded to me like a nightmare scenario out of the old Seinfeld sitcom. But nobody in Iraq was supposed to live outside a family setting. There were no bars, no dancing, nothing to entertain a person that I could discover. No man or woman who wasn't married could have sex without running the risk of being found out and maybe even killed. I would've been dead by the age of fourteen if I'd been born in Iraq, hanged as a serial sex offender. Every woman in the country had to be a virgin when she got married. I couldn't believe some of the rules that were "gospel" in the Moslem faith. If a couple got engaged there was to be no touching between them until they were husband and wife. They couldn't even hold hands and they couldn't be together except with their parents in the room. Most families arranged the marriage years in advance and most everybody married within the family, often first cousins. But that part must have worked out O.K. since I didn't hear any dueling banjo music the whole time I was there.

I kept the knowledge of how conservative Iraqi society could be in the front of my mind at all times. And I'd trained myself to control my potty mouth ever since I'd volunteered with the Salvationists anyway. The ordained Army regulars were all beautifully behaved thanks to their strict set of rules. I was so proud to be representing people like them that I wanted to do everything by the Booth. I'd only caught myself cursing in front of the Iraqi staff members once and that was when I was so tired I could hardly stand up. One of the Iraqi typists completely screwed up a letter to a local sheik. He'd written in Arabic the exact opposite of what I'd dictated. When Muntajeb read it back to me I launched into a string of epithets that would've made a drunken sailor with Turrets Syndrome blush. Luckily the poor typist didn't understand a word of it but I spent ten minutes making Muntajeb deliver an Arabic apology anyway. Luckily I couldn't be tempted by Demon Rum since he'd long since been banished by Booth and Moslems didn't tilt a glass either.

The Iraqis carried themselves with a lot of pride and they are an attractive race. From what I could see, which wasn't much, the women could be really beautiful. Sometimes the eyes of a woman would remind me of that popular photo making the rounds since *National Geographic* printed it during the first Gulf War. The one that pictured the beautiful young Kurdish girl with the haunting eyes. But of course the Iraqi women were covered from head to heels as their religion dictated. In fact even Karen had to be conservatively dressed and wear a head scarf at all times but she didn't complain since she'd found the custom as she'd observed it among Britain's Moslem women kind of fetching. The women and the men too in Iraq seemed so proud and dignified. I admired them and was happy to be accepted by them and embarrassed at the power I had over them. I could make them do anything if I wanted and it made me sad to see such intelligent people reduced to near begging for a chance to help their families.

There was nothing for an American to do at night in Al Amarah so I wondered how all the unmarrieds would come by entertainment. No singles bars to meet Miss or Mr. Right. None of this bothered me of course since even if there'd been a sin strip the size of Las Vegas and I weren't on my best behavior as a husband and an honorary missionary I would have been too bushed at night to take advantage of it.

The lack of a viable night life didn't make the time go any slower though. It was already the 19th of December when I got a satisfying surprise. That evening Major Isles called the safe house to tell me he was so impressed with my credentials and the work I was doing that he was going to write to the Army's international headquarters and tell them they should try to hire me for a three month hitch. I'd only signed up for the five-and-a-half week stint since I had to be back in the States a few months before the Matthew Hall golf tournament in May to do the planning and raise money. In fact, the St. Petersburg press was already ballyhooing the tournament and hounding Melinda about my return date so I was under a lot of pressure to make the event a success. Major Isles knew about the tournament but he thought HQ could work around the date and get me back for at least part of the interim months. Or he would be satisfied if I came back to Iraq after the tournament. But I nixed that idea because I wanted to be back in the States during the forest fire season. And besides, I knew I'd need a lot of R & R soon. In the last few days I'd caught myself falling asleep a couple of times over a spreadsheet in the middle of the afternoon. If it weren't for all those impediments though, I would have re-signed in a heartbeat for a whole year because I'd never felt better about doing a job. So many great things were happening and I was playing a small part in a history-making experiment. And for now I had enough energy left that it was hard for my Iraqi armed guard to keep up with me.

The major told me he wanted me to come back for a longer tour of duty because he badly needed my expertise. His recommendation meant a lot to me since I'd only been on site for less than ten days. And I had total respect for him. When he spoke, everybody listened. And he was held in high esteem by everybody involved in the reconstruction effort. I told him I'd think about re-upping after the tournament and the fire season.

# TWENTY-ONE

Late one afternoon word came down from HQ that seventy-six refugees were about to be transferred from the Iranian border after they met the security check and proved they lived in Al Amarah before the war. The Brits asked the Salvation Army to provide them with blankets on their arrival, which was scheduled for around six that evening. But they never got past the border. They were held up there, which happened a lot, and we just hung on to the blankets to distribute whenever or if ever they got over the line. The border situation was always in chaos. Hundreds of refugees at a time clamoring to cross into Iraq with faulty papers or no papers at all. And the Iraqi border patrol worried that the Iranians would try to lengthen the repatriation line with a spy or two.

There was so much money coming in from the U.S. as part of the eighty-seven billion that I was told by the Army's supervisors to take on another 8,000 laborers. On top of that I was to oversee the work being done on the clinics, the two small hospitals, and the thirteen schools that were about to be joined by twelve new ones in two days. But the more workers I asked Muntajeb to come up with the more he found, so manning the ongoing operations was never much of a problem. And all the workers seemed to have about the same talent level, which was passable. Still, the contracts kept coming through and I was afraid my work crews would eventually get over-burdened so I couldn't wait for the 8,000 pairs of extra hands that were due to arrive after the first of the year.

Meanwhile I was getting more and more suspicious of Muntajeb. I was almost sure he was operating some kind of major rip off scheme but I didn't have the time to check up on him. It was tough enough staying current with the paperwork connected to the competing projects without playing detective too. But one day around the middle of my stay I got a visit from one of the subcontractors Muntajeb dealt with and he told me what my erstwhile assistant was up to. First he would award, say a school rebuilding contract for 25,000 dollars, to a friend who was subcontractor. When the job was finished I'd give the twenty-five grand in cash to Muntajeb so he could pay the subcontractor. But before he delivered the money, Muntajeb would deduct 500 to a 1,000 for himself. This was gravy over and above what the Salvation Army was paying him. He only had to deal with Iraqi subcontractors because the Americans, who would have reported his shenanigans to the Provincial Authority, were all working for the big boys like Halliburton and Bechtel. So Muntajeb was free to call his own shots. It was his business and he ran it his way. And there were so many contracts being let that the chances of his getting caught were slim. And the rewards, at up to a 1,000 dollars a literal clip, could mount into real money pretty quickly.

Not that his scam was any big deal by American standards. Or for that matter much different than the way business is done the world over. When I worked in Dayton, for one example, companies were always dangling free washers and dryers as incentives for doing business with them. And certainly here in Iraq Muntajeb was dealing in chicken feed compared to what the UN was eventually alleged to have ripped off in the Oil for Food Program. But what ticked me off about Muntajeb's scam was his reputation among other Iraqis and even among some of the Coalition brass as an upstanding fellow because he was a Salvation Army employee. He was actually a fraud and a thief who stole money right and left from his struggling countrymen. All virtually undetectable because every Coalition transaction was carried out in cash, a little loophole among many that Don Rumsfeld and his pre-war "planners" had put in place. The cash only setup made for a Wild West atmosphere that was easy to exploit. When I would pick up a bundle from the Brits or sometimes from U. S. State Department guys I'd just stuff it in one of the many pockets in my Banana Republic vest. Never in a money belt. The wads were way too thick. Since the weather was cold there was always the need for a concealing jacket to hide the bulky bills. When I traveled I always had to have an armed guard because I carried upwards of a 100,000 dollars at time. God knows how much money the Halliburton contractors were toting at any given time. Or how many of the later beheadings had a profit motive mixed in with the religious hatred. But what I feared most was that Muntajeb's rip off, if it were exposed to the general Iraqi population, would somehow stain the Salvation Army's reputation in the country.

Anyway, apparently all the subcontractors knew if they didn't grease Muntajeb's palm there'd be no more contracts. Not unlike a vig for Two-Tone Clementi in the old Trafficante days. And I found out through the subcontractors that Muntajeb wasn't satisfied milking them for a percentage of the Salvation Army projects for his private fortune. It turned out that he was leaving the safe house in the middle of the night to meet with other Iraqi contractors to decide who got what contracts and to trade contracts for unauthorized jobs I knew nothing about. So he had a whole other sidebar business and he was probably making a fortune on it. Who knew how many other Muntajebs were skimming through the same sort of scams. That was a depressing thought. He was undoubtedly just one small specimen in a sea of Iraqi swindlers swimming away with U.S. assets. Need I say I wasn't surprised to learn later that billions of bucks were missing in Iraq?

The day after the subcontractor squealed on him I grabbed Muntajeb's arm and led him into a small empty office at the compound and confronted him with my findings. He was highly incensed that I was accusing him of wrong doing. But he didn't deny the basic outline of the scheme I'd figured out. Instead he chalked his cheating up to standard Iraqi practice. I couldn't believe the gall of the guy. He even offered to show me the profits he'd made on his latest swindle and then he pulled just under 50,000 U.S. dollars out of his hip pocket. I chewed his chops for over an hour and told him if I ever caught him scamming the U.S. government again I'd have his prick pickled and put on display in the town square. But I knew my threat had about as much chance of getting heeded as a holy man's sermon in a whore house. Things were too hectic in the country and Muntajeb too important to the labor pool for anyone to question his ethics. And he was too valuable as my best translator and advice-giver for me to follow through on my threats at this point. He'd used his wide social network to keep the flow of job applications steady for weeks now and his contacts were crucial in hiring the subcontractors. I had confidence in his recommendations and there'd been no major problems with the work force on his watch. I had to take his word on the laborers' skills and work ethic. In fact, my work would've been impossible without his help. And he knew full well he had me over a barrel. I had learned in those first days in Iraq, that I could be confident in approving his recommendations. The day before I confronted him over his cheating, for instance, he'd taken me outside and introduced me to two disabled men. Each had one artificial leg. Muntajeb asked me to sign off to let them work on one of the twenty-man sanitation crews. So I drafted a letter and put my John Henry on it. The two amputees were in their fifties but I'd already seen enough of their type on the job to know they were working out well and a lot better than some of the featherbedders I'd hired through other go-betweens.

I let my warning to Muntajeb sink in. My confrontation with him did accomplish one good thing. Before I'd come down on him he'd been so full of himself he'd tried to take over the whole Al Amarah operation. He'd swagger into the office every day and say something like "Sam, here's what we'll do today." And then he'd start in on his agenda till I'd have to shut him up and set out my own plan. At one point I even told him in front of the staff that I had a job to do and he worked for me and the Salvation Army and not the other way around. Everybody in the office except Mohammed kept complaining to me about Muntajeb's arrogance but after I threatened him with exposure, in two senses of the word, he was comparatively meek as an Iraqi leg of lamb. That didn't stop me from wondering what he was thinking though. With all his connections he could have had me kidnapped or killed or both. Contractors in Iraq were sitting ducks for anybody who had a grudge against them and later, of course, several of them would be kidnapped or done in or both during the insurgency. Muntajeb could have easily had me snuffed or grabbed anytime and nobody would be the wiser. So I asked the Brits to make sure I had a trustworthy guard when I made my tour of jobsites out around the province. That would be the logical place to make me die or disappear. I've often thought that if I'd stayed in Iraq longer I might have wound up beheaded in an alley somewhere.

The day before Christmas Eve an incident happened that gave me a clearer picture of Muntajeb's true nature. He was driving on a trip to a provincial jobsite with me riding shotgun and Mr. Aziz and one of the engineers in the back seat. Just after we'd left Al Amarah's city limits Muntajeb asked me about my Christian faith. I guessed it was because Christmas was right around the corner. I tried to avoid the subject like I was supposed to but he kept pressing me, I told him about getting born again back in the eighties and then about the renewal after the FBI gig in the nineties and a little about Pastor Ron and the African-American church I'd contributed to. Then I asked him about his beliefs and why he seemed to be angry at the world a lot of the time. At first he denied being pissed off but I reminded him that we'd just barreled our way through Al Amarah with him laying on the horn and waving his nine-millimeter pistol out the window and dodging in and out of traffic while his face got redder and redder. Sometimes there was a pseudo-reason for his wrath in the form of a slow driver ahead or stalled traffic but at other times he just seemed to be blowing off some steam, of which he apparently had more than Mt. Vesuvius in its glory days. He admitted that he was unhappy about the American occupation and then he began to talk about his Islamic beliefs. I found that interesting because he never displayed any piety around the office or at the safe house or when we were riding around the province together. The other Iraqi staff members were very spiritual. If one of the secretaries, for instance, was working on a problem at his desk and the prayer call came from the minarets he would stand up right away. Then he'd take off his shoes and wash his forearms and feet in the office kitchen sink and kneel for prayer with his face against the floor by his desk or, if the weather cooperated, he'd move his devotions outside. It was an impressive method of prayer, much more striking than what you'd see in a Christian church. But I never saw Muntajeb do anything like that. So when he started in on his Moslem faith I gestured to Mr. Aziz and the engineer in the back seat to let Muntajeb talk.

For a good fifteen minutes he outlined the basic Moslem beliefs and when he took a breath I asked him if he thought, like some in Iraq, that his faith would come to dominate the world. That's when he started shouting and weaving all over the road and waving his pistol again and blaring the horn though there wasn't another car within a 100 yards. His face resumed it's raspberry redness and he screamed that Islam would one day rule all the earth to the everlasting glory of Allah. I asked him how he thought that would come to pass.

"It will all start with the chaos our fighters will sew in the West!"

"You mean you will frighten us so bad we'll just surrender?"

"Yes!" His voice was getting louder and louder. "You are a Godless society and your only rallying points are sex and money! Your God is material possessions! You have no ideals! Only Allah can inspire courage because He is all powerful! When we attack we do so with Allah's greatness behind our common cause! In the end nothing can stop us! Certainly not the infidels!"

By this time Aziz and the engineer were wide-mouthed in amazement at Muntajeb's ranting and railing but they heeded my high sign and kept their silence so I could bait him some more. I'd been driving around the country-side with him for nearly two weeks and I'd never heard anything about his political beliefs. And with what I was hearing now I wanted to get him incriminated in front of Aziz and the engineer. That might help nail his hide to the wall once I got time and the right moment coincided so I could call the Salvationists' HQ in London, which I was planning to do so I could report the scamming anyway.

"Hey, come on Muntajeb. You don't mean that."

By now he was practically foaming at the mouth.

"Sam, you are an infidel! An infidel I tell you! Soon we will strike many blows against the West until your will dissolves! You have no real God, just a lesser God! The money God! You Americans and your country clubs and your big cars and mansions! In the end you are nothing because you believe in nothing! Your President Bush is sucking the world dry of its resources! Taking, grabbing, and using up everything for himself! Spitting on the rights of other countries! One day the Islamic nations will rise up and smash the power of the United States!"

"Oh, Muntajeb, you couldn't possibly mean that. Our countries will become good friends after the war. You'll see. We want to bring freedom and democracy to Iraq."

He apparently realized that he'd been saying way too much and took this second opportunity I'd offered him to backtrack.

"You're right, Sam. I didn't mean it."

Of course it was a little late for a lame apology. Muntajeb was now on record before witnesses as one of those Iraqis willing to help the Americans rebuild their country while they waited for their chance to crush or convert the invaders. There were obviously a lot of Iraqis who just wanted us off their turf and you couldn't blame them. If the yoke was on the other neck, we'd be itching to instigate an insurrection ourselves. But how many ordinary Iraqis felt the level of fundamentalist fury Muntajeb had just exposed? Probably plenty. His attitude wasn't the only one like it I'd met with. It was just a bit more rabid. And the prevalence of those attitudes made me less than confident that President Bush's noble experiment was going to work in the long run.

At any rate, Muntajeb didn't say another word that day on the way to the jobsite and all the way back to the compound in Al Amarah. But his outlandish outburst put me on my guard more than ever. It would be so easy for him to have me killed and make it look like an accident. Between my knowledge of his flimflam and his hatred of America I would certainly make a tempting target.

Despite Muntajeb's insane religious rage and the milder fundamentalist froth I'd heard once in a while around the compound and the safe house, I didn't judge the Muslim faith negatively. By now I'd read quite a bit of the Koran Muntajeb had given me and there were lots of wonderful spiritual ideas about love and compassion in it. So much so that you could imagine Jesus writing some of the verses. And it wasn't Mohammed's fault (the first one, not number 43) that his teachings had been turned to terrorism by a few fanatics, including some Moslem clerics. After all, the forbidden fruit

Adam ate wasn't the only bad apple in the Judeo-Christian barrel either. Once in awhile even an Israeli rabbi or some West Bank settler would spray a mosque with gunfire out of pure hatred. You always had a few evangelists, especially the TV types, cheating on their wives or their taxes and bringing shame to their churches. And these days if you were a Catholic you couldn't be sure whether your pastor was praying or preying back in the Saint Paddy the Pedophile parish house. So Jews and Christians didn't have the shiniest slate either. And I'd met enough wonderful Iraqi Muslims to know that you couldn't judge the Koran by its cultists. Too bad more Moslems weren't living in the States so more Christians and Jews there could get to know some of them as neighbors and friends.

In a little over a week the end of the year would be at hand and by now not only were our crews spread all over the city but all over the province too. More than 3,000 were doing road cleanup and digging sanitary ditches. There were supposed to be 9,000 more of them doing the same in the next couple of weeks. There were so many twenty-man crews at work that when we drove by the jobsites with our two armed guards it seemed like we were commanding an army of our own. In fact, a lot of these guys on the construction and sanitation crews were former Iraqi soldiers that used to shoot at our troops. But I'd grown, in the few short days I'd been in Al Amarah, to respect the vast majority of them. In fact I'd become quite attached to them, with a few exceptions. I will admit that I didn't entirely trust any of them. There culture is so radically different from ours, and I knew there must have been a lot of them who secretly felt about Americans the way Muntajeb did.

On Christmas Eve I was supposed to meet with the chief tribal leaders in Mashara to go over a building plan for a civic center with a big hall attached, plus a library and sewing facility. These meetings with city elders were always a pain in the posterior. It was the custom for the contractor and the local politicos to do a dance around each other before the business began. That involved heaping hypocritical praise on the elders who would gush their equally hokey glorification of me. I was always embarrassed by these mutual admiration displays and especially of the deference I was shown. When I walked into a meeting like this one in Mashara, where the tribal chief or some other leader of the community was present, I was always seated on his left side while the British officer would be placed on his other side. The room might've had fifty people in it, all leaders of some kind or the other and they would all stand like I was the Queen of England when I entered the room, even the local sheiks.

Actually I found out that sheiks were a dinar a dozen and hardly the romantic figures like that one from Arabia in the old song. They were just the honchos in charge of various districts in the country. Their titles were passed down to them on a hereditary basis. Everybody in the district greased the sheik's palm if they wanted some favor. The sheiks were more like Chicago mob bosses that suck up protection money than the Hollywood version of Middle East mogul. But they did dress the part of the stereotype with long flowing robes and headscarves. The mullahs were fewer and further between and much more impressive. But sheiks and mullahs alike did all kinds of bowing and scraping and enabling for our translator Mohammed because of his supposed direct relationship to the prophet. I tried to have him with me as much as possible when I was bidding for contracts because he could open a barred door faster than a cat burglar. And just like Muntajeb he was a social powerhouse who knew absolutely everybody in town. And now the townsfolk were waiting on him hand and foot and jumping at his every command because he was helping bring so much work to the city.

December 24th, 2003 arrived but it was a regular work day for the Salvation Army. It fell on a Wednesday and we couldn't even justify a break for the Iraqi Friday day of rest. So I worked away at a stack of contracts and counted my blessings. Meanwhile I had so many workers at my disposal I was sure I could pull off our latest school building project, even though I had barely two weeks left in country. I wanted to see the results of all of these contracts I'd been signing before I left for the States and I was especially anxious to get the schools built. The still standing schools were in really bad shape. Half the walls were down on most of them and there were no roofs. We set the crews to cleaning away debris and bricking up walls. They accomplished all that in a matter of days. Then they put two-inch I beams across from one wall to another. Next we stretched plywood sheets underneath and in between the I beams the crews applied brick and mortar. Then the vapor barrier was created with four-millimeter plastic and four inches of mud was laid on top and next the plywood was removed. The workers laid tile in the bathrooms and the craftsmanship this time was super. We could do this kind of work and finish it in two weeks for about 23,000 dollars. There were 550 schools in the district and we'd already redone or were redoing 180 of them. That meant there were 370 to go. I found myself praying that W's dream for a free and friendly Iraq would come to pass. I sure didn't want all these schools we were rebuilding to get turned into hate spewing madrasses as soon as our backs were turned. But judging by my dealings with them, most the Iraqi people were grateful we were there and I hoped that meant they would resist the temptation to follow fanatic ayatollahs in the future. But that was in the days before the insurgency really heated up. When I was there they seemed to appreciate getting the infrastructure reconstructed for nothing thanks to Uncle Sam. Of course, Uncle Sam had deconstructed most of it in the first place and the continuing occupation was bound to turn off the locals eventually.

When I got back to the compound that Christmas Eve around nine there were a couple of pieces of good news under my imaginary tree. First the staff had been invited to have Christmas dinner at two the next afternoon with the British provincial governor. I'd always dreamed of having an English Christmas, ever since I'd read Charles Dickens as a kid, but this one in Iraq promised to be more fun than any festive meal in London. According to my invitation there would even be alcohol served. My second present was a note in my mailbox telling me that my hard work had earned me a couple of days of R & R in Kuwait just before my ship out from the Middle East, which was scheduled for the 10th of January. That time would have to be spent sightseeing since there were no more temptations in Kuwait than there were in Iraq. Both countries' liquor laws were as dry as their deserts.

The next day at dawn I woke up to Christmas prayers and I joined in with special concentration. I hated being away from my family during the holiday. Anyway, the morning began with a round of the regular inspections of jobsites and delivery of instructions to the work crews. I could hardly concentrate though because I was looking forward to visiting the leper colony later in the morning and then at five in the afternoon having Christmas dinner with the British at the Civilian Provincial Authority Compound. I'd only spent a couple of Christmases away from my family and they were the most depressing times of my life. Being in a foreign country during that festive time of the year would be a downer for most people but it was especially tough for me because those early Christmases with my brothers and parents meant so much. It was the time of our yearly trip from Ohio to Florida for our stay at the McFadden-Deauville hotel. For me, Christmas didn't equate to Norman Rockwell snowy landscapes on Hallmark cards but to fun in the sun and the warm sea. And I sure didn't associate the holidays with the Iraqi mud.

The worst Christmas of my life by far though was 1986. That's the one I spent in the Sandinista prison in Nicaragua. The only presents I got that time were a cigarette and an interrogation. And instead of the Florida sun I spent most of the day in the dark locked in the "freezer" with no one to talk to but "Maggie" the mattress. I'd vowed that day that if I ever got out of that stinking prison I'd never spend another Christmas away from my family. But here I was again on foreign soil at this time of year. I was really looking forward to getting back to spend some quality time with Melinda and my family. I'd made up my mind that I'd never spend another Christmas away from them. This one had been wonderful in many ways and I wouldn't have given up the experience for anything but the Christmas season was too special to be away from home. Though I missed Melinda and the kids desperately this time in Iraq, there were compensations I never felt in Nicaragua. This time I wasn't serving a political master but a much higher authority and feeling God's pleasure.

I don't think any Christmas could've been more emotional than this one thanks to that morning visit to the leper colony. Muntajeb and I drove out there with a security guard around nine in the morning and stayed for two hours passing out small gifts I'd bought at Muntajeb's suggestion for the kids. Soccer balls, tricycles, wagons and the like. We also gave them several jungle gym sets donated by a missionary house in Wisconsin. It didn't matter that the children weren't Christians. If ever a group of youngsters needed a toy or two, but more important the spirit of the season, it was the lepers. When you added war to the disease they endured they had it about as bad as any group of kids on earth. I was pleased to see the improvements to the facilities since I'd been there the last time. After that first visit to the colony I'd insisted that the Army install new toilets and tile the bathrooms for them. That work was almost finished now. The total cost was around $300,000, partly the U.S. government's and partly mine, but I was sure that the American taxpayers would approve in a New York minute if they could look into the eyes of just one of those leper kids. There's a indescribable glow you see in people's eyes when they've been helped in horrible circumstances. But the most meaningful time for me came when I unveiled the new generator that my kids back home had helped me get by gifting me with their 50 dollar checks. I only wished they could have been with me to see the reaction of the lepers when the director of the colony explained to them that they would now have a reliable source of heat and light. We also gave them cookware and blankets which the Salvation Army always had plenty of. They were overwhelmed with gratitude. It was one of the most emotional experiences of my life and I knew this Christmas would be etched in my memory till my dying day. I had tears in my eyes by the time we had to leave. All the way back to our compound I was making plans to come out and visit the colony again before I shipped out.

On the way back to the safe house Muntajeb surprised me by saying he'd been moved by my generous gesture. And he followed up by conceding that I was sincere in my hope to help the suffering Iraqis. He told me he liked my drive and that he was glad we'd come to be friends. It was true that we'd spent a lot of time together and that we'd chewed over every conceivable topic in our talks. I couldn't help liking Muntajeb, even if he was a rogue. I nevertheless couldn't think of him as a friend. I did appreciate his knowledge of the ins and outs of Iraqi society and the building trades and I thought he was highly intelligent. But he was what he was and I could never forgive his political extremism or ever trust him around money. And he sure wasn't about to be trifled with on his own turf.

Back at the safe house I showered and changed clothes and then stretched out on my cot for an hour thinking about the lepers and the wishing I could bring them some of the Christmas dinner I was about to enjoy. I couldn't help wondering why God gifted some people with so much while others suffered such terrible fates. I was way too undersized mentally to figure that one out and maybe everybody was but I was sure God must have reasons. Anyway, it was time to shift gears and celebrate the season in a lighter mood so I got a couple of the guards and the American team together and we drove out to the Provincial Authority Compound.

From the outside the compound looked anything but festive. Like all the Coalition bases in Iraq it was fortified with high block walls and thick strands of razor wire. The high walls were built to keep the outside eyeballs from watching the daily routine of the British forces. Every few yards there were checkpoints guarded by uniformed Brits with assault weapons. The four sides of the building had fire zones with clear views for a mile in each direction to beef up security and minimize the odds of being overrun in the event of an attack. Camouflaged vehicles were moving past the main guard post in both directions.

When we were waved through the front entrance and inside the big entry hall the atmosphere couldn't have been more different. All the walls were hung with what must have been fake holly and mistletoe and there were Christmas carols coming from a CD player in one corner. There was a crowd of around twenty-five military and others present. Brits of both sexes standing around a makeshift bar where a pretty uniformed blonde was pouring scotch and bourbon into paper cups. Another group was singing along to the carols and there were couples kibitzing in clusters. Major Isles greeted me at the door and we wished each other a Merry Christmas. Then he introduced me to some of the guests I didn't know. That didn't take long since I was on a first name basis with most of the staff. They were the ones who prepared and let the construction contracts so I was dealing with them daily. Each time I was introduced to a stranger by Major Isles he said "If you want something built fast and cheap, see Sam." One of them was a British reporter named Ian Bentley. He was with a London tabloid and he was doing a series of stories about the Coalition mission.

After I'd met all the other special guests I headed for the bar with Ian. I hadn't had a drink since I'd left the States and by this time I was parched past all portraying. When I checked the bottles standing at attention on the typing table turned drink dispenser I got a big jolt of joy. There among them was a gleaming, untapped bottle of Old Granddad. I nearly crushed the paper cup grabbing it off the table but I managed to pour a snort and swished it around my mouth a full thirty seconds before sending it on its way to my stomach. After a couple more swigs I was definitely ready to party. I joined a group talking about soccer, or football as the Brits called it. Some of the younger staff members had formed a league around different units of the Provincial Authority. To stage their matches they searched out the few soccer fields that weren't under water thanks to the Iraqis' insistence on ignoring higher ground when they built them. Of course before every match the perimeter of the area would have to be secured and the field swept for mines. But that didn't stop the Brits from scripting some highly competitive meets that only lacked the howling fans and the hooligans from home for a full feel of the pro sport.

Pretty soon it was time for dinner. Before I joined the crowd moving toward the dining room though I made sure I didn't neglect the other senior citizen present at the party. In other words, I made sure Old Granddad joined me at the table. The two of us sat between a couple of good old blokes from the Provincial Authority who wanted to know how the contest for contracts was going and what the new housing for the Iraqis looked like. They'd been tied to their desks since they'd been in country so they had no idea what the outside world was up to. I got them caught up on the latest developments just as the dinner was served. It'd been prepared a few miles west of Al Amarah at a British military base and trucked to the Provincial HQ in thermal containers. But the turkey and dressing and mashed potatoes and all the trimmings tasted to me like they'd been prepared in Paradise. And they all went down even better thanks to my Old Granddad. Then came the dessert of fruitcake and pudding.

As the dishes were being cleared Ian Bentley sat down in the relinquished chair beside me and asked what an American was doing among all these Brits. After I explained we really hit it off and got into an animated conversation about all of the exotic places we'd been and we exchanged details about our backgrounds. Ian had grown up in a small hamlet north of London and he'd always dreamed of being a journalist. But he'd married early and never had the money to go to college so he'd tried and succeeded to get jobs on small weeklies before catching on with his paper in London. He'd been pounding out stories for the tabloid for over ten years and he was in his mid-thirties now. He'd just come back from an assignment in Namibia when he got the word he was headed for Iraq. We talked about everything from the great scuba diving off the Malawi coast to the political situation in Britain. He told me that a big slice of the British public was adamantly against the war though their polls hadn't put a dent in Tony Blair's enthusiasm for it any more than opposing opinions had changed W's mind.

Half an hour into our talk the dining room had emptied and Major Isles motioned us into the reception hall. Before we complied, Ian suggested we stay in touch.

By now the laughs were reverberating off the walls of the compound and in the reception hall the staff females dragged the reluctant males out on an improvised dance floor and shuffled to the sounds of American standards on the CD player. The whole party from start to finish lasted around four hours but it passed in what seemed like a nanosecond. Back in the car headed for the safe house in town I wondered what the coming week would bring.

In most ways it brought more of the same. The chaos on the streets of Al Amarah wasn't showing many signs of abating. There were no police cruisers and very few cops on the beat and nothing like crowd control and there was a lot of looting still going on. Not a single traffic light had been repaired in the weeks I'd been there. Whose job it was to repair them I never found out. There was complete pandemonium on the roads and annoying traffic jams. In the past I'd been scared out of my wits on wild cab rides where some of the world's worst drivers were sharing the streets. Lagos, Tokyo, Bombay, Bangkok. But sitting in the back of a hack in one of those places was soothing compared to riding the shotgun seat through Al Amarah with Muntajeb or some other Iraqi at the wheel, horn honking and pistol waving the competition out of the way.

The amazing thing was, though, I never saw an Iraqi driver flip another driver the bird and since they didn't swear I wondered how they took out their frustrations. They all, except for Muntajeb, seemed to accept the situation since I never heard a voice raised in protest. If you wanted to speed through town when the coast was clear of cluttering cars you could hit ninety and do wheelies and there was nobody to talk you out of it. The only thing the driver had to watch out for was losing the car in mid-wheelie to one of the hundreds of carjackers prowling the streets, and being taken hostage at the same time. The hostage taking was beginning now up north but also along Highway 6 coming out of out of Basra to the south. People were being kidnapped for ransom there with increasing frequency. When the Salvation Army staff traveled they had to have armed guards with them and a trailing vehicle with other gunners aboard to scare off thieves or kidnappers or just plain folks out to kill anybody that fanned their fancy. If we were traveling between cities we'd regularly hit speeds of up to 90 miles-an-hour with a second vehicle not more than 20 yards behind. Fast moving targets are hell to hit.

During the late morning of the twenty-sixth I met with Coalition force commanders to plan the spending of their part of 87 billion dollars that Congress authorized for the rebuilding effort. That money had been earmarked and had already begun to flow before I arrived in Iraq. The local take came to a cool 80 million-dollars for the province leaders to spend after it got funneled through the Brits. The Salvation Army had contracts to spend most of this money.

The rest of the day was typical. I got an armed escort to travel with me to the city of Kumiat to bid on the emergency rebuilding of a water treatment plant. I was hoping for some scenery on the way but it was just another sea of mud and more bombed out buildings. I wondered how Iraqis who didn't have the means to travel ever got the psychological staying power to live in places like Kumiat. On one bank of the river that ran through the city the people had water and on the other side they didn't. I took four Iraqi engineers with me to assess the job. I met with the British officer in charge at Kumiat and told him we'd have a proposal submitted by five that evening. Getting the contract awarded was a slam dunk since it was an emergency situation and the big contractors like Halliburton had full plates at the moment. The Iraqis needed the work and like everyplace in Iraq, Kumiat needed fixing. On the way back to Al Amarah we stopped off at a school that had fallen down and submitted a tender, or bid, of 10,000 dollars to repair it. The kids were forced to go to school in three four hour shifts each day. They actually liked the setup but their parents' weren't happy about it. Our new clinics were treating patients for the first time, but a major problem was the shortage of medicines, especially for tuberculosis, which had been stamped out in much of the rest of the world, but not in Iraq.

# TWENTY-TWO

Around noon the next day we got word that a horrendous earthquake had hit Iran just before dawn. There was said to be terrible devastation in a town I'd never heard of called Bam. I felt terrible about it and more so since it'd happened while I was sleeping off the pleasures of the Christmas party. Once again I questioned why God worked the way he does. I wanted to do something to help, but I wasn't sure that an American could get into Iran, even on a mission of mercy. We were hated by the Iranian ayatollahs and not just because of our government's support of Israel. We'd also supplied Saddam with weapons during the eight-year Iran-Iraq war in the 1980s. In fact, I thought it was unlikely that even Iraqis could get across the border. But the news was reporting as many as 25,000 deaths in Bam and I was sure the Iranians would be overwhelmed by those numbers. I found out in the early afternoon, from CNN, that the Salvation Army had received an invitation to send some supplies and an assessment team by truck to the earthquake site. The reason for the invitation no doubt had to do with the Army's reputation and the fact that our operation in Al Amarah was relatively close to the disaster site. But the shipment and the team bringing it in would have to be closely monitored and would have to keep a low profile and leave the actual relief work to the Red Crescent, which was the Middle Eastern version of the Red Cross. The mission would involve taking in the load of supplies and doing a quick assessment of needs with the whole trip taking just 36 hours.

*Sam in Iran/Iraq 2003-2004.*

*Sam in Iran/Iraq 2003-2004.*

The chance to help out in a terrible crisis combined with the adventure of being one of the few Americans in recent years to get inside Iran was too exciting to pass up. I sent an email to my Salvation Army boss in London, Major Mills, and followed up with a couple of phone calls. At first the major told me my work in Al Amarah was too important for me to be considered for the Iran mission but I reminded him I'd only be gone for a little over a day and he reconsidered. The more he thought about it and the more I cajoled the more he had to agree that my work with other earthquakes, like the one in Mexico, and my construction expertise made me the perfect person, not only to be a part of the Bam team, but to be its leader. So that very day Muntajeb and I started to make plans for a group to leave for Iran on the twenty-ninth aboard three trucks packed with supplies for the earthquake victims.

Part of my preparation for the trip included learning all I could about my destination. As usual, Muntajeb was a big help. One side of his brain held an atlas and the other side an encyclopedia. He told me Bam was a city of around 200,000 in southeastern Iran near where the country borders Afghanistan and Pakistan. It was a historic gem located on the so-called Silk Road where traders had met for centuries. This wasn't the first devastating earthquake in Iran, which was crisscrossed with fault lines. Muntajeb told me all about a temblor in the northwestern part of the country in 1990. That one killed around 40,000 people. Getting to the victims this time in Bam would be tough since the city was more than 500 miles from Tehran where we were to go on the first lap of the trip to pick up a Salvation Army official at the airport.

Before I could leave for Iran I had two days of work in Al Amarah. I had to go to Coalition HQ to pick up cash for two new contracts I'd recently bid on. I'd just won an award for twelve school reconstructions plus one for a new clinic and two water treatment plants. The morning of the twenty-seventh I picked up a bundle of cash and put it in the safe back at the compound. According to our plan Muntajeb would be running my work crews while I was in Iran and I'd have to have arrangements made for them in advance. It crossed my mind that he would have a great opportunity in my absence to rip off some more of Uncle Sam's money. Over and above the routine chores I had to finish before the trip I had to wrap up a lot of paper work so the new team coming in on the eleventh of January would have a smooth transition. When I came back from Iran I'd be a short timer with a little over a week before I was to leave for those two days of winding down in Kuwait prior to heading home to the States. But there was no time at this point to worry about any future events beyond the next hour.

There were lots of preparations for the inevitable hassle at the Iranian border. I had to put together a thick set of credentials that included letters of introduction and visa entry stamps and various IDs. Muntajeb took care of most of the letters and entry documents, including a letter that explained what our team planned to do in Iran. And I assembled every ID I had from my fake international reporter's pass to my Florida fishing license. The plan called for a caravan of four trucks to leave the next morning. I was to ride in the lead truck with Mr. Aziz at my side as my Farsi interpreter and one of our engineers, Hamad Hussain, as our driver. The other two trucks would bring Bill, Don, and Karen along with Ian Bentley who'd heard about the mission from Major Isles and wanted to try crossing the border with us to get the story for his paper. Each truck would carry two body guards with AK47s. The guards were to leave us at the border and then wait for us there. The trucks were loaded with 6,000 blankets, tents, sleeping bags, 250 space heaters, canned food, and 6,000 pounds of wheat and rice. And enough bottled water to re-float the Titanic. Once we were in country we were to make an assessment of the needs in Bam for the International Office of the Salvation Army. There was evidently nothing standing in the city. So during the stay we'd be checking on what additional supplies would be needed there and sleeping in a cold tent at night. Once we were in Iran we were to keep as low a profile as possible because of the Iranians' sensitivity. They apparently didn't want the world to know that they couldn't handle the Bam catastrophe on their own. We were supposed to take a quick look and get out of the country. I had no earthly clue how long this latest adventure would last or what kind of reception we'd get across the border, or if we'd ever get back to Iraq or even into Iran in the first place. But I wouldn't trade the tingle for the world. And any hardships ahead would be nothing compared to what the people of Bam had apparently already gone through. But the long road trip to Bam via Tehran would take me out of the communication loop for a while. So I called Melinda to tell her about my latest adventure.

The night before we were to leave we got a couple of messages that confused things completely. One was forwarded from the Salvationist brass in London. It was from a Dr. Jabbar Nessy, who was head of the Iranian Red Crescent Committee. Nessy's letter made it sound like we'd be welcomed with open arms at the border.

*Our Greeting to the International Salvation Army HQ in London and the Iraqi team. We ask God for progress and mercy to you then we ask you to help us for the urgent requirements.*

*1 – Tents*
*2 – Medical treatments*
*3 – Clothes for general*
*4 – Food*
*We want to thank you very much for your humanitative dononories*
*for those who suffered in the earthquake of Bam.*


When we read Dr. Nessy's letter we loaded some medical supplies in the trucks and the few clothes that were on hand at the Salvationist compound in Al Amarah for charitable distribution.

HQ appended a response that they'd sent the Iranian border authority along with a copy of the Nessy letter asking them to allow us "easy access" to Iranian roads and to "facilitate where possible" our entry into the country.

But we soon we got the second message. It was a wire from London HQ informing us that we needed to redraw our plans because the Army official we were to pick up in Tehran had been denied entry into the country. That news sent Muntajeb grumbling to his atlas to map out a road route directly to Bam. By midnight he had an alternate path plotted a little to the north and then southeast directly to the stricken city. Then we all tried to catch a few of hours of sleep.

At three the next morning the caravan was ready to leave. But overnight its makeup had grown. Now we were to be followed by a truck carrying an Iraqi TV crew and its equipment because there was going to be a big celebration at the border to commemorate the crossing. News of the coming event had been playing on Iraqi TV for days so there was a lot of interest built up all over the country and our mission was being viewed as something of an historic event, though there was no assurance the Iranians viewed matters in the same way. Muntajeb had even arranged for a small choir of Iraqi children to accompany the TV crew to sing ceremonial songs for the cameras at the border crossing. By six everybody was aboard the trucks including half a dozen guards carrying AK-47s and side arms. They were former Iraqi soldiers and I prayed their presence wouldn't spark a rerun of the 1980s war. I thought the Iranians would have to be really desperate to allow this entourage across the border.

When Mr. Aziz engaged our truck's clutch and hit the accelerator on that cold and dreary morning I had no idea what I'd got myself into, but soon we were tooling briefly north and then southeast toward Iran. As we approached the border we came to the ancient land of the Madan, the formerly swampy area where the legendary Marsh Arabs had lived before the Iran-Iraq war. I'd been there several times before but never on this route. As

I looked out the window I could see once again how difficult it would have been for the Marsh Arabs to survive in the now forbidding environment Saddam Hussein had created by draining hundreds of square miles of marshes right down to the confluence of the Tigris and Euphrates. For hundreds of years these marshes had been a haven for slaves, Bedouins, and others who had offended the state in some way. As the truck rolled along, Mr. Aziz began to fill me in on the history of the marshes and their people.

"Mr. Sam, this area used to be accessible only by boat. No army, no matter how strong, or determined, had ever successfully operated in the treacherous swampland. It was the perfect sanctuary for renegades who wanted to steer clear of the central authority. Saddam could never abide having this hiding place from his tyranny."

I asked him about the Iran-Iraq war.

"It was terrible. It lasted eight years. They were eight of the worst years of our lives. And it gave Saddam an extra incentive to drain the marshes in this part of the country. He saw it now as the solution to the threat of Iranian invasion. He had the rivers diverted and built gigantic canals. Look over there."

Aziz pointed to a long stretch of brackish water that formed a canal.

"The idea was to cut off the water supply to the whole Amarah marsh. The result was all this dry, arid, silted up land you see all around us. The whole ecosystem was thrown into confusion. There used to be a huge population of wading birds, storks, pelicans, even eagles. Not to mention a vast range of edible fish. And people. All of them lost their homes."

There was deep sadness in his voice as he talked about the destruction of a proud part of Iraqi history and culture.

"Mr. Sam, the Marsh Arabs lived here for thousands of years. But Saddam thought the marshes had become a haven for deserters from his army and spies as well as insurgents from Iran. But in the 1980s the army of Iraq drove through the dried up swamps, laying down great causeways for armored vehicles to move easily to the east to reach the enemy in Iran. What a blow to our history and civilization."

Aziz pointed out the window.

"Look there, Mr. Sam. The marshlands are making a comeback. Slowly the waters are returning. There are still gangs of army deserters here but soon, God willing, the Marsh Arabs will be coming back in great numbers. I hope you will thank your fellow Americans for this"

He pointed to a watery area full of tall reeds and there were several long, slender boats in view.

"Those boats are called mashoufs. They are very useful as poling canoes.

They are about the only kind of boat that can operate in the long lagoons and shallow lakes. Not many designs hold up for 6,000 years. But these have been used here for that long."

Eight hours after our departure from Al Amarah and just past the marshlands our caravan rolled up to the border, a God-forsaken guard post in the sand manned by about fifteen Iranian soldiers. A couple of allegedly important mullahs and two representatives from the Red Crescent were also waiting in the little guard house. There was a scattering of trucks and a lot of other vehicles in the desert nearby. Mostly Iraqi taxicabs waiting to transport returning Marsh Arabs to Al Amrah and other cities. Hundreds of land mines were visible to the naked eye near the road. Mr. Aziz and I got out of the lead truck and Aziz talked to the lieutenant who seemed to be in charge of the post. I couldn't tell what was being said, but I noticed that the conversation seemed to be getting more heated by the minute. Aziz tried to show the lieutenant the letter from Dr. Nessy but he wouldn't even look at it. Finally Aziz told me that the officer had said that he had direct orders from the Red Crescent that no Iraqis would be allowed over the border but that we could offload our cargo and it would be repacked in four of the Iranians' trucks to be transported to Bam. So we asked to talk to the Red Crescent reps and they backed up the lieutenant's refusal to listen to reason. They said they'd been given instructions not to let the Iraqi trucks across the border.

There was apparently no changing their minds but I thought I would try a different tack. I told Aziz to tell the lieutenant I was an American and not a Salvation Army rep but a Red Cross volunteer. I thought just maybe I'd be accepted to go along with the Iranians as an observer to make sure our supplies were delivered in Bam. I knew from news reports that the International Red Cross was already on the earthquake scene. In fact I'd worn my Red Cross vest for just such an eventuality.

There was another long conversation between Aziz and the lieutenant and the Red Crescent twosome. All this time the rest of our team and Ian Bentley had been trying to figure out what was causing the holdup and they joined us at the guard post. Along with the Iraqi TV crew which didn't please the Iranians. The Iranians made sure there were no pictures taken of our confab. Then the lieutenant asked to see my Red Cross ID. I started rifling through my credentials and pulled out the pertinent papers and my badge and passed them to the Red Crescent types. They looked the papers over as if they could read English and finally came to the ID badge. The lieutenant turned it over and tried to read what I'd written in pen on the other side, English translations of Farsi phrases I thought might be useful in Iran. I'd made a ritual out of filling the back of my credentials with helpful local language when I was crossing borders in the Middle East and Central America and Africa during the eighties. This time I'd written the Farsi versions of "How are you?" and "That's good" and "Thank you" and "I hope we meet again" and "God's will." The lieutenant wanted to know what the English words meant so it was obvious he'd been faking reading the other papers. Mr. Aziz translated the back of the badge to his seeming satisfaction. About then I was breathing a sigh of relief that the translations I'd gathered this time were post-Melinda. In the old days I'd have included things like "Your mother raised a beautiful daughter" and "Where can I buy reliable condoms?"

But all my preparations for entering Iran were in vain. After another Farsi conversation and a lot of gesticulating the guard told Aziz there was still no way I was going to be passed through the gates, Red Cross or no Red Cross. So we all left the lieutenant at the checkpoint and went back to our trucks for a conference. There seemed to be nothing to do but to let the Iranians transfer our cargo to their trucks so I sent Aziz back to the guard post to get the process started. At about that point Ian had an idea. He wanted to try convincing the Iranians they should let him go along with the cargo to Bam since he was a journalist and his reports from the earthquake site could help mobilize more international aid. At the same time he could make sure that the shipment of goods reached their intended destination in Bam. I didn't have much confidence that the gate keeper could be swayed but as soon as Aziz had a dozen Iranian soldiers emptying our cargo I called him back to translate for Ian. They walked back to the guard post and I stood by the truck and watched another animated conversation. Ten minutes later Aziz and Ian came back to the truck with surprising news. Ian had been cleared to accompany the Salvation Army supplies as an international report filer and confirmer of the shipments' arrival. I couldn't believe he'd managed to coax that stubborn Iranian lieutenant into giving the O.K. for the trip. I was sorely tempted to try flashing my phony international journalist credentials so I could go along too but I was sure that wouldn't work after I'd already identified myself as a Red Cross rep and it might just queer the whole deal for Ian.

What came next surprised me even more. Ian had apparently convinced the Iranian lieutenant through Aziz's interpreting to O.K. the camera crew and the children's choir staging a little ceremony after the trucks had been unloaded and reloaded. So the cameras rolled and the kids sang and the mullahs prayed and we all shook hands while I jabbered "*Salam sleikum*" over and over. Which means peace. Then the festivities, such as they were, broke up as quickly as they'd materialized and the four Iranian trucks pulled out for Bam with Ian, the Red Crescent folks, and the mullahs aboard. As the convoy disappeared in a cloud of dust I wondered if Ian would ever get back to Iraq or if he'd wind up with an Iranian wife and kids. Then we boarded our empty trucks and made the eight hour return trip to Al Amarah totally disappointed.

When we got back to Al Amarrah from the border on the thirtieth the bid presentations I'd worked on before had already been submitted and accepted by the Coalition bigwigs. The project involved was huge by American standards. It called for seventeen major business complexes connected to warehouses. Each complex would cost 100,000 dollars. The package was part of a six-million dollar authorization the Coalition was giving to the Salvation Army. It was the biggest award in the Army's history. What a shame I was leaving before I could see the project through to completion. I sure wanted to come back in a few months and check on the progress of all this ongoing activity and on the general reconstruction of what was supposed to be by then a free and democratic Iraq. And to put a cherry on top of all my efforts, the next day I landed a contract for the army to redo thirteen more schools and two more clinics for another bunch of Marsh Arabs who were headed home from Iran.

The Marsh Arabs had a long and mostly happy history in their small slice of the Middle East. For 5,000 years they'd lived in the wetlands in what was now southeastern Iraq. They'd made their watery way farming and fishing and hunting birds until the 1990s when Saddam did all that draining and salting and chemical contamination of the marshes, and had over a 100,000 of the Arabs killed and their houses leveled. All because the Marsh Arabs were less than enthusiastic in their support of the regime. And of course there were oil reserves to be tapped beneath the marshes too. During the previous January, Human Rights Watch had done a report that counted around 40,000 Marsh Arabs still in the area and another 40,000 living across the border in Iran and in Saudi Arabia and all of them poised to return. It was the exiles in Iran that we were supposed to prepare for now.

With Saddam gone and the Coalition in charge there'd been an attempt to restore some of the marshlands by bringing water in from the dams in northern Iraq. But there was little to no hope of getting the area back to its former fertility. In their original state the marshes had covered 12,000 square miles but by the time Saddam's sadistic "reclamation" project was completed they'd been reduced to around 1,000 square miles and the rest was desert. So the Arabs would be returning to a land they wouldn't recognize and there'd be a lot of psychological damage for Coalition counselors to deal with. Before the war the Arabs had relied on Baghdad for some services, such as health care and education and basic banking. But now Baghdad was in chaos, and the last thing you could count on there was basic services. So there'd have to be lots of planning to reestablish the Marsh Arabs' society. My job was to come up with a plan for constructing a 100 temporary housing units to ease their transition.

On the thirty first I put together a spread sheet for yet another new project. Like all the other plans I'd been drafting, this one had to take into account the fact that every bit of the labor would be done by hand. There were no cement mixers in Al Amarah. The men would have to hand mix the cement in big bowls and pour it into roughly hewn frames. But that was good in a way because it took a lot of men to do what one cycle of a cement mixer could do and one of the ideas behind the rebuilding process was to provide employment. The proposal I was working on had to do with a new sports complex for the city. It was supposed to include a new basketball court. The total cost to frame and pour the whole court was only 600,000 dollars. To redo the soccer field next to the complex by removing the sod and replacing it with fresh turf imported from Lebanon came to a mere 700 dollars. The crews were happy to have work, even at two dollars a day.

All of this progress I was helping coordinate was clouded by a reality that was becoming clearer to me the longer I stayed in country. I was getting more and more certain that George W. and his neo-cons were wrong about the prospects for a free and democratic Iraq. From reading the more violent parts of the Koran and studying the Iraqis on a day to day basis and listening to Muntajeb's tirades and watching the BBC at the safe house about what was happening in the Sunni triangle, the car bombs and the mortar attacks, I'd just about concluded that "liberating" Iraq was a losing proposition. There would never be peace between the Kurds and the Sunnis and the Shiites. They're like the Hatfield's and the McCoy's with the Mafia added to the mix. I might not have been the sharpest nail in the pail but I'd been reading the signs over there for too long to believe in the Bush administration's pipe dream. It was noble ideal, but one that just wasn't going to happen. When I'd worked under a UN contract in Israel for six months during the eighties I'd felt the same way about the chances of peace with the Palestinians in the Sinai. I was sure there would never be an agreement among the parties there. The seething hatred I saw on both sides convinced me that the Bible was right-on where it said there would always be wars and rumors of wars. And that went triple for Iraq. Here you had three major groups that detested each other's ethnicity or religious beliefs and were itching to initiate a civil war.

Not a day passed in Al Amarah that I didn't hear dozens of diatribes against one of the other ethnic or religious factions in the country. Most of the Kurds in the north and the Shiites in the south and the Sunnis in between wanted the U.S. out as soon as the rebuilding was finished so that they could get at each others' throats. National sovereignty wouldn't make a bit of difference unless the country was ruled by another Saddam-like strongman and even then the odds were the place would break apart. Probably the spark that would set the country on fire would be one of the religious leaders getting assassinated. After the U.S. pullout no indigenous infantry could hold things together more than a month. The Kurds would demand autonomy which would tick off the Turks, the Shiites would hook up with Iran, and the Sunnis would make trouble any way they could. Put the three groups together without a tyrant to keep them in line and you'd have a real cluster f – – –. The only way to pacify the place was to apply the strategy Rome used against the Carthaginians and kill all the fighters, enslave everybody else, raze the cities, and sow the fields with salt. But if you did that in Iraq some other Middle Eastern groups would come in and soon start fighting over the salt. It was sad but true. Everyday I witnessed the situation I grew more depressed about the prospect of so many American GIs losing their lives in this lost cause. Not to mention all the Iraqi civilians that might still be alive if Saddam had been left in place. It was a cliché back home in those days that the Iraqis were far better off with Saddam toppled but, that only had a chance of being true for the ones that were still alive.

Every day in Al Amarah I was made aware that I was part of a foreign occupying wave even while I was being thanked for the rebuilding effort. Some casual remark by one of the crew at the compound or a jobsite would remind me that the combination of foreign invaders and an unelected government was eating away at the Iraqis even while they appreciated the help we were giving them. Muntajeb told me once that even an election, if it was held too soon, could make the situation worse. He thought the people were torn two ways, wanting the Americans out and wanting them to stay for fear of the blood bath that would follow their exit. But there was no way we were trusted or thought of as friends by the Iraqis. If I heard it said once I heard it a hundred times during my stay: "You people are biased toward Israel."

Yet during all the time I was in Al Amarah I never felt threatened by the fighting that was going on in other parts of the country. Our Salvation Army compound staff was made up of a total of seventeen employees and we always had four well armed guards looking out for us at all times. I felt no threat whatsoever to our operation or to us personally. But a meeting called by Major Isles just seventy-two hours before my departure date gave me some food for thought. He wanted to let the contractors know that we might be entering a new phase of the insurgency.

"Be on the lookout for masked men. The terrorists and the insurgents have established free reign. For some time now they've been targeting foreigners and Iraqis who work for foreigners in the north. But we're getting reports that the attacks will be getting more frequent and more brazen in the south. The same kind of threat; car bombings, mortar and rocket attacks, bombs hidden under trash or asphalt, in goat carcasses, in date palm logs, inside barrels."

Before Major Isles's meeting I'd realized things were getting a lot worse in Baghdad but he was warning us that Al Amarah might get to be a hot spot now that 2004 was upon us.

On the third of January I got called to meet, for the first time, with the governess of Maysan province. Iraq was divided into eighteen provinces and each one was led by a State Department appointee who was in charge of the military, the independent contractors, the volunteer organizations, and every aspect of the Coalition's project in country. It turned out that because I'd made a reputation for getting hospitals and water treatment plants put up quickly the governess wanted me to talk to a visiting rep from the World Health Organization and member of the European Parliament, Baroness Nicholson of Winterbourne. When I arrived at the British compound for the meeting I was surprised to see Ian Bentley among the knot of people seated around the governess's desk in her small office. A quick round of introductions told me that the others included the imposing baroness and three World Health Organization doctors. After I'd answered a lot of questions about the way I'd pushed the reconstruction work, the subject turned to the Bam earthquake. One of the doctors, a Pakistani man named Faruki who'd studied medicine in Minnesota, had been on site right after the disaster. He'd met Ian briefly in Bam and he was interested in the reporter's take on the situation. The governess and the countess wanted to hear about the relief effort too. Of course I was all ears myself. I wanted to find out what I'd missed by being denied entry into Iran. Doctor Faruki had flown into Tehran and come down to Bam by truck from the north. He gave us a short travelogue but didn't get into his sense of the relief effort. So I asked Ian what his trip from Iraq into Iran had been like.

"The drive from the border to Bam was fascinating. Or I should say the drive from the border to Kermn, which was the staging point for the relief operation. Such a contrast to Iraq. The cities we passed through like Fatahr and Yazd had clean streets and controlled traffic and there were no signs of destruction anywhere. And the countryside was lush and fertile with beautiful high mountains visible to the north."

I asked if it was difficult dealing with the Iranians on the trip in.

"Not a bit. One of the soldiers spoke a little English. I think the lieutenant at the border post must have ignored him on purpose when we were trying to communicate. Probably jealous of his ability speak the language a bit. But the soldier turned out to be a good bloke. Helped me get the story of the quake once we got to Bam."

Dr. Faruki began putting the tragedy in perspective for us.

"You know, ten times more people died in Bam than in the terrible World Trade Center disaster. We are accustomed to earthquakes in our part of the world. But occasionally there is one that defeats the imagination."

Ian Bentley agreed.

"When we pulled into Bam the sight was worse than any war zone I'd ever been in. The scene was filtered through a thick pall of smoke that gave no sign of abating. We could see hundreds of emergency vehicles, fire trucks and ambulances everywhere. A triage was set up in the center of the town expecting many injured but there were a lot fewer than expected because such an high percentage of those caught by the quake had died. The ambulances from outside the area didn't have to transport bodies to other cities because all the dead were being buried on site. The temperatures were near freezing and survivors were living on the streets or in cars or in buildings that were in danger of falling in around them at any moment. Some of the survivors had bonfires going in the streets to keep warm. The night with the wind blowing in from the mountains was brutally cold. We were told there could be up to 100,000 homeless. Every kind of disease threatened to spread. Rescuers were still searching for survivors but they were pulling very few out. And most of the ones that were rescued had injuries that probably doomed them."

Dr. Faruki took up the grim description of the situation.

"I was busy treating the survivors but I learned a lot about the situation nonetheless. I was told that the Iranians were appealing to the international community to send more searchers. The situation cried out for every volunteer that could be mustered. The stench from the dead clogged the nostrils. A mechanical digger was preparing mass graves. The victims who hadn't been buried yet were lined up in long rows on the ground. At one point I saw a line of dead babies."

That triggered a unwelcome remembrance for Ian.

"I saw those babies also. The sight made me retch and weep at the same time. I knew that the scene would give me nightmares for years to come. That was the point where I put aside my role as reporter and pitched in with the relief effort, distributing the blankets and wheat and rice and space heaters along with the Iranian soldiers. We were told that the death toll might hit 50,000. It looked like that was a real possibility, which would make Bam the biggest earthquake in history. The townspeople had just concluded three days of official mourning declared by the national government but there were still wailing women in black chadors and stunned old men walking aimlessly around or rooting through the rubble up to their knees. And scores of orphaned children crying and begging."

Dr, Faruki continued the grim narrative.

"Yes, the wave of weeping was unbearable. It seared my soul and I knew I'd never get it out of my mind. It looked as if three-quarters of the city was rubble and some of the collapsed buildings were still smoking. There was no water or gas or electricity and no latrines. The Red Crescent was distributing food from large caches and since there were so few survivors it seemed that no one would have to go hungry."

Then Ian again with some information that fascinated me.

"I was surprised when some of the International Red Cross personnel from Europe told me the quake had only hit 6.3 on the Richter Scale. The damage seemed to indicate something much stronger. But I soon learned the reason for the collapse of so many buildings. The Iranians were worse than the Iraqis at construction. They built with bricks made of crushed mud and it was a wonder the buildings could withstand a moderate rain shower, let alone an earthquake. And when a whole city like Bam collapsed the mud bricks would disintegrate so there would be few air pockets created to provide any breathing space for those trapped in the debris. Besides the initial destruction, it looked like the structures still standing would be hard pressed to make it through the wave of aftershocks that were shaking the city. People were being warned to stay out of the few buildings that were intact. We were told by the Iranian military that one of the buildings that had collapsed was a historic gem. The quake had brought down and completely destroyed the ancient Citadel near the center of the city. It was a 2000 year old fortress called Arg-e-Bam and up until a few days before it had been one of Iran's main tourist attractions. It had a place on the UN's Educational, Scientific, and Cultural registry of important sites. So sad to lose such a treasure."

I asked Dr. Faruki about the medical situation in the city.

"There were many complications. Nearly all of Bam's medical personnel had been killed in the quake. The nearest city with doctors and nurses was Kermn, which was a 100 miles to the southeast. There were not nearly enough doctors on hand but the shortage of relief workers was more disturbing. The Red Crescent was setting up hospitals but they were barely functioning by the time I had to leave, which was after three days. A U.N.

Disaster Management team from Tehran was due in shortly after I left. They would be bringing more blankets and supplies, including the high energy biscuits they always passed out in these situations."

Ian described the living arrangements at the site.

"We camped out and slept in the truck parked in the rubble during the two nights I was there. For some reason I never understood, we weren't allowed to set up the big Salvation Army tent we'd brought. The weather was freezing with a cold wind blowing in from the mountains to the north but I'd brought plenty of heavy underwear and a warm coat with me and we had a supply of Coleman heaters. What a challenge the relief workers were in for. It was clear that a true assessment of the need in Bam would take at least a week and I only had two days. I would have liked to stay for a week helping out but the Red Crescent was making it clear that this was their responsibility, that I should get back to London and file my report. They did manage to thank me for my help."

I said that Dr. Faruki's and Ian's descriptions brought back memories of my time searching the rubble at Ground Zero. The governess and the countess wanted to hear all about that experience and I obliged with a short recap. Ian put the Bam earthquake in perspective with the World Trade Center disaster.

"One difference, Sam, in Bam all the recovered bodies were intact. I don't know whether that would make the work there more tolerable or less so. There's a certain anonymity about body parts I imagine that might make dealing with them less traumatic. But I was never allowed to go near the bodies in Bam. Some sort of religious restriction. Non-Muslims are apparently proscribed from touching dead Muslims. I couldn't get near those that were being excavated and reburied. I watched the operation from the truck. The bodies were stacked like cord wood and lay in open trenches and quickly covered with bulldozed earth. And there were many open graves. But that actually made these matters worse. Some of the children hadn't died immediately and they suffered horribly before they did. Many of them died while their hearts were still pumping and their heads and limbs were swollen to three times their normal size. After three days in their crumbled homes the bodies of the victims were so scarred they were unrecognizable as humans when I watched them pulled from the debris. In the two days I was there the soldiers warned us again and again not to touch anything except the supplies we brought. The fear was that contamination from the exposed bodies would swell the death toll even further."

By the end of our conversation I was more disappointed than ever that I hadn't made it across the border into Iran. The situation in Bam was exactly the kind of thing I'd trained for all these recent years and I wished I'd been allowed to lend a hand to those poor souls who'd survived the quake only to realize they'd lost their families and their friends and their city. I made myself a promise that the next time that kind of need for assistance surfaced, I wouldn't let anything stop me from serving.

# TWENTY-THREE

Despite missing the opportunity to help out in the Iranian earthquake relief I was proud to have contributed to the rebuilding effort in Iraq and proud of what the U.S. government and a private relief agency had combined to do for the Iraqi people by the time I left. Hundreds of schools had been renovated and attendance was up above pre-war levels and the kids were getting immunized, and the ports were getting back in the business of receiving grain and other goods while they shipped out the oil that was the lifeblood of their economy. Most of the hospitals were reopened, there was more electric power than there'd been before the war and communications equipment was proliferating. The major cities were beginning to get sewer and water lines; oil was being pumped again when the pipelines weren't being blown up by terrorists and the insurgents, and the new Iraqi army was beginning to patrol the streets. That was the kind of progress you didn't see much news about back in the States on "lead with the bleed" TV. Of course I was heartbroken later by the insurgency's success in reversing so much of the progress I'd witnessed.

I was sure back then that in spite of all my pessimism about the future of Iraq that we'd put in too much effort to pull out. Too much blood had been shed to end the experiment in democracy even if I thought the chances of success were miniscule. At the same time this idea bothered me because it was the same one that had kept us in Vietnam way past the point of diminishing returns. At least the kids in the schools we'd built in Iraq, which we'd never done in Vietnam, should have a chance at a better life before the probably inevitable civil war breaks out. So I made up my mind to volunteer to come back to Iraq when I made my final report to Salvation Army headquarters in Washington.

I looked forward to a few more sixteen-hour days before I shipped out. The only rest I got during those times was a bit of a nap when I laid my head back in the car traveling from one part of the province to another to put in bids for new projects. Yet at the same time the sleep was fitful since I couldn't be sure what Muntajeb was thinking about. Apparently if he was going to see to it that I died in Iraq he'd see to it himself.

I'd been working sixteen hours a day seven days a week for five weeks now and loving nearly every minute of it. I hadn't had a drink in all that time except for the Christmas party and a rare snort with Major Isles. I must admit though that my thoughts drifted back to my Old Granddad back in the liquor cabinet at home every time something went wrong. But I managed to suppress the urge. By this stage of my deployment I'd only sworn on four or five occasions and it made me feel great to know I was not only using the construction skills my dad had taught me but the spiritual training from my mom too. That was testimony to the positive influence of the Salvation Army. If they could make me straighten up and fly right they could pretty well accomplish anything they wanted to. For sure if I ever got asked in the future by one of my wealthy friends what charity I'd recommend for a big donation there'd be no hesitation on my part to put in a persuasive word for the Army.

It was January 6th, and only two days were left before I was to head for Kuwait. Then there would be two days in Kuwait City for R & R. After that it was board a plane for London and then a day of debriefing before flying to Miami on the 9th. I couldn't wait to get home. Even though I pushed myself and told myself I wanted to stay and help the Iraqis recover, I really needed a long rest at this point. And my golf game was getting rustier by the day. I couldn't afford to look like a complete duffer with the big tournament coming up in a little over three months.

Things were beginning to get wound down by the seventh when we met the new team that would replace ours. The group consisted of two Brits and two Americans plus a guy from Amsterdam. They were as anxious as I'd been to start helping the Iraqis put their lives back together.

The eighth of the month arrived far more quickly than I'd ever thought it would. The time had passed in a flash and now I was packing for the trip to Kuwait and then on to London and Miami. The wee hours of the rainy morning were spent saying our goodbyes to Major Isles and Ian Bentley and the rest of the Brits at the base along with the safe house staff and the Iraqi office workers. We wished the new team the best of luck carrying on the work that we'd expanded during our time in country. By seven o'clock that morning Bill, Don, Karen, and I were ready to pile into the line of four Chevy Caprice sedans waiting outside the office door. By this time the insurgency was closing in on the area and I made a mental note that the Chevy's were rolling ducks since they didn't have reinforced windows or body armor. But they were the same cars that had brought us into Al Amarah six weeks earlier so there was no overwhelming worry that any harm would come to us on the way to the Kuwaiti border.

I was supposed to ride in the back seat of the lead Chevy driven by a big Iraqi driver named Karim with Muntajeb riding shotgun. In the car behind us were Bill and his replacement team leader and their driver and a guard. The replacement leader was to return to Al Amarah with the caravan after we reached the border. The third car held Karen and Don with their driver and a guard. The trailing Chevy held a driver and four guards with AK47s. The drive would take about five hours with one stop to check out the legendary Garden of Eden one more time before we left the country.

For about an hour we were tooling down divided, four-lane Highway 6, the infamous road of death, without incident. These sorts of caravans were always a thrill because of the eighty five to ninety mph speeds we had to maintain to avoid potential snipers or kidnappers. And today the roads were slick from the rain and strewn with patches of slippery mud. But now the scene was all peace and quiet, no need for our driver to scatter slower traffic like he usually did with horn blasts. There were just a few shepherds moving flocks on either side of the road.

We had just passed through Basra and Muntajeb and I were talking about the new replacement team members when we noticed a pickup truck clogging the fast lane about 200 yards ahead. Karim hit the horn but the truck driver gave no sign he was even thinking of moving over. Muntajeb got on his hand held walkie-talkie and told the drivers behind us that we were going to pass the pickup on its right but to stay alert since it was unusual for a slow moving vehicle in the fast lane not to yield to an oncoming car. Then he produced his nine-millimeter pistol in case of trouble. My first thought was that Muntajeb had finally arranged for my "accidental" death but there was no time to resist. As soon as he gave the word our driver made his move, veering into the right lane and closing fast on the truck. Just as the nose of the Chevy reached the back bumper of the pickup it accelerated and two Iraqis with their heads fully wrapped in scarves jumped up in the bed and trained AK47s on us. They apparently thought we would stop once they had us in their sights but Karim floored the Caprice because there was no way to stop quickly on that slippery road without doing a 180. Right then Muntajeb yelled something in Arabic through the walkie-talkie and I stole a quick glance out the rear view mirror and saw the rest of our caravan do an abrupt left turn over the median strip and head back toward Al Amarah. We roared around the truck on its right with the AK47 muzzles trained on our heads no more than 6 feet away. At the same time Karim hit the accelerator the guy driving the pickup did the same but his truck fishtailed in a muddy patch of highway and I heard the phtt, phtt, phtt of an AK47 discharge and bullets bouncing off the rear roof of our car. I leaned forward and grabbed Karim's shoulder and yelled, "Go! Go! Go!" But we were well by the shooters now and they'd be hard pressed to keep up in their little four-banger after they got it righted. The driver of the pickup didn't give up though. He tried to stay behind us though his truck was getting smaller and smaller as I watched it out the rear window.

Karim was all shook up and he kept yelling as he steered and floored the Chevy, "They fired at us! They fired at us!" Muntajeb said in a controlled voice, "Just keep driving and don't slow down." I tried to calm Karim by telling him he was doing just fine and he was because we were losing the pricks in the pickup fast. Not only that, they were stupidly trying to catch us instead of the other three cars that might get slowed down in the morning traffic that'd be building up around Al Amarah by now. Muntajeb got on the horn to them and told the others to keep driving north and to stop any military convoy they met and to give the brass a description of the pickup that was following us. It stayed far behind us for at least twenty minutes before it pulled off on a side road. Then Muntajeb lost contact with the rest of the convoy. So we were flying along the "Highway of Death" with no other cars in sight. The whole thing had happened so fast I didn't even have time to break a sweat. But then I started thinking about my Muntajeb suspicions and wondering whether I'd just escaped the plot to kill me I was always attributing to him. I didn't trust anybody in Iraq anymore anyway. Too much was happening what with the revved up insurgency.

I'd been shot at about twenty times in my life before that morning on Highway 6 in Iraq, but this one was the scariest time. To see the muzzle of that AK47 leveled at my head and to here the sound of the bullets hitting the car roof provided a never to be forgotten experience. Iraq in 2004 had to be the most dangerous place I've ever been. There were so many directions from which death could come at any moment. But I stayed calm throughout the experience because I knew I wasn't ready to check out yet. And to think I'd been saved on this morning by that awful Iraqi mud that I'd complained about so bitterly for six weeks. There must have been a lesson from God in that.

Once Muntajeb was certain we'd ditched the ambushers he had Karim pull off at an exit and drive to a small town police station. We all went inside and I heard a lot of excited talking in Arabic. Then a squad of policemen ran out and jumped in a van and headed for Highway 6. We followed back north in the Chevy in hopes of finding the insurgents and getting back in touch with the rest of our caravan. About half-an-hour later we'd found no sign of our attackers but we did spot the Salvation Army caravan cars on the side of the road next to a British military convoy. We all made reports and then rolled back south and crossed the Kuwaiti border without any more incidents. We even made the stop for that last look at the Garden of Eden. About a week before the shooting I'd been having doubts about ever coming back to Iraq but now I was more determined than ever to sign up for a longer tour of duty. I made up my mind to get back one way or another. I was sure the Salvation Army would supply my return ticket.

But I got word the next week that because of the shooting incident when I was leaving the country, the team that replaced ours was pulled out as part of a total withdrawal of Salvationists. And no Army volunteers have been assigned there since because of the beheadings and other atrocities that began just after I left. Far too dangerous. And guess who took over the Coalition reconstruction effort around Al Amarah? That's right, my old pal Muntajeb. The kingpin ! The Iraqi don ! Fugheddaboutit!

I thought about Iraq a lot after I got back to the States. Was it a good thing that Saddam got put out of power? Absolutely ! Would W's plan to bring democracy to the region work? Of course not. Establishing democracy in that part of the world would be like steering a loaded logging truck with bad brakes down Denali, with the whole mountain mined. Outside of Great Britain we were going it alone in Iraq. Or maybe outside of Tony Blair. The Poles had the third largest tally of troops over there and the Polish people were nearly ninety-percent against the war. It was true that there was no country on earth we couldn't smash without help from anybody. But there was also no country the size and complexity of Iraq we could put back together again alone. And of all the countries in the region Iraq was the Humpty Dumpty. The Sunni and the Shiites and the Kurds were just too volatile a mix.

And the more we failed to bring stability to the situation the more our position would go from bad to worse to apocalyptic. We might be making a few friends building schools and hospitals but we were making more enemies fighting the insurrection. A guerilla who opposes an invading army on his own soil isn't a terrorist, he's a resistance fighter. Just like I'd be and I hope you'd be too if the North Koreans invaded America to teach us their style of government. I might not have had as much education as those neocons in the White House but I could sure figure that one out. A while after I got back from over there I read an article in the *St. Petersburg Times* that quoted Lawrence of Arabia. The author of the piece, Rasid Khaladi, thought the quote applied to America's invasion of Iraq as much as it did to the British nearly a century earlier. And I couldn't have agreed with the *Times* reporter more in the context of the situation on the ground as I knew it from Ian Bentley's letters since I'd left the country. Old T.E. had said in 1920, "The people of England have been led in Mesopotamia into a trap from which it will be hard to escape with dignity and honor. They have been tricked into it by a steady withholding of information. The Baghdad communiqués are belated, insincere, and incomplete. Things have been far worse than we have been told, our administration were more bloody and inefficient than the public knows. It is a disgrace to our imperial record and may soon be too inflamed for any ordinary cure. We are today not far from a disaster. Our unfortunate troops, Indian and British, under hard conditions of climate and supply, are policing an immense area, paying dearly every day in lives for the willfully wrong policy of the civil administration in Baghdad …" File that one under, "The more things change the more they stay the same." Vietnam should have taught us that no modern war of occupation will ever be won. Suppose we killed all the insurgents in all the cities in Iraq and captured Bin Laden and Omar and al-Zarqawi. Would we then be able to say that democracy would flourish in the Arab world? Not a chance.

And when the Abu Ghraib prison scandal broke I was more convinced than ever that the Iraq occupation would end very badly. When I saw the pictures of the unthinkable abuse those prisoners suffered at the hands of American troops I wanted to throw up and cry at the same time. I'd never been more ashamed and fearful for the future of my country. I knew the troops were under terrific stress what with roadside blasts and suicide bombers to worry about. But there was no excuse for humiliating prisoners. For one thing, I knew from my own personal experience at the Managua Marriott that physical abuse doesn't necessarily induce information. And there was no danger of an enemy attack inside Abu Ghraib. After all the effort I'd given to convince the Iraqis I'd met and worked with that America had their best interests at heart, a few out-of-control pricks had probably undone all the good for their own perverted purposes. Or were they really out of control? I was one of those who suspected the torture wasn't random but resulted from orders further up the chain of command. I didn't buy the "few bad apples" explanation. Lots of bad apples fall off a rotting tree. Whenever the army faced a scandal the S.O.P. was to find some enlisted scapegoats to cover their commanding officers' potentially exposed butts. If investigators ever find out there was an order given by some big shot up the chain of command to use torture in Iraq or, for that matter at Gitmo or anywhere else, I'd like to have a few minutes alone with that person. I can still crush a windpipe with the best of them.

# TWENTY-FOUR

For the next six months, after I got back from Iraq, I kicked my training up another notch to get ready for the return trip west to fight forest fires and to be all set for any of the other disasters that were bound to come. I took some extra counterterrorism classroom work in St. Pete, some more Red Cross courses in Tampa, and some instruction in first aid with the Largo police department. But I also needed some personal time; something to burn off the energy I still had plenty of at age sixty-eight. I was still doing a lot of weight lifting, at least four times a week in fact, but that wasn't enough to keep me occupied. I wondered if there weren't some other sports activities I could take up. I think if you ask any former Olympian they'll tell you that they try to keep in shape and I was no exception. The Senior Games were beginning to peek my interest again, though I'd become bored with them a few years earlier. They were those events held in certain cities for older ex-jocks, hobbled has-beens who couldn't give up the competition though they weren't competitive in any real sense anymore. The events were usually broken down, pardon the expression, by age groups. For instance there would be a series of games for thirty-five to forty-year-olds and forty to forty-four-year olds and so on up to and including centenarians.

When I was a sophomore at Ohio State, in the fifties I was into several team and individual sports. It's impossible for a student these days to be so diversified, because when you sign a letter of intent to play a sport at a university now you have to concentrate on that one because of all the specialized training. My goal at the time was to make the Olympic diving team for the 1960 games. But I wasn't satisfied with the level of my performances. I was only rated number four in the country and the team that would be selected for Rome was made up of just two divers. So I also began concentrating on track and field events with the intention of competing in the decathlon. I wasn't good enough in the shot put, discus, or javelin so my chances of an Italian trip through that route were slim to none. What's more, most decathlon athletes weighed at least thirty pounds more than I did but if I bulked up to that size I'd be too big for the diving events. So I was between a rock and a hard place but thank goodness my diving improved so that by the time the choices were made for the Olympics I was ranked number one in the world.

Now forty years later I decided to start competing again. Melinda and I had just made a big land purchase, seventy-seven acres on the bayou in Seminole. We were set to put up 330 condos there but I was burnt out with the construction business. Besides, Melinda and the kids were doing a sensational job of running things so I felt free to try my hand at some personal needs. I set about constructing my own training track at the Seminole construction site. There was plenty of empty space there so I put in landing pits, discus and shot-put concrete pads and a javelin run. Then I really got into the training and started entering some events around the country for sixty-five to sixty-nine-year-olds. I also got into swimming as well as track and field meets and in just a few weeks I started winning, especially in swimming. Then I started competing in other sports like shooting and horseshoes and I twice entered the world championship trapshooting events in Vandalia outside Dayton. I was doing so well I was getting bored winning or coming in second so I needed something that would be more of a challenge. I started competing internationally but that didn't last long. I went to the International games in Bermuda and won nine gold medals in swimming and six silvers in track and field. I even participated in the World Senior Games in Utah and set two world records in triathlon relay but even that level of competition began to bore me. Back at Ohio State I'd been one of five athletes in the school's history to letter in four different sports, diving, track, gymnastics, and soccer. Now in my late sixties I was in the midst of a brief fling at perfecting some of those skills again. By the time of the Matt Hall golf tournament in May I was in my best shape in years. And my mental outlook got a boost when the second year of the tournament netted 55,000 dollars for our two charities.

✳ ✳ ✳

By the early summer of 2004 I'd perfected my storm and fire watch system. Every morning before dawn I'd check the weather and related condition reports Annie prepared the previous day from reading the right publications and web sites. Like the *National Fire News* put out by the National Emergency Fire Center and the *NIFC News* from the National Interagency Fire Center in Boise and the various regional fire intelligence reports. Then there was the daily scoop Annie got via email answers to my questions from NIIMS, which stands for National Interagency Incident Management Systems. The summaries told me how many fires were being fought all over the country and how many men and women were fighting them. I could even tell how much and what kind of equipment was involved in a particular fire. How many tanker trucks and helicopters and C-130s and CL-215s. Things were pretty quiet all over the country for awhile in the first half of 2004, especially in Alaska which was a place I'd had in the back of my mind ever since I'd passed through the state on my way to Korea for a diving meet years earlier. But back then I'd landed in the state at night and we took off two hours later still in darkness. From what I'd seen of its mountains and rivers and lakes in picture books and friend's photographs since then though, I knew I'd have to return some day. So after I got into firefighting I kept one eye tied to the top of the U.S. map in case God's secret scenario would call for me to play a scene up there.

I'd even boned up on the way a fire typically started up in the North Country. It was all related to the changes in the world's climate and mostly to the fact that we've warmed up a few degrees Celsius in the last quarter-century. That meant longer summers and warmer winters and earlier springs. In those earlier springs the top layer of still frozen tundra couldn't absorb the rains so they'd run off to the rivers like a downpour through a downspout. When the rains relented the soil dried out quick and left the tundra and the grasses exposed for longer periods to the sun and wind. That made most of the state a tinderbox waiting for a match to strike. When the right kind of wind condition came to pass all hell would break loose up there. It would usually start with millions of electrical volts from bolts of a hot summer day's lightning blackening the tundra. Some tiny wisps of smoke would rise from the earth and make way for a few flames that would join together and grow into grass fires that could turn thousands of acres of birch and black spruce and aspen into ashes in a matter of hours. And I'd been told by a friend who'd fought fires up in the state that conditions were so bad in western Alaska for the past couple of years that the folks up there talked about the "twenty-minute time lag." That meant that you could grab a hunk of moss off the ground and hold it in your open hand while you stood in the sun for twenty minutes and then squeeze and the moss would crumble to powder.

In the early 2004 fire season Annie's printouts only pointed to a small outbreak of five relatively minor flare ups in the no man's land of northeast Alaska around the famous pipeline. Those fires were being evaluated by the forestry people up there. Then just as July began one of Annie's morning reports alerted me to the fact that those five fires had multiplied a hundred-fold and now over a quarter of a million acres of the forty-ninth state were in flames and the fires were out of control. And to make matters even worse over 300 new fires had been ignited overnight. I went straight home to tell Melinda what was happening up north and that I had to get on the first flight Annie could arrange. Melinda rubbed the sleep out of her eyes and said she understood and that I should ask God to keep me safe. What a wife! We were supposed to entertain the family over the Fourth with a swimming party and a big buffet and then end the evening with about 500 dollars worth of fireworks. Now I wouldn't be there to help Melinda with the prepa-rations, yet she understood that I had to do my duty and even downplayed her disappointment with well wishes. Furthermore I'd left to fight fires in five different states over the past couple of years and Melinda always under-stood and encouraged me. Any other woman would've told me to go to blazes all right, but with a whole different tenor and tone.

At any rate on July 3rd I took a flight with more legs than a Broadway chorus line, from Tampa to Atlanta to Phoenix to Seattle and over the Aleu-tian Islands and the Bering Sea to Anchorage and then on to Fairbanks. That made for fourteen hours of flight time, not to mention the long lay-overs. By the time I got to the airport in Fairbanks late on the still sunlit night of the third I was stiff as a sequoia but the trip was far from over. Twelve of us firefighters from the lower forty-eight were plucked off the plane and packed into a van headed for the military base at Fort Wainwright north of Fairbanks. And then taken to the main office of the Alaska Fire Service where we were registered and issued some equipment and sent to our sleeping quarters. The next morning we got a Forest Service briefing so detailed I thought we'd get a diploma when it was over. We found out we'd be moving still further north 200 miles from the polar ice cap and the same distance from the Russian border. I was surprised to find out there were huge forests of fir and spruce that close to the pole. We'd be working sixteen hour shifts with eight off for R & R. But the briefer also filled us in on the state's flora and fauna and fed us facts about Alaska's geography and people. For instance we learned that only twenty-five percent of the state can be reached by road. And only thirty percent of the roads in that twenty-five percent are paved. The two ways to get to Juneau, the capitol, are by boat and plane. Or if you have an amphibious car. If you're in an ordinary car somewhere in the state and ask an Alaskan for directions to Juneau you'll get the same response the Maine guy gives the tourist in the old joke: "You can't get there from here." That's just one of the reasons why a high percentage of Alaskans, compared to people in other states, are licensed pilots. One out of every forty-five residents is qualified to fly. We learned from the briefer too that every year on a May morning the sun would rise and it wouldn't set for three months. No romantic candlelight dinners for a while. The briefer also told us that the state has the point furthest west in the U.S. at Kiska Island and the point furthest east at another island called Diomede that straddles the International Dateline. And that Point Barrow is the northernmost spot in the country. Besides that most of us were surprised to find out that Alaska has seventeen of the twenty highest mountain peaks in all of North and South America. In the next couple of weeks I'd see for myself how majestic and totally isolated some of that high country is.

After we'd been inundated with information, Barry, our briefer, began to bring us up to date on the particular places we'd be sent and what they were like and what we'd be taking there. If we didn't have sleeping bags and personal tents those would be provided; along with enough food for a week, and a supply of bug spray big enough to neutralize Mothra, the monster from the old Godzilla flick. We were told about the customs and habits of the Eskimos and other Native Peoples who lived in the state and that some of them would be fighting fires alongside us. We were told too to stay alert when we walked or worked in the assigned areas because they were all pierced with old vertical gold mines. If you weren't really careful you could easily fall into one and possibly be lost forever. Barry said to make sure if any of us met up with one of the mines to mark it with red ribbons to warn the others about it. In addition we were supposed to be aware of the bears in the area. There would be big browns and grizzlies galore in the mountains and polar bears in the far north. Then Barry broke the growing tension with a little levity. He said in Alaska they call a ground squirrel a "grizzly granola bar." That story was calculated to keep us a respectful distance from the big bears so we wouldn't wind up human haute cuisine. If the bears wouldn't cooperate and insisted on socializing with us there'd always be a "shooter" with a high-powered rifle standing by the crews while they worked. But the one encounter I had with Alaska's grizzlies gave me a thrill drained of danger. On one of my breaks I walked to a gorgeous spot above the banks of a rushing river and a couple of miles back from the containment lines. When I looked downstream in the dim distance I saw two big grizzlies, each gorging themselves, on three-foot long king salmon. It was a sight I'll never forget. You can see all the Discovery Channel specials on bears that were ever filmed and you'll never appreciate what it's like to sight one in the wild. Their size and the thickness of their shoulders and haunches beggar belief.

Anyway Barry brought the briefing to a close by reemphasizing the importance of safety on the containment lines. He repeated a caution I'd heard at other orientations the year before in the west. The old firefighter's saw went like this: "If you don't know don't go because it might blow." That meant to curb your curiosity in the back country and keep concentrated on your trenching or dumping or hosing. More than one firefighter had been lost by wondering off in the woods to check out the lay of the land. We were told too to "think outside the box," by which Barry meant to always put the wellbeing of fellow crew members first. That was the kind of advice every firefighting team I'd ever worked with put into practice. It made for the incredible comradeship I loved so much on the containment lines. It was the same feeling I'd got from fighting with a platoon of soldiers in Israel or Central America. Only out in the wilderness fighting fires there was no political ambiguity to pollute the purpose of the fight. And as my firefighting skills got better and better the highs I experienced matched the mountains where the battles were fought.

The camaraderie of the crews was most especially on display on those nights after tough times on the containment lines. The day of our, "think outside the box" briefing we put in a really stressful day. I'd been taken off animal rescue duty to join in what turned out to be a botched try at stopping a secondary blaze that ended in a temporary retreat. That night the need to cut the tension was intense. The men were exhausted and aching from their efforts but they knew the best medicine was to tell tall tales to each other as they lay in their tents. One of the Native People in the tent next to mine started on this night with a story I wouldn't forget because of where and how I heard it. It went like this:

"A fire chief came home one night and found his wife relaxing in bed. That wasn't unusual but the big burning cigar in the bedside ashtray was. So the chief says to his wife, 'Where did that cigar come from?' Right then a male voice from under the bed says 'Havana.'"

That started a string of stories told from tent to tent and I still remember them all. The butt of one was the longtime joke-suffering Poles.

"There was once a report that a two-seater airplane crashed in a Warsaw cemetery killing a couple aboard. The report also said the local fire department had already recovered 300 bodies and they were still digging."

And this one:

"A fireman climbs a ladder into the bedroom of a burning house and finds a gorgeous blonde in her bed. 'Ah', says the fireman. 'You're the third pregnant woman I've rescued this month.' "I'm not pregnant', the woman objects. But the fireman fires back 'You're not rescued yet.'"

The stories went on and on for about an hour till I told one so bad the session stopped on a dime. It was a groaner about the seismologist and the meteorologist and the fireman who were captured by terrorists. The night before they were supposed to be executed they agreed on an escape plan. They decided that when they were dragged one by one into the courtyard where they were to be put to death each one would yell something really loud to scare the executioners so bad they'd get totally confused and the prisoner could make a run for it. At dawn the terrorists dragged the seismologist into the courtyard and the executioner held a knife to his throat and asked, "Do you have any last words?" The seismologist screamed as loud as he could, "Earthquake!" and the terrorists ran in all directions while the seismologist hightailed it to the American embassy.

Once the terrorists realized they'd been tricked they regrouped and dragged the meteorologist into the courtyard and the executioner put a rope around his neck and asked, "Do you have any last words?" The meteorologist thunders, "Tornado!" and the terrorists scatter again while the weatherman lights out for the embassy.

Since there wasn't even a bit of a breeze the terrorist dopes finally figured out they'd been duped again. When they reassembled this time they dragged the fireman into the courtyard. The executioner put a pistol to the fireman's temple and asked, "Do you have any last words?" That's when the fireman yelled at the top of his lungs, "Fire!"

✳ ✳ ✳

The next day we were trying to stop a big blaze at Boundary. The fire we were fighting was part of the half-million acre inferno that was consuming some of Alaska's most valuable resources. The heat from the fire was so intense that big black spruce trees were exploding like Roman candles. When I saw them blow I remembered today was the Fourth, and back in Florida Melinda and the kids were probably swimming laps in the pool. What I wouldn't give for a dip right now. A little later the fire was getting closer and the heat was building and by my watch it was cocktail hour back home. Oh to be sitting by the pool and looking out at the Gulf with an Old Granddad and splash in one hand and my the other hand in Melinda's. That would be paradise, but in fact being almost anywhere else would beat Boundary, Alaska on a day like this. The trees were igniting so fast the forest sounded like a freight train. When I was an undergraduate at Ohio State I'd wanted to be a fighter pilot because I thought there was no more dangerous job on or above earth. But even in a war a fighter pilot in trouble could turn tail and haul ass out of harm's way at 500 miles an hour. Out here in no man's land I only had legs, not wings, and if the winds turned at the wrong time my crotch would be cooked and I couldn't do a thing about it. That made this mission all the more of an unforgettable rush.

And I loved the men and women on the crews. Half of them were either Eskimos from the coastal country or Ahatbasca Native People from the interior. Both groups shared a work ethic that wouldn't flag. The Eskimos stuffed their back packs with seal oil and dozens of dried fish both of which they needed for their diet. And since most of their lives were spent on the flat coastal terrain, working in the mountains was a big challenge. No matter what the situation or the conditions, they never complained. And they could fight a fire with the best smoke eaters in the world.

But the fires still raged out of control two weeks into my stay in Alaska. In fact when I left with a crew that was reassigned to Arizona, things were worse than ever in the north country. I hoped it wasn't because of me but when my plane had arrived in Fairbanks on the third of July there were a quarter-of-a-million acres aflame and when I boarded the bird that took me to the Southwest three-and-a-half million acres of Alaska were going up in smoke because the Boundary fire had linked up with the Wolf Creek fire to lick at forest land just 80 miles north of Fairbanks. When the two joined they created a hellish fire wall over 60 miles wide. That was the kind of frustration that the firefighter faces all the time. But for me the thrills and the service were totally fulfilling.

In Arizona two blazes called the Nuttal and the Gibson were burning out of control at the 9,000 foot level in the Coronado National Forest and they were threatening to melt the Mount Graham International Observatory's remote telescope site in the Pinaleno mountains. That was the place where an operations and logistics group offered crucial support services for astronomers. If the observatory was destroyed the work of the scientists there would need years to recover.

At our first briefing in Arizona we were told about the local Native American tribes and made aware of their customs so that we wouldn't violate their space. Even though we'd be working at very high elevations we'd have to be careful not to disturb the sacred shrines near the mountain peaks. Some of our crewmates would be from nearby reservations though. They could direct us away from any areas with religious significance. Up in the Arizona mountains the most ordinary looking pile of rocks could be an icon as important to a Indian as any Madonna in a cathedral to a Catholic. If you

got separated from one of the Indians you had to make sure the heap of
stones you were about to scatter was put there by God and not some sha-
man.

There were other things to be concerned about in the Arizona mountains. Instead of grizzlies you had to give a wide berth here to rattlers. They
could be coiled anywhere, so a misstep might be your last. And since a lot of
the trees and brush had been cleared by the fires there was always the danger
of massive rockslides. Of course the weather was far less friendly to firefighting
than in Alaska too.

Those Arizona fires of 2004 were almost fatal to twelve firefighters while
I was on site. They were fighting the flames from a secondary fire when the
wind shifted and they found themselves in the path of the main Gibson
blaze. All they could do was pull out their emergency fire shelters and let the
forest burn around them. Every firefighter has to carry one of these shelters
according to Forest Service regulations. Each shelter is a three-pound aluminum tent. When a fire is about to envelop your position and you don't have
time to make a run to safety, you have to pull out your shelter and climb in
fast. Firefighters practice doing this over and over. Each firefighter has to
have a dry bandanna with him at all times too. That's to tie around his
mouth just before he tears the protective case off the shelter and steps inside.
Then he uses his feet to stomp the four corners of the foil to spread the tent
and with his hands he grabs the roof corners and pulls to stretch them over
his back. Then he flops down like a turtle in his aluminum shell. Or more
like a beef roast on its way to the oven. In fact some firefighters call this
emergency routine the "shake and bake" because by the time the fire burns
its way past your position you're about prime to be served on a platter with
potatoes. The temperature inside the tent sometimes reaches between 140
and 200 degrees Fahrenheit. And that's despite the fact that the shelter's
aluminum coating reflects heat like a mirror reflects light. But you have to
remember that a big forest fire can generate around 1600 degrees.

The flames themselves aren't the greatest danger to the trapped firefighter.
The biggest threat comes from the hot toxic air. One accidental whiff of the
fire's superheated poisonous gases and a person could easily suffocate from
scorched air passages and lungs. More firefighters die that way than from
external burns. Even in smoke-filled situations less threatening than the one
that nearly killed the twelve crewmen in Arizona, there's plenty of danger.
The firefighter has to be trained to protect his lungs when any wind shift
sends smoke his way. The best method to protect yourself is to drop down
face first, preferably on a cleared patch of ground, and dig a hole to put your
face in. That's to take advantage of the six-inch layer of fresher and cooler air

that rises from the ground to form a buffer against the hot smoke. Once your face is buried in the hole you take short shallow breaths to try to keep your lungs clear. That way you can breathe in air as hot as 400 degrees for a short time, about twenty seconds at the most. When you can't stand the hole anymore you can try breathing into a bandanna but you have to make sure it's dry because water is a heat conductor. Breathing into a wet bandanna would actually increase the humidity around your mouth and damage your lungs faster and at a much lower temperature.

One Arizona night, around a campfire, during the attempt to contain the Nuttall and Gibson blazes I listened to a Native Person named Donald tell a true harrowing tale that involved the aluminum emergency shelters. The weather during the day had given us a break and we had time to mine our memories before the usual 10:00 P.M. dinner. Donald told about an experience fighting the famous 1988 fires in the northern Rockies close to Yellowstone. He began by calling the time "the year of the red skies." The wildfires were so many and so big there weren't enough trained responders in the whole country to resist. Whole forests and a number of ranches were lost in just a few disastrous weeks. One day Donald and his crew were just about to reach the crest of a hill on a blistering sun baked day in Montana when they all of a sudden heard the mountain roar and saw a huge wall of flame racing toward them. Retreating was out of the question and getting the shelters out from their forty-pound packs in an instant was iffy. But of course they all tried. Two men who were Donald's best friends couldn't get into their tents fast enough and they were incinerated. Another one was picked up with his shelter by the howling wind and blown like a kite a 100 yards downwind where he crashed into some rocks. Amazingly he only broke a few bones. A fourth man panicked when he saw the flames and heard the roarand had started dancing and singing lullabies. He got horribly burned, but survived to spend the rest of his days in a mental hospital. So that 1988 Montana experience taught Donald never to forget taking his turtle shell to the field. And to practice deploying it every chance he got.

Having watched his crewmates die like that had scarred his own soul for life. He said he'd never get over what he saw when he crawled out of his shell once the inferno had blasted past. There was nothing left of his friends but two blackened unrecognizable mounds of smoldering flesh. Try as he might after that he couldn't make his memory stop replaying the roar of that fire and the incredible heat it hatched and the sight of that incinerated flesh. In the years since then he'd heard scientific explanations of what happens to human flesh in the first second it's seared by the heat from a big forest fire. Eyelashes disintegrate and hair turns to brittle black ash. Three seconds later skin begins to blister and char. In another twenty-five seconds the firefighter's resistant clothing called Nomex bursts into flame because it's only designed to buy a little time to get into the aluminum shelter. Then the fire itself arrives, at a higher temperature than a blast furnace can generate. With a lot of luck the victim's bones will make it through the holocaust for burial. With less luck his family will have to accept the fact that their loved one endured Nature's cremation and thank God that they didn't have to witness the ceremony.

Listening to Donald's sad story that night on a desolate Arizona mountain ridge made me more determined than ever to take every precaution facing fires. But it didn't diminish in the least my dedication to helping fight them. And getting to know Donald around that campfire and learning about his lingering sense of loss made me more respectful than ever of Native Americans. The ones I'd met were such wonderful firefighters and such knowledgeable and likeable souls. Working with them over the past two years had freshened the lesson I'd luckily learned early on that the most mistreated minorities often produced the finest folks. But before I first learned that at the Rome Olympics I'd been the typical callous clod of a young guy who used the "N-word" and "kike" and "spic" and all the other ignorant epithets I'd picked up from my school buddies. But that changed with all the traveling I did later and especially during those years in the Middle East and Africa and Central America when I got to know some of their people personally. Travel is a great teacher if you take the time to learn about the lives that you touch, and that touch yours.

When the fire season began to wind down in the fall I went back to St. Petersburg to reconnect with Melinda and the kids. I spent the better part of the next month relaxing and playing golf with David and son-in-law Jeff. The business was still going great guns so there was no need for me to spend much time at the office. I checked in with Annie every day to make sure I wasn't missing any action out West. But I also asked her to make note of any internet references to animal rescue work that was going down anywhere in the country. This was a growing interest of mine. I'd always been a sucker for animals and especially those that were suffering. That threatened yearling at the Harkness Creek fire had stoked my curiosity about ways to help out animal welfare workers. But Annie's cyber surfing wasn't turning up any hot prospects, so I did some repairs on the beach house and a little work on the pool eased by dinner dates and dancing with Melinda until the end of July when I got called to head west to the fires again.

Two weeks into August one of Melinda's nightly phone calls to me on a Utah containment line broke the news that a hurricane was growing muscles in the Atlantic and making plans to flatten Florida in the next couple of days. As soon as I told Melinda I loved her and to stay safe I called Annie at her home and asked her to check the weather reports in the morning and to call me as soon as she'd interpreted them. I was wide awake four hours later when her call came through with word that the big storm was due to hit the mainland in forty-eight hours. And it seemed to be on a path to make landfall in our living room. It was classified as a Category Three hurricane which meant sustained winds of around 125 M.P.H. with ocean surges as high as 14 feet. Our place in Belleair Shore was perched only 60 feet back and just 6 feet above a sandy shoreline beach on the Gulf. The picture window in front might as well have had a sign painted on it "Wicked Weather Welcome." If the sea surge reached its potential it could clean the ceilings on our first floor. No wonder Melinda had seemed so nervous on the phone.

I called David and told him to pick up thirty sheets of three-quarter inch thick plywood and to meet me at the beach house the next day and grabbed a flight at the Salt Lake City airport. The big storm, now named Hurricane Charlie, wasn't due to hit for another twenty-four hours so I knew there was plenty of time for the two of us to batten down the hatches. When I got to the house at two in the afternoon David had already started pounding the plywood in place and after we finished the job on the doors and windows together we moved inland across the inlet to our condo on higher ground and joined Melinda to wait out the wind. But the brunt of the blast did an abrupt turn east away from the Tampa Bay area and headed for Port Charlotte and Punta Gorda. By now Charlie was upgraded to Category Four fury with winds clocked at 145 M.P.H. When word came from the local TV channel that it had hit just 90 miles from where we were huddled I said a silent prayer for the people in its path.

Early the next morning, while I was taking down the last of the plywood pieces from the front of the beach house Melinda ran outside with the terrible news. Hundreds of people were still missing in Port Charlotte and Punta Gorda. The towns were both twisted beyond recognition. Without another word Melinda went back inside to start packing my clothes and I ran upstairs to assemble my gear. It was a drill the two of us had been through well over a dozen times by now. In fact by this time I kept my equipment at the ready in a corner of our bedroom at all times.

As I drove southeast toward Punta Gorda I reran in my mind all the tragedies and aftermaths of disasters I'd witnessed in the past few years. By my quick count this was my tenth hurricane. And then there was Ground Zero. And the earthquakes in Mexico and Iran and the mudslides in Honduras and all those forest fires and the war in Iraq. It was enough to test my trust in God's goodness. But the doubt didn't last long. That was because I made myself think instead of Melinda and my kids and the beauty of those western mountains and all the wonderful people I'd got to know along the way. God gave with one hand and sometimes took away with the other. But the balance was always for the best because whatever the fate it was better to have been here on this earth than not.

The night before, though, God had written on the wrong side of the ledger. Damn ! Now it was a Category Four. Thousands of people homeless. Left with nothing. Hundreds of the sick and the frail worse off than the others. And the elderly. Florida was full of them and now the ones around Port Charlotte and the ones in Punta Gorda, where I was headed, would be without power or telephones or food or water. Probably without a roof over their heads. Hospitals would be without services too. Just like that time in Homestead when Andrew barreled through and leveled it. I remembered how disorganized things had been down there when I'd volunteered to help in the cleanup. I prayed for the last 50 miles of the drive to Punta Gorda that the relief agencies were better prepared for Charlie than they were for Andrew.

When I got into town I found out my prayers had hit their target. Sure the place was physically ravaged, just like I thought it would be. But at the command center set up at the local airport, Charlotte County's Emergency Management Director Wayne Sallade told a bunch of us volunteers that his folks had spent years prepping for just such a situation. That really seemed to be the case. Shelters were already sprouting and searches were underway for victims and hundreds of utility trucks with full crews from all over the U. S. were tooling toward the area. Not to mention the string of semis full of supplies streaming in. Of course it would take weeks to get power and sanitation and water to all the poor people who were dispossessed. But help was on the way faster than most of them probably thought was possible I was really impressed with what Sallade had already accomplished.

And the president and brother Jeb were touring through the whole of Charlotte County to show Floridians and the rest of the country how much they cared. Even if they did have politics in the back or maybe even the front of their minds it was important at a time like this to show support. That was another big difference from Hurricane Andrew. Back then W's father was way too slow to react to the tragedy and got hammered for his Bush league performance. Even though part of the problem back then had been the governor at the time who waited three full days before declaring a disaster. But senior's sons weren't about to make the same mistake. W earned high marks from me for what he said about Charlie, "Out of these catastrophes, the sprit of America shines, and that spirit is neighbor helping neighbor." That was the absolute truth. I'd been so proud of my countrymen and countrywomen during all the draining dramas I'd seen them put through. No matter how much they suffered they kept their spirits up and always thought of ways to help their friends and neighbors do the same.

To get back to the relief effort, everything that could be done was being done and it was being done fast. There were aid stations springing up all over the county offering everything from cold drinks to hot showers. So many garbage trucks on the move they barely avoided colliding with each other. Debris removal crews on the job picking up pieces of houses blown into neighbors' yards or down the street. Workers firing up wood grinding machines to pulverize downed palm trees. There were tent hospitals dispensing medicine and treatment. Schools were getting a lot of attention so they could reopen in the next couple of weeks. All the major roads were already clear and workers were sweating up a storm sweeping and jettisoning junk from pedestrian walkways. There were even hotlines set up to make loans to hard hit homeowners. Red Cross and Salvation Army volunteers were swarming into the neighborhoods putting up distribution centers full of food and supplies. Curfews were in force and National Guard troops were taking to the streets to discourage the latent looters. Sheriffs' deputies, by the hundreds, were arriving from all over the state and country to maintain law and order and cordon off areas for logistical purposes. Plus direct traffic since very few of the lights at intersections were working. That reminded me of the good old days in Iraq.

When I got into town the morning briefing at the Incident Command Center was still a couple of hours away but the place was already alive with activity that had begun the night before. As soon as I flashed my Red Cross badge I was pressed into action. Well, maybe delivering doughnuts doesn't amount to "action." But it seemed that all the official vehicles were tied up at the time and I had a full tank of gas so I volunteered to take fifteen dozen dunkers to a fire department staging area near the city auditorium. Getting there told me something about the degree of devastation. Hunks of houses were still strewn in some streets and the sharp objects sprinkled from curb to curb were a menace to my Michelins. But the firemen got their sinkers and an hour later I was back at the ICP in time for the morning briefing.

At the briefing the Incident Commander announced the agenda and ended with the words I wanted to hear. I'd already seen that there were plenty of relief workers on the scene, thanks to the months of preparation. And I was looking to volunteer in that other area I was so interested in. Sallade announced that the Charlotte County Animal Control Center was set up in emergency quarters and they were looking for help, I had my cue. I drove over there and asked what I could do to pitch in. The man in charge looked at me like I was even older than I was and asked if I wanted to keep some records for the Center. When I told him I'd been fighting forest fires in the west and rounding up animals for the Forest Service he didn't seem to believe me. Luckily I'd thought to bring a bunch of photographs with me for just such a slight. When I showed them to him he kept looking at my face in the pictures and comparing it with the one in front of him till he finally gave up and said, "Damn ! We need you!"

For four days after that I shared an unbelievable work load with ten other staff members and we coordinated with the Charlotte County Animal Control people and with local and national reps from the Humane Society. We only had seven vans so we were always scrounging up wheels to make rescues of stray and injured animals. In fact it got so hectic during that time some of us had to move out of the main emergency center and set up a satellite with trailers and tents in a sports complex parking lot. Then we had to add a couple of extra vet centers with operating theaters. And several more trailers to use as holding pens, plus a bunch of dog and cat handlers to feed and exercise the rescued animals and give them medicine.

I was lucky enough to get partnered with a twenty-seven-year old Animal Control Officer named Kerri Hostetter. As young as she was she knew animals better than anybody I'd ever met. It seemed like she could psych out the personality of every kind of critter from a gerbil to a giraffe at a 100 paces. Besides that I didn't need a Seeing Eye dog to tell she looked a whole lot cuter in shorts than that TV crocodile guy did. Anyway Kerri and I were detailed to crisscross the county rounding up lost and wandering pets plus all sorts of other animals for transport back to the sports complex. We got to be friends fast and when I found out her emergency call sign was 706 I told her I'd make mine 706 2. So that's what we called each other from then on.

There was so much work to be done that we had to set priorities. Animals were at risk or posed risks to residents all over the county. The first thing that had to be done was gassing up the vans, but when it became clear that nobody had any cash I paid for it, I contributed a couple of hundred bucks to set up a kitty. Another thing that had to be done right away was to check up on all the registered venomous snakes in the county to make sure they weren't slithering in the streets. But that would cost a lot of shoe leather when it wasn't clear whether a single snake had left its lodgings. On the other hand there were plenty of cats and dogs in distress so we spent the morning looking for them and left the snake handling to the National Guard.

Later that first day in Punta Gorda half a herd of cattle broke through a farmer's fence and started straying onto the city's streets. Kerri and I got the call to join two other extremely good-looking blonde female Animal Control officers for the roundup. The four of us soon found ourselves on foot following about twenty Bossies through the city and urging them toward a temporary holding pen set up on a meticulously manicured baseball diamond. We were shouting and rapping bovine behinds for five or six blocks till we convinced the cows to mosey on over to their temporary quarters. We must have looked like a promo for a new western starring Cameron Diaz, Paris Hilton, Jessica Simpson—and Don Knotts. After we got the cattle corralled behind barbed wire we set up a big water tank for them with plenty of straw nearby so they could sack out. Then we arranged to have a fire truck fill the tank twice a day and got Animal Control to rev up a crew to make regular hay deliveries. Once the case of the meandering milkers was solved we went back to the sports complex for our next assignment. I never got a chance to go back to the diamond to see if the county ever managed to coax those cows back home and away from that yummy centerfield grass they were grazing when we left them.

The next morning I was standing in the lot at the command post waiting for Kerri to come out of the headquarters trailer with our new instructions when I got a slight surprise. A photographer from the *St. Petersburg Times* tapped me on the shoulder and asked if he could tag along with me all day and take some pictures of the animal control efforts. The surprise was slight since I'd got a call earlier from a *Times* reporter who'd heard about my fire fighting and animal rescues in the west and wanted to do a story. I was just getting acquainted with the photographer whose name was Jamie when all of a sudden Kerri ran out of the trailer and yelled, "Sam get in the truck we've got a mad dog to catch." On the way to the truck I shouted to Jamie, "There's only room for two in the truck. See if you can keep up." Kerri was already behind the wheel when I jumped into the passenger seat and we sped off with Jamie's van in hot pursuit. We flew through the city streets with red lights spinning and alarm horn blasting away and we were passing cars and trucks like they were standing still. All this time Kerri was filling me in on what to expect when we got to wherever it was we were going. She said Sheriff's deputies were checking on an elderly man whose neighbors were worried about him but nobody could get near his house because a huge white German Shepherd in the doorway was in a bad mood. When we pulled up in front of the house with Jamie's van nosed in behind ours one of the deputies called out that the dog was still barring the way and might have to be put down. Those were words I always hated to hear and I hoped they were mistaken in this case.

When we got to the porch Kerri said something soft I couldn't make out and the shepherd retreated into the house. Then I went in followed by Kerri and one of the big bruisers from the Dade County Sheriff's office. I chased the dog into a back bedroom where he made his stand barking and baring his teeth. But when I got my pole positioned and dropped the loop over his head and tightened the noose he suddenly went all whimpery and started licking my hand. Ferocious dog my Aunt Fannie ! Kerri reached out and petted him while she checked his ID tag. It turned out he had a name to give mailmen nightmares and strike fear into the heart of the South's most virile sheriffs' deputies—"Snowflake." Jamie arrived in the back bedroom just in time to get a couple of flattering shots of the beautiful shepherd.

Meanwhile the deputies made a quick search for the dog's owner but there was no one in the house. Then they called for a K-9 unit with bloodhounds to scour the neighborhood for the old man. I asked them to have the murky water in the backyard swimming pool pumped out since heat exhaustion was running rampant in Punta Gorda and there was always the chance that the homeowner had drowned trying to swim off the sweat or maybe he'd just fallen in. I never did find out whether Snowflake's owner was found so I still say a prayer for him to this day. But Kerri and I took his shepherd with us back to the command post and the last I saw of him he was making love to a boxer bitch in a big holding pen.

Just before I'd got to Punta Gorda a couple had come to the command center and asked Kerri to look for another "mad dog." The woman was limping on a bandaged leg and she said she'd been bitten by a big black mongrel. Kerri had spent a couple of hours looking for it in one likely neighborhood while two deputies took the woman with them to check another area. Then Kerri got a report that the deputies had spotted the canine criminal as ID'd by the bitten woman. It was a black Lab mix running loose with two other smaller dogs so, and this is the part I couldn't believe, one of the deputies shot it in the chest. The slug slowed the big dog down but the wound wasn't bad enough to stop it from escaping. Then a little later the same woman called back and said the dog that bit her was in her front yard terrorizing her again and now her neighbors too. So the deputies were dispatched to the woman's house to deal with what turned out to be a Rottweiler. When I heard the story I was livid. Not only had the idiot woman fingered the wrong dog but the damned trigger-happy deputy had wounded an innocent animal. I couldn't see straight. I wanted to bring charges against the woman but the first order of business was to find the wounded dog and if he was still alive get him to a vet. Kerri was upset too so she said we should start looking for the Lab right away.

We got in the truck and started combing the neighborhood where the Lab was last seen. On a side street half-an-hour later a call came over the intercom from another animal patrol saying a big black Lab mix had been spotted running with two smaller dogs and then lost sight of. We drove over to the neighborhood where the dog was spotted but an hour's search bought us zilch. I wanted to keep looking because I felt so sorry for the dog. He was wandering around out there probably in a lot of pain and even if he had bitten the woman, which he obviously hadn't, you couldn't blame a wounded animal for its instincts. But just then we got called by the Command Center to round up a couple of loose horses and it was two hours later before I had time to think about the black Lab. I wanted to find him right away and get him help but it was dark now and the chances of doing that at night were nil. So I slipped into my sleeping bag on the hard Command Center floor and did a lot of tossing and turning till morning.

Bright and early the next day I asked Sgt. Katzman, who was the woman in charge of the Command Center's vans, if she could get some information that would help Kerri and me find the wounded dog. She had a handle on what was going on in all the neighborhoods and might be able to scrounge up some helpful scoop. I couldn't be sure of course that the dog we were trying to find the day before was the same wounded animal I was so concerned about but both Kerri and I had a feeling it was. I wanted Sgt. Katzman to make some calls to people in the part of town we'd searched to see if she could come up with any clues. She said she'd try and an hour later she called us on the mobile phone to say she thought she knew where the dog might be and that we should pick her up at the Command Center right away. Pretty soon the three of us were on our way to an address supplied by a man from the neighborhood who said someone in a trailer on a dead end road had a big black dog that was very mean. He'd seen it running around the day before with two other dogs and it looked injured so we were pretty sure we would at least soon find the owner of the gang of three.

Half-an-hour later we were on a lonely dirt road with corn fields on either side and in one of them we found a small dilapidated trailer. And next to it a battered wooden board that signaled the right property number. When we got out of the truck and went to the trailer door we found out that nobody was home because there was a big concrete block jammed up against it. But we could hear a lot of barking on the other side of the door. We had our capture and restrain poles with us so I put mine in my left hand and moved the block and pushed the broken-locked door open with my right. I'll never forget the putrid smell of dog shit and piss that hit me in the face just then. I almost barfed but the three dogs were barking and snarling so I motioned to the women that I'd try to lasso what was obviously a big black Lab mix. We'd have to think about the smaller dogs later since they were faster and tougher targets. Right now they were hiding under a couple of smelly torn leather chairs. We couldn't waste time trying to catch them anyway because the Lab needed treatment for his wound as soon as we could get him to a vet. As I shoved wobbly tables and rickety chairs aside I kept slipping in dog shit and piss and trying not to throw up. I could see the wound on the big dog low on his chest just above his left front leg. There was no way to tell whether any of the dogs were rabid but the filth in the trailer wasn't a reassuring sign.

The two smaller dogs kept up a barking and snarling racket under the chairs while the big Lab was leading me on a circular chase around the room. Kerri and Sgt. Katzman couldn't get at the smaller dogs so they lowered their catch poles and concentrated on coaching my efforts. One of them said, "Easy Sam. Take your time." That was good advice but I was so frankly freaked by the prospect of getting nipped by the wounded and possibly rabid Lab that I kept making what the dog had to think were hostile approaches. At one point in the slippery going I went down on all fours but the Lab gave me a pass and an opening by moving into a dark corner. I didn't want to risk trying to stand up since the Lab was finally trapped so I crawled through the shit and piss and managed to get the loop over his neck from a prone position. Then I got to my feet and dragged my catch flailing and barking outside. Kerri and Sgt. Katzman re-closed and re-blocked the trailer door on the two smaller dogs. They also posted a legal notice on the door for the owners. Then we took a minute to check out the Lab. He was actually a beautiful dog or he would have been if he weren't caked with shit and soaked in piss. And the funny thing was that once he was outside he was as subdued as Snowflake had been when we grabbed him. He was letting Kerri and me pet him and hug him and he even licked my hand a couple of times. I led him over to the van and gave him some crackers that were lying in the front seat and he scarfed them down like they were fresh baked by Emeril with help from Rachael Ray. The big dog seemed glad that somebody was finally paying some friendly attention to him. Once we had him loaded in the van and ready to roll a woman from a trailer up the road came by and said she hadn't seen the animals' owner for a week. At that point I blurted out, "If you see him tell him he's in trouble." But Kerri had other ideas, "Don't tell him he's in trouble. Tell him to contact Animal Control." That was way too gentle for my taste. I wanted to put the fear of God into the prick but when I cooled down I had to admit Kerri's way of dealing with the situation was more likely to gain the creep's cooperation.

The next move was to get back to the Command Center to report our capture and then put in a call to a vet so the big Lab could get his wound treated. It didn't seem to be bothering him too much since he wasn't whimpering and his appetite sure wasn't suppressed. He didn't make any objection when I wrestled all 60 pounds of him into the van's cargo compartment and he made himself as comfortable as possible back there by lying down on the warm metal. All during the ride back to the Command Center I was seething about the trailer trash that owned the dogs and kept them in such horrible conditions. I was even madder at the bozo deputy though. The one who'd put a bullet in this beautiful animal like it was some four-legged terrorist. Not only that but he was a lousy shot to boot. He had to know that animal control people are taught to shoot only as a last resort and to always go for the head. If I'd been able to get a wire loop around the trigger happy sap of a deputy's neck I would've tightened it till he learned his lesson in law enforcement. Over the past couple of years I'd witnessed a lot of the round-the clock pressure law enforcement was under in these kinds of post-disaster situations and usually the first stress cracks started to show up on the fifth or sixth day after the event. Then it was normal for a few unwise decisions to be taken where officers or relief workers were too quick or too slow to act. We weren't even through the third day in Punta Gorda so there was no excuse for the deputy's dumb decision.

Just before we got back to the Command Center I told the women that I really felt for the dog I'd now named Black Beauty and that I wanted him to get the best treatment for his wound that money could buy. My sympathy always went out to animals that were mistreated and this was one of the worst cases of neglect and abuse I'd ever seen. I wanted to see to it that Black Beauty got some compensation for his suffering. So when Kerri, Sgt. Katzman, and I asked at the Command Center who the best vet in the area would be we were directed to a lady with a great reputation in Port Charlotte. Naturally I insisted we take Black Beauty over there for treatment as soon as we got him cleaned up. Kerri made a call to be sure the vet had her electric power restored. She did, so we left Sgt. Katzman to her motor pool work and headed for Port Charlotte. The vet met us at the door to her clinic and I carried Black Beauty into the examining room. He wasn't able to put his full weight on his left front foot and that told me the chase he'd led me on back at the trailer was fueled by pure adrenaline.

The vet said she'd have to sterilize the dog's wound but that she wouldn't use sutures because she wanted it to seep. She told me to hold the dog down during the procedure. Black Beauty was being as brave as he could be in his strange surroundings and he nuzzled his face against my chest as soon as

Kerri got a muzzle laced over his mouth. Then the vet began the exam. Right away she found an exit hole the bullet had made and that was good news. And there didn't seem to be any damage to the chest or leg bones. So it looked like all that needed to be done was to wash the wound and sew it up. But that could be a tough job if Black Beauty didn't play along. That's why the vet asked me to lay down on top of the dog to comfort and restrain him at the same time. When I was positioned over the him the vet applied the first antiseptic swab and Black Beauty let loose with a soul-searing yelp. I looked over at Kerri and I could see tears in her eyes and I felt my own filling. All I could say to try to ease the pain was, "It's O.K. big boy. I'm here for you." It took the doc about ten minutes to clean and sew the wound and I was really impressed with her work. When she'd finished putting a cast on Black Beauty's leg to help him stand and walk Kerri and I took the dog back to Punta Gorda to be quarantined. That was required procedure since we still weren't sure if Black Beauty was rabid.

Before Kerri and I went back to the Command Center I told the vet at the quarantine facility that once Black Beauty was certified to be rabies free I wanted him to get the best treatment money could buy and that I would pay for it. The truth was that I'd fallen in love with that dog and if I could have thought of a way to take care of him while I was flitting around the country fighting fires I'd have taken him with me. Black Beauty would become famous through the article about my volunteering in the *St. Petersburg Times* and get a new home and a new name, Bullet.

That night I drove into town for dinner at one of the open restaurants in an area that still had power. When I was seated and served I thought over the day's developments. Saving Black Beauty made me feel really good inside. That and the thick steak I was putting away. What with the food and my satisfaction, my anger toward the dog-shooting deputy melted a little and I decided to forgive him even though I still intended to report him. All that forgiveness made me start to feel mellow. About that time Kerri came into the restaurant and sat down with me. She was in a better mood too and she began telling me about some amusing things that happened to her in her five years on the job. That got me searching for stories to trade but most of the ones I'd heard lately fighting forest fires were a little too raunchy so I settled for a verbal rerun of my favorite scene from a Peter Sellers movie since it related to our experiences that day. I mean the one where Inspector Clouseau is standing in a hotel lobby and sees a cute little mutt begging for attention. The intrepid inspector wants to pet the pooch but his steel trap detective's mind tells him to check out its personality first. So he asks the guy behind the reception desk, "Does your dog bite?" To which the guy answers, "No." Then Clouseau puts his hand down to pet the dog which proceeds to tear it to shreds. When Clouseau recovers from the shock and awe he says to the guy behind the desk, "I thought you said your dog doesn't bite." And the guy says, "That's not my dog." Of course telling the story reminded me of that damned woman who'd got Black Beauty shot because she couldn't tell a Chihuahua from a Chow Chow and my mellow mood evaporated so I said goodbye to Kerri and went back to the Command Center to try to get some sleep.

The next morning which was my last in Punta Gorda I attended the 7:00 A.M. briefing with a 100 or so other relief workers listening to Wayne Sallade. He was calling on the reps of different agencies for reports on yesterday's progress. I was sitting in the back of the room taking notes on what was said by the people from FEMA and the Sheriff's office and the National Guard and Animal Control and the utility companies. But then Sallade called on the Red Cross and repeated the call two or three times without anybody standing up to report. Everybody was looking around the room for the rep and right away some of them zoomed in on me because I had on my agency shirt with a left pocket logo that screamed in bold block letters "American Red Cross." About that time I wanted to burrow through the fake oak floor since public speaking, to say the least, was never my strong suit. I wouldn't waste a second thought before I'd volunteer to wear a gasoline suit through licking flames for a good cause but addressing a crowd turned my joints to jam.

My face probably showed every shade of red when Sallade began berating the agency for not having a rep in the room. He was getting more and more ticked off and finally just fumed without a word while the whole crowd hushed till you could hear a Red Cross pin drop. After around sixty seconds of silence Sallade glanced my way and for the first time noticed my incriminating shirt. Then he said in a sarcastic tone, "Oh good. There's somebody here from the Red Cross after all. Let's have your report Mr. Hall." I nearly creamed my jeans when he said that but I managed to get to my feet forced to speak for the agency. I apologized for the rep's absence and explained I was working with Animal Control and didn't have a handle on the macro state of affairs. I said I did know though that the agency was out en masse establishing aid stations all over the county and that the rep, like the other Red Cross volunteers, probably hadn't slept for thirty-six hours. I said they were all still going strong though and that the rep would probably be here soon to make a report.

Sallade seemed satisfied and said, "O.K., let's hear from the Salvation Army. Salvation Army, are you in the room?" No response. Now plenty of eye pairs were locked on me again because some of the people in the room knew I'd just got back from Iraq working for the Salvationists. I was afraid I was going to have to give another unauthorized spiel, but the Salvation Army report was the last one on the agenda so Sallade ended the meeting without it. He wished everybody good luck and said he hoped there'd be a lot of progress to report next time we met.

After the meeting I was standing in the back of the room criticizing myself because in the throes of having to improvise for the Red Cross I'd forgotten the two points I'd wanted make on my own. One of the doctors who'd volunteered to help in the hurricane aftermath approached me looking friendly and said, "Sam that was a damn good report. What are you looking so upset about?" He obviously thought I was stewing over getting chewed out on behalf of the Red Cross so I had to set him straight. The doctor asked what my unexpressed important points were and when I told him he said to follow him so I did and he led me into a room where eight men were standing and looking at a map of Charlotte County. Among the eight were Sallade's assistant director and reps from the National Guard and the Sheriff's office. The doctor pulled the assistant director and the sheriff's rep aside and said, "You boys have got to hear this. Go ahead, Sam, tell him what you just told me." So I launched into my first point while I held up a plastic bag full of housing insulation. I told them that the stuff was blown all over the county and that they needed to put out an all points warning people to clear their yards and pastures. That was because insulation was lethal if it was ingested. If some toddler or an animal happened to swallow it the stuff would act like razor blades on the lining of their stomachs and block their digestive systems. To seal the sale I told the men about a farmer back in Ohio. He'd had nine horses when a tornado came roaring through the valley and ripped his barn to shreds. But he counted his blessings because all his horses survived. Then in about a week they all started getting sick and dying off one by one. When he finally got a horse to the vet for testing all the others were dead or dying. The vet decided to operate and when he cut the surviving horse open he found a hunk of insulation hung up in its intestines. The insulation was all over the farmer's fields because it was blown there from the nearby town by the tornado. My story made quite an impression and the assistant director said he'd get a bulletin out right away. In fact, he directed one of his assistants who was standing nearby to get the message out pronto.

Then I made my second point which was about that deputy who'd ignored the first rule for putting down an animal—"Never a body shot. Always a head shot." The Sheriff's rep was almost as livid as I'd been and said he'd look into the incident right away. He said he was proud of the training his men got and that any incident like the one I'd described was a blot on the reputation of his department and he wouldn't stand for it. He shook my hand and said how sorry he was about the dog and that he'd tell his troops the story as soon as he could. So I considered my points well taken and before I left the building I made sure to thank the doctor for running interference for me.

Later that morning Jamie the photographer drove me out to the trashy trailer where we'd found Black Beauty and his run mates. The small dogs were yapping inside. And it was obvious the owners hadn't been back because the warrant was still sticking in the door jamb. That saved me from savaging them in person but I had Jamie take some pictures of the place so I could bring charges against them later, which I did. We poured the water we had with us for the poor dogs who were still stuck with the living conditions the two women and I had left them in. We couldn't take them back to the Command Post at this point because we had Jamie's car. Kerri had already made arrangements for the two dogs to be taken from the owner. Just as Jamie and I were leaving a little tan kitten tiptoed out from under a chair and voiced a pathetic purr. Somehow in all the confusion of trying to round up the dogs the day before we'd missed the little guy. Jamie picked him up and petted him all the way back to the Command Center. Kerri was there and I gave her 300 dollars to spend seeing to it that the kitten we named "Kit" and Snowflake and Black Beauty and his two anonymous friends back at the trailer got all the medical attention they needed. Then I said goodbye and gathered up my gear for the return drive to St. Petersburg. I had to get back there soon or miss the Olympics on TV. Ever since Rome I'd seen every diving competition and all the other events I could lay my eyes on and I didn't want the 2004 games to be the exception. And I had another major charity golf tournament to host later in the month too.

# TWENTY-FIVE

At one point during a break in the Olympic coverage I was working on the beach house roof and soaking up the sun when a female pool service worker came by do some maintenance. But before she got started she told me she'd heard about my work in hurricane relief and wanted to talk to me about it. I said sure and told her a few of the stories about rescuing animals. Half-an-hour later, after she'd finished cleaning the pool, she handed me a twenty-dollar bill and said, "Please see that this gets to somebody who needs it in Punta Gorda." I was really moved by her gesture and told her I'd do what she'd asked. The minute she left though I went right in to my office and wrote a letter to her boss and told him to give her a fifty-dollar bonus for her pool job and to bill me for it. I couldn't let the woman's thoughtful gesture go unrewarded, especially since she most likely couldn't afford it.

I also used this down time to catch up on all the news analysis about Iraq, since I was still hoping to get back over there soon. I tried to avoid the hysterical screeching heads on TV because most of them didn't know what they were screeching about. I made it a practice, when I had the leisure, to read the *New York Times* and the Washington *Post* and *The Wall Street Journal* and *The Weekly Standard*. The war against the insurgents was going from bad to worse and I really felt for the families of the soldiers and marines who were coming home in coffins or so badly banged up they'd never fully function again. The best slant on the rebuilding effort from my first hand experience in Iraq was in a column by Tom Friedman of the *Times* where he said in order to succeed we'd need more real partners than the Brits and the handful of Poles and Italians and others that made up "The Coalition of the Willing." He was right on target when he added that our military without allies could smash any country it wanted to smash but we couldn't rebuild one as big as Iraq by ourselves. And at the moment we were still pretty much dancing alone over there.

The Olympic diving events were a real bummer for me. For the first time in 92 years the Americans didn't win a single medal. It was humiliating to watch. Back in my day the top eight divers in the world were Americans and the Russians were totally outclassed. And the Chinese didn't have a single diver in the 1960 Olympics. Nowadays, with all the great facilities all over the world, there was a deluge of great divers. But you would think that among all those Tiger Woods type talents in Speedo suits there would be enough Americans to come up with at least one medal. But it was not to be in 2004.

When the Olympics were over my thoughts turned back to the Punta Gorda situation. I'd spent the week cradled in the comfort of the beach house air conditioning and a big wave of guilt was getting to me. I knew the guilt would grow if I didn't go back to the devastated town. Especially because of a certain twenty-dollar bill burning a hole in my wallet. So as soon as I could get the car packed with provisions to distribute I drove back down there and put in two more days with the animal rescue people.

When I got into Punta Gorda I went straight downtown to check on the progress of the cleanup. It seemed to be going nicely. And I got a big surprise on a particular street corner. Standing there talking to one of the Red Cross workers was John Berglund, the Salvation Army volunteer I'd replaced in Iraq. John's Army title was Territorial Disaster Training Coordinator. He was down here volunteering help in the relief work. We'd overlapped for a couple of days in Iraq and before he'd gone back to the States he'd shown me what my duties would be. After we'd renewed acquaintances we went over to one of the soft drink stands nearby and he told me the sad news about what was happening to the post-war relief effort. He said because of the bleak security situation the Salvation Army had no one left on the ground in Iraq and only a skeleton crew manning the organization's office in Kuwait City. I asked after Muntajeb but he didn't have any info on the Al Amarah Mafioso. I told him what a shame it was that the Army had had to abandon Iraq and how proud I'd been to represent it over there. And that if the situation on the ground improved enough for the organization to restart its work in Iraq I'd be sure to submit a request to be included.

Then John mentioned another world trouble spot that had been getting more and more attention at the time. He said the Army was thinking about sending a relief crew to Sudan. I'd been reading about the terrible conditions there, the mass murders and starvation. And I'd seen the soul-searing pictures on TV of the dying children who were nothing but skin and skeleton. In the old days I'd have put together a military strike force pronto and led it on a mission to wipe the tormentors of those poor people off the face to the earth. But I'd had enough of killing in my life, and now the best way for me to contribute, in cases like this, was to volunteer to help feed and care for the victims. One thing was no different from the old days though. That was the unwillingness of the U. S. government to intervene in Africa no matter how inhumane the injustice or sadistic the slaughter. And Sudan gave every indication of rivaling the Rwanda tragedy. Too bad neither country had enough oil to make them enticing. Anyway, I told John Berglund that if he led a relief crew to Darfur or Khartoum to count me in and that night in my motel room I wrote a letter to Major Kiddo at Salvation Army headquarters in Washington to make my Sudan application formal.

But before I did that I went back to the Command Center to check on the action there. Sergeant Katzman said that the Animal Control operation could still use my help and that she'd put me back with Kerri on loose critter patrol right away. So when Kerri got back to the center from her rounds I joined her and we spent the rest of the day tooling around in the van checking on which vets had reopened after the storm and which still had no power.

The next day we were back on the beat looking for another loose dog supposedly making trouble. This was a sixty-pound mixed breed who'd been barking at passersby from a house that looked abandoned. When we got to the area, in a low income part of town that had been hard hit by the hurricane, the dog was still yapping up its own storm from the doorway. Kerri got the big dog settled down and when we checked inside the house we were half expecting some helpless sick person whose plight the dog was trying to signal. But there was no one inside to be found so we lassoed the dog and led it back to the van for the trip to the pound.

I asked Kerri what percentage of animals at the pound ever got adopted. She surprised me by saying nearly all of them. That pleased me because I hated to think of them leading the rest of their lives in captivity, even if it was compassionate captivity. I'd been impressed by the professionalism of the Punta Gorda pound's employees. They all seemed to be genuine animal lovers and dedicated to seeing that their charges got the best of care. I knew that wasn't the case at all facilities. Some of them were run and staffed by sadists.

Later in the day we rescued two of the smaller victims of the storm. A homeowner called to say her husband had picked up a couple of baby ground squirrels after they ran out of a blown-over palm tree. Kerri mentioned that while I was back in St. Petersburg she'd had several calls about little squirrels separated from their mothers. When we got to the house in question the woman wanted to make sure we had a good home in mind for the squirrels and Kerri had to assure her they would go to a local family that was already feeding several such survivors through baby bottles. When the woman was satisfied that we weren't going to harm the tiny critters, I put them in my vest pocket and we drove over to the other side of town where the private squirrel hospital was already treating a ward full of chirping patients. I told Kerri I was pleased there were some people left in this too often callous world who felt responsible for the welfare of the smallest of God's creatures.

The next morning we were called to transport water and feed to a group of eight quarantined horses. They were being kept on a small privately owned farm nearby because they'd come down with a mosquito borne disease something like West Nile. Nobody was sure whether their sickness was brought on by the hurricane or not but the storm had knocked out power to the farm's water pump and the horses were in a bad way. We took Punta Gorda's 400 gallon tanker from Animal Control's HQ to the farm. The horses drank the water so fast I thought they would empty the tanker and drown themselves in the process. After we got back to the Command Center we had to scrub down because we couldn't be sure the horses' disease wasn't transmittable to humans.

The next day I got caught up in Operation Eagle. An anonymous caller had phoned the center to say that if we went to an address on the outskirts of town we'd find a big bird with an injured eye. When Kerri and I got there we knocked on the front door but got no answer. We went around to the back yard and there on the lawn big as life was a full grown eagle beating its wings against the bars of a metal cage. Obviously, since it was illegal to "own" an eagle, somebody had dumped the bird, cage and all, behind a house where the owners were probably out of town. And maybe in the throes of conscience pangs whoever had caught or found the bird had called Charlotte County Animal Control. Just when and how the eagle's bloodied eye had been injured couldn't be determined. But what a magnificent bird. Its wingspan was incredible. It didn't seem too happy with our rescue efforts though. When I picked up the heavy cage the wing beating got even more frantic. The bird didn't settle down till Kerri slipped her vest over the top of the cage. At that point I carried the cage to the van and we drove the bird to its new temporary quarters at the Peace River Wildlife Center, just north of Port Charlotte below Venice. We were met there by the center's rehabilitator

Karen Ziober. She thanked us for delivering the bird and told us she'd feed and water it and give it some rest in a big wire enclosure. While Kerri and Karen talked about the eagle's eye problem, I decided to take a tour of the grounds. It'd been hit hard by the hurricane and there were bent and battered cages and Karen's office was a mess. When I rejoined the women Karen told us about the many animals that'd been sent to the Center after the storm and how she'd had to put them in home care with various volunteers. She'd kept those that she could handle, four raccoons brought in by the Humane Society and some baby squirrels brought in by individuals who'd found them. But several owls and crows and vultures and a couple of opossums had to be rerouted to some rehabbers around Tampa/St. Pete. Kerri said everybody in Punta Gorda thought Ms. Ziober was the very best at the kind of work she did. I was so impressed with her skills that I gave her several 100 dollars to get the damage to the grounds repaired so she could carry on her work. And I recommended that Kelley Benham, the reporter for the *St. Petersburg Times* who was following me around, write an article for the paper about Karen and the Center. In appreciation Karen kept me up to date on the eagle's progress. Which was so fast it was released the next week in the same area where Kerri and I had picked it up.

Just before I left Punta Gorda Keith Larson, who was the Director of the city's Animal Control and Rescue Center, made me an honorary member of his staff and gave me a shoulder patch to prove it. I really appreciated his gesture and hoped the people of Punta Gorda would get their lives back together soon. And I hoped my contribution to their animal population had helped.

A few weeks later back home, Annie called one night to say another hurricane, this one named Francis, was pointed in our direction but in a stationary stall just off the east coast. It was a Category Four and it packed the wallop to punish the already reeling state of Florida with more wind and rain. That night I hit the supermarket and bought fuel for my Coleman stove and bottled water and coke and canned goods and bread and milk. Then I hit an all night deli and grabbed some cooked chicken. By the time my shopping spree was over I had enough supplies for four days in case there was no power near the landfall site. The next morning I jumped in my Jag and drove four-and-a-half hours to get to the bulls eye on the storm's target. I checked into a hotel just off U.S. Highway 1 south of Palm Beach near Boca Raton. By the time I'd got to the hotel, Francis had been downgraded to a Category Two but the Weather Service was still wary because it was such a slow moving storm. It seemed to be in suspended animation and I had to wait it out like the locals. While I was cooling my heels I rode around with an EMS crew and moved a hospital full of sick, mostly senior folks to another location. Their care facility had lost power and their backup generator had refused to kick in. Most of the patients were in their eighties and nineties and they were pretty shook up about having to be moved. But we got them safe and sound out of harm's way.

When the storm finally hit it stayed around for ten hours punishing the area with high winds and torrential rains that refused to move on. Thanks to my Red Cross ID I was waved through all the secured areas manned by the National Guard or the local police so I could lend a hand with the cleanup effort.

The next day I drove out to the Peace River Center and fed the raccoons and ibises and flamingos and all kinds of other birds from wrens to herons. The volunteers there were still overwhelmed with the post-Charley chaos. People were bringing in more animals than they could handle but they were still finding other volunteers to do home care. Roaming around the Center was the most fun for me. This was my best time during Francis. I loved feeding the animals and rooting for their release.

The third day the power went out and we all had to wear helmets with searchlights attached. I didn't need to be issued one. By this time I knew to bring one on all my trips. In fact, it was the same one I'd worn at Ground Zero. I never left home without it.

More than thirteen inches of rain fell during Francis. Winds exceeded 150 M.P.H., ripping off roofs and flooding streets up to 4 feet deep. Similar downpours up in Alabama and Georgia. And the there were the tornadoes, around twenty deaths in Florida, Georgia, and South Carolina. Charley had already killed twenty-seven and cost 6.8 billion dollars. Florida financial officer Tom Gallagher estimated insured damages from Francis would run between two and four billion dollars. That wasn't counting the Florida citrus crop that suffered damaged fruit and flooded growing fields. The good news was that houses seemed to withstand Francis better than they did Charley. And Congress quickly passed a two-billion dollar aid package.

Thousands of folks were trying to get back to their homes and the highways, especially I-95, were clogged with southbound traffic. It was a bad situation because it made it tough for emergency vehicles to operate. People's tempers were short and more than one fight among returnees broke out.

A guy looking for ice shot the lock off a freezer at a gas station. People were waiting hours for a fill up and cars in line were running out of gas moving a few feet at a time. Kids were crying and people were losing patience fast. And to make matters much worse, word was coming over the radio and TV that yet another hurricane, this one named Ivan, was prepping to blast the state. This would be the third big blow in a little over a month.

The radio was also reporting that it would take over a week for full power to be restored to the affected areas. All of the store shelves were picked clean by this time. There was no bread or ice or water. People were being arrested in droves for violating curfew, which was a no-go stretch from ten in the evening until six the next morning.

As the brunt of the new storm bore in toward the coast I was listening to radio reports and found out it was headed right through the state on a path to make a direct hit on my beach house with 50 to 70 mile-an-hour winds. So I got back in the car and headed home. The drive back was hairier than Sasquatch because the rain made it tough to see out the windshield and the wind kept threatening to blow the heavy Jaguar off the road. When I finally pulled into my driveway I could see much was already amiss since part of my second-story roof was sitting in my neighbor's yard across the street. And when I walked around the back of my place I found a big hunk of the beach clogging my swimming pool.

That's when Annie called to say that now the other hurricane named Ivan was being billed as a Category Five and it could possibly hit Florida within the week. I had a hard time believing that we'd be blasted again until I remembered Xenia, a small town just outside of Dayton. Back when I was living in Ohio, Xenia had been decimated by a tornado and since then the same swath of the city had been hit at least two more times by twisters. But those examples of Mother Nature's focused fury were years apart. This was the third hurricane to hit Florida in a little more than six weeks. If another one had to hit, why couldn't it target the Carolinas for a change? Or skip right over the coast and whip through West Virginia?

That thought reminded me of the trouble my brother Tony once got in when he was a Congressman. There was a barrel of pork being considered on the House floor and it included a twelve-million dollar appropriation for West Virginia. Tony didn't like the bill since he was a fiscal conservative even though he was a Democrat. So he stood up on the floor of the House and said he'd be voting against the bill because the whole state of West Virginia wasn't worth twelve-million bucks. Needless to say the next day he had to apologize to the governor and the other West Virginia reps.

It was around the time of the third hurricane that I made a decision about a longstanding dream of mine to climb Mount Everest. Months earlier I'd begun mulling the idea as a way to show my fellow fogies in the most dramatic way possible that life didn't have to end at retirement. For years I'd devoured every *National Geographic* and other magazine article about Everest and now it seemed like Nepal was the place to make the boldest possible statement to the world about what could be accomplished despite advancing age. But honestly the sharpest spur was my need for the personal challenge because all the hurricane chasing and firefighting and animal rescue work weren't enough to keep me from getting bored. And for the past two years I hadn't been able to get the vision of the majestic mountain out of my mind. Could I actually conquer it? I knew I couldn't without an even more rigorous training program than I'd ever undertake because there was so much against me physically. Hell, I was sixty-seven years old, an officially disabled veteran with two knees that had bone on bone caps and that'd been operated on four times and looked like they belonged on a stork, a left leg that had been shot twice and never properly healed. That leg and those knees were a constant source of pain, especially in cold weather or on humid summer days. Besides these impediments I'd had a third of my left lung removed during a cancer scare thirty years earlier and more recently I'd been diagnosed with emphysema thanks to a still active smoking habit. I was not a picture of health.

When I started thinking seriously about finally doing the Everest climb, I knew I had to kick my training up a number of notches if I expected to succeed. But when I began to feel and see the results of my expanded effort, I decided to turn the tempo up some more with the best personal trainer I could find. I'd need an orthopedic surgeon too and a good nutritionist. I made some inquiries and lined up the best in their respective specialties.

Meanwhile I kept one eye on the situation in Iraq, hoping for an opportunity to get back. But things there kept going from horrendous to worse according to the newspapers and TV. The major relief organizations had long since pulled out. The security on the ground ranged from iffy to suicidal depending on what part of the country you looked at. One day I came across an article in the paper about one of the outfits still operating with some success in Iraq. It was called the Mercy Corps and it was run by a Portland, Oregon do-gooder named David Holdridge. He headed a work force of ten ex-patriots and one-hundred-and-sixty-three Iraqis What snapped me to attention was the fact that one of the areas where the Mercy Corps continued to operate was Maysan Province. They were still building schools, health centers, and parks in places that hadn't seen an American contractor or Coalition reconstruction force for months, since April to be exact. They'd pretty much taken over the area that used to be the active stomping ground of Bechtel and the Research Triangle Institute. Holdridge blamed squabbling between the U.S. State and Defense department officials inside the fortified Green Zone in Baghdad for mismanaging the reconstruction effort, squabbling that could sink the whole operation in Iraq. The article stood out as the first time I'd seen in print what I'd witnessed with my own eyes over and over again in Iraq.

Even though Holdridge insisted his group was making progress on the ground, he was also quoted as saying exactly what I thought about the Iraqi endgame, that the country was headed for a civil war that might draw in Turkey and Jordan and Lebanon and Israel and Iran and Saudi Arabia. One scary scenario. That's why he also thought like I did that there was no way the U.S. could pull out of the mess it'd made until the situation turned around. Meanwhile the Mercy Corps kept up its good work despite the fact that Holdridge and his American staff members had to avoid sleeping in the same place every night for fear of kidnapping and they had to travel in an inconspicuous battered car to avoid losing their lives in a hail of bullets. The more I read about Holdridge the more an itch to look into joining the Mercy Corps intensified. But the article indicated that the Corps was in the process of drawing down its staff and turning its activities over to the Iraqis. So the prospects of helping Holdridge hold the fort didn't look promising. I thought about writing Holdridge to see if in his rounds he'd run into my old buddy, Muntajeb. But I decided not to. I was afraid of the answer I'd be given.

# TWENTY-SIX

In a little more than a week Hurricane Ivan hit with terrific force. Even though it was being tracked 350 miles out in the Gulf the waves it produced broke over my seawall at the beach house and dumped 3 feet of sand in the pool and yard. This time the fist of the storm hit in the area around Pensacola and especially in its upscale suburbs, so after an afternoon of shoveling sand I asked Melinda to pack my things again and I rolled toward the landfall site in the new Jaguar I'd bought a few weeks earlier. On the way I reflected on the fact that this would be my twelfth hurricane service, starting with Andrew in August of 1992. But three in a matter of weeks would sorely test the will of Floridians to fight.

When I pulled in to Pensacola on the seventeenth of September the devastation reminded me of what Andrew had done to Homestead. Aside from the several deaths brought by the storm the physical damage was awesome. Thirty-story condo buildings had been flattened. Well over half the homes in some neighborhoods weren't fit for occupancy and nothing on the north side of town appeared to be undamaged. Boats in the harbor piled on top of each other or reduced to kindling. Other boats on dry land blocks from their moorings. Cars floating or half submerged in the Inter Coastal Waterway. A lot of this destruction was caused by the tornadoes that were spawned by Ivan's outside rim, which had created wind bands 100 miles from the eye. As far as Panama City 150 miles away over thirty tornadoes had touched down. And the hurricane still hadn't been satisfied. After it made landfall in Pensacola it's havoc headed north through the Carolinas and even caused several deaths and major flooding in Pennsylvania before it curved out into the Atlantic. My recently purchased mountain home in Toxaway, North Carolina was drenched with fourteen inches of Ivan's rain when the actual eye passed right over it. And then out in the Atlantic Ivan turned and hit the Gulf again with high winds and torrential rain before blowing itself out.

Once I'd checked out the general scene in Pensacola I drove directly to the check point at the bridge to the barrier islands. I figured I'd find out how much destruction there was there before heading to the Emergency Management Operations Command Center in town. I flashed my ID and was waved over the bridge to the Center on the other side. I asked what I could do to help the torn up community. The devastation was really severe here too. Condo buildings were flattened and there was so much blown sand that a couple of cars were buried up to their hood insignias. Next I learned that the situation was even worse than what I could see. Another hurricane, this one named Jeanne, was out in the Atlantic aiming for Florida. But there was work to do before she arrived. When I checked in with the Animal Control people I happened to overhear a conversation between two Fish and Wildlife workers. They were talking about their assignment which was an endangered species operation being mounted to relocate some gopher tortoises that were threatened by the rising river waters already above flood stage. I did a double take when they mentioned the tortoises since the little nine-pound cold-blooded reptiles once cost me 28,000 dollars.

Melinda and I had bought a 77 acre site about ten years earlier so we could put up a couple of 100 upscale condos. Only 22 acres of the land was suitable for building and the rest was designated by the state as a wetland area. Before we could develop the site we had to pay a licensed habitat engineer to make an ecological study. That's how it was discovered that the acreage O.K. for development was pocked with 16 gopher tortoise burrows. Thankfully only four of the burrows were active but even so I had to pay 7,000 dollars per burrow to relocate the critters to new homes. Needless to say I was not too happy when my lead engineer called to tell me what those damn reptiles were going to cost me to move. That was nearly as much as I'd paid at times in the past to relocate people.

But none of that stopped me from introducing myself to the Fish and Wildlife reps there in Pensacola and volunteering to help them round up and relocate the relatives of those reptiles that had cost me so much money years ago. I told myself how ironic this operation would be for me but what the hell. I'd never actually shaken hands with a gopher tortoise before. I'd only seen them on the Discovery Channel. If I actually found some of the little bastards I could give them a piece of my mind. Anyway, when I gave the Fish and Wildlife guys a thumbnail sketch of my animal rescue volunteering, they invited me to come along on their mission.

I followed the Wildlife Department's truck in my car to Torrence. When we got there the two officers whose names were Ted and Brian offloaded a few items. Brian was a new recruit and Ted's job was to fill him in on the gopher tortoise situation and I decided to sop up the info Ted was putting out. I'd already begun calling Ted "Ringer" because he reminded me so much of my son David, Not only did he look a lot like him but he had the same way about him, the same trusting, congenial nature.

Anyway as we started walking the fields and scouting out tortoise habitat Ted launched into an instructive canned monologue about gopher tortoises for Brian's benefit and I listened and learned at the same time. The little reptiles counted themselves members of the turtle family even though they shunned water. They were only about ten-inches long and they weighed nine pounds. They were long-lived animals just about making it to Medicare status in the wild and sometimes reaching 100 years in captivity. The biggest concentration of the gopher tortoises is in Florida where they can be found in all sixty-seven counties. And there are scattered populations from Louisiana to southeastern South Carolina. Wherever they hang out they're federally protected under the Endangered Species Act as "threatened" and under the Florida Conservation Commission's listing as a Species of Special Concern.

One of the more interesting things about gopher tortoises is the fact that like many other reptiles they have temperature-dependent-sex-determination. When their eggs are laid they're neither male nor female. Their offspring's gender is determined by the temperature of the sand where the eggs are laid. If the sand temperature is above eighty-five degrees, the hatching tortoise will be female. If the sand is cooler the tortoise will be male. Maybe this is where the idea of a "hot female" comes from but if so Ringer overlooked that fact. The tortoises are called "wildlife landlords" because their burrows are rented out by other species. Over 300 kinds of invertebrates have been found living in gopher tortoise burrows. Including snakes and other sorts of turtles and frogs and small mammals and even some birds like the Florida scrub jay and the burrowing owl. These renters are called Commensals. The burrows are like a cafeteria for predators who never know what's being served until they get up to the counter. The burrows are about 15 feet long and usually about 6 feet deep. They're dug down at a 30 degree angle and so they provide protection against predators and fire and weather, except of course flooding. Each male tortoise builds from seventeen to thirty-five burrows and females slightly fewer.

As we stalked the area Ringer steered us away from patches of ground overgrown with vegetation. He said these places were too thick with growth to support the tortoises. They needed open space with sandy soil and lots of sunlight to provide more food for them and other scrub dwellers like snakes and jays and lizards. Ringer picked out a sandy area and we followed a set of tracks to a hole in the ground and started shoveling. I was surprised when his shovel produced a dull thud and then he scooped up one of the tortoises. It looked a lot like one of the lake-going turtles I used to hunt as a kid in Ohio but Ringer treated it like it was a Hollywood star. He set down his shovel and carefully cradled the tortoise and turned it upside down to show Brian and me how he could tell its sex, "See this concave bottom shell. It's called a plastron. That shape means it's a male. If it were a female, the bottom shell would be smooth. It takes a tortoise ten to twenty years to reach maturity."

At that point Ringer put the tortoise back on the shovel and took him over to the state pickup truck and placed him tenderly in the bed before I had a chance to ask the critter what had happened to my 28,000 dollars. We went back to searching the scrub brush and over the next two hours Ringer came up with six more tortoises using a shovel and a net and his hands to demonstrate the various ways you could corral them. At one point I stepped on a snake and jumped so high it would have had a tough time striking, which Ringer said was a good thing since he identified it as poisonous.

Then Ringer pointed out a few dry animal bones on the ground and said he thought they'd been eaten by tortoises. He said the tortoises were strictly vegetarians except for dessert which was sometimes animal bones. Nobody knew for sure why they sucked on the bones but Ringer said the best theory was that they extracted needed calcium from them. By this time I'd built up a great respect for Ringer. He was a real credit to the state's wildlife service. He was proud of his knowledge and his job and so was I. He probably didn't make a lot of money and he knew I was quite well off from checking out the new Jag but he treated me just like he did Brian, with respect and growing friendship.

At one point he was on his knees in a grassy spot and pulled some stringy material out of the soil.

"See this? This is what they eat, low growing weeds and herbs. But they also like gopher apples and palmetto berries and when they can get them the pads and fruits and flowers of the prickly pear cactus."

Ringer was a born professor and if he weren't so vital to the Florida wildlife service he should have been lecturing in a university classroom somewhere.

"What makes these tortoises so important is the fact that they spread the seeds of a lot of plants in their droppings."

On the second day of my field work with Ringer and Brian the water table was rising fast and we knew we had to push ourselves. All of the rainfall from Charlie and Francis and Ivan was too much for the streams and rivers to absorb and they were overflowing more dangerously by the hour. And by noon of the second day we'd only located two more tortoises. Ringer was disappointed because he'd expected to find more in the scrub area we were searching. We worked rapidly, spread about 10 feet apart, walking a straight line from one end of a stretch of sand to another. The process reminded me of the time in Texas I'd spent helping search for the metal debris from the Space Shuttle disaster.

We headed back to the truck at noon for our quick bagged lunch and some much-needed water. After four hours of searching I was cramping up from lack of water and I promised myself I'd carry a big container of the stuff from now on. We were soaked with sweat and the three of us were a mass of cuts and abrasions from the prickly plants we'd just been exposed to. On the way to the truck I got a big surprise when I looked down at a little outcropping of grass in the sand and saw a beautiful yellow butterfly. I stopped and admired it and asked myself how in the world that creature had made it through all of the wild weather that had ravaged its haunts over the last few weeks. It was the only butterfly I'd seen in three days of barreling through the brush outside Pensacola.

On the third day I wore a long sleeved shirt and buttoned it up to the neck for most of the day to fend off all the spiders and briars and mosquitoes. The fact that I'd finally learned that lesson made me question my IQ. A few years earlier my writer friend had recommended a book by Frank Norris called *McTeague*. The main character was a dim-witted dentist who murdered his wife and was being chased by a posse through Death Valley in California. On the third day of the chase he has a brainstorm and takes off his wool shirt. The writer and I'd laughed about McTeague's slow uptake but I had to admit I wasn't much better since it took me three days to figure out I should cover my upper torso with a shirt on the tortoise hunt. At the end of the first day I'd looked like a Band-Aid ad. But on this third day at least we'd bagged four more tortoises. The work was exhausting but I was really enjoying what I was learning from Ringer who was still into his monologue broken only occasionally by a question from Brian or me.

By the middle of the third day I could tell that Ringer was not only exhausted like me but out of sorts too. When we stopped for lunch we were sitting around a fallen tree trunk. Over the three days we'd talked a lot and got to know each other well. I'd grown quite fond of my two companions but especially of Ringer who reminded me more of my son with each passing hour. I'd told him I was retired but that I did volunteer work for the American Red Cross. I'd been ashamed to tell him that I wasn't retired at all but was an active developer because I could tell he was a dedicated ecologist. Now we were watching the rising Perdido River and we knew we only had the rest of the afternoon to save as many tortoises as we could. As we three soaked souls sat devouring our prepared lunch and drinking water by the pint trying to recoup the pounds we'd lost during the morning, all of a sudden Ringer told us what was bugging him and it was the subject I'd been dreading for three days.

"The worst threat to these tortoises is habitat destruction."

I knew my conscience would begin to burn if Ringer ever started in on developers. And in fact now I wanted to bury myself in a burrow so I wouldn't have to admit my dirty secret.

But Ringer was just getting warmed up.

"These tortoises can't live if they don't have undeveloped land with plenty of flora and room to dig their burrows. Another thing that threatens them is 'land fragmentation.' Buildings like condos and roads and landfills and parking lots and all kinds of man-made facilities break up the tortoises' natural habitat into fewer and fewer empty parcels of land that are big enough to sustain them. They can't live out their lives without coming into contact with humans or, worse yet, their cars. The biggest loss of tortoises is through road kill."

I was feeling smaller and smaller as Ringer talked because it was me he was talking about, the pitiless predator, the dreaded developer.

Before I could confess though, Ringer jumped up and started walking fast. Then he beckoned to Brian and me to follow.

"Let's go. If we hustle we can get in another sixty acres before the water gets up here. That's about all we can do."

I forgot my embarrassment for the moment and we got back to our systematic grid search. As we worked through the last acreage I wondered whether I should confess my sins to Ringer. Two hours later we'd done all that could be done and we had another six tortoises in the back of the pickup, ready for relocation. When we were finished packing the truck and collecting our lunch debris I made my confession.

"Ringer, I told you earlier that I was retired. That's mostly true. What I didn't tell you was that I'm still semi-active as a land developer. My wife and kids run the business while I volunteer with the Red Cross and the Salvation Army doing animal control work like we've been doing for the last three days and fighting fires out west."

I finished up by telling Ringer and Brian about the 28,000 dollars those gopher tortoises had cost me a few years back.

Ringer didn't miss a beat. He didn't judge me at all. He just explained how the state code dictated the relocation fee so there'd always be a pot of money to buy land for the tortoises. Then I told him that my initial reaction to having to pay was anger and I apologized for being so stupid and I tried to reassure him that all developers weren't so ignorant. Then I told him the state of Florida should be proud to have someone of his quality working for its wildlife service. And I said that the last three days had been a great experience for me, which was the simple truth. That's when he said something that brought a lump to my throat.

"Sam, my dad died when I was three-years old. I'd like to think he would have been a father like you.'

By that time the tears were running down my cheek and I was thinking how off the mark Ringer was in seeing me as a good father. Hell, I was on the road so much that my kids didn't even know me anymore and my tears now were mingled with pride in Ringer's acceptance and embarrassment over my neglect of David and the girls. Then came an emotional scene with Ringer and Brian and me hugging each other. All started by a bunch of needy reptiles.

✳ ✳ ✳

When I got back to St. Petersburg from Pensacola I checked with the Weather Service about the projected path of Hurricane Jeanne. By this time all of Florida was in a stunned state what with all the weird weather that had hit over the last six weeks. Now Jeanne was poised to bring more misery. Like Francis she was a slow mover out in the Atlantic but the best predictions had her hitting somewhere around Stuart in the Panhandle. That would mean I wouldn't have to worry about my place since the suspected landfall would be 40 miles to the north. The next morning around three Melinda helped me pack my gear and while I was shaving I luckily turned on the Weather Channel and found out that Jeanne had changed her mind and was headed straight for the bathroom where I was standing. Luckily it was being clocked as a Category One but still that meant sustained winds up to 75 M.P.H. and lots of potential damage.

I was definitely getting fed up with this endless hurricane season. Our beach house had already taken three good shots in the last five-and-a-half weeks. Charlie had hit a 100 miles south of our place but had still done plenty of damage dumping sand in the yard and pool. Then Francis had refilled the yard and pool with sand and taken part of the roof off the house. Next Ivan blew another 2 feet of sand in the yard and pool and another section of my roof flew down the street. I'd had to have the pool drained twice during all this and I wasn't looking forward to spending more money doing that. Now Jeanne was poised to find us, the fourth blow in six weeks.

So before I could think about driving to wherever Jeanne would eventually make landfall I had to shore up the beach house to defend against Jeanne. I got busy and built a temporary silt fence at my seawall and fortified it with stiff bracing that would hopefully hold back the breaking waves and stop the beach from invading our pool again. I threw all of the outdoor furniture in the pool where it would be relatively safe and boarded up the house once more. Then I drove Melinda and our dog Casey to our new condo penthouse 5 miles inland and went back to the beach house to wait out the storm. Jeanne finally came ashore that evening with 50 mile hour winds but also with four hours of sustained 75 mile per hour blasts.

I hunkered down during the storm in the beach house since I'd decided to draw a line in the shifting sand a la Winston Churchill who'd defied the Germans in World War II by "fighting them on the beaches." In fact the beach house had been built in 1939. We'd had it only six months when Jeanne hit and I was to find out that it wasn't such a good idea to stay in it during the storm. For one thing it had been grandfathered in under the old construction codes and it wasn't up to facing strong winds. If I'd known the house was going to take a head-on hit I wouldn't have been so foolish as to stay even though the danger gave me a shot of the old adrenaline. But I thought the storm would hit a little to our north which was what the Weather Channel was saying in its revised forecast. I was thinking that if I stayed there might be something I could do in case part of the place flew apart or broke or leaked. I was willing to take a chance in order to save the house. It had become a favorite hideaway for Melinda over the past six months when she wanted to put the pressures of the development business out of her mind for a while.

As soon as the storm hit, around nine in the morning on the twenty-fifth of September, I knew it'd been a bad idea to stay. The house was shaking like a dish of Jell-O as the wind howled through the eves. After a few minutes watching the storm from the seaside window I went into a back bedroom and listened to the wind rip off roofing and watched the rain water begin to leak through. During a lull in the wind velocity I went out and checked my silt line and it seemed to be holding up well but a couple of hours later during another lull I went back out and discovered the fence had been breached and the sand was once again piled up in my pool. Four hours of winds that maxed out at 74 miles per hour had been too much for the fence even though I'd braced it well.

Back in the house I had more leaks than I had buckets and pans to catch them with. As it was there were so many sitting under the drips the place looked like a Food Channel set. Just about every fifteen minutes I'd have to run outside and empty the pans to catch the next gusher pouring through the roof. And the back yard was slowly filling with sand again. When I looked out one of the side windows there was a big chunk of my roof laying in my neighbor's yard.

The aftermath was pretty much the same as before. Drain the pool; shovel the sand out of the backyard. But this time rather than repair the roof I had a brand new metal one installed. Talking with the neighbors I was told that in the seventeen years they'd lived in their places before this hurricane season they'd never seen the waves break over the seawall. Yet this year it had happened four times. It was true you should never fool with Mother Nature but even if you didn't it obviously wouldn't stop Mother Nature from fooling with you. Finally the weather settled down and I began to think about new adventures.

# TWENTY-SEVEN

For several months during the hurricane season I'd had Annie augmenting my morning weather, hurricane, and forest fire reports with info off the internet that had anything to do with animal rescue operations. One October morning before sunup I went into the office to get an update on her downloads and found she'd printed out an item and stuck a sticky note to it. The note had a name and phone number scribbled on it plus a message from Annie that wondered if I'd be interested in the attached pages. They turned out to be part of a bulletin headlined BADLANDS NATIONAL PARK CONDUCTS BISON ROUNDUP. According to the release from the park superintendent, William Supernaugh, a big posse was set to mount horses and scour the park the following week for bison to be culled from the herd there and relocated on Indian reservations. The operation had been worked out between the park service and the Intertribal Bison Cooperative, a non-profit in Rapid City, South Dakota that represented fifty-one member tribes engaged in reestablishing the animals on Indian lands to "promote cultural enhancement, spiritual revitalization, ecological restoration, and economic development."

The bulletin went on to say that according to a 2003 count there were around a 1,000 bison roaming the Badlands and that was at least 300 more than the ideal number for herd health and happiness. Though the wilderness area had enough grass to sustain 1,800 of the big bruisers, a severe water shortage in recent times had reduced the viable herd size to between

500 and 700. So the National Park Service was set to corral fifty cows, fifty bulls, and twenty-five yearlings of each gender for transplanting. The numbers and ratios were worked out by resource managers to maintain the maximum genetic diversity and improve the balance of sex and age within the park herd. That involved culling some of the best stock and giving them new zip codes on the reservations. To remove any more than the proposed 150 would negatively impact the park herd in terms of its genetic makeup.

Annie was sure right to think I'd be interested in joining in a bison roundup. What she'd scribbled on her sticky note was the name and phone number and email address of the Incident Commander, someone named Scott Lopez. And underneath the bulletin Annie had put a printout on my desk of a Badlands map with a schedule of flights into South Dakota. I had no idea if I'd be welcomed on the roundup since it sounded like a government operation that would be strictly limited to Park Service rangers. But it was well worth a try. When I got Scott Lopez on the phone he was very friendly but he hit me with a couple of disappointing sentences. "Sorry, Sam, the roundup is strictly limited to federal rangers. No outsiders can participate." Since I've never been known to take "no" for a final answer, I asked Lopez if I could overnight him copies of my credentials and some photos of my animal rescue work. He said sure and so I had Annie send the stuff along, including a picture of me on a mount rescuing other horses from a forest fire in Montana. That was to show I knew which end of a nag was which. The kicker in my presentation packet though was a proposal I thought might open a corral gate or two. When we'd talked on the phone, Lopez had told me the week-long roundup would involve thirty rangers and they'd be fed in the field chuck wagon style. In my proposal I offered to spring for all of the food for the operation if I could saddle up with the rangers.

The next day I had a call from Lopez and he said "Sam, you're on. I'll pick you up in Rapid City airport if you can get here tomorrow." He didn't add anything about whether it was the prospect of free hot dogs or my foot-long résumé that clinched the deal but I couldn't have cared less. I was so excited I almost forgot to tell Annie to make the plane reservations but I got her on my cell phone on my way home to start packing. Melinda was surprised and pleased that my offer to pay for the chuck chow had seemingly turned the trick and she helped me get ready for the trip over the weekend. We threw a couple of pairs of Levis and three or four rough shirts and some rain gear into a duffle bag. And I added a couple of seat saver Kotex packs I'd picked up at the drugstore. All the while we were filling my suitcase I was thinking how I loved the thought of working with bison. I'd not only played

*Bison Roundup in the South Dakota Badland, 2004.*

Patton shooing those buffalo off the road in the Yellowstone, I'd also done several sculptures of bison. Most of them were rejects now sunk in the Inter Coastal but a couple of the better ones were still standing in my office, grazing on a windowsill. And the opportunity to help in the roundup had come at just the right time. Without a fire to fight or a hurricane in sight I'd started feeling like a couch potato. I think it was H. L. Mencken who said something about it not being the length of a life but its width and depth that counted. So I thanked God for showing Annie the superintendent's bulletin and Melinda for letting me play cowboy to help some Indians put bison burgers back on their tables. Then I waited impatiently for departure time.

Sunday night I boarded a red eye bird flight out of Tampa bound for Chicago and hooked up with a smaller early morning flight for Rapid City. Lopez had offered to meet me at the airport and drive me to his house in Wall, South Dakota for dinner but I opted to rent a car and find a motel since I didn't want to burden anybody. And on these trips I liked to be alone to prepare myself for the action to come. As I've gotten older too I've come to like my alone time. I don't even listen to the car radio much anymore since the savored silence beats blather and even music now. So I drove my rented Honda to Wall, just 60 miles from the park, and checked in at a Best Western. Lopez picked me up Sunday mid-morning for breakfast at a local hash house and we got on a first name basis right away. We traded animal stories over scrambled eggs and coffee for the better part of an hour before getting down to the business of the day. Which involved first of all finding a local store to pick out my roundup gear. Soon I had everything I needed including a tack room saddle, reins and chaps.

Next we drove up close to the bison holding pens so I could meet the horse who'd be my buddy for the next week. He was a beautiful brown full grown stud, not the quarter horse I assumed would be used on a roundup. His name was Riddle and when I asked why, Scott said because it was always a crapshoot as to how he'd behave for a different rider or even the same rider on a different day. So I said "Thanks a lot good buddy" but Scott just laughed and started saddling his own horse while I tried to make friends with Riddle by rubbing his head. He seemed laid back enough to mount so Scott helped me saddle up and I got atop Riddle for a test ride alongside Scott on his horse "Johnny." We rode out a little ways into the park and I got used to Riddle's pace. He handled more like a quarter horse than a big stud. When I leaned to the right or left he'd go that way and I was feeling really comfortable astride him till he took a jump over a three-foot prairie dog hole and almost threw me. That's when Scott reminded me that he'd mentioned before to watch for those dog domes. By the end of the ride though I was sure Riddle and I would get to be pals.

We spent the rest of the day driving the dirt trails in the Badlands Park while Scott explained the impending roundup and gave me a telling tour. His government-issued enclosed Jeep was equipped with a lot of impressive communication gear in case of a back country breakdown. And he had other conceivable crises covered by the items between our seats. One was a slug-loaded twelve-gauge shotgun and the other was a thirty-round-magazine- fitted M-16. As we headed into the heart of the park, Scott told me what an honor it was for me to be included in the project since I'd be the only non-federal employee involved. In fact, no visitors would even be permitted to view the operation for safety's sake. The rangers wanted to keep human activity and especially noise to a minimum to avoid stressing out the animals. Then Scott told me what kind of conditions we'd be in for. The roundup would work like a regular cattle drive but I was to prepare for freezing rain or snow in the mountains. Each rounder-upper would be assigned one night of standing watch over the bison herd while the others slept under the open sky.

As we headed down an offshoot road, Scott launched into a lecture about the park and the animals in it.

"Sam, in 1963, fifty-three bison were introduced here. There were originally hundreds in the area but they'd all been hunted to extinction. Most of them brought in during the sixties came from the Theodore Roosevelt National Park in North Dakota. Then in 1983 twenty more were trucked in from Colorado. They've been a big tourist attraction ever since. They're officially called bison and not buffalo, which is what most people call them. They survive on sedges and they move continually looking for a good graze. The herds usually live in subgroups of twenty to fifty animals with the cows leading the family group. The bulls usually hang out together in small groups most to the year. A herd will travel tremendous distances over time in the wild. They're the largest land mammals in North America. A big male can weigh over 2000 pounds."

Scott was turning out to be a walking encyclopedia of bison behavior and he was far from finished with his explanations.

"Historically there were an estimated twenty to thirty-million bison. Today there are about two hundred fifty thousand left in the U.S. The herds were decimated in the nineteenth-century from unregulated hunting and by 1890 they were almost extinct. The very first efforts to protect them were in 1893 and they weren't all that effective back then."

As he went on about the bison, I surveyed the prairie that stretched as far as the eye could see. I hadn't been here since a family vacation over fifty years earlier and naturally I'd forgotten the wonderful vistas of table top land broken here and there by a lonesome tree, and the beautiful cliffs and low mountains in the background. Scott pointed off to the right and identified the Sage Creek Wilderness area that he said could support 700 bison. I asked at one point why the bison couldn't be counted on to control their own numbers and Scott had a ready answer.

"Because bison don't have any natural predators to worry about, the population picks up every year. We have to make sure there's enough feed and water for the whole herd so we have to remove a certain number of animals. That's what you and I and twenty-eight other men will start doing tomorrow."

Just before sunset we started back toward Wall in the Jeep and Scott surprised me by taking another tack in his talk.

"Damn it, Sam, I really love this job and this park and now the government says I have to retire in two weeks. This is my last roundup. Hell, I'm only fifty-seven and they're putting me out to pasture. Damn the feds."

I kept quiet for a minute and let him set his own pained pace.

"I don't know how I'm going to accept saying goodbye to all this. But I guess I should be satisfied with all the great years I've had riding these trails."

I spent about ten minutes consoling Scott with descriptions of some of the adventures I'd had long after my Medicare card arrived in the mail. That seemed to help and we got back to our earlier conversation about animals. Then with the evening light nearly gone, he pulled off the side of the dusty dirt trail edge and switched off the ignition.

"Come on, Sam, I want to show you something."

He grabbed a set of big binoculars and got out of the Jeep as I followed suit. We walked up to a small rise of earth and he handed me the binoculars and told me to point them to the right and give them a slow sweep to the left. I did as directed and in the middle of my maneuver I was rewarded with a spectacular sight. In the distance hundreds and hundreds of buffalo fed on the prairie grass as the sun dropped below the horizon behind them. Scott asked me what I thought of the view and all I could say was "Wow!" Then he put the prospect in perspective.

"What you're looking at is the 63,000 acres of the Badlands. And some damned government regulation says I have to retire. Who in the hell would want to leave all this?"

Now I was getting depressed too. But I just kept quiet and with the binoculars trained on the herd I let him get control of his emotions. In a minute I heard him blow his nose and I knew he'd been crying. But after a little while he headed back to the Jeep and I followed.

On the way out of the park again, Scott got into more specifics about the upcoming adventure.

"Tomorrow we'll take six others with us for a bison drive through this area here and we'll send them into a big holding pen. Would you like to see it now?"

I said sure and we headed up another dirt road as the light began to fail. Scott floored the Jeep, because he wanted to make the pen before it got too dark to see it well. Within a few minutes we topped a small hill and looked down on a huge enclosure just outside the park boundary.

"Take a look, Sam. There's nothing like it anywhere else in the world."

It was humongous. It had to cover a couple of acres. And it looked to have been put up fairly recently. In fact when I asked, Scott said it was only about a year old. As we drove up to the entrance, he walked me through the enclosure and I discovered there were around sixteen sub-pens constructed of steel posts welded together and covered with thick plastic sheeting. The sub pens were all tied together by long runs that looked to have been de-signed by an engineering genius. There were chutes and ramps, even hy-

draulics to squeeze the boxed in bison and hold them in place one at a time
for tagging and testing. There were walls in between pens and they could be
moved to herd the bison in whatever direction called for. It would be tough
for a Mack truck to break out of these pens so I was sure they could easily
detain even a 1,600 pound buffalo with an attitude. Over all the pens there
were steel walkways so the rangers could persuade any bad-ass bull or cantankerous cow to keep moving.

Scott switched on some electric post lights so I could get a better look at
the pens in the gathering twilight. Then he told me how they figured into
the coming events.

"Tomorrow eight of us will ride out to that herd you saw tonight and
drive it and another herd about 6 miles to the west into that temporary
holding pen off to the right. We'll do that on horseback since it'd illegal to
use a four-wheel-drive vehicle in the park itself. Then comes the exciting
part. We'll use trucks to herd the bison into the main holding pen. There'll
be nine trucks involved in all. When we get the bison where we want them
we'll divide them into small groups and herd them into the pre-processing
corrals. Then each animal will be worked through a hydraulic chute that
squeezes him in place while two steel bars grab him by the neck. That's
called a 'head catch.' Then one of the rangers will grab the buffalo by the
nose with a pair of pinchers that act like pliers to hold him still. That tool
doesn't hurt the animal at all. When he's locked in the nose grip a vet will
take blood and hair samples to make sure we're dealing with a healthy specimen. Then the animal gets a hypodermic shot and a computer chip im-
planted just under the skin behind his ear. There'll be three licensed vets on
hand all during the roundup."

"How do you decide which animals go to the Indians and which go
back to the park?"

"The animals are sorted by sex and age. The blood test tells us which
animals should be separated and sent to cut down on the chances of too
much inbreeding. Then the cull animals are sent on their way to tribes in
New Mexico, Montana, and Arizona. Each tribe gets forty grown males,
forty grown females, twenty young males, and twenty young females. There's
no cost to the tribes, just a rule that they can't sell or kill any of the bison for
food in less than twelve months."

The more I learned about the operation I was about to join the more
excited I got. I couldn't wait to help send a new shipment off to the Indians
so they could turn part of last year's herd into buffalo burgers.

After Scott doused the lights at the holding pen we got back in the Jeep
and headed to his ranch house just outside Wall where barbecue and beer

were waiting for us. There I met Scott's wife Ann and a former female employee named Jeanne who'd since moved to Hawaii but had been temporarily rehired for the roundup. While we sucked on our beers Ann and Jeanne threw some chicken parts on the grill and we all traded life histories. I parried Scott's questions about my adventures with my own about his life as a park ranger and Ann's as a park ranger's wife. Long after the chicken parts had been stripped to the bone we were still at it. Scott wanted to be a world traveler like me and he'd even had an ambition in his youth to train for the Olympics in wrestling. At the same time Scott envied my Olympic experience I was jealous of his vigorous life on the prairie that had made him so straightforward and honest, and as tough as a big box of nails.

That night, need I say, I tossed and turned and only dozed off for short stints and then woke up in a sweat. At one point I dreamed I was riding a buffalo down the street in some Ohio town and my mount crushed a United States senator driving a Mini Cooper. I came back to reality and then managed another doze that had me sharing a pancake breakfast with a bison at a Waffle House. The bison had a hard time pouring his syrup. Finally my alarm that I thought I'd set for five in the morning rang at three. Since I couldn't sleep anyway I threw on my Audie Murphy movie getup and headed for "downtown" Wall which consists of two streets three blocks long. After fifteen minutes I'd had the complete tour so I headed for the all- night gas station where I was supposed to meet Scott at six. That left me with about two-and-a-half hours to kibitz with the attendants and the trickle of customers. And drink coffee while I shifted from one foot to another. About a quarter to six it occurred to me that I'd forgotten to bring my butt buffer Kotex from the motel. Since I didn't have time to go back and get them I decided to try the tiny convenience store attached to the station. I walked up to the counter and asked the woman, "Do you sell Kotex?" She looked at me like I was an asteroid alien and then she said "No" in a less than sympathetic tone. Always quick on my feet though, I asked, "How about cotton balls?" Without a word she reached under the counter and produced a bag of same and snapped "I've never met a cotton-balled cowboy before." But hey, the little white puffs proved a Godsend later in the morning, at least for a little while.

About the time the critic-clerk handed me my change Scott showed up and we drove to the corral where we met the other six rangers who would be our fellow drivers. They looked like they'd been selected by central casting for the part of western rangers, tough as tungsten but good men all as I would discover later in the week. They listened patiently while Scott gave me my last minute instructions.

"This morning will be dangerous, Sam. Hang on hard to your mount. Don't get too close to a running bull. If you do, he'll charge you and try to gore your mount. Keep enough distance so you can react. Follow my lead. These animals can run at speeds up to 30 miles an hour. If some of them break off in another direction from the main herd, head them off but keep a safe distance from them, say 40 feet or so. That will be tough to do at times when the animals break in different directions. But your life depends on staying out of their way. If they won't turn back to the main herd, forget them. We only need around 550 head this morning. And by the way, don't think the females are less dangerous. They're always smaller, but they can be mean as any bull and they'll charge you in a heartbeat too."

"I can't wait. Anything else I need to know?"

"Yes, the prairie is pocked with dog holes. Riddle will handle those. Just give him his head. He knows what to do. If you try to guide him he's liable to step in a hole and break a leg."

All this time the horses were whinnying and shuffling and finally Scott explained.

"They're getting excited. They've done roundups before and they know what's in front of them this morning."

I wondered if I'd been whinnying and shuffling myself because I was as excited as the horses. Finally, five minutes later the six of us were saddled and mounted and Scott yelled "Move 'em out" so we headed into the park to find the first herd. Dawn gave way to a bright sun above a rock outcropping in the distance as we rode up small hills and down depressions toward our quarry. Riddle was behaving like an angel and the cotton balls stuck in my butt crack were doing their job. About twenty minutes into our ride Scott signaled a halt and pointed to two large herds up ahead. They were a gorgeous sight standing in the sun with its rays playing on their ranks.

Scott pointed to the herd and gave me another lesson.

"See those calves out there? They were born in April and May. The gestation period is nine-and-a-half months. They'll stay with their mothers for up to three years. They've got a lifespan of twelve to fifteen years."

With my quick course in bison family life complete, Scott pointed to the rear of his horse to tell me he wanted me right on his ass for the foreseeable future. Apparently he wanted to watch over me personally to keep me out of trouble. In just twelve hours we'd formed a strong bond and I trusted him like a brother. So I coaxed Riddle in behind Johnny while the four other rangers aligned their horses in a single file behind mine. Then we headed for the herd and made an ever so slow sweep off to their left. With a kind of military echelon maneuver that consumed an hour-and-half we rode around their flank at a distance of about 500 yards. Then we turned toward the herd with Scott on my left and the others on my right. Next we rode at a relaxed pace straight toward the herd. We each had a rope or a towel to wave and we started whistling and yelling at the bison.

They didn't move off right away and we got within a 100 feet of them. I got a good look at them at that point and saw all the open sores seeping through the fur on about a third of the herd. That figured since bison were highly cantankerous cusses that were constantly goring one another out of all-consuming aggression. I also knew they were easy beasts to agitate so I was surprised we'd gotten this close without spooking them. But Scott let me know that this was the whole idea of the slow approach. He didn't want the animals scattering which he said they would have done if we rode at them hell bent for leather. Now they just stood and stared at the bunch of whistling and shouting intruders. A few of the bulls were shifting their feet and others were head butting each other. And my old buddies the butterflies were flitting around my stomach. But the herd finally started a lazy walk in the direction of the holding pens. I had a fleeting thought that this roundup was going to be easy. Then all hell broke loose.

With the whole herd headed for the holding pens about fifty bison suddenly broke away from each side of the ranks. Scott, another ranger, and I rode off at a gallop after the group that veered left while the rest of rangers tried to redirect the rebels on the right. We were screaming and waving towels and ropes and the dust was blinding and the sound of bison and horse hoofs pounding the ground was deafening. Then Scott yelled above the thunder "Watch it Sam!" and I realized that a few of the bison in our splinter group had stopped to face me and one was a bull pawing the ground with his head lowered for a charge. Out of instinct I pulled back on the reins and Riddle hit the brakes so hard I almost went over his head to the ground. We were less than 30 feet from the bad ass bull when for no real reason he turned tail and took his cows back to the pack of mavericks we were chasing and then they all rejoined the main herd. About the same time the rangers who'd gone after the fifty head that'd broken right had them back on track. All that bison bedlam hadn't lasted more than ten minutes but I still thrill to the recall. The ear-splitting hammer of the hoofs and the choking dust. The shouting and waving and the teamwork of the rangers. And my sore butt pounding up and down on those now useless cotton balls. I could sure understand why Scott was so reluctant to retire. What a wonderful life he had here in the Badlands. It made me sad though to think that my first roundup would be his last.

The rest of the ride passed without anymore major beefs from the bison. A couple of times an animal or two would leave the herd on the left or right or drop behind but we rerouted them without incident. At one point Scott cantered up alongside me and said, "I guess I won't have to baby sit you from now on. You did real good back there." That meant more to me than I could ever express. I really respected Scott and coming from him I counted the compliment among my most prized ever. But I didn't have time to savor it just then because we were crossing the dirt road right before the funnel fence that forced the bison one by one into the acreage they'd occupy for the night. That field was just in front of the steel-enforced holding pen with its multiple gated chutes where the culling would take place in the morning. The bison cooperated and moved through the funnel fence into the field. Except for a couple of huge bulls. They insisted on loitering on the wrong side of the fence. So Scott got behind the big swing gate and told one of the rangers, a big Indian American named Vincent Littlewhiteman, to run over to the motor pool shed and get his van. Then he said to me "Watch this, Sam. This'll be a learning experience for you."

Two minutes later Vincent tooled up to the gate in a white government-issue four-wheel-drive Interior Department Chevy and started slowly closing in on the big buffalo. When he'd maneuvered in 50 feet behind the bull he began to prod it forward by revving the engine and blasting the horn. The bull ambled in the right direction until he got within 30 yards of the swing gate. Then he stopped dead in his tracks, did a one eighty and faced the van for a pawing and snorting showdown. The Indian must have known what was coming because he gripped the steering wheel hard just before the bull charged. POW ! The 2,000 pound specimen crumpled the right front fender with a love tap that sent a headlight flying in shattered shards. A couple of days later Vincent would be bitching about the forty two hundred dollar bill from the body shop even though the feds would pick up the tab. But at the moment he managed to use the van's broken bumper to turn the buffalo around. Then he used the grill to goose the beast and hit the gas. The buffalo from a dead start rumbled toward the open swing gate but at the last minute he must have seen Scott and he took a detour toward the eight-foot fence itself. From 20 feet away the bison took a flying leap and made it 7 feet up and into the holding field taking the top of the fence with him and loosening its stationary poles. Scott was as unhappy as Vincent was over his van because we had to take time to repair the fence. When that chore was done and we'd helped Vincent pull the fender off his right front tire, we turned our attention to the other bull who was still standing a couple of 100 yards on the wrong side of the fence. That's when Scott dangled a dare.

"Sam, I'll bet you can't corral that one."

"Me?"

But he wasn't kidding. He wanted me to use Vincent's battered van to herd the lone holdout through the swing gate. Since I've never been known to turn down a taunt I said sure and Vincent threw me his keys. For the next half hour I played motorized matador trying to coax the buffalo's 2000 pound combative carcass into the holding field. The ground outside the fence was all grass and scrub brush dotted with small hills and prairie dog homes and I was bouncing along backward and forward in drive and reverse trying to convince the big bull to cooperate. At one point I floored the van thinking I'd pass the bison on the right to get him to move left but he took off the wrong way and I had to swerve over a prairie dog hole. That's when the van went airborne and I hit my head so hard on the dome light I saw stars. After the van landed I could hear Scott and the rest of the rangers laughing and one of them yelled, "Hey Sam, you're supposed to use the safety harness." So I belatedly buckled up and cut back to the chase. After ten more minutes of maneuvering I finally had the bison headed for the funnel fence when he did a 180 intent on a pawing, snorting face-off at 50 feet. For a full minute I sat there with the van idling and the bison staring. Then I did one of the dumber things I've ever done. I unbuckled the safety harness and got out of the van so I could take my coat off to wave it at the bison like a Spanish bullfighter. But I couldn't get my coat off before the bison started rumbling in my direction. Luckily I wasn't standing far from the driver's side door so I jumped back in the van and waited for the impact and another repair bill for Vincent. But the bison checked his charge a few feet from the front bumper and just stared at me through the windshield. After a few seconds he tired of that and resumed his slow motion romp outside the holding field with me in hot pursuit honking the horn and banging the outside of the driver's side door with my fist. Ten minutes into our renewed duel he must have decided he needed a roll in the sedge since he suddenly bolted through the funnel fence and joined a cluster of contented cows grazing on the other side. I got out of the van and walked over to the rangers standing by the fence. They were all laughing up a storm at my less than professional performance. So I decided to rub some of the egg off my ego by bragging a bit.

"Did you see me get out of the truck? I felt like a toreador taking a bull's ear."

Scott had a cutting comeback.

"That bull almost took your ass."

It was only a little past noon and now we had the whole herd grazing in the fenced field and the gates closed behind them. Scott pronounced the first phase of the roundup a rousing success. We took the rest of the day off to clean our equipment and rest up for the Tuesday's official start of the culling operation.

Before dawn the next morning some thirty men assembled for a hot meal at the chuck wagon next to the holding pens. The meal would be appreciated because a cold front had moved in and dropped the temperature to around twenty above zero with a lot lower wind chill. But if the weather pattern held the afternoon would bring T-shirt working conditions. Scott took the time to introduce me to all the men I hadn't met the day before, including a couple of vets who'd be vaccinating the bison. Breakfast consisted of bacon and eggs and flapjacks and black coffee that went down so well they made the twenty four hundred I'd kicked in for a food fund seem like the bargain it was. The talk around the log fire was all about my bullfighting antics the day before. Apparently Scott had filled the others in when he called them the night before so I got peppered with good natured potshots. But once the food disappeared things got serious. Scott stepped on a small platform and began the briefing that would orient the rangers and the rest of us to the task at hand.

"Good morning, people. Let me have your attention. Welcome to the 2004 Bison Roundup. Most of you have been through the drill before but some haven't and those who have could use the review. The first item on the agenda is always safety. Let me remind you there's no hurry carrying out the cull. The animals are contained and the corrals are waiting. We've got plenty of food and shelter from the wind and cold. So let's focus on the job ahead and enjoy the experience. And if you notice some safety concerns tell me or Tucker about it right away."

Here he paused and pointed to the dozen or so four-wheel drive vehicles parked near the outside the containment fence.

"During the herding you need to maintain a steady speed. Use a slow and constant push to move the animals toward the target. Be patient and methodical. The herd will have to be run over and over toward the pens until there all inside, just like last year. Remember, the faster the animals are pushed through the process the more chance of a breakdown in communications between the chute operators. So take it easy. That way the animals will be less stressed and they won't need as much recovery time when they get to the chutes. And they'll be easier to work with. And besides that if they're pushed too fast the chance of an accident gets greater. And make sure you're strapped tight into your safety harnesses. Right, Sam?"

With that he looked at me and there was a general guffaw. I'm sure my face turned crimson but I managed to say "Right, your Worship" and Scott proceeded with the briefing.

"And remember to keep the noise under control as much as possible. It's unavoidable that a lot of yelling people and roaring engines are going to spook the animals, especially the older ones and the calves. But the idea is to keep the decibels down as far as you can. A couple of years ago there were some bison seriously hurt and they had to be destroyed. And we've had damaged vehicles too when bison turned out of the herd and charged the trucks. A big bull can crush a vehicle if it hits it from the right angle. Isn't that true Vincent?"

Another big yuk. Apparently Scott had told the group earlier about Vincent's van bout with the bison too. But the Indian already had a red face so we couldn't tell if he was embarrassed. Now Scott began to hand out the assignments.

"Here are the drivers and their partners. Twiss and Buck, Logan and Richards, Myers and Kiya, Row and Wojtowicz, Griswold and Ken, Gartner and Sharp, Littlewhiteman and Hall."

My heart did a somersault. Scott had included me in the culling crew. I'd be riding in a truck with Vincent at the wheel. Spurring the animals toward the target. I hardly heard the end of Scott's briefing.

"Well, that's it. As you know I'll be retiring in a couple of weeks and I'll pass off a lot of my job to Tucker over the next four days. He'll be Incident Commander next year. Good luck, boys. Let's rock and roll."

Vincent motioned with a nod of his head for me to join him on the walk to his van. Together we must have looked like Mutt and Jeff. Weighed wet I hit 165 and I topped out a shade south of 6 feet. Vincent was a man-mountain at a rock solid timberline tall 250 pounds. It's a wonder the van didn't tilt to the left when we got situated inside.

As soon as Vincent got the engine energized and the van rolling up to join the others in front of the swing gate he reached for the sun visor and pulled down one of his CDs and slipped it into the player. The result was a surge of strange sounds Vincent identified as Sioux chants. Apparently we were going on a buffalo chase with musical accompaniment. But it turned out we could use something soothing with what was about to happen.

The idea of this phase of the roundup was to have the seven twosomes in their four-wheel-drive vehicles herd the bison over the rough terrain toward the first holding pen that connected with the maze of chutes. The co-pilots in the vans had the job of hanging out the window on the passenger side and banging buckets or waving towels and shouting at the herd. If the bison scattered it was up to the van drivers to coax them back in the right direction.

As soon as the swing gate opened the organized mayhem and fabulous fun began. For the next forty-five minutes we chased the animals toward the target. All the while I was thankful the rangers had reminded me the day before to strap myself into the safety harness because we were bouncing over rocks and prairie dog mounds, sometimes at high speeds to get into position behind the herd or to head off a stray here and there or breakaway groups of up to fifty animals. When we were positioned behind a group we'd give them a slow shove in the right direction. But most of the time the noise was a total assault on the ears. Between the pounding hoofs and the screaming engines it was barely possible to hear Vincent's CD player at full volume. The only sound to compare I'd ever heard was the roar of a big forest fire when it got too close for comfort. Or maybe a couple of high speed freight trains running side by side. At one point we almost rear-ended a big cow and another time we had to face down a pawing bull. But when the action finally slowed we'd pushed all but a dozen or so strays into the first holding pen. The strays would be dealt with later by a couple of other rangers on horseback.

Once the herd was penned in their big corrals the rangers let them simmer down for a couple of hours while they munched on fresh baled hay and washed it down at strategically located watering pools. That was because they needed to be calm for the next stage of the operation. That next stage took up the following three-and-a-half days. Small groups of bison would be shuttled through a maze of smaller corrals toward their final destination, the hydraulic squeeze chute. The method used to send the animals on their way and then systematically divide them was an art in itself. The biggest bulls were prodded through thick swinging steel walls moved by heavy equipment. Those walls had to be thick because a big buffalo will attack anything, including the wall-moving equipment itself which had to be encased in an inch of plastic sheeting. The smaller bison were waiting in a 50 yard by 50 yard enclosure and they needed to be funneled into a three-foot-wide chute. So the equipment operator would slowly push one wall in to a fifty-by-twenty space as individual animals made it through the narrow outlet chute. As the waiting group got smaller, the wall would be pushed in some more until the last bison was through the opening. That left a line of bison filling a narrow chute. At this point hinged walls would be lowered to separate each animal. Then a ranger would prod the lead bison with a kind of whip on a long stick and administer a love tap on the butt to start the animal on its trip through the rest of the maze. The whole operation was a long and tedious process but it was vital for getting the bison culled and cared for. At the end of the maze came the hydraulic squeeze chute, a congested area where vets with needles and scalpels and rangers with air guns got each animal vaccinated, blood-tested with a neck poke, DNA-inspected with a hair sample, and computer-chipped on one ear while a photographer snapped the bison's' graduation pictures. Two steel collars were lowered from the catwalk above the chute and the devices wrapped around a bison's head. Then an animal doc rendered each bison incapable of moving by fastening a tool something like pliers in both nostrils. The tool really doesn't hurt the bison like Scott had said but it gets their attention and makes movement uncomfortable.

On the second day of the roundup one of the vets asked if I wanted to try the technique myself. He showed me how to apply the grip and I spent a few hours getting acquainted with buffalo snot. Mucous Gracias!

The hydraulic squeeze chute was the most dangerous part of the maze. If an animal went down for some reason, everybody backed off and Scott or Tucker would assess the situation. A couple of times while I was doing nose ring work an animal collapsed in the chute and had to be brought back to its feet. I was lucky again that Scott trusted me enough to let me work in this phase of the operation since the catwalk was off limits to non-professionals and protected from the public by chain link fencing. No one was allowed in the small support building next to the hydraulic squeeze chute either. All the technicians were housed in that space.

Beyond the hydraulic squeeze there was a fleet of federal trucks waiting to transport the culled bison to their new homes in Montana and New Mexico. The whole operation was organized to perfection. I stood for ten minutes watching the trucks pull away and sucking satisfaction from the work we'd done.

By the time the roundup wound down on Thursday I'd been hoping for a couple of days that it would never end. I'd become good friends with Scott and Vincent. I had nothing but respect for their professionalism. Scott and I had shared deep feelings and grown close over the week's work. We promised each other to stay in touch. And the whole experience in the Badlands had proved one of the most exhilarating and enjoyable times in my life. I made a promise to myself that I'd try to arrange a return engagement the next year. In fact, I took to the cowboy culture so enthusiastically that on a break in the middle of the week I drove over to the nearby Black Hills and took a look at a 2000 acre ranch that was up for sale. I'd always dreamed of owning a place like it with animals of my own to take care of and I decided to keep checking real estate ads when I got back home. But the time had come to flush my cotton balls and fly to Florida.

# TWENTY-EIGHT

By Thanksgiving everything was in place for my crash Mount Everest training program. I had about six months to get ready for an attempted ascent in May of 2005. I'd selected for my personal trainer one Jeremy Reardon, a taut and tanned thirty-something who had a reputation in the Tampa area as a stern conditioning taskmaster, just the kind of difficult disciplinarian I needed to help me work my way into top shape. He had more degrees in his field than you'd think one person could amass in a lifetime. The day after I'd stuffed myself with traditional turkey and all the trimmings we began an unbelievably arduous program that involved some of the most difficult stretching and balancing exercises known to man. And I had to do them practically around the clock. Now my every day began at four in the morning with thirty-two incredibly tough stretches and balances pictured for me in a Reardon photo brochure I'd taped to an office wall. That warm up routine took forty-five minutes at my office which was the clubhouse at a new condo Melinda and the kids had just put up. The condo was just a ten minute walk from the Lifestyles Fitness Gym where Reardon met me at five Monday through Friday to put me through another rigorous workout that included the same thirty-two exercises I'd completed just an hour before. But this time they had to be done under Reardon's severe supervision. And to top it all off, the exercises had to be repeated a third time by myself in the late afternoon.

All of this exertion five days a week was designed by Reardon to, in the words of his brochure, "create optimum levels of stabilization strength and postural control in a multiplaner, proprioceptively-enriched environment that allows optimum recruitment of joint stabilizers that establish high levels of neuromuscular control and functional strength." That was gibberish to me but it boiled down to Reardon being the most demanding son-of-a-bitch I'd ever dealt with. He was relentless in pushing me to my limit but then that was what I'd hired him to do. And I didn't like the regimen he'd set up for me at first because it was all new to me. I was from the old school and I thought I knew the best exercises. But over the years I hadn't kept up with all the effective new workouts and treatments that sports medicine had developed. If the amount of pain paid in Reardon's plan equaled the conditioning acquired, though, I thought I'd be able to chew tin cans and climb with the best mountain goat in a matter of months. By the time the weekends came around my aches and pains had aches and pains and I didn't have the strength to do much beyond flopping on a couch to rest until it was time to drop into bed. Then on Monday the whole hellish routine began anew.

＊ ＊ ＊

At the same time I'd retained Jeremy Reardon I also hooked up with an Asian-American orthopedic surgeon named Yi. He had a great reputation in Florida for patching up injured athletes. I hoped he was as good as the doctor who'd helped me out a dozen years earlier with rotator cuff surgery that allowed me to compete in the World swimming championships in England just six weeks after the injury was diagnosed. When I went to see Doctor Yi right before my Everest training began I took Jeremy with me so the two of them could discuss the feasibility of various extra exercises for my regimen. The range of options didn't look promising when the good doctor looked at the x-rays he had me submit to that morning. When the display light showcased my gnarled knees he asked right off, "What are you taking for pain?" Both knees had disintegrated badly since my last checkup a couple of years before, so much so that I would never be a candidate for knee replacement surgery. Doctor Yi had me try to walk a straight line for him and those results weren't good either. For years I'd been walking bowlegged to offset the pain in my knees. That had to change if I was ever going to make it up Everest. Now Dr. Yi looked at Jeremy and said that I would need to be taught to walk correctly. So he stabbed me with a cortisone shot in each knee and told Jeremy it was up to him to set me straight through exercising special leg muscles And the doctor said that before every simulated mountain climb, not to mention the real thing, my knees would have to be shot full of cortisone.

Then there was the matter of the right foods. After my Olympic training in the sixties I'd paid less and less attention to proper nutrition. And at times my intake was really awful. Living holed up in the jungle with the Contras or endlessly barhopping for the FBI wasn't exactly conducive to maintaining a balanced diet. My old health nut hero Bernard McFadden had always lived by the motto "you are what you eat" and if that was true I was a sorry stew marinating in Old Granddad. Now I was directed by a friend to seek out a nutritionist named Doctor Jerry Balduf who was billed as one of the best in the business. He set me up with a healthy diet and Melinda followed it meticulously in preparing meals. Lots of vegetables and fruits. But mostly protein which meant a lot of red meat. And if fish are full of mercury these days I was well on my way to qualifying as a thermometer. Melinda saw to it that I followed the doctors' loathsome advice not to let a drop of Old Granddad or any of his relatives pass my lips. Doctor Balduf also prescribed pills that would supply my blood with more oxygen, which would be vital for the Everest ascent.

So Jeremy's training and the consultations with Doctor Yi and Doctor Balduf's diet became routine over the next month. Or as routine as the fiendish program could get. When I'd met Jeremy I'd told him I was sixty-seven but that I wanted him to think of me as a twenty-five-year-old athlete in top shape and to work me accordingly. In fact, I told him if he coddled me in any way I was walking out on him and looking for a tougher tyrant. I can't recount all the times I cursed myself for making that demand. Or the number of times I cursed Reardon for meeting it. The prick took me so seriously that by the end of the first week I had homicidal urges toward him. But I knew I had to do everything he set out for me if I was going to climb the highest mountain in the world.

The next preparation problem had to do with my lack of experience climbing on ice. I'd been scrambling up more welcoming peaks for years, like Kineo in Maine which was a sheer rock formation I'd managed to scale straight up in a driving rain, and more recently the mountains in North Carolina where Melinda and I had bought a home. And I'd taken a lot of climbing lessons from some fine instructors for the past two years. But in order to qualify for Everest you have to fill out an application that summarizes you're climbing experience and to assure a committee that you've attained a certain skill level. There are a number of different teams that take on the mountain and the regulations to join them are tough because safety is all important. If there's any hint your lack of experience and ability might put another team member in jeopardy you'll be rejected in a heartbeat. Of course the fee involved in joining a team tends to discourage amateurs. The cost runs up around 55 to 60,000 dollars. Not to mention the time involved. In addition to the months or years of training, the climb itself can consume up to six or seven weeks. And you had to have spent some time mastering icy inclines to qualify. So I spent a lot of my scarce free time in late November sitting in libraries trying to lay out plans for a logical progression of climbs leading to Everest.

December and January proved to be an emotional rollercoaster for me. The first week of December was spent training and spending some quality time with the family but one Monday I got the word from Cedric Hills at the Salvation Army HQ in London that my planned trip to the Sudan would have to be put on hold. No one was being allowed into the country because of the continuing violence. The news was a deep downer for me. My heart went out to all the suffering people over there with no outside help forthcoming. That night visions of bone thin children disturbed my sleep. I vowed I'd try again to get Sudanese permission as soon as the situation improved enough to go. Then in the middle of the week Annie's internet surfing turned up another adventure for me. And one that could be used to forward my mountain climbing agenda at the same time. I was so excited about Annie's discovery that I told her to call the travel agent right away and I wrote a check for 3,000 to sign on. It was an Earthwatch Expedition research mission run by Doctor Dan Rubenstein of Princeton University to assess wildlife habitat in the Wamba area of Samburu District in Kenya. It seems the region was suffering under the population pressures that plagued the country. Kenya had one of the highest population growth rates in the world and the land with its wonderful biodiversity was at risk. The Samburu people had coexisted for years with lions and elephants and giraffes and an ark load of other native animals but now new settlement patterns and deforestation and overgrazing livestock were a dire threat to this African paradise. The mission volunteers would be monitoring the ecological conditions and managing wildlife for a couple of weeks around the town of Lewa 200 miles northwest of Nairobi. The idea was also to analyze the vegetation in the area so that its ability to sustain herbivores could be assessed. There'd been a longstanding problem with ticks and other disease carrying parasites that threatened the already declining two species of zebras around Lewa. The volunteers would identify and list individual zebras and monitor their movements and interactions so researchers could psych out the relationship of the two species to one another.

The mission sounded like a wonderful way to combine adventure with service, just the kind of opportunity that juiced my joints. I was sure I could continue my training regimen while I helped out with the team's work. And the thought occurred to me that since the mission would take me to Kenya, I'd start focusing my training right away for the caper I'd dreamed about for years, namely climbing Mount Kilimanjaro in neighboring Tanzania. In fact, the research study would be located on the slopes of Mount Kenya where I would be able to practice some high elevation climbing in preparation for Kilimanjaro. Then if I could manage to get up Kili I could qualify for Everest in May. Kili would give me some experience in snow and I could augment that with a trip in the early spring to the Grand Tetons for some real ice climbing practice. As soon as Annie had the arrangements for the African trip made I went to an indoor facility with virtual peaks made of plastic for climbers in Tampa and then back to our place in North Carolina for more practice. In the meantime, everything was arranged for me to leave on January the seventh for what used to be called, "The Dark Continent."

⁂ ⁂ ⁂

One day the following week Harry called and said he an Jimmie were coming into town from Miami and wanted to meet me there for a pre-New Year's Eve celebration at an Indian restaurant bar. I said I was taking Melinda out on the town later in the evening but that I could spare a couple of earlier hours for my old buddies. Once we were seated in a leather-lined booth the conversation and the booze began to flow. The booze in their direction, not mine and at one point Jimmie asked a question that must have been on his mind for a while.

"Sam, you sick f—, you do the things you do? Why fly your ass around the globe looking for trouble? Why not sit back and enjoy? You've got a great life waiting for you right here in Florida."

I looked at him over the rim of my mango milkshake glass and gave him part of the answer I'd been giving myself when I thought things over.

"Somebody has to do the things I do. I was born to do them. I'm led to do them. I do them because you two won't do them."

That became my mantra whenever, after that night, I was asked about my motivations.

⁂ ⁂ ⁂

The 2004 version of Christmas was the best I'd spent in years because it contrasted so starkly with the lonely 2003 holidays in Iraq. This time I had Melinda and the kids gathered around the hearth at the Hall Compound most of the day and the exchange of feelings with family beat any gift giving on Christmases past. But there were great presents around the tree and two big turkeys for the carving. And a lot of trimmings I had to pass up. But I got caught up on all the pride producing activities that Melinda and David and Kelly were pursuing. That evening Harry and Jimmie stopped by with their latest love interests and the conversation flowed along into the wee hours of the morning. When Melinda and I finally climbed into bed the hallway clock was chiming 2:00 A.M. and we were both fast asleep before our heads hit the pillows. At four I was up again doing my killing workout but at least I didn't have to meet Reardon because of the holiday. So I went back to the compound and rejoined Melinda in bed.

It was around noon when the ring of the bedside telephone woke me out of a deep sleep. Through my mental fog I recognized David's agitated voice and when I finally focused I tried to process the news that a powerful Indian Ocean earthquake had produced a huge tsunami that'd hit the coastlines of several countries. And that the death toll was already estimated at 9,000. I thanked David for the information and left Melinda to her sleep while I went over to the recreation room and snapped on the TV. The reports from Asia were slow in coming in so details about the tsunami were hard to come by but it sounded like the death toll would be rising. I sat by the TV for the rest of the afternoon as the numbers of victims rose and the first pictures of the disaster started filtering in. At one point Melinda joined me, and we worried together about the extent of the tragedy. By evening the numbers of reported victims had more than doubled. That's when Melinda started prodding me to think about volunteering to help.

"Sam, you've got to see if there's anything you can do for those poor people over there."

"But there's not much I can do. The Africa trip begins on the eighth of next month. By the time any relief effort is organized I'll be on top of Mount Kilimanjaro."

"But Sam, those people are going to need help right away."

I went to bed that night with an itchy conscience. It was true that I might be able to be of some help to the tsunami survivors but the Africa trip was a once in a later lifetime opportunity that I didn't want to give up under any circumstances. I did a lot of tossing and turning and when I did get to sleep I had visions of huge ocean waves inundating scores of people and carrying them out to sea.

The next morning the TV was counting up to 50,000 victims and my conscience was switching from itching to outright pain. But since I now knew the relief effort was in progress and even after David and Kelly called asking if I was planning to go to the stricken areas, I held back. Did I really want to go off again so soon and to a part of the world I knew very little about while I wasn't sure whether I could be of use anyway. The international relief plan was apparently massive. Would I only be in the way if I managed to get to the afflicted areas?

On the twenty-eighth predictions were that the death toll would rise to well over a 100,000. In the middle of the morning I got a call that gave me the final push. It was from my writer friend Larry in Ohio.

"Why aren't you in Sri Lanka?"

"O.K., you're the fourth person who's tried to prick my conscience. But I've got to be in Africa on the eighth. I'll be going by way of India, though, so maybe I'll see if there's anything I can do there. And in Africa Somalia's been hit hard too and they're not getting the press that some of the other countries are."

But I knew when I said it my rationalization wasn't good enough. For no other reason than that my friend had focused on Sri Lanka, I called Annie right away and had her make reservations for a flight the next day to Colombo, the capitol. Why I hadn't decided on Thailand or Indonesia or India I don't know to this day. But 24 hours later with a file folder of notes and news clippings and internet fact sheets under my arm I kissed Melissa goodbye and boarded my flight out of the Miami airport. For the next 42 hours I was in and out of planes. When I'd boarded in Miami the newspapers had the tsunami deaths at 12,000. When I deplaned at Heathrow after the first leg of my journey the newspapers there had the figure at 50,000. After I completed the next leg in Nairobi the papers there had upped the toll to 77,000. Then when I got to Bombay the figure was "near on 100,000."

When I finally sighted the Sri Lankan coastline I couldn't believe the devastation. For what seemed like miles inland there was nothing but uprooted trees and shattered buildings and mounds of debris. As we deplaned one of the flight attendants told me the pilot had got word while we were in the air that there were at least 125.000 lives lost and the numbers were still climbing. This disaster was obviously going to make last year's earthquake in Iran look relatively benign.

Once on solid earth I made a quick inventory of my small carry-on backpack that held everything I'd brought. Now my only possessions consisted of a little medical kit, an extra pair of pants, two pairs of underwear, one shirt, and an extra sock pair. The rest of the space was taken up by rainwear since the northeast section of Sri Lanka was said to be plagued by monsoons and mudslides at this time of year. My big duffel bag full of clothes and other necessities had been sent on ahead for storage in Kenya. I was foolishly worried now that by the middle of my week here in Sri Lanka such a limited wardrobe, with little or no chance of keeping or getting it clean, would turn me into a social pariah. I had no idea then how the smell of rotting human flesh here would put my own body odor in perspective.

At the airport terminal I hired a driver through the tourism office and booked myself into a four-star hotel in downtown Colombo. Although it might strike the reader as callous to stay in such posh surroundings under the circumstances I was only using the hotel as a place to hang my pathetic proverbial hat. I knew there would be very few free hours for sleeping or hanging around the bar looking longingly at the booze bottles. I would mostly be living out of the car I'd hired or makeshift shelters but I booked the room because I've made it a practice to spend as much money as possible while I'm in disaster areas as a way of giving the economy a little boost in its hour of need. In addition to my noble ideals for booking the room, I had also learned that having a place that was able to provide room service meals at any hour could be invaluable!

After I checked in at the hotel my driver Phutee took me straight out to one of the badly hit coastal towns to view the devastation. I'd seen a lot of destruction in my time but this was unbelievable. Not a building was standing and there was twisted wreckage everywhere. If I could only have brought a fleet of front-end loaders with me from the States to remove some of this rubble. But far more disturbing than the debris were the many mass graves. Not to mention the bodies visible in the twisted wreckage of the towns or tangled in the forest mangrove roots. The stench was overwhelming. It was obvious that if I was going to be of any use here I would have to blot out the sights and ignore the smells. Everywhere Phutee drove me along the coast the situation was the same. Buildings sheared off to the foundation and broken cars and buses everywhere. And more bodies. Later Colin Powell would describe the tsunami devastation as the worst sight he'd ever seen and from the small swath of Sri Lanka I saw I couldn't have agreed more.

Back in Colombo I went straight to the Sri Lanka Red Cross office and volunteered my services. There I was told I'd be paired with a relief worker named Mark from British Catholic Charities. Our job would be to advise the locals on temporary and permanent housing for the displaced poor. That suited me fine since it meshed with my experience in Iraq and was probably the best use of my talents. But I soon discovered that the main relief effort was so disorganized, which was understandable given the scope of the disaster, that I could best help in other ways. I could see that some of the supplies that were being flown in from all over the world were just sitting around in empty fields and not getting delivered to survivors. And one of the Red Cross volunteers put me on to the fact that lots more supplies were gathering dust in warehouses around the city and they could be taken and distributed with no questions asked. So I took the initiative and hired Phutee's brother and his fairly big truck for 300 dollars a day and the three of us began loading it with supplies from out of the fields and warehouses. Though

I didn't know it at the time, there were other volunteers improvising in the same way. Once we had a load of commandeered food and water and clothing in the truck, we set out for the coast looking for survivors to distribute it to. On the same truck trips, we cleared as much debris as possible. We also took a bunch of machetes with us so we could give them to survivors so they could cut bamboo for tent poles. And we stuffed the truck with canvas tarpaulins for the tents themselves. Plus plastic buckets to carry boiled water. And light medicines and cooking fuel and blankets.

A number of times on our distribution runs we saw dead bodies on or next to the roads but there was nothing we could do about them except to alert the overwhelmed officials of their presence. Nearly always there were bodies buried in the wreckage but the worst experiences came while we were searching the mangrove forests for survivors. We never found one living person there but more dead ones than I want to remember. In Florida, our mangrove roots are only a foot-and-a-half to two-feet tall but here in Sri Lanka they rose as high as 9 feet from the ground and the coastal forests were dense with them. Their role in the tsunami was both positive and negative. On the positive side, they acted like a wall that protected some of the coastal communities behind them. But on the other hand, they also acted like a sieve when the tide went out, leaving bodies tangled in their tentacles. By the time Phutee and his brother and I began searching the forest for survivors the bodies of the unclaimed victims there were so bloated that it would probably be impossible for them to be identified. They looked like they would explode if you stuck a pin in them. And the stench was overwhelming. We wanted to bring as many back to the truck as possible for their surviving relatives but we'd been warned not to touch any bodies for fear of disease. The mere sight of them grotesquely caught in the mangrove roots had already sickened my mind and it gave me nightmares a lot like the ones I suffered after Ground Zero. Every morning in Sri Lanka I woke up in a cold sweat reliving the previous day's grisly scenes.

I'll never forget what I witnessed in Sri Lanka. Adults and children clutching battered pots and pans as they made their way through the rubble of flattened neighborhoods. Scores of others looking through tears at photos of unidentified victims displayed on the few still standing walls. But also the rebuilding that had already begun despite the terrific trauma these poor people had suffered. I asked myself if I would've had the guts to go on if my child had been ripped from my arms and swallowed by the sea, as many of these survivors' children had been. Most of the women who were searching the debris or helping distribute building materials or checking photos for missing relatives and friends had taken the time to pin fresh flowers in their

*Aiding Tsunami survivors in Sri-Lanka, December 2004-January 2005.*

hair to symbolize their commitment to life. Watching them left me floundering for an answer as to how a loving and forgiving God could allow a disaster of such proportions to befall a continent. So much overwhelming suffering. What could be the explanation?

One night back in Colombo I decided to tap an old source for the answer to my question. I emailed Pastor Ron back in Dayton from the hotel's business computer center and told him I'd seen more devastation and death than I could bear this time and that I was looking for an explanation of God's supposed mercy, that it was all too much for me to understand. I reminded him that he'd comforted me after Ground Zero and other disasters but this one was of a magnitude that had me doubting more than I ever had. I told him that all of the old assurances were powerless in the wake of this Sri Lanka experience. I said that I was openly weeping a lot of the time now while I was trying to apply all the lessons he had taught me about letting God be God and trusting that all things will work out for the best if we believe in the glory to come. And I told him I'd prayed every chance I got lately and asked God what I was supposed to be learning from this Sri Lanka experience. But I told the pastor that I needed more, namely a really compelling explanation of the "why?" of this disaster. Then I ended the email by signing it "Desperate."

While I waited for Pastor Julian's reply I went to my room and locked up all of my IDs and passport and expensive camera and a fat bundle of cash for Africa and for helping out tsunami sufferers because for the next three days I'd be living and sleeping in the truck. Phutee and I were scheduled to set out on a long trip to the northeast tip of the coastline where the rebels fighting the government were hell-bent to set up an autonomous state. These were the brutal Marxist Tamil Tigers or LTTE. Their hatred for the ruling powers was so great that a couple of days earlier they'd made a raid on government territory and burned down a warehouse full of relief supplies. It was a seven-hour drive from Colombo over barely passable roads that were in constant peril from massive mudslides. But we had to make it through because we had the truck loaded with supplies for tsunami victims on that part of the coast. Phutee was leery about my traveling through the rebel stronghold but I assured him there'd be no trouble. I'd dealt many times with rogue outfits like the Tamils when I was doing the U.S. government's bidding in Central America.

Phutee knew the back roads well and he maneuvered the truck through debris and mud. Within a few miles of our target we met up a couple of times with squads of AK-47 wielding Tamil Tigers decked out in their mismatched camis and face-hiding bandannas. One of the forlorn groups demanded my cheap camera and the three twenty-dollar bills I was carrying so I obliged them since they didn't seem interested in the 500 dollars worth of rupees hidden in my shoe. Thanks to the rebels' oversight I got to hand out the rupees later along with the supplies we'd brought to the survivors.

After spending two-an-a-half days in Tamil Tiger territory we went back to Colombo and Pastor Julian's email reply was waiting for me at the hotel. Here is what it said.

> *Sam,*
>
> *God bless your efforts in Sri Lanka. Because of Him, here is my answer to your question. There is a conflict in the world between good and evil. There is a holy, good God and there is an Evil, destructive Devil. There are good Angels and there are Demons. There is an eternal Heaven and eternal Hell. In past history Satan rebelled against God and influenced one-third of the Angels to join him. Adam and Eve and the human race were created by God in His image and they were given free choice to obey Him or rebel. As a result of their sin they were separated from their loving Heavenly Father. The world was so wicked in God's sight that He was going to destroy it all. But Noah found grace in the eyes to the Lord. The human race was saved from the great flood through the faith of Noah. This Bible record of history tells of Lot and Sodom, Moses and Egypt, Israel and surrounding nations defeated with David the great King as great warrior.*
>
> *In the New Testament we have Jesus, the perfect man, mocked, tortured and killed. Some early disciples were beheaded, imprisoned, tortured, etc. Church history is filled with extreme violence and injustice. Natural disasters take place because of natural elements. But in the midst of all this suffering, pain, questions, we see the love of God, forgiveness, strength, hope, compassion, etc. It has always been that there are people who know God and reflect God to their generation and in the midst of their circumstances. The eternal future will be a place of great joy and great sorrow but they will not be intermingled. It will be sorted out by Jesus and we will not live with the awareness of evil as we now know it. God bless you, stay safe.*
>
> *—Ron*

I can't say that Ron's explanation did a whole lot to ease the pain of my horrible experiences in Sri Lanka but it did make me appreciate some of the good that had come out of my stay. One of those goods was my growing friendship with Phutee. Over those eight days in his country we became very close. Phutee was a Ceylonese Christian and we kept up a running conversation about Christianity as we passed out relief supplies and when we were on the roads together. And we talked a lot about why God had brought on this devastation. Phutee could see what the situation was doing to me and he knew I was trying to control my anger that God would allow such a calamity. I was a mess and Phutee showed me great compassion. I was exhausted from lack of sleep and I wasn't eating anything because I was worried about getting sick from contaminated food. I had plenty of bottled water but I'd twice made the mistake of brushing my teeth with tap water at the hotel. I expected to fall ill at any moment and I prayed I could hold up long enough to help the tsunami survivors and still have enough left to make the Africa trip. But throughout my mental anguish Phutee would always buck me up with encouraging words. On the morning of my sixth day in Sri Lanka he said "Sam, don't take this wrong but you need a break and I have a friend who has an amazing farm. It's on our way tomorrow so we could take about three hours off and go there if you want." Phutee's suggestion sounded great to me and anyway I was way too tired to argue so I agreed.

The next morning Phutee, his brother and I loaded up the truck and Phutee's car with food and water from a new storage center leased to the Sri Lanka Red Cross at St. Joseph's University in Colombo and then we headed south. About three hours later we drove through an archway that formed the entrance to a huge plantation. That's when Phutee delivered the big surprise. His friend's farm was a breeding center for elephants. There were about seventy-five of the pachyderms in residence and for the next four hours I was in seventh heaven, riding bareback, washing elephants in a three-foot deep creek, and having water fights between "my" animals and "Phutee's." All of the negative energy that'd plagued me over the last week vanished and I felt totally rejuvenated. On the way back through the big archway I thanked Phutee and his brother over and over and gave them each a fifty-dollar bonus in rupees out of the stash of cash in my shoe.

Later that afternoon we delivered our last batch of supplies to a southern coastal fishing village. Then I went back to the hotel sad but fulfilled. I'd had a deeply satisfying week helping people despite the horror and my spiritual trauma. And the day's recreation at the elephant farm was an unforgettable experience. I was leaving the next morning for more adventures in Kenya and my only worry was that the time spent in Sri Lanka might have undone all the conditioning I'd endured to make the Kilimanjaro climb. I'd lost ten pounds in eight days from lack of sleep and food. But then I felt guilty about this worry in view of all that the Sri Lankan people had suffered. I thanked the Lord for letting me have the satisfaction of the trip and for the opportunity to meet so many courageous souls. I'd grown quite fond of the Sri Lankans and I had confidence in their ability to come back from their terrible loss.

# TWENTY-NINE

By the time I reached Bombay to catch the second leg of my flight to Nairobi I was thoroughly depressed again. Even though I was about to meet other volunteers for what had once promised to be an exciting research project in the heart of Africa's animal kingdom I was so exhausted I was sure I wouldn't enjoy the work. At the same time I was aware that I wasn't hitting on all my mental cylinders and that with a little rest I might look at things differently. The lack of sleep and adequate food at the tsunami site had negated nearly all the training for the Kilimanjaro climb and I had to make that ascent to qualify for Everest. I wanted to bypass the research project and head straight to Tanzania so I could use the two weeks I was supposed to be in Kenya to try to get back into mountain climbing shape. I'd already coughed up 3,000 dollars for the research gig, though, so I talked myself into staying the course but with the thought in the back of my mind that if I couldn't find the time to work out in Kenya I'd pack up again and head for Tanzania.

When I got into Nairobi I met up with the research team at the Fairview hotel. The team consisted of eight people besides myself, including four Ph.D.s, three school teachers and one physician, five women and three men. We all hit it off right away and had a cordial talk over coffee while we waited for our host, who would fly with us to our first camp in Kenya. One of the women, a perky redhead from Oklahoma City, had lost her luggage en route and I volunteered to lend her some of my gear and clothes. Luckily I had my duffel bag now and wasn't so strapped for wardrobe items as I'd been in Sri

*Sam helps Tsunami victims in Sri-Lanka, December 2004-January 2005.*

Lanka. Several of the team members were repeat participants in Earthwatch projects and they all bubbled with enthusiasm for the work ahead. After our greetings were exchanged we were taken to a small airport and piled on to a puddle jumper for a short bumpy flight to a dirt strip in Wamba. That's where six of us were to be stationed. In Wamba two of the women and myself were loaded into a van and driven to Lewa. We met our guide and porters there and set off for a two-hour drive to our base camp. Things were looking up already. The sights out the van window were an animal lover's dream. Herds of giraffe and elephants and antelope and the tiny ten-pound deer called dic dic. Also an occasional rhino or lion. The guide pointed out three different kinds of cheetahs. At another point he pulled off the side of the rutted dirt road and stopped near a clump of bushes and whispered "Don't make any sudden movement and look over there." Under the bushes were three cheetahs napping. They were three brothers who roamed the area together and they'd become so regular in their habit of dozing under those bushes that tour guides counted on them to provide a thrill for the tourist trade. The guide said we were lucky to get such a close up view of them. The sight of all the magnificent animals around the Lewa camp made the horrors of the tsunami disaster recede in my mind.

The base camp accommodations were beautiful too, very much like a romantic Hollywood set with big thatched-roofed huts that featured spacious rooms. And a cluster of smaller thatched-roofed huts where the support staff lived and worked and prepared mouth watering meals. A sort of grand resort out in the middle of wild country. The whole huge enclave was enclosed by electric fences to keep the big game at bay though the wire did nothing to deter the tribe of monkeys that gained entrance through the nearby tall trees.

Once we were settled in I got a burst of bad news. Our guide told us that for the foreseeable future we would have to do our observation work from the team's Jeeps because there was a pack of marauding lions on the loose in the vicinity and though they hadn't been spotted in a few days the coast couldn't be declared clear yet. This put a crimp in my exercise plans since I was hoping to do a lot of walking to help me get back in shape. On the way to the base camp the guide assured me I could do a little climbing around the base camp since it was located on the slopes of Mt. Kenya. That was still a viable option because the sprawling camp grounds were enclosed by electric fences and any lion that tried to intrude would get zapped into changing his or her mind. The fences worked in fact on all the animals except the thieving little monkeys, but they were a lot of fun to watch as they practiced larceny around the camp mess. They would even steal your gear if you didn't keep it firmly attached to your body at all times.

That first afternoon in camp I discovered a huge cliff inside the compound and for the next three days I would go out by myself and practice scaling it before breakfast. The high altitude in the area was also a plus because it would simulate the environment for the Kilimanjaro climb, at least the earlier stages of it. But here at the research base camp the lack of exercise during the animal observation work was weighing on my mind. Riding around in a Jeep didn't do much for muscle development or endurance enhancement. Fifteen days of this would be enough to ruin my chances to tackle the big mountain across the border. So on the morning of my fourth day at the camp I decided to call it quits. My conscience hurt me because I wasn't sure my leaving wouldn't put a crimp in the team's work but I was sixty-seven years old and I didn't have that much time left to realize my most dramatic dreams. I explained my decision to the team leader and she said she was sorry that I wouldn't be able to help out as planned but also that she understood my reason. So a few minutes later I called and arranged through the local conservancy game preserve office to hire a bush pilot to fly me back to Nairobi so I could catch the one hour flight from there to Tanzania.

It was the 11th of January when I landed at the airport in Ashura, Tanzania planning to go straight to a hotel and make arrangements for a climb. But when I got off the plane two African men surprised me in the middle of the tarmac and introduced themselves as Remy and Solomon. They wanted to know why I was in Tanzania and if they could assist me with bookings or other needs. When I told them I wanted to climb Kili they gave me their card and said they could arrange everything. They even drove me to a hotel they recommended, which took about an hour so that we got to know each other a little. The ride gave them time to arrange for a guide and a couple of porters through a cell phone call. When they dropped me at the hotel we agreed to meet the next morning to firm up arrangements for a climb the following day. Before I checked into my room I asked the hotel owner to vouch for Remy and Solomon and he said they had an excellent reputation and were especially well thought of by tourists. The rest of the day and evening I explored the hotel, a cute little thatched-roofed affair with a gorgeous flower garden, an excellent restaurant where I put away a big steak, and a patio bar where I unfortunately had to restrict myself to a couple of non-alcoholic pineapple drinks.

The next morning Remy and Solomon arrived bright and early and we made a deal that would put me on the mountain the next day. They said they had already lined up a great guide and a porter and they asked me to pick out a menu for the climb, including meals at three way station huts and on the trail. Then they left and I spent an anxious day wandering close to the hotel and anticipating the climb to come. Finally the next morning arrived and I found myself rolling over two hours of rough roads in Remy and Solomon's BMW up to the gates of the national park. Right inside the gates I got my introduction to the guide, a slight fellow named Minja, and our equally small porter, Noah. Minja explained that he and Noah would carry the food, water, and gear, which were purchased in advance and waiting at the climb site. The gear would include lots of snow stuff, heavy duty boots, enough down clothing to ward off the freezing weather at the highest elevations, sleeping bags, a portable cooking stove, pots and pans and plates. So considering the size of the load compared to the size of Minja and Noah I arranged with Solomon and Remy for thirty-dollars to take on another porter named Patrice. That was no problem since porters hung around the main gate at the park looking for work. The four way split would lighten our loads considerably. I wasn't absolutely sure Patrice would be needed but I figured he could probably use the work and if he and Noah performed well I could leave them with a handsome tip. That only seemed right since the whole cost of the six day climb was a paltry 1,200 dollars. Besides, the trip up the mountain would give both Patrice and Noah a couple of useful entries for their dossiers. To work your way up to being a guide on Kili you had to climb regularly as a porter for five years.

Once the details about fees were worked out we all sat on some benches just inside the park and Minja described the coming ascent. It seems there are two routes up Kilimanjaro. One is called the Coca-Cola route and the other one is the Whiskey and I think you can guess which is the toughest. Naturally I chose the easier Coke path since after my time in Sri Lanka I wasn't sure I could make it up a steep staircase let alone a 19,000 foot mountain. As it was the soft drink route added up to thirty-three kilometers up and, naturally, thirty-three back. Of course the climb would have to be accomplished in increments. The first day would take us up a 7 kilometer grade to the first camp which would turn out to be accurately called a hut. We would bed down there at a settlement called Mandara at 8,920 feet above sea level. Then the second day would bring another nine kilometer climb to the next camp, the Horombo hut at 12,370 feet. Then on day three another twelve kilos to stop number three, the famous Kibo hut at 15,510 feet. Minja smiled and said "The next level is the peak and its only five kilometers from Kibo, but straight up."

Next Minja filled me in a bit on his qualifications and experience. I was interested in what he had to say because he looked so small I wondered how he could possibly conquer a high hill let alone a mighty mountain. He told me he was 42 years old and weighed 135 pounds, though I would have guessed his weight at 110. But he also told me he'd made the trip to the top of Kili over a 100 times with 45 kilos of gear and supplies on his back and he thought of those treks as a job like any other. But the average worker in the average job should have been so lucky as to be able to have the glorious mountain as their work site. At every lull in the conversation I kept sneaking a peek at the summit glistening white in the sun. I couldn't believe I was finally looking at the sight Hemingway had loved and described so well. Needless to say I was anxious to get started but I had to bide my time until first light the next morning.

By sunup we were making good progress up through dense jungle and into one of the most beautiful forests I'd ever seen, at first an easy almost horizontal climb that quickly became fairly steep after about an hour. I told Minja as we set out that there would probably be times up ahead when I'd beg him to let me quit and backtrack down the mountain but that his job would be to talk me out of it. I added that I'd be serious about canceling the whole venture but that he should keep saying "You can do it, Sam." And then give me a good reason for going on. And that each time he succeeded in prodding me forward and upward I'd give him five bucks. Little did I know that first morning that I was about to make Minja a millionaire by African standards. Or that he'd also almost get killed on Kilimanjaro since several times when he prodded me as requested I would have thrown him off a cliff if I'd had the strength. But most of that deceptively easy first day I'd been pushing at such a pace that Minja was constantly reminding me to "pooley, pooley, pooley," which was Swahili for "take it easy."

We reached the first hut at sundown and I was feeling good about my conditioning after all. I'd accomplished those first seven klicks without a hitch or too much discomfort. My fourteen pound pack full of water, and clothes, and camera, and soap, and toothpaste, and toothbrush was feeling heavy, but tolerable on my back though the higher we climbed the heavier it felt. Toward the end of the day I was glad I hadn't packed any shaving equipment. Another ounce would have done me in. The hut was equipped with thin mats, for sleeping, spread on a hardwood floor but when I stretched out on mine after the day's steady climb it felt like cloud nine. The Mandara hut, like all the others along the way up the mountain was a small wooden A-frame building. Once we had our bedding ready and waiting the porters broke out the butane stove and cooked a meal to be served in the hut's little "dining room." I never tasted a better buffalo steak in my life and it was just part of a three course meal that would form the pattern of our food service for the rest of the climb. Always delicious chicken or buffalo steak brought to me on a tray at a table with a special cloth bearing Minja's design. Each guide had his own distinctively designed table cloth. So it seemed that I'd be living in relative luxury on my way up the mountain. Except for the fact that there was no heat in the huts and my long johns were way overmatched by the cold when it was time to shiver off to sleep, in addition to the fact that there was no running water. As it turned out the lack of running water was no problem, because the porters always heated bottled water on the butane stoves and brought it for my bath before we started out each day.

Bright and very early the next morning we were off toward the second level. For the first couple of kilometers I felt fine and I was enjoying the nearly perpendicular trek through tundra pocked with low bushes. Minja was giving me climbing lessons all along the way. Every chance I got I took my eyes off the trail to take in the gorgeous vistas off to our east. But at around 10,000 feet I began to feel some dull pain in my chest and I knew I was in for a lot worse very soon And nearly half the climb was still ahead of me. I only hoped that Dr. Balduf had seen to it that I had the right nutrients to make it to the top and that I could take in enough oxygen on the way. But at the same time I knew that now that I'd got this far, nothing was going to stop me from conquering Kili and qualifying for Everest. So I kept plugging through the pain and at sundown staggered into the Horombo hut for a rejuvenating sleep. That night on Kili reminded me of the ones over in Iraq because I had to sleep with all of my bulky gear on to keep from freezing to the sleeping bag. There was a rule on Kili against having fires in camp. The only heat we would see for five days came from the small portable stoves the porters used to cook the meals. I'd never been so cold in my life as in those first few nights on Kili. I had to wonder how much colder the air could get in the higher elevations of Everest.

The next day I hit a wall less than an hour into the climb at the 13,000 foot level. My chest was exploding and my knees felt like bones were grinding into bones. About that time I remembered that because of the tsunami distraction I'd forgotten about getting the cortisone shot Dr. Yi had scheduled me to take before tackling the mountain. When we came around a turn in the tundra trail I told Minja for the first time that I couldn't go on, that I was going to quit. But he'd learned his role well. He sat down next to me and said, "Come on Mr. Sam, you can do it. Only 6,000 feet more." That wasn't exactly what I wanted to hear but he kept pressing the point that I'd come this far and it would be more than a shame not to push on. "And the next phase is easy. Just a slight incline." Then it was up a few more feet. Straight up. But I couldn't deny Minja was doing just what I'd wanted him to do.

And I wanted to conquer this mountain in the worst way. The trouble was I was in the process of doing it in the worst way all right, on a lung-and-a-half and creaky knees. But Minja kept prodding me and the next thing I knew I'd dragged myself back to my feet and onto the trail. All the while I was trying to climb and walk in the special way that Minja recommended to conserve energy. There was a knack to it and after the first few hours on the trail the day before I'd learned it pretty well. The technique is called 'the rest step' and it methodically moves you forward. The idea is pretty much like it sounds—a step at a time followed by a second's stop. It's used whenever the climber needs to recuperate between steps. At the lower elevations it's usually your legs that need rest—step therapy but when you get higher up it's your lungs that need help. High up or lower down on the mountain, though, you have to be well balanced to move without inviting inhibiting pain.

We were making slow progress toward the third camp when I had to pee. That hadn't been a problem so far because I'd sweated so much despite the temperatures freezing my snot in mid-drip. There wasn't much fluid left in me. I'd only had to stop once to urinate the first day. Now, though, when I unzipped I had a hard time finding my pisser. Because of the cold and the thin air it had shriveled to a size where I could have used a thimble for a condom if there'd been a willing woman within 12,000 feet of me. When I finally located my poor prick and tried to pee it produced a piercing pain. Then I almost fainted and I got hit with a blinding headache that was probably started by my lungs. That's when I decided that if I ever climbed another high mountain I'd rig up a little heater and attach it to my fly zipper or failing that tie a string around the incredible shrinking shaft so I could at least locate it when nature called.

My chest was hurting so bad now that I stopped every 5 to 10 feet and begged Minja to let me quit altogether. But each time he urged me back to the climb, first with "honey" and then with "vinegar." At one point I'd give up and he'd say "We may see some animals on the next stretch" and then I'd falter again and it would be "Wait till you see the view around the next bend." But after half a dozen failures of will he'd say something like "White men can't climb as well as black men" or "You aren't in very good shape, are you?" or "I brought some British women up this far last year." Then it would be "Get back on the trail or you'll never qualify for Everest." I wanted to strangle him or throw him into the next crevasse. Not only was he getting more and more obnoxious he was costing me five bucks every time he insulted me. He was beginning to remind me of one of my old swimming coaches who I'd hated with all my heart. He would walk the length of the pool as I swam, screaming at the top of his lungs to induce my maximum effort and beyond. But I remembered that he'd managed to improve my performance to Olympic level so I resolved once again to try to accede to Minja's taunts. But the higher we got on the mountain the harder that became, especially when I began to trip or slip at which point I'd fall over backward on my pack like a helpless turtle. Or when I'd just keel over trying to stand up after a rest. And every few 100 feet I'd have an overwhelming urge to throw up though I never produced the puke. There were times too when I wanted to pitch the camera I'd brought to get rid of the weight but Minja talked me out of that too. Besides I knew that I didn't have the strength to wrestle the damn thing out of my backpack. But just before we reached the next camp I thought of pitching the new Rolex Mariner watch Melinda had given me for Christmas because my wrist felt like it was dragging a concrete block along with it. I even thought about ditching the bottled water in my backpack but that would involve another expenditure of effort. Most of the way toward the third camp I wanted to lie down and roll over on my stomach and die because I hurt too much to go on or even to start back down the mountain.

More than once I got mentally confused and hallucinated. Fortunately I'd been warned that this might happen or these moments might have been scarier. At one point I thought I was back in my Florida condo climbing a stairwell and started calling for Melinda. Another time I was convinced that Minja and the porters were bent on stealing my backpack. And once I thought I saw a herd of elephants charging at me from the rocks above us. I also thought my chest would burst at any moment and my knees were throbbing while my legs shook from the effort and all that was no hallucination. On top of everything else I was worried about getting really sick so I'd have to be carried back down the mountain on a stretcher. I'd had altitude sickness once in Colorado and I'd been laid up in a hotel room for two days. I'd finally decided back then that sick or not I had to drive to a lower elevation and so I did and didn't feel any better till I hit Kansas. But up to this point on Kili as far as that crippling altitude malady was concerned I was doing O.K. Still I told Minja that I thought I should rest up for at least twelve hours when we got to Kibo camp so I could get some of my strength back. And after the third day's horrific twelve hour climb we finally reached the fabled Kibo hut. It was the storied spot where climbers rested up for the final assault on the summit, confident in the knowledge that they could reach it with relative ease. I'd read about Kibo in all the outdoor magazines for years. And now I'd reached the hut, which was perched precariously on a steep incline. I said a prayer of thanks to God that I'd reached this point and hadn't broken down.

When we got situated in the hut I headed straight for the sleeping quarters and arranged my mattress and laid down intent on a twelve hour rest but Minja came and stood over me and insisted that I eat something first. I told him I didn't think I could eat and when we went into the dining room Minja found out I was right. There was a small steak set out in front of me but there was no way I could touch it. The very thought of food made me want to throw up and Minja got very concerned about me. He said I would have to eat even if I couldn't swallow very much because eating would give me something to think about and ease the pain by taking my mind off of it. Then he brought over s couple of cookies and a bottle of water along with half a Diamox pill. After I'd choked down the cookies at Minja's insistence one to the porters brought a wonderful bowl of meat and vegetable soup. It took me half an hour to get the soup down but when I'd finished I did feel a little better. So it was off to sleep with the assurance that Minja would allow me a full twelve hours of oblivion.

Late the next morning I woke up sufficiently restored to thank Minja for pulling me through the previous day and to tell him to make sure I made it to the 18,000 foot Everest qualifying level even if he had to kick me the rest of the way up the mountain. He was all smiles and said he knew I'd change my mind about quitting. I had to admit that he'd proved to be as good a mental guide as he was a trail blazer. And the tougher the going got and the more he spurred me on the deeper our friendship became. By the fourth day we were trading good-natured insults. He would imply that I was a white wuss and I'd threaten to throw his black ass off the peak of Kili once we got there. But I knew I'd never forget this little man and that if I ever made it up to the top of Everest I'd have to drink a toast to Minja for making it possible.

As we set out on that fourth day of the climb Minja had given me the other half of the Diamox pill and I'd washed it down with some garlic soup he carried in a thermos jug. Then it was five straight up hours till we stopped around noon for lunch. But I couldn't eat a thing and while the others did I gazed up at the snowcapped heights and said another silent prayer that I could make it all the way to the end of this journey I'd dreamed about for so long. Then it was into the climb again. By the early afternoon the sun glistening off the snow piled all around us was so blinding I lost track of Minja and the porters a couple of times. I'd been warned not to look at it straight on for more than a second or two because it could actually burn your eyes. The idea was to focus on exposed rocks or keep looking down at the bare trail or at the horizon off to the left and right or the clouds below us. Three or four times I tripped while I was scanning the horizon and went over backward and more than once I almost fainted from the lack of oxygen. I hurt all over now and it took me two hours to cover the same amount of ground I'd taken an hour to cover the day before. Minja kept urging me to put one foot in front of the other and take about five rest steps, then quit altogether for a minute or two. I'd bought a walking pole at the Kibo hut and after every few steps now I'd lean on it for support. It was the only way I could keep standing. Minja would shout at me from behind to "pooley, pooley, pooley" as if I needed any coaxing to go slowly. But I couldn't afford to take too long a break at this altitude for fear of freezing. The idea now was to keep moving to make the blood circulate. Tears froze to my face thanks to the howling wind. That was the only sound, aside from Minja's voice, I'd heard for days.

Late that afternoon we reached the little barren plateau where climbers rest before the final 900-foot ascent to the summit. When I fell down on purpose to rest it took me a while to realize that I'd just qualified for the Everest climb with a few 100 feet to spare. We were now well above 18,000, really closer to 19,000 according to Minja, and I can't describe the feeling of accomplishment at that moment. All that training and denial had paid off big time. There was so much welled-up emotion that I cried and again the tears joined the others frozen to my face. But I also knew I couldn't go any further. My lungs felt like they weighed a 1,000 pounds and I could barely lift my arms. I'd walked straight up thirty kilometers and now I was desperate to get down to a level where I could breathe without intense pain. My energy and willpower were totally tapped out. I laid there for half-an-hour before I told Minja that this was it, that I couldn't climb another inch and that he should give me fifteen minutes more rest and then we'd head back down the mountain. He was thoroughly disappointed that I would come so close to the goal and then quit but I didn't think I could take the terrific pain in my chest a much longer before I'd be dead.

Minja agreed it was time to turn back, not only because he'd spotted weather front coming in and we'd be cutting it close trying to make the summit before we got hit with a lot of wind and snow. Besides that, as I learned later in the day when we'd reached a lower level, Minja was concerned about me. It seems my face and lips had turned very blue. So now he helped me to my feet and when he withdrew his supporting arms I almost keeled over before he caught me. I laid back down and the porters produced some hot porridge that I managed to choke down even though I hated it. Anything for body fuel at this altitude.

Once I felt a little better I remembered a promise I'd made to Melinda's best friend, our housekeeper Nancy, back in Florida. Her father had died of a heart attack just before I'd left for Sri Lanka and I'd promised her I'd say a prayer for him when I reached the highest point I could make. I told her that altitude might offer me the best chance I might ever get to gain God's ear. My promise consoled her and she thanked me again and again and urged me not to forget. So I as I looked down at the clouds enveloping the foothills I asked the Creator of this great mountain to bless Nancy's father and for good measure reminded the Lord that my own dad was still residing in Heaven.

At that point Minja pointed down the slope and I heard voices coming our way. I managed to roll over on my side to get a look and saw about seven heads appear over the edge of the little plateau one by one. It turned out to be four Germans and an Aussie, all apparently in their twenties, and a couple of guides. They all looked fresh as spring colts and they were talking up a storm. They were exhilarated by being so close to their goal and they sat down and rested for about fifteen minutes with me. They were fascinated when they learned my age. They couldn't believe I'd made it so far up Kili. As we talked, their youthful excitement began to rub off on me. I started having second thoughts about quitting but now Minja was warning me that an assault on the last few 100 feet wasn't a good idea because of the approaching storm, which was coming toward us faster than it had appeared to be doing a few hours earlier. But I was convinced there would be safety in numbers so decided I could make it after all.

The guides agreed that the weather didn't look good and that all of us should retreat down the slopes as quickly as we could. But the young hikers were set on making the top and they didn't want to be talked out of it. They all argued that we had plenty of time before the storm hit and one of the Germans yelled, "Let's move out," which meant upwards. The Aussie said to me, "Come on lad, you're going with us." I was too tired to talk and too flattered being called a lad to resist so I just nodded an O.K. and stood up to follow them. Their enthusiasm was irresistible. So what if I was about half a century older than they were? I felt a burst of confidence in their company. The porters stayed below but Minja and the other guides reluctantly followed the six of us as we started clambering over rocks toward the top. The summit was only about 200 yards away but it was straight up.

About twenty minutes into our climb everything suddenly disappeared. We'd wandered into a total whiteout, a rare but horrendous happening on top of Kilimanjaro. The wind was ferocious and snow and rain and sleet all together blasted us so hard that we all fell down at once. There was no way we could move either up or down the mountain. The only course of action we could take was to try to get into a sitting position and hold on to each other for dear life. No one could move more than a few inches from the others for fear of losing contact with the group. Luckily we were all practically bumping into each other on the climb when the snow hit. At Minja's command we were able to scoot into a circle with our backs to the incredible wind. No one made a move for fear of losing track of the group and being stranded alone. I was sitting between the Aussie's guide and Minja, my hands in theirs for warmth and to make sure none of us got separated. The freezing sleet hitting the back of my neck felt like it was being fired from an AK47. At one point I moved my left hand to the front of my face but I couldn't see it. I was having a hard time breathing.

As the hours wore on, Minja directed us to take turns making a row of four facing the wind in order to give the other four a little shelter from the brunt of the blast. At one point the Germans tried to construct a snow wall to protect us but even though the snow caused pain when it hit us it was too fine to pack. And it kept coming in an endless sheet. Worse yet was the total blindness. I was sure we would never leave the mountain alive. It seemed as if Mother Nature was intent on replacing in one day all the snow pack Kili had lost to global warming As the waiting dragged on, we told stories to the person next to us in order to take our minds off our plight. But the howling of the wind made hearing almost impossible. About then I led a prayer that probably went unheard but made me feel better. There was no telling how long the storm would last and whether we'd be found dead up here a few days from now, our carcasses frozen like the legendary leopard's in Hemingway's story.

It was four hours after the start of the whiteout that it lifted to reveal an African sunset of unforgettable beauty. All of us were on the verge of exhaustion from the tension and the terrible wind and the fear but we managed to pick our way back down to the little plateau we'd started from and regrouped. The young people decided to bed down for the night and then make another stab at the summit in the morning while Minja, my porters, and I headed on down the mountain after saying our goodbyes and pledging to stay in touch with each other. As we began the two-and-a-half day descent, Minja again cautioned "pooley, pooley, pooley" but I was hell bent to get to the lowest altitude on the African continent as quickly as I could. That was a big mistake. I'd thought coming down a high mountain would be like coming down a river like the Rogue in Oregon where a boat might take three struggling hours to make it to a destination upstream and only half an easy hour coming back with no problem. It turns out that descending too fast from a high altitude can be just as dangerous as climbing too fast. And I would pay for my haste in a hospital back in the States. But when I reached the bottom of Kilimanjaro all I could think about was my accomplishment and how soon I could get back to Florida to see Melinda and the kids.

* * *

Once home again I settled into family life and got caught up on the world news with frequent timeouts to hone my climbing skills in preparation for the Grand Tetons in March and Everest in May. The papers and TV and Annie's internet surfing were turning up stories about the "wild west" world of contractors in Iraq and how the tsunami relief effort was being stymied by incompetence and corruption. I worked out my frustrations about those fiascos by fast walking with a backpack full of water bottles and other weighted items up and down the six-story fire escape stairwell at our high rise condo. I did the walk three straight times each exercise period, pretending all the while that I was on Everest. The closer I got to the Everest expedition, the more weight I added to my stair-climbing backpack. And I kept doing Jeremy Reardon's thirty-two exercises every morning at 4:00 A.M. and every afternoon sandwiched around sessions with the training tyrant himself. Each workout pained my knees enough to keep me reminded to get a couple of cortisone shots from Dr. Yi right before attacking the Grand Tetons.

In mid-February I picked up the paper and noted a disturbing article about King Gyanendra of Nepal. He'd dismissed the government and declared a state of emergency. That effectively cut off the country from the rest of the world because the king had shut down most of the air links and even suspended phone and internet connections, not to mention freedoms of press, speech, assembly, and privacy. Not a positive development for the Nepalese people. Not for me, either. The king had used a Maoist insurgency as an excuse for the crackdown that he'd probably had in mind all the way back in the days when the local Reds were just slightly pink. The U.S. government and the Indians and the Brits and even the U.N. were on the king's ass over his power grab but all that condemnation wasn't changing his mind. If the situation on the ground didn't change by May, I might be denied access to Everest. It was a worry I'd carry with me as I made my preparations.

But my enthusiasm for the trip and the climb got another boost when the Tampa paper carried an article about a local lecture by the first woman to reach the summit of Everest from the north, or the Tibet side. She was Nepalese and her name was Pemba Doma Sherpa. She'd accomplished the feat in 2000 after she'd been a young Sherpani and trekking guide for a few years. Twenty-four months after her 2000 triumph she'd become one of only six women to ever scale the mountain twice. Unfortunately the article about her was published after her talk and I wasn't alerted beforehand so I missed it. I would have loved to meet her and pick her brain for helpful hints. Just reading about her got my juices flowing like they did every time I heard about someone conquering the 29,035-foot monster. In 1953 I was just a raw teenager with Olympic dreams when I read the story and saw the photos in *Life* magazine about the historic first summit success accomplished by the great Sherpa Tenzing Norgay and the intrepid New Zealander Edmund Hillary, from then on to be known as Sir Edmund. Since that time many had tried to duplicate their achievement and a few had scored but a lot more had failed and some had died in the attempt. And every time I heard or read about an expedition to the mountain my determination to one day make my bid to reach the top of the world was refreshed. I think I must have read *Into Thin Air* a dozen times to make the climb vicariously. But still I had the gnawing feeling that assaulting the mountain was a selfish thing at this stage of my life. It would fulfill my personal need for adventure and danger but it would also take me away from the volunteer work helping others. I also knew, though, that I had to attack the mountain or I'd always wonder if I could have won the battle. And I knew too that if I could make it I'd at least show other seniors what could be accomplished by a beat-up bozo pushing seventy.

About this time another letter arrived from Pastor Ron. It was his second attempt to explain why God allows disasters like the tsunami to occur. I took the letter out to read on the beach where our own stretch of ocean glistened peacefully in the sun.

> *Dear Sam:*
>
> *Just a few ideas to help you with your effort to understand the evil experiences of life in light of a loving, good God.*
>
> *We live in a fallen world—as my children remind—now that they are adults and have children of their own.*
>
> *Read just three chapters of the book of JOB. It is right before the book of Psalms in your Bible. Read chapters one, two, and forty-two.*
>
> *Beginning and end. The rest of the book is Job and his friends trying to understand what is going on ! Let God be God. There are things going on we will never see or understand in this world.*
>
> *Early in my ministry I was getting very discouraged with all of the real evil I was uncovering. A short scripture got my attention and changed my life. 'Do not be overcome by evil, but overcome evil with good.'—Romans 12:22. At that point I decided that I would give all of my energies to doing good and let the chips fall where they would. The twelfth chapter of Romans is a great chapter to read.*

*The Bible says that God causes the rain to fall on the just and the unjust. Read Luke 13:18.*

*Satan is not Good. Only God has all power, all knowledge, and is everywhere. Satan is powerful and wants to think He is as good and great as God but this Is His problem in failing to acknowledge that God is in a position by Himself. God does not necessarily cause everything to happen but nothing happens that is not within his permissive will.*

*This is why I wish we could see each other more often but I know that God is with you all the time—you have the Bible, the Holy Spirit, other Christian friends and the circumstances of life that are meant for you. Thanks for being a friend to me …*

*May God bless you as you work your way to the Mountain. Hope to see you soon.*

*—Ron*

I appreciated Ron's ongoing attempt to explain God's ways and I made a promise to read the Bible sections he recommended. But I had to admit that so far despite his words which were meant to comfort me, I still saw bodies tangled in mangroves in my nightmares. And at least once a month a grotesque vision of that fireman with his knees inside his chest at Ground Zero. I doubted if I'd ever understand or accept what God allowed in Sri Lanka and New York and too many other places. But I also knew the only way to defend myself from being crippled by those sights was to keep helping the victims and to try to inspire others, regardless of their age, to do the same.

March finally arrived and I flew out to Jackson Hole to train on the Teton ice. There on the 10th, my birthday, I met with my instructor, Evan Howe, a rock solid six-foot-three specimen who divided his time between teaching skiers the fine art of swooshing down the slopes, giving classes in avalanche safety, and trying to clue in novices like me in the ways of ice climbing. A few years earlier he'd spent two months scaling the highest summits in Pakistan. And taking great photographs since he'd also built a reputation as a world class shutterbug. I liked him right away. He was very friendly and perfectly polite but he insisted that I do things the right way, which, though it was what I wanted, nonetheless took a tremendous amount of effort. His brand of discipline was just what I'd had in mind when I'd told him I had only four days with him and that if he expected a big tip he'd better make sure I learned everything correctly and thoroughly. I'd asked him to treat me like a thirty-year-old but naturally when he took me at my word there were times when I hated him because the training was as difficult as any I'd done in my life. If I made a mistake or did something that wasn't up to his standard he'd make me back down a slope and come up again, but this time do it perfectly. The bottom line though was a big plus for me because he taught me a thing or two that saved my life later on the ascent toward Everest.

Among the things Evan taught me was the technique climbers use to save themselves after falling on the ice, something I did more times than I like to remember. I was taught how to manage a fall once a slip was in progress. The climber needs to know that drill in order to keep from sliding off a ledge or down a shale embankment. Evan showed me how to do it if you were pitching forward and a different method for a back flip. Pitching forward you had to land stomach first onto your flattened pick and try to dig it into the ice or snow as deep as possible to prevent or stop your slide. If you landed back-first on the slick surface you had to roll over right away, and then use the same flattened pick technique. And no matter which direction you were falling, you never wanted to try to prevent your drop or slide by digging your boot spikes into the ground because that's a prescription for breaking a leg or two or severing an Achilles tendon.

I learned in the Tetons too to make sure that my sun glasses were extra dark. The sun can be blinding at high altitudes and the first time up on the Wyoming mountain I had a few anxious moments because the tint in my lenses was too light. And speaking of the sun, you learned fast on the high slopes that the sun on your back can be damned hot while your front is solid ice. The first time I experienced that phenomenon I felt like a TV dinner cooked in a substandard microwave oven, my buns burning and my meat balls frozen.

Evan taught me a number of knots to tie that were new to me and how to position items in a backpack for easy access. He told me always to hang my knife around my neck to get at it quickly and to greatly lessen the chances of losing it. And he even threw in some tips on recognizing the warning signs for potential avalanches and how to test for them. This turned out to be a fascinating process. Two people would stand side by side on a fifteen to thirty-foot ridge top snow drift with their arms linked tight together. Then they would jump up at the same time and pull their legs into a sitting position or what's called on a trampoline a seat drop and land on their butts right where their boot prints were. The weight of their bodies slamming the top of the drift would cause an avalanche. Pretty clever.

A couple of weeks after I got back to Florida, things in Nepal were still looking iffy at best. There was an article in the Saint Pete *Times* about a major rebel assault on a Nepalese army base a few 100 miles west of Kathmandu. Eight Nepalese soldiers had been wounded and three of them were in bad shape. It was the fiercest fighting in weeks so the insurgency looked to be heating up just in time for my trip. But apparently none of this was having an effect on the tourist business because two days later my private climb contract with a May third starting date arrived in the mail. Guy Cotter, the adventure organizer in New Zealand, summed up the costs at 9,215 dollars for the ascent to a 21,000 plus foot crag called Island Peak. And there was a stipulation in the deal that gave me the option, if I could hack it, to bypass the fork in the trail that led to Island Peak and forge on to the Everest base camp at 250 more per day and then on to the summit of the big mountain for another 500 dollars per day. That all depended on whether I was feeling my oats by that stage of the trek. I'd already priced plane fares at 8,000 dollars and looked into insurance costs and the like. Cotter described Island Peak as a beautiful spot with some scant facilities at the head of the Khumba Valley. I would have another New Zealander for a guide and a Sherpa plus porters to carry loads and assist with the climb. Cotter thought that because the climb "wasn't too difficult" *(Right, by his thirty-something age perspective!),* it would be suitable for someone with "my background and desires." I was pleased with the plan because if I could make it to Island Peak I could sure push on a few 1,000 more feet to realize my dream of making it all the way to the top of the world.

I arranged some preliminary adjustments to the agenda and included a day of shopping for some of the equipment on the list of necessities Cotter had sent. That would be done in Kathmandu so I didn't have to drag a heavy load through airports. And that way I could check out the city before starting the climb. The shopping list Cotter provided called for, among a lot of other things, an ice axe, crampons, extendable ski poles, climbing harness, four kinds of boots and shoes, thermal underwear, enough camping equipment to outfit a third-world army, plus personal hygiene items and first aid kit.

Now my anticipation was reaching a crescendo. I was tossing and turning every night as the time for the flight to Nepal got closer and closer. Luckily at this point, I had no way of foreseeing what a harrowing experience on the mountain I was in for.

# THIRTY

Finally, after three weeks of nervous anticipation and fitful sleep, I boarded a flight at the Tampa airport for Miami. From there I flew on to London, then Dohar, then Kathmandu, the last leg by way of Indonesian Airlines, an outfit that made the other carriers seem like magic carpet companies.

A couple of minutes after the aged, creaking 747 touched, or rather slammed down around seven in the morning on the Kathmandu landing strip, it rolled to a shuddering stop. After I cleared customs I saw a tall, ruddy-faced thirty-something man standing in the reception area and holding a sign with my name on it. It was my New Zealander Himalayan guide, Steve Moffat. Sure enough when I reached the bottom of the exit ramp he ambled up and offered me a powerful handshake. On the way to the hotel he told me what to expect for the next couple of weeks and I responded with my overflowing eagerness.

Once I got unpacked at the hotel we set off on an exploration Kathmandu. I was glad to get out into the streets, not only to see the sights but also to give my legs a workout after the long flights. One of the first buildings that caught my eye turned out to be King Gyanendra's palace with its beautiful adjoining gardens. That made me muse on the fact I'd learned just before I left the States, namely that the king's son was a graduate of Schiller University. A month or so earlier I'd got word from the president of Schiller, which is located in Dunedin, Florida and has campuses and programs in London, Madrid, Switzerland, Heidelberg, and Paris, that I'd been recommended for an honorary doctorate in humane letters. Now here in Nepal, I could have called on the King's son and suggested we drink a couple of toasts to our alma mater, except that he was probably busy helping daddy confront the Maoist insurgents and maybe advising him to back off his power grab. Or not.

The King's compound was a stark contrast to the rest of the city. Like all of the countries I'd visited in the past three years, Nepal was desperately poor. The city was a cesspool of foul smells and the streets, like the road into town, were crumbling, unpaved, pothole pocked tracks. Most of the buildings in the city, none of which was over four or five stories high, looked like the next gust of Himalayan wind would blow them to China. Neighborhoods could have passed for Baghdad with all the filth in the streets, the poor rain runoff, the stopped-up sewers and stifling stench. But I took an instant liking to the Nepalese people. They moved with such great dignity and went about their business in a pleasant way. There was no hassling of foreigners like I'd come to expect in so many of the poor nations I'd visited. And Steve and I didn't get a single pitch from the sellers behind the street side stalls as we bargained for my kids' and Melinda's gifts with hand gestures. Steve explained that most of the people in Kathmandu were Hindu but that once we started our trek up the mountain we would meet mostly Buddhists.

After an hour's sightseeing Steve took me to a low building that housed an outfitter's business where you could rent anything connected with mountain climbing. Steve's company, Adventure O, had hired international consultants that in turn had hired this local agency to handle all the necessary paperwork like trekking permits and to sell all the essential gear, including special radios for communication between the climbers and the first responders in the city in case of emergencies. The agents spoke good English so there was no problem filling my shopping list. I rented an ice pick, a pair of hard plastic boots within another pair of plastic boots, crampons (the ice spikes that attach to the boots), and all the other necessities right down to a plastic urine bottle. When I'd finished my buying spree that afternoon at the outfitter's shop I was chafing at the bit to get started on the climb. I told Steve I'd meet him in the morning to begin the ascent and hired a rickety cab to get all the stuff I'd bought and rented back to the hotel.

The next morning I met Steve in the lobby at the stroke of eight and he introduced me to my Sherpa pathfinder whose name was Pemba. His height surprised me since I was expecting the usual slight figure so common among Asian men. Pemba, on the other hand was a strapping six-foot-two and his handshake just about crushed my fingers. He was around thirty and he spoke excellent English. He said he was looking forward to getting to know me on the trek. Then Steve told me a little about Pemba's background as the Sherpa smiled and listened. He'd been on a number of great climbs in the past. He'd never been to the top of Everest, but he'd been closer than most of his peers in the profession. His great strength came from several years in his youth when he joined a relay team toting up to fifteen six-pound air tanks that weighed around a 100 pounds each up the mountain two days in advance of climbing parties. Then along with others among the best climbers, he would carry a couple of the big air tanks up to a staging area for the last leg of the trek to the top of Everest. Only the strongest were selected for that last chore and Pemba had been one of them. From the look of him, he could have carried me up and down the mountain at a jog and never broken a sweat. After a few years of air tank ferrying Pemba had decided to exploit his familiarity with the mountain and switch to guiding climbers. Steve said he got excellent pay for his expertise, which I took to be a hint and I made a mental memo to tip him handsomely at the end of the trek.

At breakfast Steve laid out the details of the trek for me.

"This morning we take a short flight to a small village called Lukla. We'll start our climb from there. Lukla is around 8,000 feet in elevation. Most of the summits we'll attack are in the heart of the Sherpa country. We'll follow the classic Everest approach through Solo Khumba. Then we'll trek to the Gokyo valleys. Wait till you see those, Sam. Some people think they're the most beautiful valleys on earth. The lakes and glaciers will make you want to stop and spend the rest of your life there."

I doubted that. Maybe on the way back down from the summit, but not before. Steve kept the itinerary moving.

"After a little village called Chhukuma La Pass we head for the Everest base camp and then up to Kal Patthar at just over 18,000 feet. At Chhukuma La Pass you can look down on the Maoist army encampments. After the Everest base camp we'll make a slight descent to Dingboche by way of Pangboche (Boche means village) and then through the Chhukung valley to the Imja Tse or Island base camp. We'll spend the night at the high camp on the South West Ridge and then attempt the Island Peak at 20,350 feet. If we make the summit there we'll get magnificent views of the Khumba. And then the trek back down to the Lukla airstrip."

An hour later we picked up the two porters we'd contracted for and boarded a twenty-seater twin prop, just the kind of workhorse to carry a heavy load of gear, plus the dozen or so other climbers who were a part of other parties. Once we were airborne and headed for the tiny runway at Lukla I took advantage of my window seat. For the first few minutes the view out my cabin window turned up lots of low hills but within a few minutes the landscape below transformed into a maze of high mountains. The high terrain below could have been Cambodia with its terraced rice paddies except that here there were tiered potato patches. But about the time I was making the comparison between the two countries I got a horrendous pain in my gut that just about doubled me over. Actually I'd been worried about getting sick the first day in Kathmandu when I got to feeling queasy in the afternoon. Now I was really upset at the thought of some bug coming between me and my dream after all my arduous preparation. So I decided not to mention my symptoms to Steve.

As the plane approached Lukla I noticed a number of sandbag emplacements manned by Nepalese soldiers protecting the airstrip. Steve gave me a thumb up to communicate the good news that there were no insurgents storming the strip at the moment. Once we touched down there was a final check of our gear and we were on our way to the little nearby settlement of Phukding. There Steve took the lead with me right behind him, Pemba behind me and the two porters bringing up the rear. At first the trail seemed to head straight up but then it leveled out a bit though not all that much. It was a steady incline for much of the first day. Early on I had to let Steve know about my worsening sickness because at one point I felt a searing pain in my gut, so sharp that I nearly fell down. Pemba saw me lurch and called to Steve to stop. Everybody gathered around me and I explained what had happened. Steve told me to sit down and rest a minute but there was no way I was willing to do that. But he added that since I was feeling bad that I should call the speed. He knew about my success climbing Kilimanjaro at a "pooley, pooley" pace so he wasn't concerned about making good time up the slopes.

"I sure hope whatever that was, it was nothing serious. Let's keep moving."

Steve said O.K. and we started back on the trail. Ten minutes later I was dry-heaving and struggling to get my pants down to shit. Steve had to help me and I shot a foul smelling stream next to the pristine trail. Steve made a quick diagnosis.

"You must have picked up a bug here or on the trip in. Let's turn around and get you some medical help."

I told him "No!" It was May, the only month that gives a window to reach the peak, the rest of the year it's like a hurricane everyday. No one would ever climb Mt. Everest in any other month than May. I refused to pack it in. I was getting too old to defer to the next year. Besides, when you added up the high prices of the guide from New Zealand, the sherpa, head guide, and his three "packers," my transportation and other costs I had already laid out at least 60,000 up front! I wasn't about to quit. No freakin' way.

"O.K., Sam. It's your call. But don't stress yourself too much."

For the rest of the day I fought severe cramping while I puked and shit my way up the trail. When we quit for the night after an exhausting eight-hour trek broken by a rest stop at Manche Bazaar, I managed to get half a bowl of soup down but ten minutes later I deposited it just beyond the campsite. I was barely aware enough, at the mid-point of the march, to appreciate what a wonderful village Manche Bazaar is. It's the most important place in the trade business that follows the trails up the mountain. It's loaded with shops for the climbers who stop there for two nights to get their bodies tuned to the elevation. But the only thing I craved from the Manche Bazaar markets was a lifetime supply of Imodium.

The next morning I felt worse and barfed my boiled egg before it hit my stomach. Steve asked again if I wanted to pack it in. So I had to tell him again that that was out of the question. Especially since this day would be spent, as per the schedule, resting at Manche Bazaar. I figured the day off would give me time to recuperate and be ready for the next day's trek. I couldn't figure out why I kept feeling worse with each passing hour but then I thought back to that first morning in Kathmandu. About halfway through brushing my teeth I'd realized I was using tap water instead of the bottled stuff I'd brought specially for that purpose. That was probably what accounted for the god-awful pain in my gut. Or maybe it was those exotic looking green bananas I'd bought later that morning in a street side stall. One thing for sure, if it was a bacterial infection, I had to hand it to the Nepalese for breeding microbes that could have gone fifteen rounds with Muhammad Ali in his prime. Still, I was sure the cramps and puking would pass once I got a good night's sleep. But I spent half the night gagging my guts out.

The third day it was back to the trail but it proved to be a continuation of the first one as far as my condition was concerned. I moved as fast as I could between upchucking and crapping and resting periodically. And talking Steve out of turning back. Every chance I got between barfs I checked out the magnificent scenery and promised myself I'd return here with Melinda sometime soon. Steve had understated the beauty of the climb in his run-up descriptions. If I lived through this trip I'd have to survey it again as a simple sightseer. The good news at this point of the current climb was that my legs weren't protesting too badly and my lungs were relatively pain free. But Steve started making me drink electrolytes and he gave me energy bars to munch for strength. He had brought a powdered mix with him that dissolved in water and made something that looked a little like urine and smelled like raw sewage, and tasted like pond scum. I dubbed it Yak Aid. I kept mixing it with the spice gum drops I'd brought from the States. The combination of energy bars, Yak Aid, and gum drops produced a series of abstract paintings next to the trail when I barfed them up. Some day archeologists may find them and declare a long lost civilization found.

On the fourth day things hadn't stabilized a bit. I was till upchucking and dumping at unpredictable intervals. But the worse news was that now all that misery was accompanied by horrendous headaches and I began taking an extra strength compound for those. I kept a Diamox pill pressed against my gums all the time now, hoping that would dissolve the severe cramps. And Steve was making me take lmodium for the awful diarrhea. Now my lungs were beginning to burn and my knees ached worse than they had in years. None of the medicines were working. But Steve had brought enough alternatives to supply a first rate hospital. Bucastem for nausea, Cipro that he started me on the second day, Nepiphen and Dexamethod for altitude sickness, Amoxicillin for a broad spectrum antibiotic.

Besides that he'd brought along a 6.6 pound oxygen tank and a device called a Gamon Bag to use in case of an emergency. The bag is a unique inflatable capsule/chamber that you put the injured or ill party in. It has special filters and a foot-operated air pump that for twenty minutes or so would provide the injured person 100 percent oxygen and bring him down to an artificial elevation level where he could survive. The gizmo looks like a body bag made of a hard, coarse material and in fact if the patient dies on the slopes the Gamon Bag can double as a casket. It gave me a lot of satisfaction to know that thanks to the bag if I didn't survive the shits Pemba could carry my corpse back down the trail in style. But I didn't want to get to the point where Steve had to use the Gamon Bag on me because that would be a signal that I'd have to give up the climb. So I pushed on as the incline on the trail steepened. Always up and up, higher and higher. These mountains weren't like Fuji in Japan. It just rises to its peak right out of a plain but here there were high peaks leading to higher peaks and then still higher peaks to ascend the closer you got to Everest. That's why it takes three weeks just to get to the base of the giant. Far more trekking even than the Kilimanjaro climb in Tanzania that, if you could stretch it out over a flat plain, would amount to 32 kilometers. The mountain we were climbing at this point didn't even have a name since it was only one of hundreds of towering piles in the Himalayas. But around an occasional bend or in a high clearing we would catch a glimpse Everest, tantalizing us from afar.

Somehow I managed to fight my way for five hours to our next stop at Deboche via Thengboche. Some of these so-called villages have only eight or ten stone huts, one of which will be a kind of mini-hostel, and maybe twenty hardy residents. The idea was to have three meals at these wayside stops on rest day or one if you were just taking a trek break. Unfortunately, I can't vouch for the cuisine since I never got any of it much past my tonsils. And that was a worry because I knew I'd need some fuel to keep going. That night in Thengboche I couldn't sleep for the vomiting because the sight of my supper had brought on a non-stop urge to purge. I'd literally collapsed into my sleeping bag expecting to drop off instantly only to toss and turn between heaves.

The next morning I skipped breakfast altogether. I couldn't face another boiled egg at this point and in fact I promised myself I'd never look another egg in the yolk for the rest of my life, which might not have been that much longer the way things were going. Steve had me try some different multi-grain bars that came out of something like a toothpaste dispenser, the kind of fast energy source that athletes and astronauts rely on. But I couldn't keep those down either. Despite all that we got back on the trail for the five-hour trek to our next stop which was Dingboche. Steve suggested we slow up even more so I could keep going. By now he'd given up on trying to make me give up. But he kept checking my vital signs. With an Oximeter that he clamped on to my middle finger twice a day now to measure my oxygen saturation and pulse. He was always noting the color of my tongue in case I displayed severe dehydration, which could become the main danger. He checked my pupils too. And he worried that I would suffer frostbite. The cold was getting worse and worse and there was only a small heater/burner for warming tea. That night we stopped at a little climbers' hostel along the trail a little short of our target of Dingboche.

The sixth morning we made the rest of the trek to Dingboche by ten o'clock and laid up there for the rest of the day. I struggled in and out of my sleeping bag to barf and shit. The short walk to the village had been enough to add to my miseries. My left eyelid froze shut and refused to reopen. I'd been retching so violently that I was tearing up all the time and now at this extreme altitude the tears had turned to ice and the one lid had closed automatically. Steve's warning not to touch my eye came seconds too late because I'd just rubbed ice over it in hopes the friction would loosen the lid up. I'd removed my thick mittens and inadvertently pressed my palm against my eye socket to melt the ice that formed from my tears and in the process I'd ripped straight across the retina. So now partial blindness was added to my list of ailments and it may have been the most dangerous as the trail was now sometimes no more than a foot-and-a-half wide with 1,000 foot drops to the left or right.

Climbing parties, mostly Korean and Japanese, would pass us occasion-ally and ask how we were doing. And of course knots of Nepalese bearers, their backs bearing goods for the hostels and equipment for the climbers. This time a German group of climbers asked if Steve and Pemba needed help getting me to a medical facility.

That sixth day was when the sickness got to my head. The whole time on the trail I'd been climbing in a robotic daze. At one point during a break in the early afternoon I was resting my back against my backpack in our makeshift camp. I reflected on how sick I was and then got profoundly depressed. Here I was at age sixty-eight, puking and crapping and fighting an incessant migraine and cramps that had me doubled over a lot of the time, shit stains in my drawers, smelling worse than a yak, with halitosis breath and blurred vision in one eye, walking along these razor-thin trails looking off at infinity. I couldn't eat and I was having trouble sleeping. Plus I didn't even know at the time that I had three broken ribs from the convul-sions. And I was only a third of the way to my goal. That's when it hit me that I could make all my troubles go away by taking a flying leap off one of the ledges we would be climbing the next day. Dying would be a lot easier than what I was going through. But the more I thought about it the more suicide seemed a totally selfish way out. Not to mention cowardly. This whole trip had been selfish to start with because it was a personal quest having nothing to do with my promise to help distressed victims in danger zones. I had to get this climb over so I could get back to that work. If I didn't have the stuff to go on, I wasn't good for much else either.

Earlier in my life if I were suffering like I was now, I probably would have done away with myself, simply ended the misery. Three times that morning I'd written in my notebook, "suffering sucks" and, "I just want to die." But I had too much to live for now so I banished the thought of suicide by calling myself a dozen names for "chicken." The challenge in front of me demanded fortitude, endurance, and skill but I told myself one out of three wasn't bad. I knew I should be happy just to be on this mountain, painful as my ordeal had become. In fact in my more lucid moments I regretted not discovering mountain climbing until so late in life. I wondered what I could have accomplished if I'd started in my thirties. But just thinking about how far I'd come in my life in other more important ways since then made me feel rejuvenated. I knew I was going to be all right because I had a destiny mapped out for me by God. There were so many more people whose lives I could touch in a positive way. So I got up and said to Steve and Pemba "Let's get going."

# THIRTY-ONE

But Steve reminded me that this day off was part of the schedule. And he took the timeout for some refresher coaching for the following day's climb.

"Sam, take three breaths with each step. Breathe, breathe, breathe. Step off and plant your walking stick. Lock your knees"

He told me he knew how much I was hurting the day before. He remembered me at one point sitting on a flat rock, both hands on the head of my staff, my head hanging from exhaustion between my shoulders, my one good eye staring at my feet, my mouth gaping open, unable to summon any soothing saliva.

Pemba kept reminding me to take it easy too. He'd turned out to be a very concerned and caring person and I counted it a privilege to have had the opportunity to climb with his aid. I can't count the times he encouraged me and asked after my condition and he was always reminding Steve to make sure that I stayed within my capabilities given the situation. He had great dignity and never betrayed a negative emotion. I admired his demeanor and wished I could be more like him. One night we talked to each other about our families as we crowded next to the small stove for warmth.

The seventh morning we headed up toward Chhukung, which was another four-hour climb into the clouds. By this time I was moving more slowly than ever. I would take about ten steps and rest for thirty seconds or so, then another ten steps and rest. It was an exhausting effort because I was so weak. We would stop periodically in the small huts that lined the trail at

*Climbing Mt. Kilimanjaro in Tanzania, 2005. (Photo Credit, Evan Howe)*

several kilometer intervals. These were tiny stone buildings with plywood walls, very cold inside. The locals called them hostels but that was an exaggeration. There was always a slightly larger dining hut. Sometimes the buildings would have two stories because of the slant of the mountainside. Or a one-story unit would have a little loft. The food would be served to Steve and Pemba by Sherpa cooks there but not to me because the sight of food sent me reeling.

Steve kept Kathmandu aware of my condition on the special radio he carried. I tried to nap in the sleeping quarters just below Chhukung during a break but the result was more fitful tossing and turning. Our eight-by-ten or so sleeping room was inside a small separate hut with a narrow, blanket/bedroll with a sheet and a pillow. The bedroll reminded me of my maggot-infested Sandinista mat "Maggie" except any maggot that ventured this far up the mountain would've long since been turned into a wormsicle. The toilets were outside but we never used them during the night because it was around forty degrees below zero out there. Climbers are advised never to wash on the trail either, except to use baby wipes. They worked well except for the nights they froze solid.

And we never undressed at night. At the higher elevations it gets so damned cold after sundown that no one ever takes off their clothing. When I crawled into the sleeping bag I would have on two pairs of socks, three pairs of pants and at least five layers on the upper body plus a knit cap. The only thing removed were the boots. And still I froze my butt off. You had to keep your drinking water canister and 32 ounce piss bottle with you inside the bedroll because if you left them sit out they would freeze solid. Everything froze if you didn't keep it next to your body to catch its heat. Of course, you had to mark the containers with identifying duct tape so you didn't wind up slaking a midnight thirst with your own urine. What passed for personal hygiene was a quick swipe or two under the arms and across the crotch with baby wipes. Shit would cake to your a – – hole and I had the added pleasure of plenty of dried blood from a burst hemorrhoid. Needless to say, I was rank after the first day on the trail but at those altitudes the only time you can actually smell yourself is in the sleeping bag. After this day of headaches that felt like somebody was using a jackhammer on my frontal lobe and the non-stop stomach cramps and diarrhea that had me on a double dose of Imodium, the onset of dry heaves and dizziness intensified. I looked forward to getting inside one of those bedrolls as if it were a 1,000 dollar a night honeymoon suite at the Waldorf.

During the day I always carried a butane lighter and my knife suspended from a cord around my neck. The idea, which you'll remember I learned on the Tetons from my guide Evan Howe, was to keep the two between layers of your sweat shirts. That served a couple of vital functions. The knife wouldn't freeze shut like it would further from the relative heat around your chest. And the knife and the lighter wouldn't likely get lost hung around your neck as opposed to carrying them in a pants pocket. You had to make sure the lighter was the butane kind too because any other wouldn't function in the extreme cold. The lighter served to fire up a cigarette (yes, you're right, I was still stupidly smoking) or a butane stove. The knife might save your life if you had to cut yourself free from a support rope tying you to the others in your party on dangerously narrow trails. If you ever saw the movie *K-2* you'll know what I'm talking about. It's about a father and his two kids that are roped together and the father and son fall into a crevasse while the daughter is anchored above on a ledge. The daughter doesn't have the strength to pull both of them up so the father cuts himself loose and falls to his death to save the children. The movie illustrates an unwritten rule among climbers that they carry a knife for situations like that. The first thing a climbing instructor will say during the first lesson is "Show me your knife." And I learned that whenever I climb with someone I should ask to see their knife just after I say hello.

One critical item Steve made me use was a piss-measuring bottle. Every morning he would check the output of my bladder after he took all of my vitals. At first I'd been urinating over twenty-five ounces per night but that headed dramatically downward until by the fifth day I was only generating four ounces. Since I couldn't keep anything down I wasn't getting enough liquids. I kept on pushing myself onward and upward, but at a snail's pace. Steve and Pemba kept urging me to pack it in. They said no one as sick as me should continue. But I told them a dozen times my illness was probably only temporary and slogged on.

✳ ✳ ✳

On the morning of the eighth day, amazingly we were still less than one day behind the originally plotted schedule. It was much colder outside than the day before and it had snowed during the night. When I tried to pee I couldn't produce more than a drop or two. I didn't want to let Steve in on this latest symptom, so I mixed about three ounces of drinking water with the night's urine output. Once a cheater always a cheater. When Steve checked me the urine bottle passed muster but my vitals were worse than ever. I told him, though, that I thought I had at least twenty-four more hours in me and we would decide whether to quit the climb that night or the next morning. He said he'd heard me retching and coughing during the night and wanted to come in and give me some pain medicine to knock me out. But he said he didn't because he knew that I would be pissed if he did (although pissed was the wrong word entirely). He knew that I wanted one more day hoping that I'd take a turn for the better. He was dead right about the problems I was having that previous night. What he didn't know was that my vision was starting to go altogether. I'd tried to read the night before (I'd brought a couple of W.E.B. Griffen military history books along). Everything was so dim when I started on a biography of General MacArthur that I'd changed the batteries in my head lamp thinking they'd run down. But the new batteries didn't help. What I was to find out later at a Kathmandu clinic was that both my eyes had taken a beating from the Himalayan jet stream. That was because a couple of times I'd stupidly forgotten to wear my sunglasses. And, through the special phone Steve used to call his girlfriend in New Zealand and I used to call Melinda and my kids, we learned by way of updates from the Everest base camp that there were violent hurricane winds blowing at us off of Everest. Not that we needed to be told as we were nearly knocked down more than once. Those radio reports had provided me with entertainment throughout the climb. It was fascinating learning about how other climbers were faring and if any were making the assault on Everest itself. Learning about the others helped take my mind off my own pain. Barely.

On the ninth day we laid up in the Sherpa hamlet of Chhukung and rested and critiqued our next move. Steve alerted our agents' in Kathmandu that I was in terrible shape and though I didn't want to quit I would decide in the next day or so whether I would have to. If there was no going on we'd call in a chopper for an evacuation. I'd been put on extra Cipro that morning in hopes that the medicine and the layover would do me some good. My decision would be whether to call the climb off the next day or leave in the morning for Island Peak at just over 20,000 feet. I'd decided not to call my kids because I knew they would try to talk me out of going on. Besides, the one time I'd tried to call I got nothing but static. Steve and Pemba said they'd understand if I quit because I'd already proven myself the toughest old codger they'd ever seen. That's when I told the two of them if they thought I was tough they should meet the other Halls. We all got back on the trail heading up.

We were at around the 18,000 foot mark by late afternoon and decided to stay there for the night. The next day was a rest stop that Steve had planned before we resumed the climb so I'd have some time to think about my situation. I was hoping the medicines would kick in and I would feel better and be able to eat and get a little energized. When we'd started out more than a week earlier I could keep up a fairly good pace despite the illness and sometimes I could go without a rest break for half an hour. By the third day I'd begun playing a game with myself to see how far I could get without a break. I would talk to myself as I was climbing and say, "All right big boy, let's see you take a 100 steps without stopping." Then I would add another ten steps between rests, but this didn't last very long. Once I got up to 135 steps before the stomach cramps doubled me over. I quickly went down to 40 or 50 steps by the middle of the sixth day. And ten or so by the eighth. Then I collapsed that night just getting out of bed to produce a pathetic pee for Steve's measuring bottle. But now we were within striking distance of Island Peak.

On the morning of the tenth day I had another turn for the worse. The pain in my gut was just about unbearable now and I was shooting liquid projectiles out of my mouth and butt. My knees were on fire and at this altitude my lungs gave me the feeling that I was being smothered. But the scenery was getting more and more awesome as we got closer to Island Peak. Sick as I was I still had the faculties to take in the sights. I was walking in the clouds looking down on God's green earth from a height I 'd never imagined possible. The sight of the valleys below us couldn't have been much less spectacular than what the astronauts see from an orbiting capsule. I knew I couldn't give up until I experienced that vaunted view from the summit of Island Peak. So we started climbing again.

Around noon Steve said, "Sam, you can't make it any further." He told me that my face was grey and my lips were blue. That's when I told him about my mother's saying, "Can't never *did* anything." And I told him, "My face may be grey and my lips may be blue but at least I'm not as ugly as you."

Apparently he didn't like my little verse so he called me a, "bloody asshole" and told me to pray over the decision I'd have to make in the next twenty-four hours. He didn't have to coax me to do that. I'd been petitioning God over the last nine days to give me the strength to keep going. At any rate, we were still on the trail making upward progress, slow though it was.

At the end of the day Steve called a conference and told me I had to make a decision about going on toward Private Island. I had to admit at this point that my condition wouldn't allow me to go much further, though the prospect of giving up was as painful as my gut. Toward the end of this day's climb, I'd been so weak that I could only take a step or two without having to stop and rest. And when I'd sat down it was impossible to get up again without a wave of dizziness that almost keeled me over. The combination of pain and lack of oxygen had been almost too much to take. Once I'd actually fallen back down after getting up and Steve had walked back beside me and begged me to stop. But I'd insisted on going on so he demanded that we rope ourselves together, Steve and Pemba and me, in case one of my fainting spells hit me on a narrow ledge, some of which were now no more than a foot wide. With up to 2000 foot drop offs.

As darkness set in I fell into my bedroll to try to get some sleep and maybe, by morning, some perspective. Should I try to push on or tell Steve to put in an emergency call for the French Ecureuil evacuation helicopter? As I was mulling that question, I heard a knock on the plywood door of my sleeping room. It was Steve and he had a woman doctor with him. She was on her way down from the Everest base camp after spending a couple of days there with friends. Steve had met her at the main dining room of the "hostel" and explained my problem to her and asked if she would check me out. She had the added expertise of a lot of climbing experience so Steve trusted her judgment. After her mini-exam she said I shouldn't continue and that Steve should call for my evacuation. I thanked her for her opinion, even though I hated it. When she left, I convinced Steve to wait until morning before making the call, just in case I made a miraculous recovery in the meantime.

Towards morning I decided I couldn't make it to Island Peak and I reluctantly told Steve when he emerged from his bedroll a little later. He told me right away he'd help me pack for the return trip. It was while I was getting some things together that I looked into my backpack and discovered the American flag I had my daughter Kelly buy me before I left the States. The sight of it depressed me at first because I felt like such a failure, so guilty. During our time on the mountain we'd got news of two deaths and ten people had been covered by an avalanche and seven of them had to be evacuated due to severe injuries. Those were all climbers who were headed for the top of Everest. They were the real heroes. They'd tackled the big one. And I'd been beaten by this insignificant, nameless mountain, probably because of a microscopic bug. I felt like the soldier that goes into combat for the first time and takes a bullet in the ass. That was me. The doughboy who'd taken one in the buttocks. So I couldn't start back down the mountain without one more quest. I sprang a surprise on Steve.

"I forgot something that I have to do."

"What's that?"

I held up the American flag. I'd promised my kids and myself I'd plant it on top of one of these mountains. I pointed up to a ledge about 500 feet above us and said:

"Steve, I'm feeling a little better (another lie). I want to plant this baby up there. I'd like to make a final climb up this ridge. It's not that far from here and this mountain has my name, not to mention my barf, all over it."

"But Sam, you need to get medical attention ASAP. My God, man, you've done far more than I could have in your condition. What more do you want, you crazy son-of-a-bitch?"

"I'll double your bonus if we make it to that ledge."

"That's not the important thing, Sam. Your health is the big ticket."

"It's something I have to do."

✳ ✳ ✳

Steve made a quick survey of our situation and decided to have our porters wait on this lower ground for the three or four hours it would take us to get to the ledge and back. We wouldn't try the ascent directly because that route Steve judged to be too dangerous. Instead we would attack at different angles by switch backing. There would be no trail to follow, just a geometric scramble up the mountainside.

When we moved out this time Steve let me take the lead with Pemba short-roped (which means about 15 feet between climbers) behind me and Steve bringing up the roped rear. I knew it was going to be a rough climb. No more than a third of the way up one narrow ledge I doubled over in pain and we had to wait for fifteen minutes crouching above a long drop off before I could straighten up again. Then a little further up I was rounding a curve in the trail when I was hit with a gust of wind coming off Everest at about 70 miles-an-hour. It blew me back into Pemba and nearly knocked us over a 2,000 foot drop but luckily Steve was anchored firmly around the bend and kept us from going over the side. I remember a lot of incoherent shouting but the near catastrophe had been averted just the way the text-book dictated. I should have expected to be blown over at some point in the climb anyway since we'd been talking for days about the hurricane force winds that were pounding Everest and agreeing that no one should be making a try for the summit until the weather improved. Needless to say at that moment when Steve anchored Pemba and me I was glad I'd spent all that money to hire the best guide in these mountains.

Now I was feeling so good about having survived the potential calamity that I added rock lifting to my trail blazing. With the help of a shot of adrenalin I moved a couple of big rocks from our zigzag route to clear the way for the others and Steve shouted his kudos. And he said I'd done well to resist the temptation to push the rocks over the side of the ledge where they could have created a slide that would endanger our porters waiting for us on a ledge below.

Next we stopped to rest at an outcropping and while we were sitting on a huge, flat boulder Steve pointed off in the distance and said, "That's the east face of Everest." I almost burst into freezing tears at the sight. I'd been so concentrated on the climb for the last couple of days I hadn't noticed how much closer to the great peak we'd come. The white monster loomed so large it looked like I could reach out and touch it. I'd never seen anything so awe inspiring or such a proof of God's love than that mountain on that May morning. There in front of me was the object that had dominated my dreams since I was a kid. And I had come this close to standing on its summit and no more. I wished I had another lifetime to prepare for the ultimate climb to the top of that majestic peak. But I said a prayer of thanks for the opportunity to draw so near. Now I felt satisfied to make this last effort to reach the high ledge up ahead on this nameless Himalayan height and I motioned to Pemba and Steve that we should get back to blazing our trail.

After fifteen more minutes of picking our way upward I got smacked with a violent siege of cramps and went down on my knees. Twenty minutes later I still couldn't stand up. Steve and Pemba carried me over to a big sun-splashed rock and stretched me out on it. Then Pemba got above me and pulled my arms in his direction while Steve held on to my feet. They worked my muscles for what seemed like hours but it was only a few minutes until I was able to stand and get back to the climb.

In another twenty minutes we reached the rocky pinnacle and I sat down and began dry sobbing. It was as far as I could go and it was well short of my goal but I was proud of having made it this far against all the odds. Before I had time to fully appreciate the situation Steve and Pemba began pounding me on the back and Steve shouted, "Sam, you magnificent bastard, you did it!" That's when I began to really appreciate what I'd accomplished. This was no Nob Hill. I'd beaten a real mountain. We were at about 18,500 feet, higher than anything in the U.S. lower forty-eight. Steve snapped the mandatory picture of me holding my American flag just before I planted it between two big boulders. I hope it's still waving there on that mountain significant only to me and maybe Steve and Pemba, somewhere above Chhukung. I knelt down to say a prayer of Thanksgiving and Steve knelt beside me and bowed his head in silence while Pemba looked on. When we got to our feet Pemba presented me with a white scarf, which Steve explained as the highest form of respect a Sherpa can offer a climber. As I put it around my neck I hugged Pemba and the tears froze all around. That's when I said, "I've had it. Call for the med-evac."

After about twenty-five minutes of rest we started back down from the ledge. It took us a good two hours to reach the ridge below where our porters were waiting. And the woman doctor who had waited with the porters to check on my progress and condition. She said she was concerned about me after she gave me my checkup and decided to stick around to make sure

I made it to safety. She'd even monitored with her binoculars my climb up the final ledge. I hugged everyone and thanked them and gave the porters each a couple of 100 dollars apiece for their services. They were all smiles because I'd made it with Steve and Pemba up to the high ledge. Then the three of us sat on the cold ground and waited for the helicopter while the porters and the doctor started back down the mountain on foot. Within minutes we heard the sound of copter blades and saw the bird squeezing between two shear mountain walls. When the chopper landed a surprise passenger stepped out. It was the highest ranking Buddhist monk of the province. His temple was on the other side of the mountain we'd just scrambled down. The holy man was a short and stocky seventy-something and he was decked out in beautiful red robes. The moment he stepped down out of the helicopter Pemba fell to his knees. He was shocked to see such a high ranking figure in his religion make an appearance near the climbing trail. And it was an experience that I'll not forget either.

Just before we boarded the chopper Steve and I put our heads together (which added up to one good head) to try to record what I'd eaten during the climb. It amounted to one half of a boiled egg daily and no lunch and at night one third of a bowl of soup. None of it had stayed with me. Of course I'd been stuffing gum drops in my mouth all the way and I was getting a reputation as the culprit who puked up more sugar and spice on the slopes of the Himalayas than there were yak patties. At any rate, Steve helped me through the copter door and climbed in beside me. As we took off we waved our goodbyes to Pemba below. I hoped my path and Pemba's would cross again because I'd come to love him over the past ten days. I couldn't muster the words, though, to tell Steve how I felt about him and Pemba because my body was in a state of total collapse. But I was happier than I'd ever been in my life. I'd walked in the clouds and planted my flag and now I was going home.

When we arrived at Kathmandu I was helped off the chopper and rushed, with Steve at my side, to a wonderful clinic run by westerners. We were met at the door by a great team of doctors and nurses. My main doctor was an Israeli named Michael Alkan. He did a series of exams and tests and his findings could have filled a medical text book. I had severe gastroenteritis; partial blindness in the left eye; three frost bitten fingers; high altitude cerebral edema or HACE; ataxia or loss of coordination; advance symptoms of AMS (which means lots of vomiting); and three separated ribs from the violent convulsions. But at the bottom of the diagnosis sheet was the good news, "Full Recovery Expected."

I got to know Doctor Alkan quite well over the next two days. At first he talked exclusively to Steve because I was incoherent a lot of the time (some people say I'm always that way). He needed to know all of my symptoms to make a diagnosis and he pumped Steve for a description of them. But a little later the good doctor and I talked at length about my efforts on the mountain and about my experiences in Israel. Before we parted company after the final checkup he asked me, "Sam, what drove you to accomplish what you did with what you had?" I told him I couldn't answer his question. Then I said, "What do you think?" And he answered, "Divine intervention." I promised myself that the next time I saw Pastor Ron I'd tell him about Dr. Alkan's explanation.

In order to speed my recovery time I was advised to stay in the Kathmandu clinic. That time was spent relaxing and sleeping and waiting for my strength to return. During those hours in the clinic much of my experience on the mountain came back to me through waves of unconnected images. Some of the memories were wonderful and I want to remember them always. But for sure I want to forget the sickness and the pain.

The flight back to the States rewound the tape, including Kathmandu to Doha aboard Indonesia Airlines. But now I couldn't have cared less about the plane's amenities. I just wanted to get back home.

# THIRTY-TWO

After a month of lazing around the beach in Florida and getting in some running I was feeling tip-top again. That's when it occurred to me that it would be a shame to let all that pre-Everest training go to waste and so I started thinking about other adventures that would allow me to live on the edge once more. And do some gooding at the same time. I'd been fascinated by the Far North ever since I'd read Jack London novels as a teenager and I'd been dreaming for years of doing some personal exploring at the Pole. So it seemed like serendipity when, after an invigorating run, I flopped in a lounge chair on the beach and picked up a *St. Petersburg Times* that carried an article about harp seals, those pathetically vulnerable looking creatures with the enormous eyes. The article talked about the fact that they were being killed to the point of near extinction off the coast of Quebec. And about how they were being killed. The pups, before they were three-weeks old and still in pure white fur, would have their heads brutally bashed in with a club. So their fur could be made into a coat to please some rich bitch. Or the males' penises sliced off and sent to Asia to make aphrodisiacs so a few limp louts over there could perk up their own privates. That waste of beautiful animals really steamed me. And the more I read the more steamed I got. So I decided I had to get more familiar with the harp seal predicament than I could just reading a newspaper article.

I had Annie pull up all the information she could find on the internet about the slaughter and she came back with info from thirty-three different

*Happy polar bears.*

lobbying groups dedicated to stopping it, all linked into a "Protect the Seals Network." Outfits from all over the world, from Asia and Australia to France and Spain and Holland and Russia. By the time I finished the brochures I knew I had to join the fight. Maybe go up north myself for some fact finding. And do some fund founding too. I knew I'd always been good at raising money for a variety of causes so why not harp seals? My first move was to have Annie write a letter to each seal saver organization saying I wanted to get personally and financially involved in the cause. And of course the answers practically crossed Annie's letters in the mails because the groups were so much in need of backers with pockets deep or shallow.

Of all the responses from the Network, including one from Jacques' son Jean-Michel Cousteau, I was most impressed with Inez Robinson's from the Humane Society of the U.S. She described the slaughter in detail and listed the laws being broken and identified the ways the Society was responding, including filming for the purpose of provoking wider outrage, and lobbying for a boycott of Canadian seafood. Those were some of the reasons I chose the Humane Society to be the recipients of my seal fund even before the first penny was solicited. But within hours of that decision I had another letter drafted and sent to all of my friends asking them to donate. And I wanted to do something fairly dramatic to encourage folks to give. I knew from the Humane Society and the other groups that the killing took place in April when the pups were born but there was no way I was going to wait six months to churn up some publicity and maybe do some filming for the fund. So I decided to head to the North Country right away. But by this time the idea of a personal adventure was way down the list of reasons for going.

Annie contacted a travel agency called Leisure Connections and before long I was scheduled to take an August third flight out of Orlando for Reykjavik and then on, by my choice of boat or plane, to Kulusak. And next helicopter to the relatively big city of Ammassalik for a days trip to Basalt Island and the nearby mountains. Ten days into the trip it would be on to Uummannaq and the North Pole area including Grimsey and then back to Reykjavik on the sixteenth for the flight home. Little did I know as I looked over the itinerary that the trip I was making primarily for PR purposes would turn into the very kind of adventure I'd dreamed about all those years ago reading *The Call of the Wild* and *White Fang*.

While I waited for the big departure day I kept tabs on the fattening fund I'd set up and learned all I could about the economics of the seal pelt trade. Ninety-five percent of the seals killed in the hunt are between twelve-days and four-months old. I discovered that there'd been a European ban on

*Sam feeding baby seals.*

importation of these white coat seals passed in 1986 and that the fur industry was struggling for a while after that. This was right around the time that
the news footage showing hunters clubbing infant seals to death had horri-
fied TV viewers across the world. But then demand for seal products ratcheted
up again and kept growing. Pelt prices were the highest in years right then
and furriers and fashion moguls were trying to open new markets to gin up
the industry even more. In 2002, a Canadian government report stated that
nearly a million raw seal skins had been marketed in places like Norway,
Denmark, Poland, Estonia, Greece, Japan, and Hong Kong. The next year
China and Taiwan got into the importing act to produce neckties and wal-
lets and eye-glass cases.

I found out too that there were only a few major processing companies.
One was a subsidiary of the Barry Group with a plant in Catalina, Newfoundland and another was a Norwegian firm called Carino. The workers
allegedly kept a low profile and there were no identifying signs on the plants
that were located next to fish processing facilities.

Getting the seal pelts ready for market takes a few months and involves
several steps. Each pelt is around 3 to 4 feet long and 2 to 3 feet wide. They

have to be soaked in brine for over a week and some have to be dyed. When they're ready they're sold to brokers who turn around and resell them to fur coat and accessory makers mostly in China and other Asian countries but also in Russia, Siberia, and Western Europe. There are supposedly thousands of excess pelts stored in Canada and Norway. That's been denied but 300,000 seals were killed in 2002 and only 85,000 were exported, so you can do the math.

The value of all this trade to the Canadian government alone averages around three hundred thirty five-million dollars a year. The going rate for pelts is in the neighborhood of fifty-dollars per. The rest of the booty comes from seal oil for human consumption. The Canadian authorities claim the hunt on the offshore ice flows is more humane than in the old days. But that's mostly spin. They passed a law in their parliament that makes a mockery of the humane claim. The law established the "blink test," which mandates that hunters, when they stroll down a line of seal pups bashing their brains out, have got to wait until the last one they clubbed stops blinking its eyes, the sign that it's dead. Real kindhearted. And our compassionate neighbors to the north also claim that the seal population is rising and needs to be controlled. But that's mostly spin too. The government may be trying to appease fishing communities for political reasons. The fishermen blame the seals for depleting fish stocks. And the Department of Fisheries plays along, claiming the seal population is healthy and abundant and almost triple what it was in the 1970s. And that hunting should continue until the number of seals falls below four million.

Canada claims it's striking a balance between conservation and the economic needs of the maritime provinces, but the industry employs very few people. And the Canadian officials who claim the hunt is part of the indigenous cultures of Labrador and Newfoundland are blowing smoke too. Its commerce, stupid, just like any other industry only a lot crueler. The anti-hunt activists have gathered plenty of evidence that animals are still being skinned alive and that they die in agony. Their plea for a boycott of Canadian seafood includes a no-buy policy for restaurants. Hopefully our northern neighbors' government has started to feel the heat from activists' agitation. And from the 22,000 dollars my seal fund has generated at this writing.

But none of that information gleaned from books could substitute for first hand experience, so bright and early on the third of August I boarded a big bird for the flight to Reykjavik. The first week of the adventure a hired guide there took me, usually with a handful of others, to beautiful small islands and tiny villages and through settlements with names like Igloot, Tlingit, Kulusuk, Kangerlussuaq and Ilulissat. We would walk around the villages watching and taking photos of the indigenous tribesmen fishing and mending their nets and scrubbing their boats. These were scenes very little changed from the times when Admiral Perry explored the region. On the open sea between the villages my heart did some extra thumping because whales were breeching in every direction. In fact I was so excited by the sight of them I almost forgot how cold it was. But not entirely. I remembered being told that if I fell overboard I'd have to be rescued within the first minute or I'd be, I almost said toast, but that wouldn't be quite the right metaphor. With all the equipment I was carrying, though, if I slipped into the drink I'd probably strike the seabed before any would-be rescuer could react anyway.

In a couple of the villages I got a chance to see the natives put part of the harp seal population to legitimate use. These were full grown animals and they were killed by the local men for food and clothing for their families. Though I hated to see the seals die, their fate was acceptable because it meant the survival of those families. This was nothing like the slaughter on the killing fields for big profits. The locals would do some selling for subsistence, though. Before they butchered the seals they would skin them and sell the hides to middlemen for a little over fifty-dollars each. If a hide was marred by a bullet hole, which most were, the buyer would deduct two-dollars from the price.

My next stop was the gorgeous town of Uummannaq where I checked in at its only hotel overlooking the harbor. The town's located in a glorious setting on a small island with only about a 1,000 inhabitants and it's backed by a starkly striking landscape dotted with multi-colored houses. The next morning I sat sipping hot tea on the glassed-in veranda with my cold weather gear sprawled at my feet, and the scene below reminded me of the jigsaw puzzle picture of a fishing village that Melinda and I had assembled a couple of months earlier. This was Greenland's Cape Cod in the middle of its west coast, but a very cold Cape Cod. It was late "summer" up here and the third ice-free month of the season but there were freezing winds blowing in off the glaciers and the water temperature was minus-two degrees Fahrenheit. And this time of year there was no darkness at any time of night. In another month everything would turn to ice and supplies would have to be brought into the harbor by a boat being led by an ice cruncher. There are only two ways to get to Uummannaq, by boat and helicopter. I'd come in by chopper.

In the hotel dining room at lunch time I met four Danish doctors and a registered nurse who were stationed at the local hospital as part of their six-month obligation, like a military hitch in other countries. We became fast friends and they were impressed by the intensity of my interest in the harp seals. They were animal rights activists themselves, but sensible ones. Not the kind of extremists whose ideas tend to marginalize the movement and open it to ridicule. I mean people like Brigit Bardot who once accused a French mayor of "genocide" when he had a flock of nuisance pigeons gassed. Or the past president of PETA who declared that the life of a single clam was as significant as a human's. Maybe birds and crustaceans were that momentous in God's eyes. But crying "genocide" over pigeons diminishes the real wrongs in Rwanda and Somalia and too many other places. And some tyrant could use that clam claim to justify a lot of mischief too, like tossing more than just your overalls into Mrs. Murphy's chowder.

When my new friends brought up the subject of global warming and what a threat it was to the indigenous way of life in the region, I sympathized with their concern. I told them about my experience on Mount Kilimanjaro and how the mountain had lost two-thirds of its snow pack in the twentieth century. We agreed that steps had to be taken soon to begin the earth's healing process. They were surprised at my views on the subject and became still more affable. Before we'd met, they'd apparently thought all Americans were fossil fools who drove Hummers and flushed their crankcases into the oceans.

* * *

When I'd left the States on this trip I'd had to decide whether to leave immediately to join up with the crew of a Russian nuclear ice breaker called the Yamal on its scientific way to the North Pole, or depart a few days later and choose a variety of other adventures. Ordinarily the chance to sail with the Russians would have been too tempting to pass up. It involved flying to Moscow and then on to Murmansk where I'd board the Yamal with a group of scientists, professors, and other teachers. Then they crunched their way through the ice for a week till they reached the Pole too and killed another week coming back. The brochure described the destination as, "perhaps the most amazing location on our entire planet" but it wasn't enough to convince me at that point to spend two weeks in cramped quarters aboard ship, and for a cost of nearly 20,000 dollars, instead of roaming freely on my own through the North Country. There would be small boats aboard the Yamal for side trips to the remote islands of Franz Josef Land but sailing with the Russians would wipe out the kayaking and dog sledding I'd been looking forward to. So I decided to crunch my own ice to pour Old Granddad over in between paddling and mushing I'd arrange myself.

Once at Uummannaq I began my self-generated itinerary by purchasing passage on a, thankfully heated, sightseeing boat for a tour of the immediate area. Since the four doctors and the nurse and I'd turned out to be so simpatico we'd all decided go on the trip together. The boat took us along with twenty or so other tourists to various nearby islands and towns. As we sailed together we became closer still and one of the doctors suggested that he make a phone call to a friend in the Danish Coast Guard to see if he could get me embedded with them during one of their routine law enforcement cruises. That sounded like the opportunity of a lifetime so of course I encouraged the idea, even though I knew it might crowd something out of my packed schedule. And the very next morning I found myself canceling a dog sledding reservation and instead bouncing along the brine in a sleek cutter as the Danish guardsmen checked out every fishing vessel they spotted. They were making sure the fishermen were using the sanctioned size of nets and that they hadn't killed any whales. But during my morning sortie with the crew, they didn't discover any infractions.

For the next two days, in between some fun kayaking, I took a boat to the base of a couple of relatively low mountains on the west coast of Greenland around Kulusak and did some climbing. I'd wanted to kayak among icebergs ever since I'd seen pictures of guys doing it on the pages of *National Geographic*. So at Kulusak I hired a guide and a coach to take me out to the bergs. Maneuvering the kayak in these waters was kind of scary at first what with all the jagged, floating ice, but after a couple of hours I got proficient in dodging and turned it into a game.

Reaching the summits of the small mountains and getting back to the boats that took me to them consumed a mere six hours up and down each day but they did provide some gorgeous views of the water and the surrounding countryside. The major climb of the trip, though, came the next week with one of my new Danish doctor friends named Thomas Foged. This time the peak to conquer topped Greenland's tallest glacier called Beluugas. It rose to over 6,000 feet and some of the ice packs beneath it were more than a mile deep. Since there were no crampons in this part of the world, the climb up the glacier ice would be hellishly hazardous and so the thrills promised to be plentiful.

To launch the adventure Doctor Foged and I rented a large boat and hired a guide and pilot to take us on the two hour trip to the base of the glacier, a stunning mass towering over the sea dotted with ice formations. With the guide waiting at the boat, the two of us began the climb at the point where the narrow glacier base meets the sea. Negotiating the rocks at the base was tough but when we reached the lower slopes the difficulty of the climb became apparent. We were ascending extreme inclines of pure ice which meant we had to chop steps in the glacier face in order to establish footholds. That was a prescription for danger and also for a lot of expended time and energy. After every ten or so minutes of climbing and chopping, we had to stop for a break. Once we reached some appreciable height, just maintaining a slippery foothold while we rested was a challenging chore in itself. And the perpendicular view from the upper reaches of the Glacier reminded me of some of scary straight-down perspectives in the Himalayas.

Three-quarters of the way to the top of the Glacier I was rewarded with a rush that not even the Everest climb had provided. We were resting in our footholds when Doctor Thomas took out his binoculars and twisted around with the intention of checking on the guide and the pilot waiting by the boat below. That's when the good doctor shouted, "My God!" and handed me the glasses. When I turned and focused what should I see about 200 yards from the anchored boat but a huge polar bear. And he was walking straight for the guide and the pilot. I was as dumbstruck as my friend at the size of the bear. It looked twice as big as the boat, which was no child's toy by any means. We knew that the two down below couldn't see the bear because a curve in the glacier blocked their view. All we could do was try to call to them but from our height they probably couldn't hear us. I had visions of Doctor Foged and myself having to pilot the boat back to Uummannaq with what was left of the guide and pilot. That is, if the bear decided to pass up us and the boat for dessert. When it became obvious that our shouts weren't heard, all we could do was watch the situation develop. Which it thankfully did without incident. The bear just walked right past the two men and on around the glacier base. He'd apparently just come from a smorgasbord or was headed for a cold swim with a hot date.

Once we were sure the bear was long gone, we chopped and clawed our way to the summit where we were rewarded with a fabulous view. Miles and miles of blue and white stretching to the horizon. This was living on the edge for sure. It was literally and figuratively chilling to realize the ice was so deep beneath us. As we surveyed the scene and rested from the ascent, Doctor Foged snapped a photo of me that I'll always treasure. And I planted my flag. In the hotel room at Uummannaq I'd made a banner for this occasion. I'd torn up one of my T-shirts and put my "Hall expedition" badge from Mount Everest in the upper-left-hand corner and, on the lower right, one of the patches I'd received for each of the two earlier climbs here in Greenland. Running diagonally across the flag was a fold of toilet paper held together by three-inch scotch tape. Between the two tie strings fastening the flag to the staff (a brush handle bought at what passed for a supermarket in Uummannaq) was an woman's empty disposable plastic sanitary napkin bag I'd found in my hotel bathroom. I remember the bag had "OQ AFLOB" written on it. But I'd filled that humble bag with a precious payload. I'd taken a lot of ribbing from Doctor Foged, the guide, and the pilot about my flag but that ragged banner meant almost as much to me on that windswept glacier summit as Old Glory herself. Once I had it unfurled I opened the plastic bag and took out the email that I'd got at the hotel in Uummannaq. The message had been from Annie my secretary and it listed all the seal fund donors' names.

I took out a pencil (pens were unreliable at these temperatures) and wrote a prayer under the donor list: "Heavenly Father, thank you for giving me the strength and the compassion for these efforts here in the Arctic Circle. I ask that you bless these names of people who feel the way I do about the slaughter of the harp seals. I ask that you bless each and every name, their families and friends. Father we ask forgiveness for having any ill thoughts, jealousies, grudges and hates and we forgive those who have sinned against us. We pray for peace in Jerusalem and around the world and rebuke the devil in your name … Amen." I wanted to keep the flag and the names of the donors and have my daughter Kelly frame them. But instead I buried them under a rock at the summit of the glacier because I'd been told that the children up there, just before the first snowstorms and the return of the big freeze in the fall, traditionally write their wishes on pieces of paper and put them under what they consider to be lucky rocks. And I wanted the seal fund donors to be blessed with good luck for their generosity.

Once my flag was planted we made our slippery and hairy descent. I kept reminding myself of Pemba on Kili cajoling "pooley, pooley, pooley." Slowly, slowly, slowly we retraced our steps down the glacier and around the rocks at its base till we met up with the guide and pilot at the boat. After they congratulated us for having scaled the big ice, they told us how panicked they'd been when they finally realized that the big polar bear was bearing down on them. They said their immediate instinct had been to run for the boat and row for their lives, but a big swimming bear could easily overturn the boat and make short work of them. Once their thought processes started working they'd decided to freeze in place and hope for the best, which came to pass. I thought I'd give them a hard time since they'd teased me unmercifully about my flag. I told them I could have defended myself against any puny polar bear attack. I said I would've throttled the marauder with my bare hands or clamped the sanitary napkin bag over his snout and suffocated him. Nanook of South Florida ! Back at the hotel that night the three of us downed shots of bourbon and relived the day's adventures.

The next morning I found the internet station at the hotel and sent an email back to the States to let the folks back home know I was having the time of my life and to find out how the seal fund donations were shaping up by now. And I wanted to get a fix on what was happening in the rest of the world. There was only one TV channel available at the hotel and so far as I could tell the only news was local and in Danish. Wherever my travels had taken me in the past, I'd managed to keep up with global events but Uummannaq presented the biggest challenge. For days all I could glean from the tube was that Danish royalty was involved in a lot of ceremonies. But the Greenlanders were great people. Most of them spoke a little English mixed with Danish, enough to understand, and I loved getting their slant on things like global warming and the state of world politics. They were pessimistic about both.

On the fifteenth I left Uummannaq by plane thanks to a change in plans. Instead of staying four full days there I decided to arrange a flight over the North Pole itself. I'd met another traveler in Kulusak who'd suggested we hire a fixed wing aircraft and share the costs of a trip to the top of the world. That sounded like a fitting ending to my fact finding and my adventure so I agreed to meet him at Qaanaaq up near Thule where the plane was waiting. The flight turned out to be something of an anticlimax, though. Just an endless stretch of white, rarely broken ice cover, although the breaks the sea did reveal a few bowhead whales and walruses. But all in all I was glad I hadn't spent two weeks getting here aboard that Russian ice breaker.

Back at Uummannaq I asked around to see if there were any zoos or marine labs or veterinarian shelters where I could have close contact with live harp seals and I was told the best bet was over in Iceland at Reykjavik. So I arranged to fly over there and spent a day at a marine lab watching and feeding hundreds of the beautiful animals and learning more about their Arctic ecology. The experience doubled my desire to help in any way I could to stop the wanton killers of these beautiful creatures. I was appalled anew when one of the Icelandic biologists told me how the slaughterers would follow in the wake of Russian ice crunchers on their twice a year run opening channels in this area. The hunters would wait with their soon-to-be-bloodied clubs for the seals to flop onto the dislodged ice debris to sun themselves.

By the time I caught the flight home from Reykjavik I was totally exhausted. I'd spent so much time in the past two weeks climbing in and out of boats on the way to little villages and boarding planes and choppers that my back was killing me. But I wouldn't have traded the experience, including the physical exertion, for anything. Even though my conscience was a little tender around the edges because so much of what I'd done on this trip was selfish, still I'd seldom felt as fulfilled. And I'd made some important contacts with real players in the environmental movement. And checked

*Sam tries his hand at kayaking.*

out which agencies were doing the best work in the area. Like Greenpeace whose tanker I saw at several ports and whose helicopters seemed to be everywhere. Once home I offered my support to Michigan's Carl Levin who authored U.S. Senate Bill 33 condemning the Canadian hunt and I contacted my Florida senator, Bill Nelson, to make a plea for the seals. I inundated Canadian agencies like their Ministry of Fisheries, the Solicitor General of Ontario, and the Canadian Veterinary Medical Association and others to voice my vehement sentiments about the slaughter. And I made a promise to myself to continue funneling funds to the right groups. So when I sent the money from the fund I'd collected I added a sizable check of my own and sent it to Inez Robinson at the Humane Society.

# THIRTY-THREE

Less than a week after my return from the Pole, word hit the airwaves about a monster Category 5 hurricane named Katrina churning its way over the Atlantic towards the southern coast. But when it made its first landfall on the twenty-fifth of August, just north of Miami, it was diminished to a relatively benign Category 1 and everybody was breathing easier. Little did they suspect that it would re-intensify to a Category Four and slam into the Gulf Coast on the 29th, ripping up 300 miles of beachfront and flattening towns in Mississippi and Alabama and breaching the levee system in New Orleans, killing hundreds and leaving thousands homeless. For the next three weeks Katrina and her younger sisters Rita and Wilma kept me busy at some of most heart wrenching but rewarding rescue work I'd ever done.

Before the storm reinvigorated itself I was monitoring it around the clock and loading my SUV according to my usual hurricane routine just in case. I'd learned from my disaster experiences that the official agencies, and especially the government ones, were slow to get off the mark. I made it a practice to be geared up well in advance. And I'd known storms to wax and wane and then wax again before they roared ashore so I wasn't taking anything for granted. All my preparations were completed and I was ready to roll two days before Hell's swells actually inundated New Orleans. But once they did where to roll to? This was different breed of disaster because never before had there been such a massive evacuation order. People were fleeing to every point of the compass, making it impossible to find hotel rooms.

Days earlier I'd had Annie line me up a first two nights' stay at a Ramada Inn between Pensacola and the Alabama border. But after that I'd have to improvise. So I unpacked and repacked the SUV, turning it into a 235-horsepower hotel, testing its axles with ice chests and a Coleman camper stove and dozens of batteries and five cans of bug spray and a big tent and food and other supplies for two weeks. And thanks to Melinda and Nancy, who's our housekeeper and Melinda's best friend, five jerry cans of gasoline that I would've stupidly left behind. I took a number of other creature comforts too that I'd feel guilty about having once I saw the disaster up close and personal. But the three big bottles of Old Granddad I stuffed in a duffle bag would turn out to be more like lifesavers than a mere indulgence.

I also stuffed my pockets with 5,000 dollars in twenty and fifty-dollar bills to pass out to storm victims. Because my SUV had magnetic signs on its doors and a tailgate logo that announced my Red Cross affiliation, victims needing money were always approaching me at disaster scenes. If their stories of hardship added up and I was certain I wasn't being conned, I always gave them a hand until my stash ran dry.

All the way to Pensacola I was hearing radio reports about how bad the situation was in the affected areas but once I got to the hotel around eight that evening I really began to grasp the extent of the horror as Katrina slammed into New Orleans and Mississippi and Alabama. I stayed glued to the hotel room TV until four in the morning and then pointed the SUV toward New Orleans. I wasn't on the road more than a couple of hours when I got a cell call from Inez Robinson at the Humane Society. She said the planning for a stranded animal rescue operation in New Orleans was being hamstrung by the lack of grid maps of the city, those charts like the military use that show every borough and ward and the streets and the creeks and lakes and schools, everything that would provide a comprehensive overview of the area to attack. Despite the fact that a hurricane-prompted flooding of the Big Easy had been anticipated in government scenarios for some time, all the "great work" that Mike "Brownie" Brown had done running FEMA hadn't included laying in an adequate supply of city maps. Now Inez's big boss at the Society and the honchos at the SPCA, the ASPCA and the IFAW were all clamoring for the grids to no avail. They were needed to slice up the city into manageable sections that could be worked by small animal rescue teams. Once the animals in a particular grid had been saved, the team working that grid could move on to nearby locations without tripping over another team.

Since Inez knew that my construction company subcontracted its drawings to a huge engineering firm, she wondered if they could help by producing an emergency stream of New Orleans maps. I told her I'd get right on it and immediately called my friend the company CEO and asked if he could help since this was a federal emergency. He told me that his guys would take it as a civic duty to produce the maps and he would drop what he was doing and get the process started right away, though it would take a few days to craft and deliver them. I told him that the timing was O.K. since Inez had indicated that the various animal welfare groups hadn't yet picked a spot to headquarter their operation. I thanked him and kept driving toward the Gulf Coast.

With all of the van's radio reports making it clear that the Phase One rescue operation in New Orleans centered around helicopter missions, I decided to take Highway 10 and check in at Gulfport, Mississippi. I'd been at Kessler Air Force Base decades earlier and had a fondness for the place. According to the radio, Gulfport and Biloxi were devastated too and needed boots on the ground rather than choppers for search and service.

I knew from experience that it's important in disaster relief work to hit the ground running but when I got to Gulfport, there was no ground to hit. I couldn't believe my eyes. The town was simply missing. The whole physical community wiped away overnight. The only sign of the town's neighborhoods were the bare concrete slabs and water-filled basement foundations. My inspection of the region during the following week revealed town after town after town in the same shape. Or should I say former town after former town after former town. And this was a scene in Gulfport like no other I'd encountered after hurricanes. There were none of the usual soaked couches or drowned TV sets or soggy beds I'd come to expect. Nothing of the sort. All the household effects had been washed out to sea by the tidal surge. There was even what used to be a floating casino sitting at a cockeyed angle atop the shell of a Holiday Inn. But in the middle of my shocked scrutiny I remembered that I was here to do a job.

Since I was wearing my Red Cross shirt it was a simple matter of finding a group of willing citizens looking for leadership. There were a number of homeowners, or rather former homeowners, staggering dazedly around what used to be the streets. Some of the ones who'd chosen to ignore the evacuation warnings and ride out the storm. Most of them were crying and unable to talk as they poked around piles of rubble trying to locate any of their belongings that might somehow have been spared. I decided to try taking their minds off their suffering by organizing them into a search and rescue party. But first I had to give them a little lecture on safety since it's been a long since proven principle that most disaster-related injuries happen after the fact, in the cleanup operations where you have to watch that you don't step on scattered nails or dislodge a pile of debris only to have it crash down on top of you. Once I was sure my searchers understood the rules, we began scouring the immediate neighborhood for survivors, or, far more likely, non-survivors. Calling out to potential survivors under mounds of rubble and hoping to hear cries for help, we searched for the rest of the day, lifting trees and branches and heavy lumber and building materials of every size and description.

In the process we met up with a few others who'd made it through the storm only to encounter worse horrors. They were wondering through twisted wreckage in utter bewilderment. A woman whimpering, "My mother needs insulin," and an old man picking through debris and repeating over and over, "Help me find my grandchildren." We also managed to locate three bodies earlier searchers had missed. They were wrapped up in old blankets alongside what used to be their homes. Folks who'd paid the ultimate price for failure to heed the get-out-now sirens before the big winds. Even though I'd been through these kinds of discoveries too many times before, at Ground Zero and after the tsunami and other places, I still choked up when I came across a body. A nightmare is a nightmare. There aren't many gradations of horror. All my searchers and I could do when we came across such scenes was hug each other. But I couldn't afford tears at this point since I'd just managed to quell the crying of my amateur search crew.

That night I dismissed the second crew I'd organized and they headed toward their cars to get some sleep or to friends' places that were further inland and had sustained less than total destruction. At that point there was no electrical power for miles around, so in some ways cars offered more comfort than houses. I had a hotel room waiting for me in Pensacola but I was too drained to drive so I decided to spend the night in the SUV. My back was killing me. Toward the end of the search for survivors I'd felt a bit of a twinge just above my butt when I'd moved a downed telephone pole atop a pile of logs and aluminum siding. I hadn't thought much of it at the time but now I was in a lot of pain and could hardly sit down. I had just enough strength left to wrestle one of the Old Granddad bottles out of the duffel bag and take a big hit from it. That night I got less than two hours sleep thanks to my aching back.

The next morning I could barely get up and when I finally managed all I could do was curse. Earlier in the year I'd missed my chance to reach the top of Mount Everest because of illness. Now it looked like because of a bad back I might have to call off this mission in the middle of the greatest natural disaster in the nation's history. Once I ran out of the profanity I switched gears and said a standing prayer (since I couldn't have knelt, even in the presence of the Pope) that God would let me keep going because if ever I was needed to do some unselfish work it was now. But was it really unselfish work? How could it be when it left me so fulfilled?

God must have had earphones on because I managed for the next three days to lead citizen searchers and lift heavy debris in Gulfport and Biloxi and help set up food and water distribution lines in Pascagoula. All this time I'd been waiting for my engineer friend to alert me about the availability of those grid maps and for Inez Robinson to let me know where the staging area for the animal rescue operation for New Orleans would be located. Their messages came within fifteen minutes of each other. The maps were ready for me to pick up and the animal welfare groups had decided to set up their advance position at the Lumar-Dixon state pavilion in Gonzales, Louisiana. So I headed back to Florida to get the maps and to swallow as many pain pills as I could get my hands on. Then I planned to drive to Gonzales to join in the rescue effort. That decision was easy since I wasn't a helicopter pilot, what they needed in New Orleans to rescue people, and my interest in protecting animals had peaked to a passion thanks to the harp seal project.

Back at the condo, after downing more pain drugs than the average pharmacy sells in a month, I unfurled the seven huge grid maps that my friend the engineer had had his staff create. They were things of beauty. Each one had fifty 18x24 sheets that indicated every nook and cranny of New Orleans. And all in living color. But before taking them to Gonzales, I decided I'd better see my doctor because the pain was getting unbearable despite the pills. If he could get me something even stronger I could put off the more serious treatment I might need until after the Katrina crisis was over. And get right back to the front lines and do a better job. Most of the way home I'd crouched over the steering wheel and avoided letting the seat back touch mine. Needless to say, when I pulled into Largo and got out of the SUV I was hunched over like Quasimodo trying to tie his shoelaces. But when I got to the doc's office late in the morning of my arrival from Pascagoula, he didn't seem too worried. He said he thought I'd probably pinched a nerve and he recommended an MRI on my back just to make sure there was nothing seriously wrong. The problem was that the damned MRI couldn't be done for three days. So I told him I'd be sure to schedule one as soon as I got back from the Gulf Coast in about a week.

I went home from the doctor's office and spent the rest of the day watching the grimmer and grimmer news from New Orleans. A lot of the time I was in tears watching the catastrophe unfold and the rest of the time I was cursing the idiots at FEMA who didn't seem to realize that there was a problem with overcrowding at the Superdome, among other predicaments. I couldn't understand how the agency that had done such good work after other hurricanes could screw up so badly this time.

I knew deep down that I needed some time off but during a cataclysm like this it couldn't be considered. Even though I was totally unable to put on a pair of socks without Melinda's help. And to watch the TV news I had to lay flat on the floor on my stomach. All the same I had Melinda and Nancy repack the SUV so I'd be ready to return to the Gulf Coast in the morning. They did what I asked but I'm sure it was just to make me feel better. They had to think New Orleans would be rebuilt by the time I could walk upright again. I kept telling Melinda the pain was easing up and she kept calling me a lying son-of-a-bitch.

Finally after three or four hours of listening to TV news I couldn't take my short exile any more. Pictures shown over and over again of residents wading for their lives, bodies floating in the streets and strapped to abandoned wheelchairs. AWOL city police officers, the mayor and the governor fighting with each other, FEMA nowhere to be found.

Sitting around home, even for half a day, was intolerable in that situation. But by this time I knew that, fouled up though it was, the human rescue operation was over and the recovery phase was winding down. There were always three phases to such a procedure, the human rescue, the recovery of bodies, and the rescue of animals. If I could get myself up from the floor in front of the TV, I could deliver those maps and still make Phase Three.

Melinda was at work but I didn't dare call her because she would have rushed home and tried to talk me out of my going. I left her a note saying the pain had eased up quite a bit and I was headed to New Orleans. As I crept out the door, like a thief in the night, I grabbed all the pain medicine samples the doctor had provided. And on the way out of town I picked up three more bottles of Old Granddad. The way I staggered in and out of the liquor store the clerk probably thought I'd already polished off a case of the stuff earlier in the day. On the way back to the SUV I spotted a sporting goods store and decided to pick up a bigger tent to hold the extra supplies I'd had Melinda and Nancy pack a cot that could give some support to make it easier to lie down and get up to pee rather than having to get prone on the ground and then stand up from that position.

On the twelve-hour drive to Gonzales, which is about fifty minutes by car from New Orleans, I tried to convince myself that I was feeling better. And after a few prayers the pain actually did abate a bit. When I arrived at the rescue staging area I was greeted like a visiting potentate. Inez Robinson was there to welcome me at the suggestion of her boss who wanted her to thank me personally for my donations to the society. And the fact that I'd not only arranged for the grid maps and even incurred the expense of having them printed at Kinko's (the engineering firm had donated the drawings) but also had ponyed up a sizable check for the next three weeks' Society expenses, added to the warmth of my welcome.

The pavilion turned out to be a huge facility a lot like a state fairgrounds with a big rodeo building and a lot of open-sided, roofed structures that held thousands of animal pens. The place was already jumping with activity generated by rescue operations in Mississippi, Alabama, and other parts of Louisiana. There were nearly 5,000 rescued animals, mostly dogs but lots of cats and hundreds of mostly injured horses. Hundreds of volunteers caring for them, including dozens of veterinarians, reps from the Society for the Prevention of Cruelty to Animals, the International Federation for Animal Welfare and other like-minded groups. Seemingly everybody connected with animal treatment from California to Maine.

I was introduced to nearly all the players one by one. I shook so many hands I wound up with a sore right shoulder but I was so excited to be there that I didn't think about my ailing back. I met a number of officials from government agencies like Health and Human Services and FEMA. And I noticed something that would prepare me even more than the earlier short-age of maps had for a lot of the Monday morning quarterbacking of the next few months. What the FEMA folks did best was stand around apparently bewildered. Either looking lost or getting in the way of the professionals. There were times when I felt like grabbing them by the throat and scream-ing at them to do something, anything.

But the most impressive people I met that day were the five staff mem-bers and the dozen or so animal control officers linked as "Code 3 Associ-ates." "Code 3" is an animal rescue unit out of Erie, Colorado that's affiliated with the International Federation for Animal Welfare. Their founder and leader is a Carnation milk family heiress and animal lover named Nan Stuart. Hers is the most highly trained and experienced of all the rescue teams in the country. It works almost exclusively in flooded areas so they were in the right place at the right time here on the Gulf Coast. They had all of the very best equipment, including a couple of air-conditioned eighteen-wheelers that could haul a 100 big animals and sleep six people at the same time. And sleek flat-bottomed boats with different kinds of specialized motors. I knew right away that this was the outfit I wanted to work with. So I couldn't believe my luck when they invited me to join them. They'd been told I'd worked tsunami relief in Sri Lanka and that I was the one who had delivered the grid maps so that was good enough to get me a spot on one of their rescue crews.

Once all the introductions were finally finished I pitched my tent in a large open area of the complex and practically ran, bad back and all, to the staging area for instructions. Even though it was late afternoon by now, I was asked to suit up right away for a mission in New Orleans' poorest ward, the ninth, because of the urgency of the situation. The first item of business was to don the "dry suit." I'd wind up having a love-hate relationship with mine. The damn thing was so cumbersome and hot. I was told the temperature inside it could reach over 150 degrees Fahrenheit in the Louisiana sun. It was a lot different than the wet suits I was familiar with from my scuba diving days. This outfit was made of absolutely impenetrable cortex that pushed the price up to ten times more than a good wet suit's. It had a rubberized high neck and stiff zippers that took two strong hands to close. By the end of day each of the crew members wearing these outfits would have sweat at least four liters of liquid. But there was no doubt the getup would fend off more lethal diseases from the toxic flood waters than the CDC could keep track of. That's why the law required us to wear the damn things, even though it made us look like walking condoms.

After we were suited up, we all piled into a big van and were on our way to the flooded ninth ward. Once we were inside the city limits on a raised and dry freeway we downloaded our boat next to the triage area that volunteer veterinarians had set up there. Then we launched from a freeway off ramp, which became "SOP" over the next two weeks, and headed out on a cruise of several miles in between and around homes, downed trees, drowned cars and trucks. Always avoiding shallow water because we couldn't be sure what projections were lurking there to penetrate boat bottoms.

When we got into the heart of the ninth ward I realized how grisly our work could get. We sometimes found ourselves gliding among bloated bodies the human rescue phase had somehow missed. Bodies face down in the water, almost all of them shoeless which meant they probably drowned while swimming for their lives against waves of high water. And a couple of times we had to tie dead bodies to front porches so they wouldn't drift to another address. I wanted to get the bodies back to their families but we weren't tasked or equipped to do that. Leaving the floating corpses led to a lot of crying among the crewmates. I'll take on any jackass that claims a man should never cry. It's the guy who never cries that isn't a real man.

I was upset too by all the abandoned animals we were picking up. I felt so sorry for the pet owners who'd been forced to leave their canine or feline or other animal friends to the hazards of the storm. And even more sorry for those people who'd not heeded the evacuation warnings and died with their pets. But there wasn't time to reflect much on those things. There were dozens of animals in distress that needed saving pronto just in this one slice of neighborhood.

Our equipment included snare poles of different lengths. They had thick wire loops on their ends. And the boat was always loaded with empty cages. Once we located a stranded dog or cat, or sometimes a raccoon or a skunk, the pole worked beautifully from a distance of around 5 feet, give or take a half-dozen inches. The length was supposed to insure that we wouldn't be bitten. That was a concern because you couldn't be sure the animal at the end of the pole wasn't rabid. The tricky part came after the dog or cat was in the boat still lassoed to the pole. Getting it into the cage and shutting the door on it was no easy matter. And all the while we were supposed to make sure we didn't come in contact with the contaminated water.

The dry suits protected everything but our heads and hands. The problem was that we were always somewhat distracted from our work with trying to keep our hands sterilized with special solutions because they were always getting splashed with the putrid water. And that night, like every other night that followed back at the base camp, we'd have to decontaminate our gear and ourselves. This was always done in a very professional manner according to detailed instructions. And in my case there was the added problem of my back. I could go all day long in relative comfort thanks to the distracting intensity of the rescue work. But at night, back at the pavilion, the pain would come. rushing at me from behind. That's when I prayed that the next day's assignment could be accomplished without collapse. And gulped down pain killers with Old Granddad. Followed by several Old Granddad chasers. The only food I could tolerate were some vanilla cookies from a zip lock bag that Melinda had packed. She'd also packed a lot of wonderful food that I wound up giving away.

Over the next several days the rescue work became more and more rewarding. All of it done in the ninth ward which was still not fully drained by the time Rita re-flooded the city. By the time I left Louisiana I would be down to half a swig of Old Granddad out of the three bottles I'd brought with me.

Every morning, sometimes with the same group as the day before and sometimes with a new crew, I'd load up my gear back at the pavilion and climb in the boat for a grim sail down the flooded streets looking for abandoned pets or wild animals stranded in tree branches or riding on floating debris. Two particular incidents I'll never forget.

One morning we got word that a second-floor veterinary clinic had been abandoned about two miles into the ninth ward. We knew all the animals inside would be sick since that would have been their reason for being with a vet in the first place. And some and maybe all of them had no doubt died since no one had been in the building for two weeks to feed and water them. But we couldn't be sure that some of them weren't still alive so we mounted a two-team rescue mission not knowing what we'd find. We had a tough time locating the building even with our detailed city maps but we finally got there after two hours of searching. The water in that area was 4 or 5 feet deep at the time so we were able to run the boat right through the building's open door and step out onto the mid-point of the stairway for the climb to the stranded animals. When we smashed into the locked second floor area that housed the clinic, we were in Dante's hell, greeted by the most sickening death smell I've ever experienced. And I've smelled death all over the world. There were seven dogs and two cats already dead. But there were eight live (barely) dogs and two live cats. We loaded the sick survivors into separate cages and rushed them back to triage at the expressway off ramp. But I convinced the rest of the crew to make one emergency stop on the way. I'd spotted a big mixed breed dog standing forlorn on a soggy wooden front porch. The crewman at the motor maneuvered us within 20 feet of the porch but couldn't get any closer. And the dog had retreated and was standing at the front door of the house. That's when I decided to wade in and get the mutt. When I picked him up I felt a searing pain in my back but the two of us whimpered our way to the boat. The last I saw of the poor pooch he was scarfing down a big bowl of Kibbles at the triage and that sight gave me a lot of satisfaction.

A couple of days later we got word that there was a cat menagerie stranded in an abandoned house one ward away. It seems a woman who lived in the house had some fifty feline pets and before the evacuation all of her neighbors had brought their own cats over to be gathered up together after everyone returned to the area, which they all thought would be just a matter of days or even hours. But for two weeks now the water around the place had been chest deep and no one had been able to check on the crowd of cats. There were supposed to be around sixty of them including some kittens all caged with food and water but we packed up sixty carrier cages in case the ones at the house would turn out to be too cumbersome to transport. Just finding the house wasn't that easy because our maps didn't show the right street name. No fault of the engineers or Kinko's, just a previous error they'd reproduced. It took our four three-man teams forty-five minutes of searching till we arrived at a well-kept two-story frame house in a fairly nice neighborhood. There was a huge oak tree downed in front so we had to do a circuitous entry through a neighbor's yard. And that presented problems because a submerged wrought iron fence separated the places and it had to be knocked down to gain access to our target. Once the boats were tied to the neighbor's porch and the fence pushed over, we entered the front door with bolt cutters. Inside on the first floor, the extent of the damage was disheartening to say the least. Floating furniture and picture albums. Flooring that collapsed under our feet. Everything we touched crumbling to a wet grainy sludge. The howling of the cats upstairs assaulting our eardrums and the appalling stench from the kitty litter already inducing nausea.

After half an hour the crew leader and I had fashioned a makeshift path through the floating debris. We grabbed a cage in each arm and climbed the stairs together. That was a real chore because they were steep and narrow and partly under water. At the top of the stairs each of us voiced a simultaneous, "Holy Shit." Cats were running everywhere, over furniture and fixtures. We didn't have time to count tails because about a third of the cats were comatose so we had to get the animal technicians and veterinarian assistants (there was one in each boat) busy right away injecting the down-for-the-count animals with dextrose to revive them. Then the technical types took the worst of the cats by boat back to the triage center at the off ramp. While the rest of us went to work literally herding cats. And that turned out to be just as tough as the old saw said. The cats were scared out of their skins and running in every direction and they wouldn't stand still long enough to permit a crewman with a pole to get a noose over their necks. If you managed to get close to one it'd get its back up and spit and scream and, if you gave it half a chance, take a chunk out of your hand. In one stairwell a group of about thirty cats and kittens with bared teeth and flailing paws held off their rescuers for half an hour until they were picked off one by one with the pole nooses.

It took us a full two hours to get all of the feisty felines locked down in the portable cages, sometimes two or three to a cage because there'd obviously been an undercount by the woman who'd agreed to board the neighbors' brood. But eventually the bunch, including the twenty or so the vet assistants had revived, were doing a lot of mellow meowing and munching in their cages. That's the point where we finally did a count and discovered there were eighty-five of them, including twenty-four kittens. Apparently the cat woman had either not known there'd been a lot of expectant mothers among her new boarders or had lost track of the total cat collection as it mounted. And who knew how many more cute kittens would be born in the next few months thanks to the other kind of mounting that was no doubt going down on that second floor cat house for two weeks.

We weren't quite ready to congratulate ourselves on a successful mission at this point though. Not a single cat had died so far as we could tell but we still had to get them all to triage. That meant a tricky descent down the slippery stairs and a tough wade back to the boats by a caravan of crewmen carrying a couple of cages at a time. But on an earlier trip up the stairs with a cage I'd spotted in one of the bedrooms what might be made into a labor saving device for the removal process. It was an inflatable mattress and I didn't even have to waste my breath pumping it up since it was already full of air. I told the rest of the crew what I had in mind and proceeded to cut and clear away the heavy fallen branches and thick vines that blocked access to an outdoor balcony off a second-floor bedroom over the side yard. Then I had to saw off a section of the balcony railing big enough to fit the mattress through. Once I'd accomplished that, my improvised raft was put to good use for the evacuation. We lowered cage after cage from a window and down the side of the house from the balcony and onto the air mattress below and then floated it trip after trip to the waiting boats. My ingenuity gained me some good natured ribbing. For the rest of the day I was called MacGyver after the TV hero who fashioned anything handy into a situation- saving device. And for the next few hours I was congratulated on what the crews called "MacGyver's floating pussy wagon."

We said our goodbyes to our feline friends back at triage after they'd been treated and were being packed into air-conditioned trucks to be driven in style back to the pavilion and eventual reunion with their owners. By federal law no rescued animal can be delivered anywhere unless it's in a specially built carrier that's air-conditioned. Nothing but the best for God's furry friends. And I'm sure that after what this bunch had been through they really appreciated the royal treatment.

It turned out that the cats fared a lot better than the crews in the rescue operation. Each of us wound up with multiple scratches and bites. I had three deep puncture wounds in my left hand. All of the wounded had to be treated back at the triage center and again at a public health tent at the pavilion. That meant too that rabies shots were a must. They had to be given within twenty-four hours of contact with a rabid animal so the crews formed a line at a local hospital waiting to get stuck. And we had to return four more times because rabies protection requires five shots.

The night of the eighty-five cats I was down to the last dregs of Old Granddad and the pain in my back was excruciating. I decided at that point I probably needed professional attention. I could go on working with the Code 3 crews but at the risk of doing something permanently disabling. I knew I could get the rest of my rabies treatment back home. Besides, Melinda and I were scheduled to receive Citizen of the Year awards at a Largo banquet in three days. In the morning I told my crew mates for the first time that I'd been suffering with my back and was worried something serious was wrong. They were surprised and said they hadn't noticed I was in pain but they understood and gave me their email addresses for future reference. The drive back home was another exercise in trying to keep my flipside from coming anywhere near the upholstery on the SUV seat back and by the time I pulled up to our condo I was so stiff and aching I could barely get to my bed. The next morning my doctor managed to get me into the hospital right away for an MRI. And with Melinda's help I managed to make the awards ceremony. But I couldn't eat much of the banquet food, not only because my back had wrecked my appetite, but also because the news was now all about the approach of Hurricane Rita.

Rita hit and broke the New Orleans levees again re-flooding the city while I was waiting for the MRI verdict and I was too antsy to stay around the house. Melinda helped me repack the SUV and after a call to Inez Robinson for instructions I headed to an area around Beaumont, Texas and spent another five days arguing with my back, chugging Old Granddad, and rounding up horses and the scattered remnants of a 35,000 head cattle herd. The rescues were both on foot and in boats at places where the storm waters had flooded stables and corrals. In most spots the surge had obliterated streams and ponds so the animals hadn't eaten or drunk for too long. And many of them had been blinded by the salt that soaked their eyes when the sea water reached its maximum surge. There were lots of dead cattle and a few dead horses but I was glad to see that the blind survivors were able to smell the fresh water and hay we put out for them. And they seemed to be doing well by the time I left for home.

When I got back to Florida I called the doctor and he told me to come in for a conference. That didn't sound good but if a conference could get my back feeling better I was all for it. When the doc had me seated in his office he pulled out my chart and started reading from the MRI report but I had to stop him at points so I could try to figure out words like; "multilevel degenerative disease," "spondylolisthesis," "degenerative annular bulging," and "paracentral protrusion." When he seemed to be finished I said, "O.K., doc, I don't speak Greek. What the hell does all that mean?" That's when I got the wonderful news.

"Sam, remember when you broke your back years ago?"

"Well, you just re-broke it in at the same two spots."

After the shock subsided I asked what I'd have to do to get healed and he advised complete rest for the next few days while he did some checking.

Two days later his head nurse called. She was usually breezy on the phone but over the years I'd learned not to count on the cheerfulness of her voice. This time she got straight to the point.

"Sam, the doctor wants you to come in for a dexascan right away."

"What for?"

"Just to be certain."

"Certain of what?"

"Just to be certain."

"Come on, Bonnie. Level with me. What will the test show, that I have a bad back? I already know that."

"Please, Sam. Come in at eight in the morning. And take two calcium tablets with your meals in the meantime."

This didn't sound good to say the least, but I finally agreed and the next morning I had the scan. While I was waiting for these new results, the Weather Channel was tracking Hurricane Wilma bearing down on the Florida coast. It was scheduled to make landfall near Naples in the next twenty-four hours so I had Nancy, our housekeeper, pack my van with the usual hurricane supplies, food, water, sleeping bag and the like. That night I went to bed at ten but couldn't get to sleep. Around one in the morning I carefully rolled over and switched on the Weather channel. Wilma would make landfall close to Naples around 6:45 A.M. With a rush of the old adrenaline I carried my bags out to the van and by two o'clock I was ready to roll. I told Nancy that under no circumstances was she to let Melinda know I was heading for Naples for fear she'd try to stop me. I knew my back would only allow light work but I had to volunteer for my own sanity. Driving to the potential disaster and doing what I could sure beat waiting around for word from the doctor.

A couple of hours of driving later I called Melinda to let her know I was doing fine. But she gave me an ass-chewing that made me wonder if I'd ever be let in the house again. She was worried sick that this time I'd gone too far and would undo in advance anything Doctor Price could do for my back. But I assured her I'd take it easy and just pass out supplies. By this time I was close to Exit 107 to Naples off I-75. And the eye of Wilma was a mere 10 miles to the south. I pulled the SUV under a bridge just north of the ramp to escape the sheets of rain driven by 80 mile-per-hour winds that made driving just about impossible. I felt safe enough under the bridge. Safe from the storm. But not safe from my thoughts. What if that test at the doctor's office revealed something serious, even life threatening? By life threatening I meant threatening to the life on the edge that I'd been living. Death itself is a little thing. I've stared it down any number of times over the years. But how would I cope with a situation where I had to slow down, even stop in my tracks? The highway ahead wasn't the only thing obscured by those sheets of rain that morning.

Once the downpour and wind slackened a little I pulled back on to I-75 and drove straight into Naples. The guards at the already erected security barriers checked my Red Cross ID and waved me through. Then I dodged downed power lines and fallen trees to reach one of the distribution centers and had a couple of workers there load cases of bottled water and ice into the SUV to be passed out to harried homeowners. But all I could contribute to the relief effort was my ability to drive hunched over the steering wheel. The cartons of water and bags of ice were too difficult for me to pick up. I had to ask the volunteers at the site to do the lifting. Humiliating as hell.

Three hours into shuttling supplies to devastated Naples neighborhoods I nearly jumped out of my skin at the sound of my cell phone ringing. I knew right away that it had to be the doctor's office with news about the dexascan because the results were due by now. Nurse Bonnie's voice deepened my anxiety.

"Sam, we have the results of your test. Doctor Price wants to see you. Can you come in later this afternoon?"

"No I can't, Bonnie. I'm in Naples. Tell me the results."

"No, Sam. I'll have to let the doctor tell you."

"Bonnie, please. Give it to me straight."

"I can't."

"Is it bad?"

"It's osteoporosis."

The word hit me like a punch to the pit of my stomach. It was a worry I'd been trying to suppress ever since I'd done the dexascan. I hung up the phone without uttering so much as a thank you or even a goodbye. I just slumped further over the van's steering wheel and began to quietly cry. I started thinking again about my dad's death and how I'd promised myself mine would be totally different. Toward the end dad was a helpless diabetic with seventeen major complications. And then came the heart problems that left him bedridden till he passed away on an operating table while he waited for a pacemaker. I know everybody's on a one-way trip to the coroner's office and most can't dictate the way they go but I'd promised myself I'd never put my own kids through my dad's kind of goodbye. I didn't want to make my exit holed up in a hospital ward. Don't get me wrong. Those medical people do noble work. But I wanted to make my own pace to the end, thank you very much. Now a doctor's diagnosis painted a picture of my own last days as an invalid. Maybe a shrink would tell you that was the fear that fed my romance with risk.

With that thought and a hundred others racing through my mind I decided that I wasn't doing anybody any good here in Naples. Instead I was driving around numb and totally unable even to help myself. So I packed up through my pain and phoned Annie to search the internet for articles about osteoporosis. And I asked her too to see if there were any vacancies in our condo complexes that might be donated to house some of the New Orleans evacuees that were homeless now. The government was asking for property owners to volunteer any extra space they could and though I knew nearly all or maybe all of our units were rented and the ones under construction a long way from completion, I wanted to make sure there wasn't something we could do for the poor displaced souls from the storm.

The next week after a depressing session with Doctor Price in his office I settled into a sun-drenched lounge chair by the pool at the beach house. Melinda was staying at one of our condo penthouses overseeing our new construction project. Still a little pissed at me for going down to Naples during Wilma. So I was alone except for Nancy. She knew I wasn't feeling well and all about the diagnosis so she didn't disturb me as I began reading Annie's printouts. And as the tears began flowing again.

"The human costs of osteoporosis are significant. As many as 20 percent of patients who break their major bones die within a year. Among patients over age seventy, the mortality rate may increase to as high as 50 percent. Another 30 percent may require considerable help for daily living. Twenty percent of patients may not be able to walk for a year after a break and up to 50 percent will not be able to walk as well as they did before the fracture."

That last part already applied to me since one of my legs was now refusing to keep up with its partner. Statistics like the ones I was reading about were unsettling to say the least. As I lay there in all my discomfort, not just from the back pain but also from feeling sorry for myself and guilty about lasting only one day volunteering during Wilma, all the terrible things I'd experienced in the last few years came rushing back in a kaleidoscope to me. The fireman with his knee thrust into his chest at Ground Zero, the tangle of bodies in the mangrove roots after the Sri Lanka tsunami, the floating human flotsam in the aftermath of Katrina, and all the other soul-searing sights I'd witnessed. But I knew if I dwelt on those thoughts I'd be way down below the dumps and I couldn't let that happen. I tried to replace the dark memories in my mind's eye with images of Minja on Kilimanjaro and of Pemba pointing to spectacular Himalayan vistas and of a lone polar bear silently gliding among glaciers. There was no doubt I'd piled up enough positive memories to more than compensate for the horrors I'd seen. I'd lived a life of incredible privilege. And I had a loving wife who indulged my every desire (well, up until a week earlier) when most women would have long since left me in the lurch. And wonderful kids and a close extended family. Who was I to feel sorry for myself? Still I couldn't quite cope yet with the possibility that my work for others not to mention my selfish adventures might be coming to an abrupt end.

So I closed my eyelids on my tears and started a silent prayer.

"Lord, take away this pain I have, not just from the back but from the guilt of coming home early from Wilma. Make me strong and give me more time to carry out your work. I pray for healing of my osteoporosis and for peace in Jerusalem."

As soon as I finished my prayer I felt a little better, knowing in my heart that the Lord wasn't finished with me.

Then Nancy opened the pool deck door and shouted, "Is there anything you need?"

"Not now, Nancy. I think I have everything I need." And I knew at that moment it was true.

So that's where I was when I finished prepping my writer. After that, while we were finding a publisher and then, once that was accomplished, waiting for the book to come out, I got my back treated among other offending body parts including a problem leg that almost led to an amputation. The back and the leg have kept me from several places where I could have been of help and it tears me up that I wasn't able to offer it. Places like Pakistan where that awful earthquake and its aftermath killed so many destitute people. I cried a lot watching the TV pictures from there because I'd come to love the Asian mountains and the people who live there. And of course the misery in Iraq and Afghanistan that had me itching to get back into counterterrorism. Not to mention the still disregarded genocide in Darfur.

But there will be lots of places where a helping hand will be badly needed

*Sam in Isreal on the northern border with Lebanon*
*during the August War, 2006.*

*Outside Beriut, Lebanon, two weeks after ceasefire, September 2006.*

# Afterword

*A recent letter from Sam Hall to his family*

I want to share with you a wonderful experience I had today on the Texas border working with survivors from hurricane Ike.

Children, as you know I wear many hats regarding what I do in the aftermath of a disaster. I have clearances/identification to work as a volunteer with the Red Cross, Salvation Army, firefighter, etc. Usually I pick according to what needs to be done. Several years ago, I was burnt out from burying victims in mass graves. I helped with the earthquakes in Iran, mud slides in Central America, the tsunami in Asia and ground zero here at home. Like the old expression, the more people I meet (and bury) the more I love my dog … so mostly, these last three years, I've been rescuing animals.

Today, in Texas, I pulled into a small Incident Command Post (ICP) where many of the rescued survivors (mostly from the Houston area) were sequestered and being well-cared for. There were doctors and hot meals, donated clothing and the people were given all the major things like soap, toothbrushes and a cot and blankets. They will stay there until it's safe to return to their homes. I was asked to be a social worker. That entails walking around the tents or, in this case, a large temporary shelter. Outside the shelter were a number of tents with 50 or 60 picnic tables where people could eat or just sit and congregate.

(I have done this a number of times. All the survivors are extremely distraught and suffer from trauma that's hard to understand unless you have been through it yourself).

When you do this type of social work you should do it in a way that makes people comfortable at the first meeting. An example is, if they are eating off a plastic plate then you do the same. Always do things on their level. If they are sitting then you sit. If they are standing then you stand. If they fold their arms, you fold your arms … if they put … well, you know what I mean!

The weather was horrible outside. A shower just went thru and we are still getting gusts of more then 30 mph at times. Most everyone went into the shelter to avoid the rain. I had just gone thru the Salvation Army truck and had a plate of two sandwiches and some twinkies. I noticed a young girl (around Samee's age) who was sitting at a picnic table with a tent over it which kept it fairly dry. However the humidity was so bad that, with the hot air from the Gulf, it made you sweat something fierce. I watched her for a minute and saw her dabbing at her food with her right hand. Her left hand, elbow propped on the table, was holding up her head. I was behind her so couldn't see that she'd been crying. She was all alone so I went over and sat down next to her ... not real close, though, for she smelled of fear and sweat and probably hadn't showered for two days.

I was wearing my Red Cross shirt and name badge. I wanted to leave because of how much she smelled. I understood, then, why she was alone.

Being professional, however, I said, "May I join you?" She didn't say anything, she just lifted her head up and nodded. I introduced myself and told her I was known as "Sam, the Red Cross Man." She smiled at that but still didn't say anything, so I ate my sandwich and waited her out. After a few minutes, I said I was going to get another fruit punch. I asked her if she would like me to bring her one. She didn't have any tissues or napkins so she was just wiping her tears and her drippy nose with her wrist. She looked at me and finally said something like, "Yes, I would like that."

I came back to the picnic table with two punch drinks and some napkins to wipe her eyes and nose with. We just talked about little things. I asked if she was getting everything she needed and could I get anything for her. She asked me where I was from and I told her. She was really interested in why I would come so far from Florida and did my wife complain about me being away ... so we talked. Well, actually I did most of the talking—about me. I was trying to get her to laugh. Then I turned the conversation towards her. Slowly her story came out and what she told me floored me. I will never forget it and never want to.

She was rescued by the National Guard in an area near Houston. She had to swim to stay alive because the surge was coming in so rapidly. The Army Personnel retrieved her and brought her here to this staging area.

I waited for her to go on. A couple of minutes later she said that this was the second time she had to be rescued. She said that she had to swim for her her life during Katrina. She and her family did not evacuate their rental home in New Orleans. Just like this time ... they decided to take a chance and believed that they would be all right. They were wrong on both counts.

I should say that she was bedraggled and not at all a pretty girl, especially with no make-up, no jewelry, or decent clothes ... she was just a plain, short, plump young girl.

Several minutes later she started sobbing, real intense ... tears really coming off her cheeks ... three paper napkins soaked. I reached over and put my hand on her shoulder and said, "What's wrong?" I told her, "You're here and you're safe."

She looked me in the eye and said, "… at Katrina we were swimming to stay alive." She told me "Me and my brother made it. My mother drowned that day and I couldn't save her."

I didn't know what to say so I kept quiet and waited. She looked over at me, glanced at my name tag, and said "Sam, yesterday, before I was rescued, while I was trying to swim to safety, I thought about my mother drowning three years ago. And during my swim to safety I didn't care if I made it or not. I thought about giving up so I could be with and in the arms of my loving mother once more."

Tears kept falling down my face. She had so much guilt. I didn't do anything except try to hold back my own tears.

We sat there together, quietly alone, both of us sniffling. I finally said that her mother in Heaven was looking down on her right now and was proud of her daughter for not giving up. I said she probably said "You did good, girl. We have plenty of time. I will wait for you. Live your life to the fullest."

She said, "Oh, Sam, I hope so! Thank you for being here and listening to me!" I reached in my pocket and grabbed some twenty dollar bills and put them in her hands. She started to refuse and I said, "Remember what I said earlier. I am Sam, the Red Cross Man. I am allowed to do that."

I got up, grabbed her hand and pulled her to her feet. And that poor, sad, little smelly girl reached out, wrapped her arms around me and kissed me on the cheeks, both of them—our tears wetting each other. Suddenly she didn't smell anymore. I walked away and she yelled "God Bless you!"

I couldn't look back. All I did was keep walking, raising my hand up in the air like a wave. I was feeling ashamed that earlier I had thought of her as a smelly, plain, fat little girl when, in truth, she was nothing less than a little angel.

Later, when I was driving the car, I couldn't get her out of my mind. I am not ashamed to admit to you, my children, that in the confines of my car, I cried like a baby.

I want to share with you one more thing about this wonderful experience. I know, with all my heart, that the Lord put the two of us together today.

Let me say it like this. During the aftermath of 9/11, while I was on the site for those three weeks, Mayor Rudy Giuliani was always coming down. He would approach us workers who were digging. He was King. He always went up and touched each of us and said, to everyone, the same thing, "Hey, you done good."

I believe God wrapped his arms around me today and kissed me on the cheeks. He had that wonderful girl do it for him … and I like to think that he looked down on me and said, "Hey, Sam. You have had the best of everything. Now things are different and time for you to make the best of everything."

And for sure I know he said "Hey, Sam. You done good."

Your loving father in Texas …

P.S. I am heading for Nacogdoches tomorrow up in northern TX, where there's an Animal Shelter Command Center. I'm going off to work with the animals … humans sap to much of my strength.

Printed in the United States
135448LV00003B/14/P